WORKSHOPS IN COMPUTING
Series edited by C. J. van Rijsbergen

Also in this series

continued on back page...

Ursula Martin and Jeannette M. Wing (Eds.)

First International Workshop on Larch

Proceedings of the First International Workshop on Larch, Dedham, Massachusetts, USA, 13–15 July 1992

Published in collaboration with the British Computer Society

Springer-Verlag
London Berlin Heidelberg New York
Paris Tokyo Hong Kong
Barcelona Budapest

Ursula Martin, MA, PhD, MBCS, CEng
Department of Mathematical and Computational Sciences, University of
St Andrews, North Haugh, St Andrews, Fife, KY16 9SS, Scotland

Jeannette M. Wing, SB, SM, PhD
School of Computer Science, Carnegie Mellon University
5000 Forbes Avenue, Pittsburgh, PA 15213-3890, USA

ISBN 3-540-19804-0 Springer-Verlag Berlin Heidelberg New York
ISBN 0-387-19804-0 Springer-Verlag New York Berlin Heidelberg

British Library Cataloguing in Publication Data
First International Workshop on Larch:
Proceedings of the First International Workshop on Larch, Dedham, USA,
13–15 July 1992. – (Workshops in Computing Series)
   I. Martin, Ursula II. Wing, Jeannette M. III. Series
   005. 1
ISBN 3-540-19804-0

Library of Congress Cataloging-in-Publication Data
International Workshop on Larch (1st : 1992 : Dedham, Mass.)
   Proceedings of the First International Workshop on Larch, Dedham, USA,
13-15 July 1992 / Ursula Martin and Jeannette M. Wing (eds.).
      p. cm. — (Workshops in computing)
   "Published in collaboration with the British Computer Society."
   Includes bibliographical references and index.
   ISBN 3-540-19804-0 : $62.00 (approx.). — ISBN 0-387-19804-0 :
$62.00 (approx.)
   1. Automatic theorem proving—Congresses. 2. Larch prover—
Congresses. I. Martin, Ursula. II. Wing, Jeannette Marie.
III. Title. IV. Series.
QA76.9.A96I58   1992   92-36174
005.13'1—dc20   CIP

Typesetting: Camera ready by contributors
Printed by Antony Rowe Ltd., Chippenham, Wiltshire
34/3830-543210 Printed on acid-free paper

Preface

The papers in this volume were presented at the First International Workshop on Larch, held at MIT Endicott House near Boston on 13–15 July 1992.

Larch is a family of formal specification languages and tools, and this workshop was a forum for those who have designed the Larch languages, built tool support for them, particularly the Larch Prover, and used them to specify and reason about software and hardware systems.

The Larch Project started in 1980, led by John Guttag at MIT and James Horning, then at Xerox/Palo Alto Research Center and now at Digital Equipment Corporation/Systems Research Center (DEC/SRC). Major applications have included VLSI circuit synthesis, medical device communications, compiler development and concurrent systems based on Lamport's TLA, as well as several applications to classical theorem proving and algebraic specification.

Larch supports a two-tiered approach to specifying software and hardware modules. One tier of a specification is written in the *Larch Shared Language* (LSL). An LSL specification describes mathematical abstractions such as sets, relations, and algebras; its semantics is defined in terms of first-order theories. The second tier is written in a *Larch interface language*, one designed for a specific programming language. An interface specification describes the effects of individual modules, e.g. state changes, resource allocation, and exceptions; its semantics is defined in terms of first-order predicates over two states, where state is defined in terms of the programming language's notion of state. Thus, LSL is programming language independent; a Larch interface language is programming language dependent.

The Larch toolkit includes syntax checkers for LSL and for various Larch interface languages including Larch/C, Larch/Modula-3, Larch/ Ada, Larch/Smalltalk, Larch/ ML, and the Generic Concurrent Interface Language (GCIL). Most significantly, the Larch toolkit includes a semantic analyzer in the form of the Larch Prover (LP), developed by Steve Garland at MIT. LP is based on a fragment of first-order logic and its design derives from a long series of theorem provers based on rewrite-rule theory.

This lively and productive workshop was attended by active Larch users and developers in industry and universities from Europe and the USA. Papers were presented covering all aspects of the Larch project, and seventeen of these are presented in this volume.

We should like to thank many people for their help with the workshop. We thank Digital Equipment Corporation and the National Science Foundation for their financial support. We also thank Olga Guttag and Anne Rubin, who took care of many of the local arrangements, William Ang who designed the Larch logo, and Mimi Pierson and her staff who maintain such a splendid conference facility at MIT Endicott House. Rosie Kemp of Springer-Verlag and Margaret Anderson of St Andrews University were unfailingly helpful in the preparation of these proceedings.

November 1992

Ursula Martin
Jeannette M. Wing

Contents

Is Engineering Software Amenable to Formal Specification?

John W. Baugh Jr.

Department of Civil Engineering

North Carolina State University

Raleigh, NC 27695-7908 USA

Abstract

Unwieldy, incomprehensible, spaghetti-like Fortran code is very likely the image conjured by the term "engineering and scientific software." What could the purveyors of such monstrosities possibly want with formal methods? Written from the perspective of a civil engineer, the following is a discussion of the potential role of formal specification tools, such as Larch, in engineering applications. The discussion also includes some examples of specifying engineering software components, and some comments on the potential benefits of formal specifications in engineering program design.

1   Introduction

Engineers are accustomed to dealing with specifications of behavior—they define the minimal requirements for a product to be considered "correct." For example, bridges must span certain distances, limit deflections under prescribed loads, and so on. During design and analysis, these specifications provide an integral source of information that guides the project and ensures that the product design is in the set of acceptable designs. An additional aspect of traditional engineering design is that the bridge engineer can argue rigorously that the conceptual "bridge" satisfies its specification even before the actual product has been built. This ability is founded on Newton's laws, theories of deformable bodies, and other tools that are available for describing the behavior of the conceptual bridge, or mathematical model.

Given this intimate relationship between engineering and specifications, it seems likely that civil engineers could benefit from the use of formal specification tools, which provide some assistance in representing and manipulating formal objects. This paper attempts to answer the question, "Is Engineering Software Amenable to Formal Specification?" first by describing three potential civil engineering applications, and then by giving some detailed examples in one of these application areas, engineering software development.[1] The discussion also includes some observations and some mention of the likely benefits of formal specification technology in civil engineering.

---

[1] Parts of the example and some corresponding observations have been taken from an article to appear in *Computers & Structures* (Pergamon Press) entitled "Using Formal Methods to Specify the Functional Properties of Engineering Software."

2 Potential Engineering Applications

A dichotomy often used in engineering is the separation of analysis and design aspects, and both parts of the process may benefit from the use of formal methods. Other applications, such as electronic data exchange, may span the entire engineering process. Some of these applications include:

- *Analysis software*—civil engineering analysts often use large and complex numerical programs to characterize and understand physical and chemical systems. Support is needed to help manage software complexity and to promote reliability and reuse.

- *Design standards*—certain constraints must be imposed to guarantee the safety and serviceability of engineered products. Although current design standards are represented textually, computer representation and processing of standards could both improve their quality and enhance their use.

- *Electronic data exchange*—civil engineering projects are characterized by large teams that span several disciplines and involve a number of organizations and government agencies. Any improvement in communication, such as electronic data exchange, will dramatically improve the engineering process.

The potential use and benefit of formal methods in these broad areas are described below.

2.1 Analysis Software

A large class of engineering software analyzes and simulates natural phenomena and man-made objects, such as the diffusion of contaminants through porous media or the structural behavior of buildings and bridges. To analyze these systems, engineering programs typically convert representations of physical systems into mathematical models which are then approximated. For example, the behavior of a structural system may be described by partial differential equations that are approximated by finite element methods. Although many concepts arise from the various domains included in these programs, they are almost always structured around procedures rather than data, and without abstraction barriers in either case. For example, it is unlikely that one could reuse the network representation of a structural analysis program in a transportation application—it is in there somewhere, but you "can't get your hands on it." Nevertheless, a methodology of data abstraction generally produces better program structure for this class of programs [5].

2.1.1 The engineer as computer user

While routine use of commercial software is common, many problems encountered by engineers require program development or modification. For example, programs are often extended to analyze additional phenomena, such as a new building component, which may complicate the governing equations and require additional approximation methods. What appear to be local additions may in fact send ripples throughout the implementation. Thus, "the engineer as computer user" can often be replaced by "the engineer as programmer."

2.1.2 Enter formal methods?

If program development and modification are important components of engineering, and if engineering programs are notoriously difficult to develop and modify, what can be done to improve these processes? One possibility is to identify appropriate data types and formally specify their behavior [2, 3], which may help us not only to communicate our intentions, but also to improve our understanding of the overall computational process. For example, the process of moving from the physical to the mathematical is embedded in our programs but hardly noticed otherwise. Representations of physical systems, and their mathematical interpretations, can be readily defined in a formal yet abstract manner using equational specifications. System validation is another potential benefit, since these specifications might be used as a workbench to experiment with new analysis strategies, physical systems, computational models, and computer architectures. Because many of our functional requirements can be stated formally, the necessary proofs of use may be easily stated.

2.2 Design Standards

Analysis and simulation, as described above, are part of a more general design process that imposes limits on behavior to ensure satisfactory designs. For example, to design the supporting structure of a steel frame building, civil engineers follow an 800-page standard produced by the American Institute of Steel Construction [1] (other standards may also be applicable in certain situations). The standard does not prescribe the loading requirements for which structures should be designed, but rather the allowable stresses, deflections, and factors of safety. Of course, other design constraints, such as social, economic, and political constraints, are beyond the scope of standards and fall within the realm of "engineering judgment." The steel design manual consists of the following components:

- *Tables*—properties of standard sections (i.e., the cross-sections of standard members) such as I-beams, angles, and channels are given, which include depth, weight, area, and so on. Tables also list welded joints and fasteners, such as rivets, bolts and threaded parts, and their respective properties.

- *Formulas*—the standard prescribes allowable stresses (e.g., for tension, compression, shear, bending, etc., and their combinations), allowable deflections, stability factors, and the placement of rivets and bolts.

- *Text*—the proper use of tables and formulas is described informally by associated text and commentary, whose logical steps are relatively complex. The standard also says which effects should be considered in a given situation.

2.2.1 Are standards consistent and complete?

The answer to this is, "not very likely." Because their text is open to multiple interpretations, and in the absence of standards-checking tools, design standards are simply checked as thoroughly as possible by review committees. Professor Steven J. Fenves of Carnegie Mellon University has said in effect that the "carefully considered" aspects of standards are indeed sound, but that the more obscure aspects contain inconsistencies and omissions [10]. Given this, one may ask if these inconsistencies and omissions have led to any structural failures. Although the answer is, "probably not," because of safety factors and established practices, standards are now being used in ways other than what was originally intended by standards organizations. For example, the allowable stress standards were developed before designs could be so highly optimized by computers, so structures today are designed much less conservatively than those of a decade ago.

2.2.2 Computer representation and processing

Computerization of standards can potentially benefit:

- Standards committees, by assisting in the checking process.

- Implementors of computerized design aids, by providing standards that are amenable to machine manipulation.

- Steel designers and engineers.

As early as the 1960s, Fenves advocated the use of decision tables for representing and processing design standards [9]. Such a structured approach is suitable both for proving the soundness of a standard and for processing it. Although some portions of standards have been represented by such, decision tables have been criticized for their lack of expressiveness, both in a logical sense and in a data modeling sense, and as a result have not been considered by standards-defining organizations. Given the need to represent domain specific objects in a standard, such as structural shapes and materials, current research in standards representation has taken on a more procedural tone, borrowing from concepts of object-oriented programming [11]. The combined strengths of data modeling and formal manipulation provided by the Larch Shared Language and Prover make them obvious candidates for representing and validating engineering design standards.

2.3 Electronic Data Exchange

As previously mentioned, the large teams required by engineering projects mean that communication must be precise and efficient. Some steps have been taken in the direction of electronic communication, e.g., standards for CAD data exchange such as IGES. These modest but effective standards have enabled the communication of product drawings across machines, software packages, and organizations, and have thus significantly improved some parts of the communication process. The acceptance of these standards has led others to propose more comprehensive standards that would enable the sharing of all product data, from ships to silicon chips, instead of simply arcs, lines, and points.

An international effort in this direction, referred to as STEP, has been under development since the mid-1980s. As described in the ISO document "STEP Part 1: Overview and fundamental principles":

> "The Standard for the Exchange of Product Model Data (STEP) is a neutral mechanism capable of completely representing product data throughout the life cycle of a product. The completeness of this representation makes it suitable not only for neutral file exchange, but also as a basis for implementing and sharing product databases and archiving. There is an undeniable need to transfer product data in computer-readable form from one site to another. These sites may have one of a number of relationships between them (contractor and subcontractor, customer and supplier); the information invariably needs to iterate between the sites, retaining both data completeness and functionality, until it is ultimately archived."

The US effort is led by the PDES organization (Product Data Exchange using STEP), which has over 600 participating members, and which is coordinated by the National Institute of Standards and Technology (NIST). To represent product data, such as those needed by the architecture, engineering, and construction (AEC) industry, PDES has developed a procedural data modeling language called EXPRESS. Although EXPRESS has been successfully used to describe volumes of data models, there is increasing concern over the soundness of those specifications. Kent Reed of NIST recently mentioned the need for tools that can both ensure consistency and completeness, and validate implementations of the data models [19]. Tools and methodologies produced by the formal methods community could have a substantial impact on this and similar endeavors.

3 Engineering Software Development

As implied in the preceding discussion, specifications have a fundamental role in the development of engineered products, including computer programs. This section describes some of our experiences in developing a handbook of reusable software specifications for engineering analysis. The use of high-level notations allows us to focus attention on the design of domain-specific software components such as topology, coordinate systems, spatial transformations, discretization techniques, material models, and so on. Such a handbook can be used to guide software implementation and to promote discussion on designs and design strategies. Because they are formal objects, these specifications may also be used for validating functional requirements, verifying program correctness, representing knowledge about program components, and prototyping complex software systems, since some formal notations also have an operational interpretation.

3.1 Specifications

Not only must notations be considered in program specification, but also the level at which programs are to be described. At the highest level are requirements that the overall program must satisfy, and these may described using a variety of mathematical notations. This task may be particularly straight-forward in engineering domains if the problem statement is already posed in terms of mathematics. For example:

> Find a function $u = u(x)$, $0 \leq x \leq N$ that satisfies the following differential equation and boundary conditions:
>
> $$-u'' + u = x, \qquad 0 < x < N$$
> $$u(0) = 0, \qquad u(N) = 0$$

Although we have an obligation to show that programs satisfy these require-ments, such high-level descriptions offer little help in structuring programs or reasoning about them, which motivates us to specify what the program does at lower levels of abstraction. For example, the program developer may choose to recast the problem in variational form and approximate a solution by discretiz-ing the domain using finite element methods. This computational approach should be represented in the program specification.

Something closer to the computational process, yet independent of imple-mentation details, is required. One approach to program development that is particularly suited to specification techniques is data abstraction, which results in a program composed of abstract data types. An abstract data type may be defined as a set of values (i.e., the domain) and a set of operators with both syntactic and semantic descriptions. While not often used in numerical programs, data abstraction has been shown to produce the same benefits (e.g., loosely-coupled, highly-cohesive modules) as it has in other application areas [5]. For example, even though their requirement specifications look rather dif-ferent, analysis programs must represent many similar concepts, e.g., topology, coordinate systems, matrices, and material properties. Thus, it is likely that we will be able to reuse our specifications in a variety of applications.

The approach used to specify these data abstractions is based on multi-sorted equational logic, which is supported by the Larch family of specification languages. Using a *two-tiered* approach to specification [16], the equational theories are separated from the interface specifications, which specify the ac-tual software components in terms of their preconditions and postconditions. Thus, equational theories remain uncluttered from error values, implementa-tion language features, etc., since they are used only to define the assertion language of the interface specification. The separation of concerns provided by the two-tiered approach allows equational theories to be reused far more easily than other kinds of computational objects.

3.2 A Simple Example

A particularly important characteristic of equational specifications is their abil-ity to describe many different kinds of behavior, from very low-level types, such as Booleans and cardinal numbers, to very high-level types that are appropriate in specific domains such as civil engineering. The following is an example of specifying engineering software components, such as those needed in network analysis and finite element methods. Although somewhat abstract, the exam-ple was chosen to minimize the need to describe substantial domain-specific details.

3.2.1 Topology

The representation of topology is a common requirement for engineering programs since they often model physical objects and processes. Typical engineering models include hydraulic systems with pipes and junctions, structural
systems with beams and connections, and construction management schedules
with activities and events. The topological relationships in these discretized
models may be conveniently represented as a labeled attribute graph. By extending graphs with the notion of a "generalized edge," i.e., one that is denoted
by a nonempty set of incident vertices instead of just two as in ordinary graphs,
the topology of two- and three-dimensional elements, such as those found in
finite element applications, may be represented. Graphs extended in this way
are referred to as *hypergraphs*.

Definition Let $V = \{v_1, v_2, \ldots, v_n\}$ and $E = \{e_1, e_2, \ldots, e_m\}$ be finite sets,
and let f be a function that maps each e_i to a subset of V such that

$$f\, e_i \neq \{\} \qquad (i = 1, 2, \ldots, m) \tag{1}$$

$$\bigcup_{i=1}^{m} f\, e_i = V \tag{2}$$

A hypergraph [6] on V is defined as $\langle V, E, f \rangle$ with vertices v_i and edges e_i.

In engineering applications we are generally interested in the order of incident vertices, and we may therefore define each e_i to be an ordered set. An
example hypergraph is

$$
\begin{aligned}
f\, e_1 &= [\, v_1, v_2 \,] \\
f\, e_2 &= [\, v_2, v_4, v_3 \,] \\
f\, e_3 &= [\, v_6, v_5, v_3 \,] \\
f\, e_4 &= [\, v_4 \,] \\
f\, e_5 &= [\, v_6, v_4 \,] \\
f\, e_6 &= [\, v_7, v_8, v_6 \,]
\end{aligned}
$$

with edge names $e_1, e_2, \ldots, e_6$ and vertex names $v_1, v_2, \ldots, v_8$. To draw the
hypergraph we represent a vertex by a point, and an edge of cardinality 1 as a
loop, of cardinality 2 as a continuous line, and of cardinality greater than 2 as
a curve enclosing incident vertices (cf. Figure 1). In the remaining discussion
we drop the distinction between graphs and hypergraphs, and assume that any
graph may have generalized edges.

Because edges and vertices may have attributes, a function from edge names
(or IDs) to edge attributes, $f_e : EID \rightarrow EA$, is provided, as well as one from
vertex names to vertex attributes, $f_v : VID \rightarrow VA$.

To specify a graph using equations, equivalences are defined between graph
terms containing constructors and observers. For example, a graph may be
built-up with the constructors

$$
\begin{aligned}
&new :\rightarrow H \\
&add\_v : H, VID, VA \rightarrow H \\
&add\_e : H, EID, EA, OrderedVID \rightarrow H
\end{aligned}
$$

8

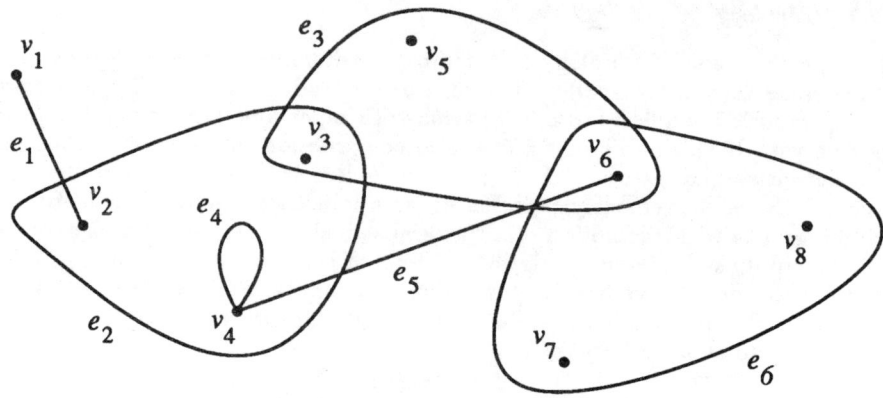

Figure 1: Representation of a Hypergraph

where H is a generalized graph, VID is a vertex name, VA is a vertex attribute, EID is an edge name, EA is an edge attribute, and $OrderedVID$ is an ordered set of vertex names (the incidence list). The primitive constructor new denotes an empty graph, and add_v and add_e are used to add vertices and edges to the graph, respectively. If vertex and edge names are symbols and their attributes are integers, the term

$$add\_e(add\_v(add\_v(new, x, 1), y, 2), a, 10, insert(x, insert(y, \{\})))$$

is interpreted as a graph with vertices x and y having attributes 1 and 2, respectively, and with an edge a that connects them having attribute 10. The operator $insert$ is a Set (or $OrderedSet$) constructor.

Because we are interested in incidence as well as adjacency information, observers are provided that access that information and the component attributes. The observers $attr\_v$, $attr\_e$, $incid\_v$, and $incid\_e$ return attributes and incidences for vertices and edges. The complete trait, a basic unit of specification, is shown below:

$Hypergraph(VID, VA, EID, EA, H)$: **trait**
    includes
        $Set(VID, SetofVID)$, $OrderedSet(VID, OrderedVID)$,
        $Set(EID, SetofEID)$
    introduces
        $new :\rightarrow H$
        $add\_v : H, VID, VA \rightarrow H$
        $add\_e : H, EID, EA, OrderedVID \rightarrow H$
        $vertices : H \rightarrow SetofVID$
        $edges : H \rightarrow SetofEID$
        $attr\_v : H, VID \rightarrow VA$
        $attr\_e : H, EID \rightarrow EA$
        $incid\_v : H, EID \rightarrow OrderedVID$
        $incid\_e : H, VID \rightarrow SetofEID$

$incid\_e' : H, VID, SetofEID \rightarrow SetofEID$

asserts

H **generated by** new, add_v, add_e

H **partitioned by** $attr\_v, attr\_e, incid\_v, incid\_e$

$\forall\, h : H, v, v' : VID, va : VA, sv : SetofVID, ov : OrderedVID,$
$\quad e, e' : EID, ea : EA, se : SetofEID$

$vertices(new) == \{\}$
$vertices(add\_v(h, v, va)) == insert(v, vertices(h))$
$vertices(add\_e(h, e, ea, ov)) == vertices(h)$

$edges(new) == \{\}$
$edges(add\_v(h, v, va)) == edges(h)$
$edges(add\_e(h, e, ea, ov)) == insert(e, edges(h))$

$attr_v(add_v(h, v, va), v') == $ **if** $v = v'$ **then** va **else** $attr\_v(h, v')$
$attr\_v(add\_e(h, e, ea, ov), v') == attr\_v(h, v')$

$attr\_e(add\_v(h, v, va), e') == attr\_e(h, e')$
$attr\_e(add\_e(h, e, ea, ov), e') ==$
$\quad$ **if** $e = e'$ **then** ea **else** $attr\_e(h, e')$

$incid\_v(add\_v(h, v, va), e') == incid\_v(h, e')$
$incid\_v(add\_e(h, e, ea, ov), e') ==$
$\quad$ **if** $e = e'$ **then** ov **else** $incid\_v(h, e')$

%% Careful here, overridden edges must not contribute
$incid\_e(h, v) == incid\_e'(h, v, edges(h))$
$incid\_e'(h, v, \{\}) == \{\}$
$incid\_e'(h, v, insert(e, se)) ==$
$\quad$ **if** $v \in incid\_v(h, e)$
$\quad$ **then** $insert(e, incid\_e'(h, v, se))$ **else** $incid\_e'(h, v, se)$

In the specification, the **generated by** clause adds an induction rule for *Hypergraphs*, and the **partitioned by** clause adds a deduction rule that says that two *Hypergraphs* are the same if indistinguishable by the given observers. The trait *Set* (from the Larch Handbook) and related trait *OrderedSet* are textually included by an **includes** clause. Of course, an alternative approach would be to model *Hypergraphs* using even higher-level traits, such as those for functional relations.

3.2.2 *Validating the Specification*

As already stated, one of the primary benefits in defining formal specifications is that it allows one to focus more attention on the *design* stage of programming. In contrast to informal ones, a formal specification can be reasoned about using ordinary mathematics, providing an alternative to testing-by-execution, as described below [14]:

> "The Larch style of specification emphasizes brevity and clarity rather than executability, so it is usually impossible to validate Larch specifications by testing. Instead, Larch allows specifiers to make precise claims about specifications—claims that, if true, can be verified at specification time."

Thus, specifications are "tested" by showing that they exhibit certain properties. For example, the following is a property that all graphs should exhibit: the set of edges is equivalent to the union of the incident edges for all vertices in the graph. Formally, we wish to show that the equational theory:

implies $\forall\ h : H$
    $edges(h) == edges'(h, vertices(h))$

where

$\forall\ h : H, v : VID, sv : SetofVID$
    $edges'(h, \{\}) == \{\}$
    $edges'(h, insert(v, sv)) == incid\_e(h, v) \cup edges'(h, sv)$

Validating this property also tests the notion of incident edges, which is not directly represented by a graph term. The definition of incident edges is needed for adjacency information, and also for certain engineering applications where vertex information (such as average nodal stresses) are computed from incident edge attributes.

For validating Larch specifications, proof-debugging support is provided by LP, the Larch Prover. After the translation to LP, proof of the theorem above begins by induction on graphs,[2] but requires a number of intermediate lemmas to prove the induction subgoals, including:

prove $edges'(add\_v(h, v, va), sv) = edges'(h, sv)$ **by induction on** sv
prove $incid\_e(h, v) \subset edges(h)$ **by induction on** h

and some lemmas on *Sets*:

prove $e \in x \Rightarrow insert(e, x) = x$ **by induction on** x
prove $(x \subset y) \Rightarrow (x \subset insert(e, y))$ **by induction on** x
prove $(x \subset y) \Rightarrow (x \cup y = y)$ **by induction on** x

As might be expected, however, the proof process eventually requires the following:

prove $edges'(add\_e(h, e, ea, sv), sv') = insert(e, edges'(h, sv'))$

which follows only if

$sv \subset sv'$

which is not known.

The inability to make proofs go through often points to design errors. In the previous case we failed to impose the necessary restriction on graph terms.

---

[2] The obvious induction rule is generated by the **generated by** clause in the *Hypergraph* trait.

We can eliminate the possibility of invalid terms at the level of interface specifications, which describe the behavior of the procedures we intend to provide in software, and this avoids complicating our theory of graphs with error terms. Thus, we can impose the following representation invariant on graph implementations to get the desired property:

$$\textbf{assert } \forall\ h : H, v : VID, va : VA, ov : OrderedVID, e : EID, ea : EA$$
$$rep\_inv(new)$$
$$rep\_inv(add\_v(h, v, va)) == rep\_inv(h)$$
$$rep\_inv(add\_e(h, e, ea, ov)) == ov \subset vertices(h) \land rep\_inv(h)$$

which ensures Equation 2 in the original definition of hypergraphs. For example, to allow only terms satisfying both Equation 1 and *rep_inv*, the following precondition would be required for a procedure that adds graph edges:

$$addEdge = \textbf{proc}\ (h: Hypergraph, e: EID, ea: EA, ov: OrderedVID)$$
$$\textbf{requires } \neg(ov = \{\}) \land ov \subset vertices(h)$$
$$\textbf{modifies } h$$
$$\textbf{effects } h_{post} = add\_e(h, e, ea, ov)$$

From the preceding example it should be apparent that equational specifications enable the precise description of complex behavior in a small amount of space. For instance, we could have defined the graph behavior using Fortran code, which is also precise, but it would have contained many unnecessary details, such as an implementation of functional relations by (perhaps) hash tables, that obfuscate communication and complicate proofs of use to the point that conventional testing methods must be used exclusively. It should also be apparent that, while a helpful design tool, these proofs cannot be effectively performed with pencil and paper, and that even the specification itself requires machine support to ensure proper syntactic construction.

3.3 Specifying Other Engineering Concepts

We have used the equational approach to specify and prove properties of other engineering analysis concepts, including many of the informal ones for finite element analysis described in [5]. Based on this experience we offer the following observations and comments.

In general, equational specifications are suitable for describing the underlying abstractions in engineering analysis programs. They offer a precise, implementation-independent way to define the variety of abstractions needed in these programs. In addition, they provide a vocabulary for defining even higher-level program behavior.

For example, using some of the specifications already defined, one might define the required behavior of a structural analysis program with the following compatibility, equilibrium, and force-displacement relations, where the states are joint displacements and the sources are loads:

- **Compatibility:**

  $$\forall\ v : vertices(h) \bullet$$
  $$(e_1, e_2 \in incid\ e(h, v)) \Rightarrow vertexState_g(e_1, v, h) = vertexState_g(e_2, v, h)$$
  $$where$$
  $$vertexState_g(e, v, h) = toGlobal(edgeVertexState(attr\ e(h, e), v), e)$$

- **Equilibrium:**

  $\forall \; v : vertices(h) \bullet$
  $source(attr \dot{} v(h, v)) = \sum \{e : incid \dot{} e(h, v) \bullet internalVertexSource_g(e, v)\}$
  $where$
    $internalVertexSource_g(e, v, h) =$
      $toGlobal(internalVertexSource(attr \dot{} e(h, e), v), e)$

- **Force-displacement:**

  $\forall \; e : edges(h) \bullet$
  $internalSource(attr \dot{} e(h, e)) = stiffness(attr \dot{} e(h, e)) \times state(attr \dot{} e(h, e))$

where *edgeVertexState* returns the displacement of the specified vertex for a given edge, *internalVertexSource* returns the internal load, and *toGlobal* converts vector quantities to a common coordinate system.

Informally, the above specification says that a program modeling a truss structure under loading must generate a (unique) solution in which the members remain connected at joints (compatibility), the internal forces are in equilibrium (Newton's Law), and the member displacements are linearly related to the applied loads (force-displacement).

3.4   Some Observations

The use of specifications to build up descriptions of complex behavior enables one to precisely state the functional behavior required of a program. For example, by doing some symbol manipulation —not program execution— one could show that a (constructive) structural analysis program (e.g., one that uses the direct assembly approach of matrix methods) satisfies the (declarative) specification above.

With all the benefits of equational specifications, however, sometimes their appropriateness is diminished either because the concept is already well-defined (and perhaps formalized), or because a direct implementation of the concept is at a high enough level to be readily understood without a specification. In the latter case, there may be situations where there are few if any details of the implementation that need to be abstracted away, so that the specification and the implementation are similar. This may happen, for example, when specifying facts about the application domain. Consider specifying the stiffness properties of, say, a plane truss element as

$$k(A, E, L) = \frac{AE}{L} \left[\begin{array}{cc} 1 & -1 \\ -1 & 1 \end{array} \right]$$

Here it makes little difference whether we "specify" this in Fortran or in an equational specification language.

In addition to these observations, there are some specific issues that have yet to be resolved regarding numerical computing. For example, a distinguishing characteristic of engineering analysis programs is that they must deal with the effects of roundoff errors, and specifications may need to account for them. For example, it would probably be wrong to specify the behavior of a routine that performs dot products as $x^T y$. Because of less than infinite precision arithmetic, we might write instead $fl(x^T y)$, *where* $\mid fl(x^T y) - x^T y \mid \leq \epsilon(u, n)$, in which $fl()$ represents the computed quantity and ϵ is a function of the unit roundoff error and the size of the vectors x and y. In this approach we may define specifications using exact arithmetic to avoid complicating them, and use interface specifications to impose limits on the precision of computed quantities. A somewhat different approach would be to simply label matrix operations by well-known algorithms where roundoff and other interesting characteristics are completely defined. For example, a routine for factorizing symmetric, positive definite matrices might be "specified" as gaxpy Cholesky or outer product Cholesky [13].

A final observation is that, unlike some other applications, such as the display types in [15], engineering programs may need a potentially large number of data types from many domains to implement useful behavior, and many of these data types, when considered in isolation, are not very "interesting" (where I measure interest by the complexity of interaction between constructors and observers). Thus, to show that module specifications satisfy higher-level problem requirements we need tools that can manage a large number of data types (e.g., efficiency, parameterized types).

4 Formal Specifications: Engineering Potential

Although equational specification techniques have yet to be applied in engineering software development, our preliminary experiences with them have been both positive and informative. Often, attempts to formalize a specification or to develop a proof have increased our understanding of a problem, leading to substantial design changes. There are also positive side-effects of the approach, including the benefits of data decomposition on program structure and modularity [5].

Our initial success has prompted the development of a handbook of reusable software specifications for engineering analysis, augmented with informal commentary and validation proofs. Such a handbook would have useful applications in a variety of areas, including:

- *Education.* Finite element textbook writers often include Fortran source code of a finite element program for "instructional purposes" [17, 22]. The intent is for students to use the program, make modifications, add new elements, etc., so that they can get experience with programs with more capabilities than what they could develop in a single semester. However, the amount and complexity of details required to fully understand these programs is enormous. An alternative to presenting inscrutable code would be to use the specification handbook to describe a high-level programming environment, allowing students to deal with concepts such as elements and nodes rather than program implementation details.

- *Research.* The increasing demands placed on finite element programs encourage researchers and program developers to experiment with new solution approaches, analysis capabilities, and hardware architectures. Research in computational mechanics is largely based on the demonstration of these novel techniques, perhaps within the framework of an existing program. A specification handbook would provide a convenient set of high-level building blocks for describing and mechanically validating new formulations, solution strategies, etc., without regard to implementation details.

In addition to these applications, there are other potential uses of equational specifications in engineering analysis:

- *Deriving Parallel Programs.* By applying correctness preserving transformations, an equational specification can be converted into a functional (applicative) program that expresses an appropriate horizontal/vertical parallelism for a given computer architecture. Annotated with strictness and process information, such programs represent a process network, or *dataflow graph* [4], that constrains evaluation enough to describe a parallel algorithm. This approach to parallelism has the advantage that it avoids the subtle timing issues that complicate control-flow parallelism.

- *Algorithm selection.* A sophisticated implementation of a computationally intense numerical program might accommodate multiple representations and algorithms, with selection based on the problem (input) at hand. This feature could then be used, say, to take advantage of matrix structure in solving linear systems. Note, however, that a precise statement of behavior is required to know when several different representations or algorithms can be used to achieve the same effect. Since formal specifications define the functional behavior of algorithms and data types, we have a basis proving whether one operator can be safely substituted for another (i.e., each terminates on the same class of inputs and produces identical outputs).

- *Correctness.* Finite element analysis programs are often used in situations where reliability is crucial, e.g., the design of high-rise buildings, nuclear power plants, and defense systems. Agencies such as the Nuclear Regulatory Commission require detailed audit trails of the development of programs written for analysis and design of nuclear power plants. Combined with automated theorem-proving technology, formal specifications provide a basis for implementing provably-correct engineering analysis software.

5   Related Work

Some related work may be found in both the application area (e.g., where engineers and scientists try to improve engineering analysis programs via numerical mathematics, AI techniques, etc.) and the approach area (e.g., where computing scientists develop program specification tools and techniques).

In the former area, little work has formally addressed the issues of engineering program design, although various tools and approaches have been advocated for implementing these programs [7, 8, 20]. Some of these approaches concentrate on low-level aspects, such as hiding hardware characteristics for portability reasons, while others extend Fortran with modern control constructs, dynamic storage allocation, and other useful features.

In the latter area, formal methods of program development are collectively a young and active area of computing science research, although their benefits have been shown for certain classes of problems. For example, formal methods have been shown to effectively support the design of programs in which data abstraction has a prominent role. However, the application and benefits of such methods in engineering and scientific computing have not been addressed. We are unaware of any other attempts to use formal methods in developing engineering analysis software, although a couple of related projects are apparently underway [21, 18].

6 Conclusions

While formal methods may eventually lead to improvements in engineering software, some may wonder if such a radical change in the development process is really necessary. After all, "engineering judgement" has taught us to view computer results with healthy skepticism, so perhaps highly reliable (or extensible) software is not so important. Of course there are obvious flaws in that argument, not the least of which is this: civil engineers are currently developing software for active structural control, automated construction systems, air traffic control, and hazardous waste processing. Because these systems operate without a human in the loop, the impact of errors can be particularly devastating. For instance, the same programs that analyze structural behavior may in fact be embedded in computers that exert significant forces on buildings, limiting vibratory effects and resisting earthquake loads. The high dependability and fault tolerance required of this class of software is significant, and has not been addressed by either engineers or computer scientists. These observations lead one to the following conclusion: Is engineering software amenable to formal specification? It had better be.

References

[1] American Institute of Steel Construction (AISC), Chicago, Illinois. *Manual of Steel Construction*, Eighth edition, 1980.

[2] John W. Baugh Jr. Program design with algebraic specifications. In Oktay Ural and Ton-Lo Wang, editors, *Electronic Computation: Proceedings of the Tenth Conference*, pages 345–352. Structural Division of the American Society of Civil Engineers (ASCE), 1991.

[3] John W. Baugh Jr. Formal specification of engineering analysis programs. In E. N. Houstis, J. R. Rice, and R. Vichnevetsky, editors, *Expert Systems for Scientific Computing*, pages 393–400. IMACS, North-Holland, 1992.

[4] John W. Baugh Jr. and Daniel R. Rehak. Applications of coarse-grained dataflow in computational mechanics. *Engineering with Computers*, 8(1):13–30, Winter 1992.

[5] John W. Baugh Jr. and Daniel R. Rehak. Data abstraction in engineering software development. *Journal of Computing in Civil Engineering*, 6(3):282–301, July 1992.

[6] Claude Berge. *Hypergraphs: combinatorics of finite sets*. Elsevier, New York, 1989.

[7] Robert H. Dodds Jr. and Leonard A. Lopez. Software virtual machines for development of finite element systems. *Engineering Computations*, 3:18–26, March 1986.

[8] Carlos A. Felippa and G. M. Stanley. NICE: A utility architecture for computational mechanics. In P. G. Bergen, K. J. Bathe, and W. Wunderlich, editors, *Finite Element Methods for Nonlinear Problems: Europe-U.S. Symposium*, pages 447–463. Springer-Verlag, New York, 1985.

[9] Steven J. Fenves. Tabular decision logic for structural design. *Journal of the Structural Division*, 92(ST6):473–490, December 1966.

[10] Steven J. Fenves. Personal communication. Discussion during the *Eighth Conference on Computing in Civil Engineering (ASCE)*, June 1992.

[11] James H. Garrett Jr. and M. Maher Hakim. Object-oriented model of engineering design standards. *Journal of Computing in Civil Engineering*, 6(3):323–347, July 1992.

[12] Joseph A. Goguen. Modular algebraic specification of some basic geometrical constructions. *Artificial Intelligence*, 37:123–153, 1988.

[13] Gene H. Golub and Charles F. Van Loan. *Matrix Computations*. Johns Hopkins University Press, Baltimore, Second edition, 1989.

[14] Stephen J. Graland, John V. Guttag, and James J. Horning. Debugging larch shared language specifications. Technical Report 60, Digital Equipment Corporation Systems Research Center, Palo Alto, CA, July 1990.

[15] John V. Guttag and James J. Horning. Formal specification as a design tool. In *ACM Symposium on Principles of Programming Languages*, pages 251–261, 1980.

[16] John V. Guttag, James J. Horning, and Jeannette M. Wing. Larch in five easy pieces. Technical Report 5, Digital Equipment Corporation Systems Research Center, Palo Alto, CA, July 1985.

[17] Thomas J.R. Hughes. *The Finite Element Method: Linear Static and Dynamic Finite Element Analysis*. Prentice-Hall, Englewood Cliffs, NJ, 1987.

[18] Terry Kubat. Personal communication. Department of Computer Science, Montana State University, June 1991.

[19] Kent Reed. Personal communication. Discussion during the *Eighth Conference on Computing in Civil Engineering (ASCE)*, June 1992.

[20] Daniel R. Rehak and Leonard A. Lopez. Computer aided engineering: Problems and prospects. Civil Engineering Systems Laboratory Research Series (CESLRS) 8, Department of Civil Engineering, University of Illinois at Urbana-Champaign, Urbana, IL, July 1981.

[21] Maarten van Emden. Personal communication. Department of Computer Science, University of Victoria, January 1991.

[22] Olgierd C. Zienkiewicz and Robert L. Taylor. *The Finite Element Method*, volume 1, Basic Formulations and Linear Problems. McGraw-Hill Book Company, New York, NY, fourth edition, 1989.

How to Prove Observational Theorems with LP

Michel Bidoit

LIENS, C.N.R.S. U.R.A. 1327 & Ecole Normale Supérieure
75230 Paris, France

Rolf Hennicker

Institüt für Informatik, Universität München
8 München 40, Germany

Abstract

In this paper, we explain how observability issues can contribute to a better understanding of software correctness. We describe a simple framework of observational specifications, and we give correct powerful proof principles for this framework: generator induction and context induction. We show how, under some hypotheses, the context induction principle can be greatly simplified. Then we focus on the proof of equations, and we show how observational equations can be directly proved with the LP theorem prover, by means of adequate partitioned by deduction rules. This result provides a deeper understanding of the relationships between observability and the partitioned by deduction rules used in the Larch Shared Language and LP.

1 Introduction

A fundamental aim of formal specifications is to provide a rigorous basis to establish software correctness. Indeed, it is well-known that proving the correctness of some piece of software without a formal reference document makes no sense.[1] Algebraic specifications are widely advocated as being one of the most promising formal specification techniques. However, to be provided with some algebraic specification is not sufficient per se. A precise (and adequate) definition of the correctness of some piece of software w.r.t. its algebraic specification is mandatory. This crucial prerequisite must be first fulfilled before one can develop relevant verification methods, and try to mechanize them.

Hence the adequacy of the chosen definition of correctness has a great practical impact, and we should therefore define software correctness in conformity with actual needs. In the framework of algebraic specifications, straightforward definitions of correctness turn out to be oversimplified: most programs that should be considered as being correct (from a practical point of view) are rejected. Indeed, when the program behaves correctly, there can still exist some differences between the properties stated by the specification and those verified by the program. Here, to behave correctly means that these differences are not

---

[1]Who would attempt to prove a theorem without providing its statement?

"observable." Consequently, more elaborated definitions of correctness, taking observability into account, should be considered. Similar issues are raised by the abstract implementation of a given specification by a more concrete one [22, 15] (cf. e.g. the well-known problem of the implementation of stacks by means of arrays and pointers).

Thus, our claim is that observability issues are fundamental to define a practicable notion of correctness. In [2], we have detailed various aspects related to modularity, observability, and their interactions with software correctness. However, the framework described in [2] is merely a first step towards putting software correctness proofs in practice. A further issue is to develop practicable proof methods on top of observational semantics. A major contribution to this issue is [14], where a uniform proof method for correctness proofs in the context of observational specifications, called "context induction", is developed. Moreover, it is shown in [14] how this proof principle can be applied to verify observational properties of algebraic data types, and how one can prove that the abstract implementation of a given specification by a more concrete one is observationally correct.

The aim of this paper is to investigate how standard proof techniques, hence "standard (and powerful) theorem provers/checkers" such as LP [7, 8], can be used to prove some properties in an observational framework.

This paper is organized as follows. In Section 2 we introduce the basics of observational semantics. In Section 3 we recall the context induction proof principle of [14], and we study how we can greatly simplify its application. Then in Section 4 we show how we can directly prove observational equations with LP, without any explicit context induction.

2 Observational semantics: Definitions and Notations

We assume that the reader is familiar with algebraic specifications [10, 5] and with the elementary definitions of category theory [18]. An algebraic specification SP is a tuple (S, Σ, Ax) where (S, Σ) is a signature and Ax is a finite set of Σ-formulas. We denote by $Mod(\Sigma)$ the category of all Σ-algebras, and by $Mod(SP)$ the full sub-category of all Σ-algebras for which Ax is satisfied.

2.1 Motivations

A specification is supposed to describe a future or existing system in such a way that the properties of the system (what the system does) are expressed, and the implementation details (how it is done) are omitted. Thus a specification language aims at describing classes of correct (w.r.t. the intended purposes) implementations (realizations). In contrast a programming language aims at describing specific implementations (realizations). In a loose framework, the semantics of some specification SP is a class $\mathcal{M}$ of (non-isomorphic) algebras. Given some implementation (program) P, its correctness w.r.t. the specification SP can then be established by relating the program P with one of the

```
spec : STANDARD-SET;                      spec : SET-AS-LIST;
   use : ELEM, BOOL;                         use : ELEM, BOOL;
   sort : Set;                               sort : Set;
   generated by :                           generated by :
   ∅ : ⟶ Set;                               ∅ : ⟶ Set;
   ins: Elem Set ⟶ Set;                      ins: Elem Set ⟶ Set;
   operations :                             operations :
   _ ∪ _ : Set Set ⟶ Set;                    _ ∪ _ : Set Set ⟶ Set;
   _ ∈ _ : Elem Set ⟶ Bool;                  _ ∈ _ : Elem Set ⟶ Bool;
   axioms :                                 axioms :
   ∅ ∪ S = S;                               ∅ ∪ S = S;
   ins(x, S) ∪ S' = ins(x, S ∪ S');          ins(x, S) ∪ S' = ins(x, S ∪ S');
   x ∈ ∅ = false;                            x ∈ ∅ = false;
   x ∈ ins(y, S) = (x eq y | x ∈ S);         x ∈ ins(y, S) = (x eq y | x ∈ S);
   ins(x, ins(x, S)) = ins(x, S);            where : S, S' : Set;
   ins(x, ins(y, S)) =                           x, y : Elem;
         ins(y, ins(x, S));               end SET-AS-LIST .
   S ∪ S' = S' ∪ S;
   where : S, S' : Set;
      x, y : Elem;
end STANDARD-SET .
```

Figure 1: Two specifications of sets

algebras of the class $\mathcal{M}$. Roughly speaking, the program P will be correct w.r.t. the specification SP if and only if the algebra defined by P belongs to the class $\mathcal{M}$. However, as mentioned above, such an approach leads to an over-simplified understanding of software correctness. Indeed, if software correctness (w.r.t. its formal specification) is defined in such a way, then most realizations that we would like to consider as being correct (from a practical point of view) turn out to be incorrect ones. This is illustrated by the *STANDARD-SET* specification given in Fig. 1.

If we consider a realization of *STANDARD-SET* by e.g. lists, we do not obtain a correct realization: this is due for instance to the axiom expressing the permutativity of the insertion operation, which does not hold for lists. However, if we notice that indeed we are only interested in the result of some computations (e.g. membership), then it is clear that our realization of *STANDARD-SET* by lists "behaves" correctly. Thus, an intuitively correct realization of an algebraic specification SP may correspond to an algebra which is not in *Mod(SP)*. This leads to a refined understanding of software correctness: a program P should be considered as being correct w.r.t. its specification SP if and only if the algebra defined by P is an "observationally correct realization" of SP. In other words, the differences between the specification and the software should not be "observable," w.r.t. some appropriate notion of "observability."

A similar problem is raised when one wants to prove that the abstract implementation of a given specification SP by a more concrete one SP' is correct. A first approach would be to compare the model classes $Mod(SP)$ and $Mod(SP')$, and to say that the abstract implementation is correct if and only if $Mod(SP') \subseteq Mod(SP)$ (up to renaming). Unfortunately, such an approach leads to reject most of the abstract implementations that we would like to consider as being correct. For instance, if we consider the two set specifications given in Fig. 1, then $SET\text{-}AS\text{-}LIST$ is not a correct abstract implementation of $STANDARD\text{-}SET$, since the axiom expressing the permutativity of the insertion operation does not hold for $SET\text{-}AS\text{-}LIST$.

Hence the problem is how to specify the "observations" to be associated to some specification, and to define the semantics of such "observations". Up to now, various notions of observability have been introduced, involving observation techniques based on sorts [9, 28, 16, 6, 23, 19, 26, 21, 20], on operations [27], [2], on terms [25, 13, 4] or on formulas [24, 25, 17]. Assuming that we have chosen some observation technique, we can specify, using this technique, that some parts of an algebraic specification are observable. An observational specification is thus obtained by adding a specification of the objects to be observed to a usual algebraic specification. The next step is to define the semantics of these observational specifications. There are mainly two possible ways to do this. We can extend the class of the models of the specification SP by including some additional algebras which are "behaviourally equivalent" (w.r.t. the specified observations) to a model of $Mod(SP)$ (*extension by behavioural equivalence*, see [24, 25, 13]). We will call these approaches **behavioural semantics**. We can also directly relax the satisfaction relation, hence redefine $Mod(SP)$ (*extension by relaxing the satisfaction relation*, see [23] [21] [27] [2] [4]). In the sequel such an approach will be referred to as **observational semantics**.

For a comparative study of these various ways of defining the (behavioural/observational) semantics of observational specifications, and of the relative expressive power of the various observation techniques mentioned above, see [3]. In the sequel we will recall the basic definitions of an observational semantics based on the observation of some sorts.

2.2 Observational semantics

Our observational semantics will be based on a redefinition of the satisfaction relation. Here we will only consider flat observational specifications (cf. e.g. [2] for the semantics of modular observational specifications). As explained above, we want to reflect the following idea: some data structures are observable with respect to some observable sorts (e.g. sets are observable by means of the membership operation).

Definition (Observational Specifications): An *observational specification* is a couple $SP\text{-}Obs = (SP, S_{Obs})$ such that $SP = (S, \Sigma, Ax)$ is a classical specification (i.e. Ax is a set of axioms over Σ) and $S_{Obs} \subseteq S$ is the set of *observed sorts*. If Ax only contains equalities then $SP\text{-}Obs$ is called *equational*. If Ax only contains axioms of the form $[(u_1 = v_1) \wedge \ldots \wedge (u_n = v_n) \implies (u = v)]$ then $SP\text{-}Obs$ is called *positive conditional*.

Example: For our set specifications, we will choose $S_{Obs} = \{Elem, Bool\}$.

As usual, the notion of *observable contexts* is crucial for observability [16, 23, 21, 13, 14, 2, 4]:

Definition (Contexts and Observable Contexts):

- A *context* over a signature Σ is a Σ-term C with exactly one variable.

- Given a context C, its *arity* is $s \to s'$, where s is the sort of the variable occurring in C and s' is the sort of the term C.

- The context reduced to a variable z_s of sort s is called "the empty context" (of sort s).

- Given a context C of arity $s \to s'$, a *subcontext* C' of C is any context (of arity $s \to s_i$) which is a subterm (of sort s_i) of C. C' is a subcontext of C will be denoted by $C' \preceq C$. Note that $\preceq$ is the syntactic subterm partial ordering restricted to contexts.

- Given a context C of arity $s \to s'$, and a Σ-term t of sort s, $C[t]$ denotes the term obtained by the substitution of t to the variable of C.

- Given a context C of arity $s \to s'$, and an element a of sort s in a Σ-algebra M, let σ denote both the assignment of the variable of C to a and its unique extension from $T_\Sigma(X)$ to M. Then $C[a]$ is by definition the value $\sigma(C)$ (of sort s') in M.

- Given a signature (S, Σ), given a distinguished subset S_d of S and a sort s in S, we denote by $C_s^{S_d}$ the set of all contexts C of arity $s \to s_d$, with $s_d \in S_d$. Hence $C_s^{S_{Obs}}$ denotes the set of all *observable contexts* of sort s.

Let us now define the semantics of flat observational specifications.

Definition (Observational Semantics): Let *SP–Obs* be an observational specification and Σ be its signature. Let M be a Σ-algebra and let ϕ be a Σ-formula.

- Two elements a and b of M are *observationally equal* with respect to S_{Obs} if and only if they have the same sort s and for all contexts $C \in C_s^{S_{Obs}}$ $C[a] = C[b]$ in M (according to the usual equality of set theory). In particular observational equality on observable sorts coincides with the set-theoretic equality;[2] for the non observable sorts, the observational equality contains the set-theoretic equality, but there are also distinct values which are observationally equal.

- The Σ-algebra M *satisfies ϕ with respect to S_{Obs}* is denoted by $M \models_{Obs} \phi$ and means that for all substitutions $\sigma : T_\Sigma(X) \to M$, $\sigma(\phi)$ holds in M according to the observational equality (defined above) and the truth tables of the logical connectives of ϕ.

---

[2] because $C_s^{S_{Obs}}$ always contains the empty context z_s, when s is an observable sort.

Lemma: Let $SP–Obs$ be an observational specification and Σ be its signature. Let M be a Σ-algebra and let $LHS = RHS$ be an equation. Let s be the common sort of LHS and RHS.
$M \models_{Obs} LHS = RHS$ if and only if $\forall\ C \in \mathcal{C}_s^{S_{Obs}}\quad M \models C[LHS] = C[RHS]$, where $\models$ denotes the usual satisfaction relation.

Example: It is not difficult to show that the algebra of lists observationally satisfies the $STANDARD\text{-}SET$ specification given above (w.r.t. $S_{Obs} = \{Elem, Bool\}$). In this algebra, ins is realized by adding the element in front of the list. $ins(x, ins(y, S)) = ins(y, ins(x, S))$ is observationally satisfied (even if these two list realizations of sets are not equal with respect to the set-theoretic equality) because all observable contexts that can be applied to these two terms have $Set \rightarrow Bool$ as arity and must contain $\in$.

Notation: Given an observational specification $SP–Obs$, $Mod(SP–Obs)$ is the full sub-category of $Mod(\Sigma)$ whose objects are the Σ-algebras that satisfy all the axioms of $SP–Obs$ w.r.t. S_{Obs}.

2.3 Finitely generated observational models

The framework defined above provides a firm basis to establish the correctness of some software w.r.t. its observational specification, or to prove that some abstract implementation of a given specification by a more concrete one is observationally correct. However, if we really want to prove correctness properties, then we need adequate deduction rules and proof techniques. This point is thoroughly studied in the following sections, but we would nevertheless discuss here some proof related aspects. It is a usual practice to introduce a restriction to finitely generated models (w.r.t. the operations specified as generators) to guarantee that "induction w.r.t. the generators" is a correct proof principle. An obvious question is whether a similar restriction can be introduced in the framework of observational specifications, and whether we will obtain a similar powerful proof principle.

As a first remark we should note that the restriction to finitely generated models (w.r.t. the generators) is not adequate since such a restriction will be somehow contradictory with the aim of the observational semantics we have developed so far (for a detailed discussion of this point, see [2]). The point is that we must allow values that are not exactly denotable by a composition of generators; but we can still obtain the desired proof principle by requiring for each value to be observationally equal to a value denotable by a composition of generators. This leads to the following definition:

Definition (Observational restriction to generators): Let $SP–Obs$ be a modular observational specification. Let $\Omega \subseteq \Sigma$ be the set of generators declared in $SP–Obs$. A model M of $SP–Obs$ is *observationally finitely generated w.r.t.* Ω if and only if for every value m in M there exists an Ω-term t such that m is observationally equal to the value denoted by t.

Notation: Given an observational specification $SP–Obs$, $Gen(SP–Obs)$ is the full sub-category of $Mod(\Sigma)$ whose objects are the Σ-algebras which satisfy all the axioms of $SP\text{--}Obs$ w.r.t. S_{Obs}, and which are observationally finitely generated w.r.t. Ω. By convention, $SP\text{--}Obs \models_{Obs} \phi$ means that $\forall M \in Gen(SP\text{--}Obs)$ $M \models_{Obs} \phi$, and $SP \models \phi$ means that $\forall M \in Gen(SP)$ $M \models \phi$.

Theorem (Generator Induction Principle):
Structural induction w.r.t. the generators Ω is a correct proof principle for $Gen(SP\text{--}Obs)$.

Sketch of the proof: The result follows from the fact that structural induction w.r.t. Ω is a correct proof principle for $Gen(SP)$, from the definition of $Gen(SP\text{--}Obs)$ and from the fact that the observational equality we have defined is a congruence.

2.4 The *SET-AS-LIST* example

Let us consider again the *SET-AS-LIST* specification given in Fig. 1. To fully understand the link between the usual satisfaction relation and the observational one, it is important to keep in mind the following remarks and examples:

- *SET-AS-LIST* $\models x \in (S \cup S') = x \in (S' \cup S)$, hence *SET-AS-LIST* $\models_{Obs} x \in (S \cup S') = x \in (S' \cup S)$, since this is an equation between **observable** terms. More generally:
  For all observable terms LHS and RHS, $SP\text{--}Obs \models_{Obs} LHS = RHS$ if and only if $SP \models LHS = RHS$.

- *SET-AS-LIST* $\models S \cup \emptyset = S$ (the proof can easily be done by induction on the generators of *Set*), hence *SET-AS-LIST* $\models_{Obs} S \cup \emptyset = S$. More generally:
  For all terms LHS and RHS, $SP \models LHS = RHS$ implies $SP\text{--}Obs \models_{Obs} LHS = RHS$.

- *SET-AS-LIST* $\models_{Obs} S \cup S = S$, but *SET-AS-LIST* $\not\models S \cup S = S$. The next sections will provide us means for proving that this equation is an observational theorem of *SET-AS-LIST*. More generally:
  $SP\text{--}Obs \models_{Obs} LHS = RHS$ *does not imply in general* $SP \models LHS = RHS$.

It is important to note that the general properties enounced here only hold for **equational observational specifications**.

Up to now, the only proof principle at hand for observational specifications is the generator induction principle. Together with the two general properties enounced above, this principle will allow the proof of some theorems. However, it is obvious that the definition of correct proof principles for observational specifications requires further investigation (at least to be able to prove that *SET-AS-LIST* $\models_{Obs} S \cup S = S$!). This is the topic of the next sections.

A last remark is that we can consider observational semantics from two symmetrical viewpoints. On one hand, as explained above, the aim of our observational semantics is to provide a better notion of correctness. For instance, in an observational framework, one can prove that *SET-AS-LIST* is a correct abstract implementation of *STANDARD-SET*. On the other hand, one could as well consider that the aim of an observational approach is to extend the theory associated to a given set of axioms, by substituting the observational theory to the usual one. In that case, more consequences will follow from the axioms given in the specification (e.g., $S \cup S = S$ belongs to the observational theory of *SET-AS-LIST*). Hence, in an observational framework, we reach a specification style which is really abstract.

3   Context Induction

In this section we recall the "Context Induction Principle" as described in [14] and we study some of its properties.

Definition (Context Property): Given a signature (S, Σ), given a distinguished subset S_d of S and a sort s in S, remember that we denote by $C_s^{S_d}$ the set of all contexts C of arity $s \rightarrow s_d$, with $s_d \in S_d$. A $C_s^{S_d}$-*context property* Φ is a property universally quantified over $C_s^{S_d}$, i.e. the property Φ looks like:
$$\Phi : \quad \forall C \in C_s^{S_d} \quad \Phi(C).$$

An obvious example of a context property is the observational satisfaction of a given equation $LHS = RHS$. Remember that we have seen that a Σ-algebra M satisfies $LHS = RHS$ w.r.t. S_{Obs} if and only if the following context property holds: $\forall C \in C_s^{S_{Obs}} \quad M \models C[LHS] = C[RHS]$, where s is the common sort of LHS and RHS.

Notation: In the following we will often have to consider contexts of the form $F(t_1, \ldots, t_{i-1}, C_i, t_{i+1}, \ldots, t_n)$, of arity $s \rightarrow s_d$, where:

- F is an arbitrary non constant function symbol in Σ of arity
  $F : s_1 \ldots s_n \rightarrow s_d$, with $s_d \in S_d$,

- i is an arbitrary integer such that $1 \leq i \leq n$,

- C_i is an arbitrary context of arity $s \rightarrow s_i$,

- $t_1, \ldots, t_n$ are arbitrary ground terms (of sort $s_1, \ldots, s_n$ respectively),

By convention, these contexts will be denoted by $F(\ldots, C_i, \ldots)$.

Definition (Inductive Context Property): A $C_s^{S_d}$-context property Φ is said to be *inductive* if and only if the two following conditions are satisfied:

1. $\Phi(z_s)$ is true, where z_s denotes the empty context of $C_s^{S_d}$. Note that if $s \notin S_d$, there is no empty context in $C_s^{S_d}$. In that case, the condition is by convention trivially satisfied.

2. For all contexts $F(\ldots, C_i, \ldots)$ of arity $s \rightarrow s_d$, with $s_d \in S_d$, the following implication is true:[3]
   $$[\forall C_j \in C_s^{S_d} \text{ s.t. } C_j \preceq C_i, \ \Phi(C_j)] \Longrightarrow \Phi(F(\ldots, C_i, \ldots))$$

---

[3] To fully understand this implication, it is important to remember that $C_i \preceq C_i$.

Let us now recall the Context Induction Principle as stated in [14]:

Proposition (Context Induction Principle): A $C_s^{S_d}$-context property Φ is true if and only if it is inductive.

Proof of the Context Induction Principle:

$\Rightarrow$ If the $C_s^{S_d}$-context property Φ is true, then $\Phi(C)$ holds for any context $C \in C_s^{S_d}$. Hence the first condition and the implications of the second condition for inductiveness are trivially satisfied.

$\Leftarrow$ If Φ is inductive, then we obtained the desired result as a direct consequence of the structural induction principle. The ordering on the set of contexts $C_s^{S_d}$ is defined by the syntactic subterm ordering.

The proposition above provides means for proving context properties. However, its practical application is not always that simple, especially because, if $s_i \notin S_d$, then $C_i \notin C_s^{S_d}$, hence the proofs of the implications of the second condition for inductiveness cannot be done by a "simple induction step" (because we cannot assume $\Phi(C_i)$). Therefore, to prove these implications, one has often to start another proof by context induction over the contexts C_i of arity $s \to s_i$. For these proofs, the distinguished subset S_d to consider is $\{s_i\}$. This is why we did not directly state our definitions and proposition for S_{Obs} (remember we are mainly interested in proving observational properties), but rather for an arbitrary distinguished subset S_d. We will now look for some simpler conditions for inductiveness that will be hopefully easier to check.

Definition (Regular Context Property): A $C_s^{S_d}$-context property Φ is said to be *regular* if and only if $\forall\, C_1, C_2 \in C_s^{S_d}$ $[C_1 \preceq C_2 \,\wedge\, \Phi(C_1)] \Longrightarrow \Phi(C_2)$.

It is important to note that **the observational satisfaction of a given equation is a regular context property.**

Proposition (Simplified Context Induction Principle): Assume that $s \notin S_d$ and that the $C_s^{S_d}$-context property Φ is regular. Then Φ is inductive if and only if the following condition is satisfied:
For all contexts $F(\ldots, C_i, \ldots)$ of arity $s \to s_d$, with $s_d \in S_d$ and $s_i \notin S_d$, the following implication is true:
$$[\forall\, C_j \in C_s^{S_d} \;\; s.t. \;\; C_j \preceq C_i, \;\; \Phi(C_j)] \Longrightarrow \Phi(\, F(\ldots, C_i, \ldots)\,)$$

Note that the condition $s_i \notin S_d$ means that we only have to consider those contexts $F(\ldots, C_i, \ldots)$ where F has at least one non-distinguished sort in its domain, and where C_i is a context of arity $s \to s_i$, with $s_i \notin S_d$.

Proof of the Simplified Context Induction Principle:

$\Rightarrow$ is obvious.

$\Leftarrow$ We only have to prove that the omitted parts in the conditions for inductiveness are unnecessary. Since $s \notin S_d$, the first condition for inductiveness is trivially satisfied. Now, let us consider a context $F(\ldots, C_i, \ldots)$.

If i is such that $s_i \notin S_d$, then the desired second condition for inductiveness is exactly the condition guaranteed by the simplified induction principle. Otherwise, to prove the desired implication, we can assume that $\forall \ C_j \in \mathcal{C}_\bullet^{S_d}$ s.t. $C_j \preceq C_i$, $\Phi(C_j)$ holds. But since $s_i \in S_d$, we have $C_i \in \mathcal{C}_\bullet^{S_d}$, hence $\Phi(C_i)$ holds. But then, due to the regularity of Φ, we can conclude that $\Phi(\ F(\ldots, C_i, \ldots)\ )$ holds.

Example: Let us consider again the *SET-AS-LIST* specification given in Fig. 1. According to the Simplified Context Induction Principle, to prove an equation $LHS = RHS$, it is enough to prove (after some obvious simplifications) the following implication, for all contexts C_i of arity $Set \rightarrow Set$:

$[\forall \ C_j \in \mathcal{C}_{Set}^{S_{Obs}} \ \text{s.t.} \ C_j \preceq C_i, \ \textit{SET-AS-LIST} \models LHS = RHS \ ] \Longrightarrow$
$\textit{SET-AS-LIST} \models e \in C_i[LHS] = e \in C_i[RHS]$

where e stands for an arbitrary ground term of sort *Elem*. To prove this implication, we will start another proof by context induction, but now w.r.t. the contexts of arity $Set \rightarrow Set$. Obviously, such proofs can be mechanized. The ISAR system [1] is a system designed and developed at the University of Passau to perform proofs by context induction.

From now on, we will assume that the observational specification under consideration has **only one non observable sort**, say s (s will be called the sort of interest). Hence we have $S = S_{Obs} \uplus \{s\}$. In that case the signature can be split into three parts:

- The set $\Sigma - O$ of operations of arity $O \ : \ s_1 \ldots s_n \rightarrow s_d$, with $s_d \in S_{Obs}$, and at least one s_i equal to s. These operations "observe" the sort of interest.
  In our *SET-AS-LIST* example, $\Sigma - O = \{\in\}$.

- The set $\Sigma - I$ of operations of arity $I \ : \ s_1 \ldots s_m \rightarrow s$, with at least one s_j equal to s. These operations "produce" values of interest.
  In our *SET-AS-LIST* example, $\Sigma - I = \{ins, \cup\}$.

- The set of all other operations. This set contains the operations involving only observable sorts in their domain and codomain, and those operations producing values of interest that are either constant or that only involve observable sorts in their domain.
  In our *SET-AS-LIST* example, this set contains all operations on booleans and elements, plus the constant operation $\emptyset$.

Remark: In that case, to apply the Simplified Context Induction Principle (with $S_d = S_{Obs}$) to a regular context property Φ, the contexts to be considered are the contexts of the form $O(\ldots, C_\bullet, \ldots)$, where $O \in \Sigma - O$ and $C_\bullet$ is a context of arity $s \rightarrow s$. The implications to prove are therefore, for all operations $O \in \Sigma - O$: $\forall C_\bullet \in \mathcal{C}_\bullet^s \ \ \Psi(C_\bullet)$, where the property $\Psi(C_\bullet)$ is:
$\Psi(C_\bullet) \ : \ [\forall \ C_j \in \mathcal{C}_\bullet^{S_{Obs}} \ \text{s.t.} \ C_j \preceq C_\bullet, \ \Phi(C_j)] \Longrightarrow \Phi(\ O(\ldots, C_\bullet, \ldots)\ ).$

The following theorem provides simple conditions to check the inductiveness of a regular context property Φ:

Theorem: A regular C_s^{Sou}-context property Φ is inductive (hence is true) if and only if, for all operations $O \in \Sigma - O$, the following two conditions hold:

Cond-1: $\Phi(O(\ldots, z_s, \ldots))$ is true.

Cond-2: For all contexts $I(\ldots, C_s, \ldots)$ built from an operation $I \in \Sigma - I$ and a context $C_s \in C_s'$, the following implication is true:
$$\Phi(O(\ldots, C_s, \ldots)) \Longrightarrow \Phi(O(\ldots, I(\ldots, C_s, \ldots), \ldots))$$

In the theorem above, for sake of clarity, we have left implicit the index i ($1 \le i \le n$, $s_i = s$) where the context C_s is plugged into O, as well as the indexes j ($1 \le j \le m$, $s_j = s$) where the same context C_s is plugged into I. Remember also that the dots stand for arbitrary ground terms of adequate sorts. z_s denotes the empty context of arity $s \to s$, which is a variable z_s of sort s.

Proof:

$\Rightarrow$ is obvious.

$\Leftarrow$ From the remark made above, to prove that Φ is inductive (w.r.t. C_s^{Sou}), we have (by regularity of Φ and the Simplified Context Induction Principle) to prove that the property Ψ is true, for all operations $O \in \Sigma - O$. Now, let $O \in \Sigma - O$ be an arbitrary operation. By the Context Induction Principle, it is enough to show that the property Ψ is inductive (w.r.t. C_s').

1. For the empty context z_s of C_s', $\Psi(z_s)$ reduces to $\Phi(O(\ldots, z_s, \ldots))$, which is is exactly **Cond-1**.

2. We have to prove, for all contexts $F(\ldots, C_i, \ldots)$ of arity $s \to s$, the following implication:
$$[\forall\, C_k \in C_s' \;\; s.t. \;\; C_k \preceq C_i, \;\; \Psi(C_k)] \Longrightarrow \Psi(F(\ldots, C_i, \ldots))$$
where C_i is a context of arity $s \to s_i$. Let us consider such a context $F(\ldots, C_i, \ldots)$. To prove the desired implication, we can assume that:
(P_1) $\forall\, C_k \in C_s'$ $s.t.$ $C_k \preceq C_i$, $\Psi(C_k)$
and we have to prove that $\Psi(F(\ldots, C_i, \ldots))$ is true, i.e., by definition of Ψ, that the following implication is true:
$$[\forall\, C_j \in C_s^{Sou} \;\; s.t. \;\; C_j \preceq F(\ldots, C_i, \ldots), \;\; \Phi(C_j)] \Longrightarrow$$
$$\Phi(O(\ldots, F(\ldots, C_i, \ldots), \ldots)).$$
Hence, we are done if we can prove $\Phi(O(\ldots, F(\ldots, C_i, \ldots), \ldots))$ by assuming (P_1) and (P_2) where:
(P_2) $\forall\, C_j \in C_s^{Sou}$ $s.t.$ $C_j \preceq F(\ldots, C_i, \ldots)$, $\Phi(C_j)$.

Case $C_i \in C_s'$: Hence $F \in \Sigma - I$. In that case, we can use (P_1) for C_i itself, hence we know $\Psi(C_i)$, i.e.:
(P_3) $[\forall\, C_j \in C_s^{Sou} \;\; s.t. \;\; C_j \preceq C_i, \;\; \Phi(C_j)] \Longrightarrow \Phi(O(\ldots, C_i, \ldots))$.

But since $C_j \preceq C_i$ implies $C_j \preceq F(\ldots, C_i, \ldots)$, the hypothesis (P_2) implies: $\forall\, C_j \in C_s^{Sou}$ $s.t.$ $C_j \preceq C_i$, $\Phi(C_j)$.
Therefore, using (P_3), we have $\Phi(O(\ldots, C_i, \ldots))$.
But then, the condition **Cond-2** (applied to $C_s = C_i$ and $F = I$)

provides $\Phi(\ O(\ldots, F(\ldots, C_i, \ldots), \ldots)\ )$, which is the desired property.

Case $C_i \in C_s^{S_{Ob}}$ **:** In that case, we can use the hypothesis (P_2) for C_i itself (obviously $C_i \preceq F(\ldots, C_i, \ldots)$), hence $\Phi(C_i)$ holds. From the regularity of Φ we directly conclude
$$\Phi(\ O(\ldots, F(\ldots, C_i, \ldots), \ldots)\ ).$$

4 Proving observational equations with LP

We will now focus on the proof of observational equations. We assume given an equational observational specification $SP{-}Obs = (SP, S_{Obs})$, and an equation $LHS = RHS$. Let s be the common sort of LHS and RHS. Moreover, we assume that all sorts but s are observable (i.e. $S = S_{Obs} \uplus \{s\}$). We are interested in the observational satisfaction of the equation $LHS = RHS$ in the class $Gen(SP{-}Obs)$, i.e. we want to prove that $SP{-}Obs \models_{Obs} LHS = RHS$. We know that it is equivalent to show that the following regular $C_s^{S_{Ob}}$-context property Φ is inductive:
$$\Phi : \quad \forall C \in C_s^{S_{Ob}} \quad SP \models C[LHS] = C[RHS].$$

Hence we can apply the last theorem of the previous section. Now, the conditions to be proved are the following, for all operations $O \in \Sigma{-}O$:

Cond-A: $SP \models O(\ldots, LHS, \ldots) = O(\ldots, RHS, \ldots)$

Cond-B: For all contexts $I(\ldots, C_s, \ldots)$ built from an operation $I \in \Sigma{-}I$ and a context $C_s \in C_s^s$, the following implication is true:
$$[\ SP \models O(\ldots, C_s[LHS], \ldots) = O(\ldots, C_s[RHS], \ldots)\ ] \Longrightarrow$$
$$[\ SP \models O(\ldots, I(\ldots, C_s[LHS], \ldots), \ldots) =$$
$$O(\ldots, I(\ldots, C_s[RHS], \ldots), \ldots)\ ]$$

Remember that, for sake of clarity, we leave implicit the index i ($1 \leq i \leq n$, $s_i = s$) where the context C_s (applied to LHS resp. RHS) is plugged into O, as well as the indexes j ($1 \leq j \leq m$, $s_j = s$) where the same context C_s (applied to LHS resp. RHS) is plugged into I. Remember also that the dots stand for arbitrary ground terms of adequate sorts.

Let us now define the Observability Kernel of the specification $SP{-}Obs$ as follows:

Definition (Observability Kernel): Under the hypotheses above, the *Observability Kernel* of the specification $SP{-}Obs$ is, by definition, the following set $OK[SP{-}Obs]$ of conditional equations, deduced from the condition **Cond-B** above by generalization (for all operations $O \in \Sigma{-}O$ and all operations $I \in \Sigma{-}I$):
$$O(\overline{x_a}, Z_L, \overline{x_b}) = O(\overline{x_a}, Z_R, \overline{x_b}) \Longrightarrow$$
$$O(\overline{x_a}, I(\overline{y_a}, Z_L, \overline{y_b}), \overline{x_b}) = O(\overline{x_a}, I(\overline{y_a}, Z_R, \overline{y_b}), \overline{x_b})$$
where $\overline{x_a}$, $\overline{x_b}$, $\overline{y_a}$, $\overline{y_b}$ are (vectors of universally quantified) distinct variables defined accordingly to the dots in the condition **Cond-B** above, and where Z_L

(resp. Z_R) is a new variable of sort s plugged to the same indexes i and j as $C_s[LHS]$ (resp. $C_s[RHS]$) in **Cond-B**.

It is obvious that the Observability Kernel generalizes the conditions **Cond-B**. The generalization is obtained by substituting the variable Z_L (resp. Z_R) to $C_s[RHS]$ (resp. $C_s[RHS]$) and is intuitively justified by the fact that we have to consider arbitrary contexts C_s (and that we are interested in arbitrary equations $LHS = RHS$). More precisely:

Theorem:
Under the hypotheses above,
  IF $SP \models OK[SP\text{–}Obs]$
  THEN $SP\text{–}Obs \models_{Obs} LHS = RHS$ **if and only if,** for all operations
  $O \in \Sigma - O$: (P) $SP \models O(\overline{x_a}, LHS, \overline{x_b}) = O(\overline{x_a}, RHS, \overline{x_b})$
where again $\overline{x_a}$, $\overline{x_b}$ are (vectors of universally quantified) distinct variables defined accordingly to the dots in the condition **Cond-A** above.

Proof: The proof of the theorem is obvious since, if $SP \models OK[SP\text{–}Obs]$, then the condition **Cond-B** above will always be satisfied (for all equations $LHS = RHS$, for all operations $O \in \Sigma - O$ and for all operations $I \in \Sigma - I$), and hence, to prove an equation $LHS = RHS$, we just have to prove the condition **Cond-A** (for all operations $O \in \Sigma - O$), and this condition is exactly equivalent to (P), since in **Cond-A** the dots stand for arbitrary ground terms (remember we are interested in finitely generated models w.r.t. Ω).

This theorem is obviously a crucial one, since it reduces the proof of observational equations to two tasks:

1. The (standard) proof of the Observability Kernel $OK[SP\text{–}Obs]$, once for all.

2. For each equation, the (standard) proof of the corresponding property (P), for all operations $O \in \Sigma - O$.

Now, we only have to note the similarity between the conjunction of the properties (P), for all operations $O \in \Sigma - O$, and the **partitioned by deduction rule of LP**. This leads to the following theorem, which provides a simple way of proving observational equations with LP:

Theorem (How to prove observational equations with LP):
Given an equational observational specification $SP\text{–}Obs = (SP, S_{Obs})$, assume that all sorts but s are observable (i.e. $S = S_{Obs} \uplus \{s\}$). Let $SP\text{-}part$ denote the specification SP enriched by the following deduction rule:
s **partitioned by** all the operations $O \in \Sigma - O$.
  IF $SP \models OK[SP\text{–}Obs]$
  THEN $SP\text{–}Obs \models_{Obs} LHS = RHS$ **if and only if** $SP\text{-}part \models LHS = RHS$

In the Appendix we show how this theorem can be successfully applied to our $SET\text{-}AS\text{-}LIST$ example, hence for instance how the observational satisfaction of $S \cup S = S$ can be proved with LP.

5 Conclusion

We have explained how observability issues can contribute to a better understanding of correctness (for either true software or abstract implementations). We have described a simple framework of observational specifications, and we have given correct powerful proof principles for this framework: generator induction and context induction. A careful study of the context induction principle has led us to show that, to prove a regular (arbitrary) context property, it is equivalent to prove two simpler conditions (if we assume there is only one non observable sort). Then we have specialized to the proof of equations, and we have shown that, once the (standard) satisfaction of the *Observability Kernel* associated to a given equational observational specification is proved, then any equation is observationally valid if and only if it is valid (in the usual sense) w.r.t. the underlying standard specification, enriched by an appropriate *partitioned by* deduction rule.

This result has many consequences. On one hand, we have now not only a suitable framework for correctness but also adequate and simple proof principles. On the other hand, this result provides a deeper understanding on the role of the *partitioned by* deduction rules systematically used in the *Larch Shared Language* [12, 8, 11] and the *Larch Prover*.

Further issues to be investigated are the extension to more complex formulas than equations (e.g. conditional equations) and to specifications where more than one sort is non observable. We believe as well that the method described in this paper can be extended without difficulty to a more powerful framework of observational specifications, where not only sorts but also operations are taken into account to specify the observations [2].

Acknowledgements: This work is partially supported by the French-German cooperation program Procope, a joint CNRS-NSF grant, and the E.E.C. ESPRIT Working Group COMPASS. Special thanks are due to Steve Garland who helped us in improving our LP script.

Appendix

In this Appendix we detail the application of our method to the *SET-AS-LIST* example. The following is a (slightly edited) LP script file.

We start by defining the *SET-AS-LIST* specification.

```
set name set
declare sorts Elem, Set
declare variables x, y: Elem, S, S': Set
declare operators
    empty:                  -> Set
    insert:     Elem, Set -> Set
    \union:     Set, Set  -> Set
    \in:        Elem, Set -> Bool
    ..
```

```
assert Set generated by empty, insert
assert
  empty \union S == S
  insert(x, S) \union S' == insert(x, S \union S')
  not(x \in empty)
  x \in insert(y, S) == x = y | x \in S
  ..
```

We first prove two useful lemmas.

```
prove S \union empty == S by induction on S
  qed
prove x \in (S \union S') == x \in S | x \in S' by induction on S
  qed
```

We now prove that the Observability Kernel of *SET-AS-LIST* is valid.

```
declare operators
  ZL: -> Set
  ZR: -> Set
  ..
```

```
prove x \in ZL = x \in ZR =>
      (x \in insert(y, ZL)) = (x \in insert(y, ZR)) by =>
  qed
prove x \in ZL = x \in ZR =>
      (x \in (S \union ZL)) = (x \in (S \union ZR)) by =>
  qed
prove x \in ZL = x \in ZR =>
      (x \in (ZL \union S)) = (x \in (ZR \union S)) by =>
  qed
```

Once the Observability Kernel proved, we can add the partitioned by deduction rule. Then the proof of observational equations is done directly with the enriched (standard) specification.

```
assert Set partitioned by \in
```

```
% This command is translated by LP into the
% following deduction rule:
% when (forall e) e \in s1 == e \in s2 yield s1 == s2
```

```
% Theorems about union
```

```
prove S == S \union S
  instantiate
    s1 by S,
    s2 by S \union S
    in deduction-rule
    ..
  qed
```

```
prove S \union S' == S' \union S
  instantiate
    s1 by S \union S',
    s2 by S' \union S
    in deduction-rule
    ..
  make inactive equation
  set ordering left-to-right
  order
  set ordering noeq-dsmpos
  rewrite conjecture
  qed

% Theorems about insert

prove insert(x, insert(x, S)) == insert(x, S)
  instantiate
    s1 by insert(x, insert(x, S)),
    s2 by insert(x, S)
    in deduction-rule
    ..
  qed

prove insert(x, insert(y, S)) == insert(y, insert(x, S))
  instantiate
    s1 by insert(x, insert(y, S)),
    s2 by insert(y, insert(x, S))
    in deduction-rule
    ..
  make inactive equation
  set ordering left-to-right
  order
  set ordering noeq-dsmpos
  rewrite conjecture
  qed
```

References

[1] B. Bauer and R. Hennicker. An interactive system for algebraic implementation proofs. Technical report, Talk at the 8th WADT, 1991.

[2] G. Bernot and M. Bidoit. Proving the correctness of algebraically specified software: Modularity and Observability issues. In *Proc. of the 2nd International Conference on Algebraic Methodology and Software Technology (AMAST)*, 1991.

[3] G. Bernot, M. Bidoit, and T. Knapik. Observational approaches in algebraic specifications: a comparative study. Technical Report LIENS–91–6, Laboratoire d'Informatique de l'Ecole Normale Supérieure, 1991.

[4] G. Bernot, M. Bidoit, and T. Knapik. Towards an adequate notion of observation. In Bernd Krieg-Brückner, editor, *European Syposium on Programming*, LNCS 582, pages 39–55, Rennes, February 1992.

[5] H. Ehrig and B. Mahr. *Fundamentals of algebraic specification 1. Equations and initial semantics*, volume 6 of *EATCS Monographs on Theoretical Computer Science*. Springer-Verlag, 1985.

[6] H. Ganzinger. Parameterized specifications: Parameter passing and implementation with respect to observability. *ACM Transactions on Programming Languages and Systems*, 5(3):318–354, 1983.

[7] S. Garland and J. Guttag. A Guide to LP, The Larch Prover. Technical Report 82, DEC-SRC, 1991.

[8] S. Garland, J. Guttag, and J. Horning. Debugging Larch Shared Language Specifications. *IEEE Transactions on Software Engineering*, 16(9):1044–1057, 1990.

[9] V. Girratana, F. Gimona, and U. Montanari. Observability concepts in abstract data type specification. In *Proc. of Mathematical Foundations of Computer Science (MFCS)*, pages 576–587. Springer-Verlag L.N.C.S. 45, 1976.

[10] J.A. Goguen, J.W. Thatcher, and E.G. Wagner. *An initial approach to the specification, correctness, and implementation of abstract data types*, volume 4 of *Current Trends in Programming Methodology*. Prentice Hall, 1978.

[11] J. Guttag, J. Horning, and A. Modet. Report on the Larch Shared Language: Version 2.3. Technical Report 58, DEC-SRC, 1990.

[12] J.V. Guttag and J.J. Horning. Report on the Larch shared language. *Science of Computer Programming*, 6(2):103–134, 1986.

[13] R. Hennicker. Implementation of parameterized observational specifications. In *Proc. of TAPSOFT*, volume 1, pages 290–305. Springer-Verlag L.N.C.S. 351, 1989.

[14] R. Hennicker. Context Induction: a Proof Principle for Behavioural Abstractions and Algebraic Implementations. *Formal Aspects of Computing*, 3(4):326–345, 1991.

[15] R. Hennicker. Observational implementation of algebraic specifications. *Acta Informatica*, 28(3):187–230, 1991.

[16] S. Kamin. Final data types and their specification. *ACM Transactions on Programming Languages and Systems*, 5(1):97–123, 1983.

[17] T. Knapik. Specifications with observable formulae and observational satisfaction relation. In Michel Bidoit and Christine Choppy, editors, *Recent Trends in Data Type Specification*, Dourdan, September 1991. Selected papers from the 8th Workshop on Specification of Abstract Data Types.

[18] S. Mac Lane. *Categories for the working mathematician*, volume 5 of *Graduate Texts in Mathematics*. Springer-Verlag, 1971.

[19] J. Meseguer and J.A. Goguen. *Initiality, induction and computability*, pages 459–540. Algebraic Methods in Semantics. Cambridge University Press, 1985.

[20] L.S. Moss and S.R. Thate. Generalization of final algebra semantics by relativization. In *Proc. of the 5th Mathematical Foundations of Programming Semantics International Conference*, pages 284–300. Springer-Verlag L.N.C.S. 442, 1989.

[21] P. Nivela and F. Orejas. Initial behaviour semantics for algebraic specification. In *Recent Trends in Data Type Specification, Selected Papers of the 5th Workshop on Specification of Abstract Data Types*, pages 184–207. Springer-Verlag L.N.C.S. 332, 1987.

[22] F. Orejas, M. Navarro, and A. Sànches. Implementation and behavioural equivalence: A survey. In Michel Bidoit and Christine Choppy, editors, *Recent Trends in Data Type Specification*, Dourdan, September 1991. Selected papers from 8th Workshop on Specification of Abstract Data Types.

[23] H. Reichel. Behavioural validity of conditional equations in abstract data types. In *Contributions to General Algebra 3, Proc. of the Vienna Conference*, 1984.

[24] D. Sannella and A. Tarlecki. On observational equivalence and algebraic specification. In *Proc. of TAPSOFT*, pages 308–322. Springer-Verlag L.N.C.S. 185, 1985.

[25] D. Sannella and A. Tarlecki. Toward formal development of programs from algebraic specification revisited. *Acta Informatica*, (25):233–281, 1988.

[26] Oliver Schoett. *Data abstraction and the correctness of modular programming*. PhD thesis, University of Edinburg, 1987.

[27] N.W.P. van Diepen. Implementation of modular algebraic specifications. In *Proc. of the European Symposium on Programming (ESOP)*, pages 64–78. Springer-Verlag L.N.C.S. 300, 1988.

[28] M. Wand. Final algebra semantics and data type extensions. *Journal of Computer and System Sciences*, 19:27–44, 1979.

Using SOS Definitions
in Term Rewriting Proofs

Karl-Heinz Buth [*]

Christian-Albrechts-Universität

Kiel, Germany

Abstract

The main property to be checked when verifying a compiler is semantic equivalence of source program and generated target code. In order to be able to decide this property, a precise formulation of source and target semantics is needed. Moreover, when an automatic proof support tool is to be used, these definitions must be expressed within the tool's formalism. We will demonstrate a way how to model structured operational semantics in the style of Plotkin by means of a special form of term rewriting systems. These systems can be shown to model the original semantics definitions very closely, and they can be implemented as standard rewriting systems within the object language of the Larch Prover. An application of this implementation is the proof of equivalence of structured operational and denotational semantics definitions for a small language. This proof becomes necessary when different aspects of verification require different ways of defining the semantics.

1   Introduction

For compiler verification, it is essential to have precise semantics definitions for the languages involved, i. e. source language, target language and the host language the compiler itself is written in. The most difficult problems to be solved during verification are problems relating semantics of different language constructs. In a simple case, this might take the form of proving equations like

$$sem_T(compile(exp)) = encode(sem_S(exp))$$

where exp is a source language expression, $compile$ is the function translating into the target language, sem_S and sem_T are source and target semantic functions respectively, and $encode$ is a function mapping elements of the source language's semantic domain into the target language's semantic domain.

When an automatic proof tool is to be used to assist the verification, the semantics definitions have to be expressed within the tool's formalism. We will show how this can be done for the Larch Prover (LP, cf. [GG89, GG91]) as the proof tool and structured operational semantics (SOS) definitions in the

[*]Author's address: e-mail: `khb@informatik.uni-kiel.dbp.de`, mail: Institut für Informatik und Praktische Mathematik, Christian-Albrechts-Universität, Preusserstr. 1 – 9, W - 2300 Kiel 1, Germany. Parts of the work reported were supported by the Esprit BRA project 3104 "ProCoS" and the Deutsche Forschungsgemeinschaft, grant La 426/12-1.

style of Plotkin (cf. [Plo83]). Here, semantics is essentially defined by a set of deduction rules, and we simulate them by a set of rewrite rules without employing LP's deduction rule feature. The main problem to be solved for this simulation is the handling of variables that occur in the premise of a deduction rule but not on the left-hand side of its conclusion (so-called "extra variables").

The context of this work is the compiler development part of the Esprit BRA project ProCoS (*Provably Correct Systems*, cf. [BHB$^+$89]). The semantics of several of the project languages have been described operationally; therefore this simulation could help to verify the translation between them. Furthermore, the need for equivalence proofs between operational and denotational semantics definitions for the same language has emerged; we will choose one of these proofs to demonstrate that LP is capable of implementing the proposed simulation.

The paper starts in section 2 with a sketch of the type of SOS definitions we will consider, followed in section 3 by a brief description of the semantics equivalence problem. Section 4 presents the methods used to simulate semantics definitions by rewrite rules, and section 5 an overview of the way the basic mathematical domains are represented. Finally, section 6 contains remarks on the actual proofs carried out.

2 Structured operational semantics

The style of operational semantics definitions we want to consider is the structured approach taken by Plotkin in [Plo83]. Here, semantics is defined by transition systems whose transitions can be labelled with actions:

Definition 2.1   (transition system)

(1) A transition system is a triple $(\Gamma, T, \rightarrow)$, where Γ is the set of **configurations**, $T \subseteq \Gamma$ is the set of **terminal configurations**, and $\rightarrow \subseteq \Gamma \times \Gamma$ is the **transition relation** satisfying $T \cap dom(\rightarrow) = \emptyset$.

(2) A labelled transition system is a tuple $(\Gamma, T, A, \rightarrow)$, where Γ and T are as in (1), A is a set of **labels**, and $\rightarrow \subseteq \Gamma \times A \times \Gamma$ is the **transition relation** satisfying $\forall t \in T \, (\neg \exists a \in A, \gamma \in \Gamma : t \xrightarrow{a} \gamma)$.

For our purposes we need not consider labelled systems since they can be simulated by unlabelled ones:

Lemma 2.2

Let $S = (\Gamma, T, A, \rightarrow)$ be a labelled transition system, and $S' = (\Gamma', T', \rightarrow')$ be the unlabelled system defined by

- $\Gamma' =_{df} \Gamma \times A^*, T =_{df} T \times A^*$ and

- $\rightarrow' =_{df} \{((\gamma_1, l), (\gamma_2, la)) | \gamma_1, \gamma_2 \in \Gamma, a \in A, l \in A^*, \gamma_1 \xrightarrow{a} \gamma_2\}$.

Then S and S' are equivalent in the following sense:

$$\forall n \in \mathbf{N}_0 \, \forall \gamma_0, \ldots, \gamma_n \in \Gamma \, \forall a_1, \ldots, a_n \in A :$$
$$\gamma_0 \xrightarrow{a_1} \gamma_1 \xrightarrow{a_2} \ldots \xrightarrow{a_n} \gamma_n \Leftrightarrow (\gamma_0, \varepsilon) \rightarrow' (\gamma_1, a_1) \rightarrow' \ldots \rightarrow' (\gamma_n, a_1 \ldots a_n)$$

In the structured operational semantics definitions we will consider, the transition relation is defined by a set of axioms and deduction rules of the following form:

$$\frac{b_1 \wedge \ldots \wedge b_p \wedge \gamma_1 R_1 \gamma_1' \wedge \ldots \gamma_n R_n \gamma_n' \wedge B_1 \wedge \ldots B_q}{\gamma \to \gamma'} \tag{1}$$

where $\gamma, \gamma' \in \Gamma, n, p, q \in \mathbb{N}_0$, and $\gamma_i, \gamma_i' \in \Gamma, R_i \in \{\to, \to^*\}$ for $i \in [n] =_{df} \{1, \ldots, n\}$; the b_i are predicates expressing conditions on the variables occurring in γ and the B_j are predicates also containing **extra variables** that do not occur in γ, but at least in one of the γ_i'. The interpretation of such a rule is that the b_i are restrictions on the "input values", i.e. the components of the initial configuration, and the B_j are restrictions on the "output values" that correspond to components that only occur in the the transitions $\gamma_k R_k \gamma_k'$ as components of the γ_k'.

Example: Consider a transition system designed for calculating the square root of real numbers. Configurations are complex numbers, and one of the rules might look like

$$\frac{x < 0 \wedge (-x \to y) \wedge y = \sqrt{-x}}{x \to i * y}$$

expressing how to take the square root of a negative number x. The value of x is the "input value", and the value of y is the "output value" that is derived from the input in the transition $(-x \to y)$ in the premise.

3 The problem

The main objective of the ProCoS project is to demonstrate a way how a fully verified computer system can be obtained. An important part of such a system is a compiler for a high-level programming language. It has to generate code in such a way that argument and result are semantically "equivalent" in a sense that has to be defined suitably to meet the user's demands.

In our special case, the compiler is written in a language called SubLisp (cf. [MO90]), a purely functional subset of CommonLisp, and it generates code for the **transputer** micro processor. The semantics definitions for these languages are very different in style: SubLisp is defined denotationally, and the machine code operationally in SOS style. Therefore, in order to ease the verification of the compiling function ("compiling verification"), another intermediate language is introduced. It is called $\mathrm{PL}_0^{\mathrm{R}}$ and is essentially the language of while-programs, enriched by input and output and parameterless recursive procedures. For verification against SubLisp, $\mathrm{PL}_0^{\mathrm{R}}$ has a denotational definition, and for verification against machine code, it has an SOS definition (cf. figure 1).

If the correctness of $compile_1$ and $compile_2$ have been proved, the correctness of $compile_2 \circ compile_1$ can be deduced provided the two semantics definitions for $\mathrm{PL}_0^{\mathrm{R}}$ have been proved equivalent in an appropriate way. In [Lak91], such

Figure 1: Compiling verification for SubLisp

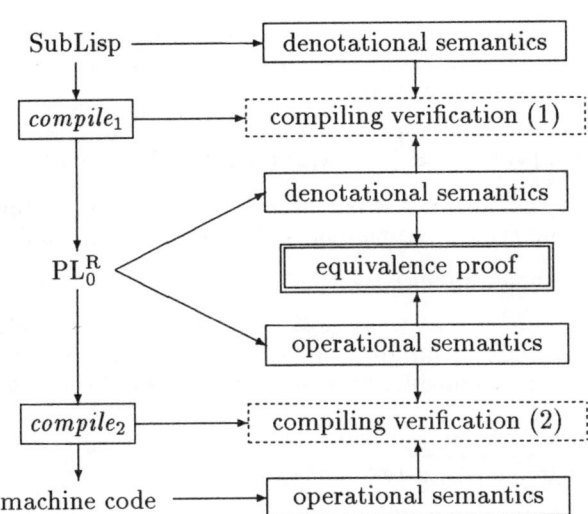

a proof has been given, and our aim is to use LP to produce a mechanically checked version of it. As a first step in this direction, we examine the sub-problem of semantics equivalence for PL_0^R expressions. In the remainder of this section, we will present those parts of [Lak91] that are necessary to define this problem.

3.1 Abstract syntax of PL_0^R expressions

PL_0^R provides the usual set of arithmetical and logical operators (monadic and dyadic):

$$mop \in MonadicOp$$
$$dop \in DyadicOp$$
$$mop ::= - \mid \text{NOT}$$
$$dop ::= + \mid = \mid \text{AND} \mid \ldots$$

Variables can be simple identifiers or array components:

$$name \in Name$$
$$var \in Variable$$
$$exp \in Expression$$
$$var ::= name \mid name[exp]$$

Expressions can be integers, truth values, variables or applications of operators:

$$int \in Int$$
$$exp ::= int \mid \text{TRUE} \mid \text{FALSE} \mid var \mid mop\ exp \mid exp_1\ dop\ exp_2$$

3.2 Static semantics of PL_0^R expressions

In our example, static well-formedness is only a question of correct typing. Identifiers occurring in expressions can either denote integer or array variables. This is recorded in static environments:

$$\delta \in \mathsf{Dict} \ =_{df} \ Name \rightarrow \mathsf{Type}$$
$$\mathsf{Type} =_{df} \{\mathtt{VarInt}\} \uplus \{(\mathtt{ArrayInt}, n) \mid n \in \mathbf{N}_0\} \uplus \{\bot\}$$

where $\delta(name) = \bot$ iff $name$ has not been declared as an identifier. $\uplus$ denotes disjoint union. The type of expressions can be either "Boolean" or "integer":

$$tp \in Tp =_{df} \{\mathtt{bool}, \mathtt{integ}\}$$

Formulas $\delta \vdash_{Variable} var$ and $\delta \vdash_{Expression} exp : tp$, respectively, are used to express well-formedness of variables and expressions w.r.t. static environments δ. They are defined by a deduction system with rules of the following form:

(ER1)
$$\frac{\delta \vdash_{Variable} var}{\delta \vdash_{Expression} var : \mathtt{integ}}$$

(ER2)
$$\delta \vdash_{Expression} int : \mathtt{integ}$$

(ER6)
$$\frac{\delta \vdash_{Expression} exp : \mathtt{bool}}{\delta \vdash_{Expression} \mathtt{NOT}\ exp : \mathtt{bool}}$$

3.3 Operational semantics

The operational semantics of an expression depends on the actual operational environment, recording the memory locations corresponding to the identifiers, and on the machine state, containing the information what values are stored at the locations:

$$val \in \mathsf{Val} \quad =_{df} \ \mathsf{Integer} \uplus \mathsf{Bool} \uplus \{\mathtt{error}\}$$
$$\sigma \ \in \Sigma \quad =_{df} \ \mathsf{Loc} \rightarrow \mathsf{Integer}$$
$$\rho \ \in \mathsf{OpEnv} =_{df} \ Name \rightarrow \mathsf{Loc} \uplus \mathsf{Loc}^*$$

The transition system for the semantics of expressions is defined relative to a given static environment δ:

$$\Gamma^\delta_{Expression} =_{df}$$
$$\{\langle exp, \sigma \rangle \in Expression \times \Sigma \mid \exists tp \in Tp : \delta \vdash_{Expression} exp : tp\}$$
$$\cup \mathsf{T}_{Expression}$$
$$\mathsf{T}_{Expression} =_{df} \mathsf{Val}.$$

The transition relation is based on the interpretation α that assigns meanings to the language primitives. The defining rules depend on an operational environment ρ; some examples are:

(EO1)
$$\rho \vdash_\delta \langle int, \sigma \rangle \longrightarrow_{Expression} \alpha(int)$$

(EO4)
$$\rho \vdash_\delta \langle name, \sigma \rangle \longrightarrow_{Expression} \sigma(\rho(name))$$

$$\text{(EO6)} \quad \frac{\rho \vdash_\delta \langle exp, \sigma \rangle \longrightarrow_{Expression} \; val \wedge val \in \mathsf{Val} \setminus \{\mathbf{error}\} \mid \mathbf{error}}{\rho \vdash_\delta \langle mop\ exp, \sigma \rangle \longrightarrow_{Expression} \; \alpha(mop)(val) \mid \mathbf{error}}$$

The last rule is shorthand for two rules, each with identical left-hand sides in the transitions. The various cases for the right-hand sides are separated by '|'.

3.4 Denotational semantics

Denotational environments and values differ from their operational counterparts by being possibly undefined:

$$\mathsf{DenVal} =_{df} \mathsf{Val} \uplus \{\perp_{\mathsf{DenVal}}\}$$
$$\mathbf{env} \in \quad \mathsf{DenEnv} =_{df} \mathit{Name} \rightarrow \mathsf{Loc} \uplus \mathsf{Loc}^* \uplus \{\perp_{\mathsf{DenEnv}}\}$$

The semantic function E for expressions is defined in the standard way. Example clauses are:

$$\mathcal{E} : \mathit{Expression} \longrightarrow \mathsf{DenEnv} \longrightarrow \Sigma \longrightarrow \mathsf{DenVal}$$

$$\mathcal{E}[\![int]\!] \, \mathbf{env} \, \sigma =_{df} \alpha(int)$$

$$\mathcal{E}[\![name]\!] \, \mathbf{env} \, \sigma =_{df} \begin{cases} \sigma(\mathbf{env}(name)), & \text{if } \mathbf{env}(name) \neq \perp \\ \mathbf{error}, & \text{otherwise} \end{cases}$$

$$\mathcal{E}[\![mop\ exp]\!] \, \mathbf{env} \, \sigma =_{df} \begin{cases} \alpha(mop)(\mathcal{E}[\![exp]\!] \, \mathbf{env} \, \sigma), \\ \qquad \text{if } \mathcal{E}[\![exp]\!] \, \mathbf{env} \, \sigma \in \mathsf{Val} \setminus \{\mathbf{error}\} \\ \mathbf{error}, \quad \text{otherwise} \end{cases}$$

3.5 The equivalence theorem

Before we can define what we mean by equivalence of the two semantics definitions, we have to introduce a compatibility relation on environments: Let $\rho \in \mathsf{OpEnv}, \delta \in \mathsf{Dict}$. Then

$$\rho : \delta \overset{\text{def}}{\Longleftrightarrow} \forall name \in \mathit{Name} : (\rho(name) \in \mathsf{Loc} \Leftrightarrow \delta(name) = \mathtt{VarInt}) \wedge$$
$$(\rho(name) \in \mathsf{Loc}^* \Leftrightarrow \delta(name) = (\mathtt{ArrayInt}, \#\rho(name)))$$

where $\#l$ for a list l is the length of l.

Now we can state the equivalence theorem for expressions:

Theorem 3.1 (Expression equivalence)

For all static environments $\delta \in \mathsf{Dict}$, expressions $exp \in \mathit{Expression}$, operational environments $\rho \in \mathsf{OpEnv}$, states $\sigma \in \Sigma$ such that

$$\rho : \delta \wedge \exists tp \in \mathit{Tp} : \delta \vdash_{Expression} exp : tp$$

the following two conditions are satisfied:

(1) $\rho \vdash_\delta \langle exp, \sigma \rangle \xrightarrow{\quad} _{Expression} t$ iff $\mathcal{E}[\![exp]\!] \tilde{\rho} \sigma = t$,

for all $t \in \mathsf{T}_{Expression}$ and

(2) $\neg (\exists t \in \mathsf{T}_{Expression} \cdot \rho \vdash_\delta \langle exp, \sigma \rangle \xrightarrow{\quad} _{Expression} t)$ iff $\mathcal{E}[\![exp]\!] \tilde{\rho} \sigma = \bot$.

where $\tilde{\rho}(name)$ is $\rho(name)$ if this is in $\mathsf{Loc} \cup \mathsf{Loc}^*$ and $\bot$ otherwise.

A sufficient condition for 3.1 is:

$$\forall \delta \in \mathsf{Dict} \; \forall exp \in Expression \; \forall \rho \in \mathsf{OpEnv} \; \forall \sigma \in \Sigma \; : $$
$$\rho : \delta \wedge \exists tp \in Tp : \delta \vdash_{Expression} exp : tp \Rightarrow \tag{2}$$
$$(\mathcal{E}[\![exp]\!] \tilde{\rho} \sigma \neq \bot \wedge \rho \vdash_\delta \langle exp, \sigma \rangle \xrightarrow{\quad} _{Expression} \mathcal{E}[\![exp]\!] \tilde{\rho} \sigma)$$

In words: If exp is statically well-formed, then operational and denotational semantics yield the same value which is not "undefined", provided the static and dynamic environments are compatible.

In [Lak91], (2) is proved by structural induction on exp.

4 Modelling the semantics definitions

4.1 Denotational semantics

In the expression example, the denotational semantics is rather simple since it does not contain fixed point operators. Therefore, the equations can be transformed into rewrite rules quite easily. Consider for example the equation

$$\mathcal{E}[\![mop\ exp]\!] \ env\ \sigma =_{df} \begin{cases} \alpha(\ mop\ )(\mathcal{E}[\![exp]\!] \ \mathsf{env}\ \sigma), \\ \qquad \text{if } \mathcal{E}[\![exp]\!] \ \mathsf{env}\ \sigma \in \mathsf{Val} \setminus \{\mathbf{error}\} \\ \mathbf{error}, \quad \text{otherwise} \end{cases}$$

It could be modelled by two conditional rewrite rules. This does not help us, however, since conditional rewriting is not supported by LP. But the unconditional solution is simple, too. The right-hand side of this equation is a conditional expression. Therefore, the corresponding rewrite rule uses an `if` term [1]:

```
dsem(mk_Expr(mop, exp), env, sigma) ->
   if(to_Val(dsem(exp, env, sigma)) = _ERROR,
      mk_DenVal(_ERROR),
      mk_Denval(alpha(mop) . to_Val(dsem(exp, env, sigma))))
```

where '.' is an application operator. The only reason that this rule looks more complicated than the original equation is the appearance of the injection and projection operators (`mk_Denval` resp. `to_Val`). This is a consequence of the multi-sorted approach that is taken by LP.

---

[1] We will write terms, rules etc. that are meant as input for LP in teletype font, so `if` is an LP operator. We will use the sans serif font to write terms in mathematical notation that is easier to read; e.g. we have the operator if ... then ... else ... in this notation.

4.2 Implementation of let terms

For the simulation of transition systems by term rewriting systems, we use a two step transformation. In the first step, a special kind of generalized systems are generated, and in the second step these systems are transformed into "standard" rewriting systems containing first-order terms and no extra variables on the right-hand side.

The generalization we introduce in the first step is the integration of terms from lambda calculus: We allow terms of the form

$$\text{let } x = e \text{ in } e_1 \tag{3}$$

which is a representation of

$$(\lambda x.e_1)e \tag{4}$$

There exists some work on the combination of term rewriting and lambda Calculus (e. g. the "λ-rewriting" of Kahrs, cf. [Kah91]), and the properties of such combined calculi have been closely examined. But we will not need the generality of this approach, and therefore we choose another direction. In [ACCL90], the "$\lambda\sigma$-calculus" is introduced that explicitly handles substitutions and β-reduction. It is based on the concept of De Bruijn indices (cf. [Bru72]) that substitute the bound variables in λ-terms, and it provides a rewriting system for the evaluation of substitutions.

The only way λ-terms can enter our term language is in terms of form (4), i. e. in direct application of λ-abstractions. Therefore we can always perform a β-reduction step

$$(\lambda x.e_1)e \rightarrow_\beta e_1[e/x] \tag{5}$$

before adding the rules containing (4) to our rewriting system, and hence we do not need an explicit β-reduction rule. What remains of the $\lambda\sigma$-calculus is just the rules for distributing substitutions over terms.

Another important concept we will need is that of **contexts** for terms. Let f be an operator. An **f-term** is a term for which f is the outermost operator. Assume that f-terms on the left-hand side of rules never contain any f-terms as proper subterms, and suppose that we want to be able to control how often f-terms are rewritten and which rules are used for this. Assume further that we have $N > 0$ rewrite rules that have an f-term on their left-hand side. Then an f-context is an $(N+1)$-tuple of the form

$$\langle \mathit{freq}, s_1, \ldots, s_N \rangle$$

where $\mathit{freq} \in \{0, 1, \omega\}$ and $s_i \in \{\mathsf{on}, \mathsf{off}\}$ for $i \in \{1, \ldots, N\}$.

In order to be able to control the rewriting of f-terms, we only allow these to occur together with an associated context; to this end we introduce a new infix operator @:

$$f(\ldots) \mathbin{@} \langle \mathit{freq}, s_1, \ldots, s_N \rangle$$

The first component of the context indicates how often the corresponding f-term may be rewritten: not at all (if it is 0), once (1) or arbitrarily often (ω).

The other components s_i are on if the ith rule may be used in the first rewriting step and off otherwise. Contexts are a useful means to ensure that f-terms are rewritten only once (by changing the frequency from 1 to 0 in the corresponding context after a rewrite rule has been applied); this will turn out to be useful since we will consider one-step rewritings. Furthermore, contexts allow us to forbid the use of certain rules (by setting its context component to off) when their use might lead to problems; for example, repeated use of the same rule can be prohibited this way.

4.3 Operational semantics

The semantics of a transition rule

$$\frac{hypo}{\gamma \to \gamma'}$$

is that (an instance of) the transition from γ to γ' is possible if (the corresponding instance of) *hypo* can be proved. In the case where *hypo* cannot be proved [2], nothing is said about transitions starting in γ.

Our aim is to simulate this behaviour with rewrite rules of the form supported by LP. This precludes the use of conditional rules

$$hypo \Rightarrow \gamma \to \gamma'$$

which would seem natural at first sight. But this is not a problem, since a in [But92a] a method for the simulation of transition rules by unconditional rewrite rules is presented. The main difficulty emerges from the presence of extra variables in the transition rule; the solution is to use **let** terms, i.e. concepts from λ-calculus. In this section, we will demonstrate the method in a small example, taken from the semantics definition in section 3.3.

Consider the rules defining the semantics of unary operators:

(EO6)
$$\frac{\rho \vdash_\delta \langle exp, \sigma \rangle \longrightarrow_{Expression} val \wedge val \in \mathsf{Val} \setminus \{\mathbf{error}\} \mid \mathbf{error}}{\rho \vdash_\delta \langle mop\; exp, \sigma \rangle \longrightarrow_{Expression} \alpha(\;mop\;)(val) \mid \mathbf{error}}$$

In a first step, we include the parameters ρ and δ in the configurations:

$$ec \quad \in \quad \overline{\Gamma}_{Expression} =_{df} \mathsf{OpEnv} \times \mathsf{Dict} \times \Gamma_{Expression}$$

$$\overline{\mathsf{T}}_{Expression} =_{df} \mathsf{OpEnv} \times \mathsf{Dict} \times \mathsf{T}_{Expression}$$

and reformulate the rules using the new domains:

$$\frac{\vdash \langle \rho, \delta, \langle exp, \sigma \rangle \rangle \longrightarrow_{Expression} \langle \rho, \delta, val \rangle \wedge val \in \mathsf{Val} \setminus \{\mathbf{error}\} \mid \langle \rho, \delta, \mathbf{error} \rangle}{\vdash \langle \rho, \delta, \langle mop\; exp, \sigma \rangle \rangle \longrightarrow_{Expression} \langle \rho, \delta, \alpha(\;mop\;)(val) \rangle \mid \langle \rho, \delta, \mathbf{error} \rangle}$$

---

[2] We assume that this means that $\neg hypo$ can be proved.

This does not change the essence of the definition; the original configurations are still available by projection on the third component of the new "extended configurations".

When setting up rewrite rules that simulate (EO6), we make use of the fact that the extra variable *val* has a very special meaning. In the case where the transition in the conclusion is deduced with this rule, it is the name of a configuration that can be reached from $\langle exp, \sigma \rangle$ in one step. So we can view it as a name for the result of a one-step evaluation of this configuration. A convenient way to fix names for such results is a let term, evaluated in call-by-value style:

$$\text{let } ec = \langle \rho, \delta, \langle exp, \sigma \rangle \rangle \text{ in } \ldots \tag{6}$$

In section 4.2, we have seen that let terms can be reduced to simpler terms. We keep them here because they are easier to understand than the reduced forms. How we can ensure that $\langle exp, \sigma \rangle$ is evaluated only once, we will see in a moment. Note that ec is not a variable in this term but a local constant (cf. section 4.2); its third component $(ec \downarrow 3)$ corresponds to *val*.

We have some more information about *val*. First, we know it is a typical variable for the domain Val. And second, we know it has to be unequal (first case) or equal (second case) to **error** if the corresponding conclusion is deduced with this rule. In the body of the let term in (6), we can express these conditions as a type check for the third component of ec, e. g. in the first rule:

let $ec = \langle \rho, \delta, \langle exp, \sigma \rangle \rangle$
in if $type(ec \downarrow 3) = $ Val $\land ec \downarrow 3 \neq $ **error**
    then $\langle \rho, \delta, \alpha(mop)(val) \rangle$
    else $\ldots$

We still have to find a suitable term for the **else** part of the conditional. This term corresponds to the case where the premise does not hold; hence the deduction rule does not apply and leaves the input configuration unchanged. One way to model this behaviour could be to take the left-hand side of the rule as the **else** part:

$\langle \rho, \delta, \langle mop\ exp, \sigma \rangle \rangle \rightarrow$ let $ec = \langle \rho, \delta, \langle exp, \sigma \rangle \rangle$
        in if $type(ec \downarrow 3) = $ Val $\land ec \downarrow 3 \neq $ **error**
            then $\langle \rho, \delta, \alpha(mop)(val) \rangle$
            else $\langle \rho, \delta, \langle mop\ exp, \sigma \rangle \rangle$

but there are two problems with this rule: (1) We do not make sure that $\langle \rho, \delta, \langle exp, \sigma \rangle \rangle$ is evaluated only once, as required, and (2) we do not prevent non-terminating rewriting arising from repeated reducing the if term to its **else** part.

Both problems can be solved by associating all the extended configuration terms with **contexts** (cf. section 4.2)[3]. Assume that we have only the two deduction rules (EO6). Problem (1) is solved by putting $\langle \rho, \delta, \langle exp, \sigma \rangle \rangle$ into the context $\langle 1, \text{on}, \text{on} \rangle$: both rules may be used for the evaluation, but it may only take

---

[3]This is possible since such terms never occur in nested form on the left-hand side of rewrite rules (see the condition on f-terms in section 4.2).

one step. Since the result will again be a configuration-context pair, we have to select its first component to access the configuration contained. Problem (2) is solved by switching the failing rule off in the **else** term. We need two forms of each rule, one for one-step evaluation and one for evaluation to normal form, differing only in the contexts used. The ω-form of the first rule is

$$\langle \rho, \delta, \langle\ mop\ exp, \sigma \rangle \rangle\ @\ \langle \omega, \text{on}, s \rangle \rightarrow$$
$$\quad \text{let } ec = (\langle \rho, \delta, \langle\ exp, \sigma \rangle \rangle\ @\ \langle 1, \text{on}, \text{on} \rangle) \downarrow 1$$
$$\quad \text{in if } type(ec \downarrow 3) = \text{Val} \wedge ec \downarrow 3 \neq \text{error}$$
$$\quad\quad \text{then } \langle \rho, \delta, \alpha(\ mop\ )(val) \rangle\ @\ \langle \omega, \text{on}, \text{on} \rangle$$
$$\quad\quad \text{else } \langle \rho, \delta, \langle\ mop\ exp, \sigma \rangle \rangle\ @\ \langle \omega, \text{off}, s \rangle$$

and the 1-step form of the second rule is

$$\langle \rho, \delta, \langle\ mop\ exp, \sigma \rangle \rangle\ @\ \langle 1, \text{on}, s \rangle \rightarrow$$
$$\quad \text{let } ec = (\langle \rho, \delta, \langle\ exp, \sigma \rangle \rangle\ @\ \langle 1, \text{on}, \text{on} \rangle) \downarrow 1$$
$$\quad \text{in if } ec \downarrow 3 = \text{error}$$
$$\quad\quad \text{then } \langle \rho, \delta, \text{error} \rangle\ @\ \langle 0, \text{on}, \text{on} \rangle$$
$$\quad\quad \text{else } \langle \rho, \delta, \langle\ mop\ exp, \sigma \rangle \rangle\ @\ \langle 1, \text{off}, s \rangle$$

The switches in the **then** terms are all **on** because the rules have been successfully applied in these cases. For the frequency component, note that $1 - 1 = 0$, whereas $\omega - 1 = \omega$.

4.3.1   Equivalence of inference and rewriting system

Let $TS = \langle \Gamma, T, \rightarrow_{TS} \rangle$ be the original transition system for a language L containing $N > 0$ transition rules. Let $\rightarrow_{TRS}$ be the rewriting relation of the term rewriting system consisting of the generated rules together with the $\lambda\sigma$-rules and a basic system B containing rules about primitive operators like constructor and selector functions for the several data domains that we use. We assume that B can be used to rewrite every simple condition not containing transitions to either **true** or **false**, and that rewritings that only use rules from B always terminate. Then we can prove that $\rightarrow_{TRS}$ simulates $\rightarrow_{TS}$ correctly and completely in a rather straightforward way.

In order to express these properties formally, let us first define some abbreviations for contexts w. r. t. configurations.

Definition 4.1   (special contexts)

Let $k \in [N]$ and $s_1, \ldots, s_N \in \{\text{on}, \text{off}\}$.

$K_1^k =_{df} \langle 1, s_1, \ldots, s_{k-1}, \text{on}, s_{k+1}, \ldots, s_N \rangle$
(one step allowed, rule k may be used)
$K_0 =_{df} \langle 0, \text{on}, \ldots, \text{on} \rangle$
(no more steps allowed, but no restriction on special rules)
$K_f =_{df} \langle \omega, \text{on}, \ldots, \text{on} \rangle$
(no limit on the number of steps, all rules may be used)

We can prove the following five properties about the derived system:

(1) **One-step completeness**:
$$\forall \gamma, \gamma' \in \Gamma \; \forall k \in [N] \; \forall s_1, \ldots, s_{k-1}, s_{k+1}, \ldots, s_N \in \{\text{on}, \text{off}\} :$$
$\gamma \to_{TS} \gamma'$ using rule k in the last derivation step $\Rightarrow$
$$\gamma @ K_1^k \to_{TRS}^* \gamma' @ K_0$$

(2) **One-step correctness**:
$$\forall \gamma, \gamma' \in \Gamma \; \forall k \in [N] \; \forall s_1, \ldots, s_{k-1}, s_{k+1}, \ldots, s_N \in \{\text{on}, \text{off}\} :$$
$\gamma @ K_1^k \to_{TRS} \gamma' @ K_0$ using the rewrite rule derived from rule k in the last
step $\Rightarrow$ $\gamma \to_{TS} \gamma'$

From these two properties it follows that every step in one system can directly be simulated in one step in the other system using the corresponding rule.

(3) **Normal form completeness and correctness**:
$$\forall \gamma \in \Gamma \; \forall t \in T : \gamma \to_{TS}^* t \Leftrightarrow \gamma @ K_f \to_{TRS}^* t @ K_f$$

No normal form is lost during simulation and no additional normal forms are introduced.

(4) **Non-termination completeness**:
$$\forall \{\gamma^{(i)}\} \in \Gamma^{\mathbf{N}} :$$
$$(\forall i \in \mathbf{N} : \gamma^{(i)} \to_{TS} \gamma^{(i+1)}) \Rightarrow (\forall i \in \mathbf{N} : \gamma^{(i)} @ K_f \to_{TRS}^* \gamma^{(i+1)} @ K_f)$$

All infinite program executions as specified by the semantics will have corresponding infinite rewriting sequences.

(5) **Non-termination correctness**:
Let *Term* be the set of all configuration/context pairs constructed with @.
Then we have:
$$\forall \gamma \in \Gamma \; \forall \{t^{(i)}\} \in Term^{\mathbf{N}} : t^{(1)} = \gamma @ K_f \wedge (\forall i \in \mathbf{N} : t^{(i)} \to_{TRS} t^{(i+1)}) \Rightarrow$$
$$\exists \{\gamma^{(i)}\} \in \Gamma^{\mathbf{N}} \; \exists j : \mathbf{N} \to \mathbf{N} \text{ strictly monotonic} :$$
$$(\forall i \in \mathbf{N} : \gamma^{(i)} = (t^{(j(i))} \downarrow 1) \wedge \gamma^{(i)} \to_{TS} \gamma^{(i+1)})$$

This means that all non-terminating rewriting sequences have an infinite subsequence that corresponds to a non-terminating program execution. Therefore, the rewrite rules introduce no artificial termination problems that are not part of the semantics.

Figure 2: "1:n" simulation of transition sequences

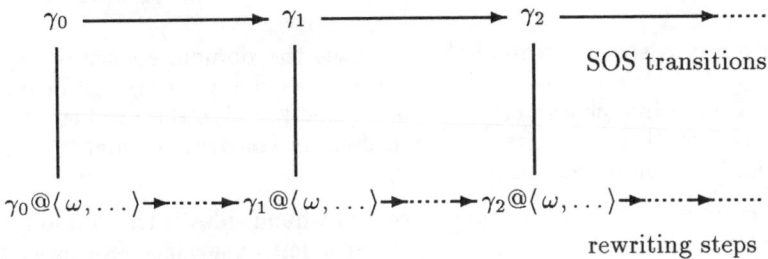

Properties 1. to 5. define a "1:n" simulation (fig. 2). The rewriting sequence S corresponding to a transition step in most cases contains more than one rewriting step. This is because transitions "in the premise" are explicit in S whereas they are hidden in the transition sequence. There they only occur in the justification of the single transitions, i.e. in the associated proof trees; S can be viewed as a flattened version of the trees. Another reason is that applications of basic rules do not occur in the transition sequence. Transitions take place modulo the equational theory generated by the basic system.

As immediate consequences of the simulation, we have that TRS is confluent only if TS is deterministic, and that TRS is finitely terminating only if all programs of L must always terminate.

5 The basic rewriting system

5.1 Data type rules

Most of the rules that are contained in the basic rewriting system B deal with the mathematical domains that are used to describe the application area and the problem to be solved. The operators occurring in these rules are constructors, selectors and recognizers for the domains. In this section, we will see how domains are defined and what kinds of definitions are needed to model them using LP.

As in VDM (cf. [Jon90]), the domains are defined by a set of recursive equations. We will not use the full general VDM form (cf. [Daw91]), but a restricted version.

Definition 5.1 (domain equations)

Domain equations are defined by the following grammar:

$$
\begin{array}{rcl}
dom\text{-}equation & ::= & idf\,'='\,dom\text{-}expr \\
dom\text{-}expr & ::= & union\text{-}expr \mid function\text{-}expr \\
union\text{-}expr & ::= & product\text{-}expr_1\,'|'\,\ldots\,'|'\,product\text{-}expr_n\ (n \geq 1) \\
product\text{-}expr & ::= & elementary \mid idf_1\,'\times'\,\ldots\,'\times'\,idf_n\ (n \geq 2) \\
elementary & ::= & idf \mid token \\
function\text{-}expr & ::= & idf_1\,'\times'\,\ldots\,'\times'\,idf_n\,'\rightarrow'\,idf_{n+1}\ (n \geq 1)
\end{array}
$$

A *token* is a special symbol that denotes the domain consisting of just this symbol. We will write token symbols as character strings beginning with a underline character, e.g. _ONE, _ERROR. '$\times$' is the product domain constructor, '|' is the disjoint union domain constructor, and '$\rightarrow$' is the partial function domain constructor.

A domain identifier only occurring on right-hand sides of the domain equations of a system denotes a domain that is left unspecified in this system. In VDM, such an identifier would be declared not yet defined.

VDM also provides constructors for set and tree domains. For our examples, we will not consider these.

The syntax is rather restrictive in not allowing complex domain constructions. But the effect of an equation with a complex expression can always be achieved by a set of simpler equations: Instead of

$$T_1 = T_2 \times (T_3 \to T_4) \times (T_5 \mid T_6)$$

we can use the equivalent system

$$T_1 = T_2 \times T_7 \times T_8$$
$$T_7 = T_3 \to T_4$$
$$T_8 = T_5 \mid T_6.$$

Union domains: In order to model a union domain, defined by the equation

$$T = T_{11} \times \ldots \times T_{1n_1} \mid \ldots \mid T_{m1} \times \ldots \times T_{mn_m}$$

where $m \geq 1, n_i \geq 1$ for $i \in [m]$ and each of the T_{ij} is elementary, we first declare the sort T (assuming the T_ij have already been declared) and the following kinds of operators:

- constructors, mapping elements of the subdomains into the union;

- projectors, mapping elements of the union into the appropriate subdomain;

- recognizers, deciding whether a union element is in a certain subdomain;

- selectors for the components of those elements that are tuples.

The rules about the operators are those frequently used in reasoning about objects of that kind of domains. E. g. we have that selecting the n-th element of a tuple made up from components $e_1, \ldots, e_m$ $(m \geq n)$ yields e_n, or that the projection onto a subdomain indeed yields an element of that domain.

Function domains: In order to model a function domain, defined by

$$T = T_1 \times \ldots \times T_m \to T_{m+1}$$

where $m \geq 1$, we declare the following operators:

- the empty partial function of sort T;

- the extension (modification) of a given function with an additional pair of argument list and result;

- the application of a function to an argument list.

Except for technical rules about types and substitutions, we only need one rule about application of an extended function.

Type rules: Type rules map every term constructed with the operators from above onto its type. This is necessary for the type checks used in the SOS rules (cf. section 4.3).

A more detailed description of the basic system can be found in [But92b].

5.2 Static semantics and other rules

In [Lak91], the static semantics of PL_0^R is defined by a system of deduction rules (cf. section 3.2). As usual, the intended meaning of this system is that PL_0^R constructs are statically well-formed if and only if this property can be proved using the rules.

In order to model the static semantics by rewrite rules, we first introduce a "well-formed" operator:

```
wf_expr: Expr, Dict, Type_ -> Bool
```

where `Type_` contains `_INTEG_` and `_BOOL_`, modelling the types `integ` and `bool`. The corresponding operator for variables is not needed since the definition of the domain *Var* has to be expanded into the definition of *Expression* in order to allow structural induction (cf. section 6).

The deduction rules are always used in a "backwards" way to prove static correctness of given complex expressions from the static correctness of simpler components and not in the other ("forward") direction. Therefore an inference rule

$$\frac{premise}{conclusion}$$

can be modelled by the rewrite rule

```
conclusion -> premise. 4
```

For the inference rules of section 3.2, this results in the following rules ('.' is the application operator; `idf` and `i` are the typical variables for *Name* and *Int*, respectively):

```
wf_expr(mk_Expr(idf), delta, _INTEG_) -> ((delta . idf) = VarInt)
wf_expr(mk_Expr(i), delta, _INTEG_)
wf_expr(mk_Expr(exp1, _PLUS, exp2), delta, _INTEG_) ->
    wf_expr(exp1, delta, _INTEG_) & wf_expr(exp2, delta, _INTEG_)
```

The first rule results from expansion of *var* in the *exp* productions. In order to capture the intended equivalence, we need some more rules. For otherwise, with only the rules from above, a term like

```
wf_expr(mk_expr(42), delta, _BOOL_)
```

is irreducible, even though it should reduce to `false`. Therefore, we have to add all the cases containing the "wrong types" :

---

[4] Since at most one rule applies to a given expression, there is no confluence problem with these rewrite rules.

```
wf_expr(mk_Expr(idf), delta, _BOOL_) -> false
wf_expr(mk_Expr(i), delta, _BOOL_) -> false
wf_expr(mk_Expr(exp1, _PLUS, exp2), delta, _BOOL_) -> false
```

The basic rewriting system does not only contain rules about data types and static semantics. It also has to provide the relevant information about the other primitive operators, e.g. arithmetical or logical operators. Another important operator corresponds to the interpretation α used to assign a meaning to language primitives in semantics definitions. Which information is actually "relevant" essentially depends on the actual proofs that are attempted; the rules must describe all the aspects of the primitive operators in sufficient detail. Ideally, however, the rules should supply a complete definition (cf. the assumption about the basic system in section 4.3.1).

6 The proof

In [Lak91], the proof of the equivalence theorem (cf. equation 2) proceeds by induction on the structure of the expression. It is not too complicated; most steps amount to application of the semantics definitions. The length of the proof is about 2 1/2 A4 pages.

Due to the very systematic description of the VDM domains and the SOS rules, the generation of LP input from these definitions could be automated. (For a description of these tools, see the full version of this paper [But92b].) With the help of the tools, we succeeded in replaying this proof with LP. The machines used were Sun SPARCstations under SunOS 4.1.1.

The structure of the proof performed with LP is very similar to the original proof. The main idea is again structural induction. There is one problem with the original syntax, however; the definition is

$$exp ::= int \mid \textbf{TRUE} \mid \textbf{FALSE} \mid var \ mop \ exp \mid exp_1 \ dop \ exp_2$$
$$var ::= name \mid name[exp]$$

The construction of an indexed variable requires the recursive construction of an expression that denotes the index. The expression is not "visible" on top level; the derivation is $exp \rightarrow var \rightarrow name[exp]$. This causes LP not to realize that the induction hypothesis can be used for exp_1 in the case

$$exp = name[exp_1]$$

and so the proof gets stuck. The easiest way out of this problem is to flatten the recursive structure by expanding var in the exp equation which yields

$$exp ::= int \mid \textbf{TRUE} \mid \textbf{FALSE} \mid name \mid name[exp] \mid mop \ exp \mid exp_1 \ dop \ exp_2$$

After this modification, the induction hypothesis is also used for the array index expression.

The proofs for the inductive cases are all rather similar. A very pleasant consequence of this was that it sufficed to work hard for one case to get the proof right. After this was finished, proofs for the other cases could be obtained by copying the LP proof script for the first case and performing some obvious modifications.

LP is a heavy user of resources; it is extremely important to use the `forget` command frequently to discard information about critical pairs. Without this command, the Unix process for LP became larger than 44 MB, and otherwise it stayed below 24 MB. But even the reduced size requires machines with at least 32 MB of memory in order to prevent paging which dramatically degrades the performance.

The size of the LP input was

- 350 rewrite rules, 8 deduction and 15 induction rules for the basic system (including the rules modelling the denotational semantics definition),

- 24 rewrite rules for the rewriting system modelling the SOS definition, and

- about 500 lines for the LP proof script.

The timing figures on a SPARCstation2 are as follows (starting from a frozen basic rewriting system):

Recent	Success		Failure		Total
------	Count	Time	Count	Time	Time
Ordering	235	0.11	0	0.00	0.11
Rewriting	2693	1:18.15	19487	52.22	2:10.37
Deductions	157	6.02	2886	16.80	22.82
Unification	14	0.08	8	0.02	0.10
Prover					3:25.96
GC's	20				
Total time					8:15.26

The semantics definitions caused no technical problems during the proof. Especially, application of the large SOS rules remained hidden under "normalization". This is about the same level of detail that can be found in the original proof in [Lak91]; there we can see statements like "the definition of the operational semantics yields ... [some result]". This means that the structure of the LP proof stays close to that of the original proof; it does not present any surprises and hence remains plausible to the reader.

7 Conclusion

In [But92a], it is proved that SOS definitions can be simulated very closely by standard term rewriting systems. The experiments with LP reported in this paper have shown that the simulation can also be implemented, and that this implementation can be used to check proofs involving the semantics definitions. The form of the SOS semantics rules did not require artificial complications in the proofs; therefore, it seems to be adequate for this purpose. LP itself provides a sufficiently comfortable proof environment. When a proof gets stuck, in most cases it is relatively easy to detect the source of the problem.

There are some obvious next steps to be taken:

- An equivalence proof for the full language PL_0^R should be performed. This does not present new problems for the operational semantics rules, but rather for the denotational semantics. For it means that we have to model loops and recursion, and hence fixed points, and therefore we cannot simply use the equations as rewrite rules.

- The SOS rules should also be applicable for proofs that only use operational semantics. An example from ProCoS is the compiling verification for the translation from PL_0^R into machine code; this correctness proof has also already been carried out manually (cf. [Frä92]).

- Even full PL_0^R is still deterministic. Modelling the operational semantics of a non-deterministic language in the way presented in this paper results in a non-confluent rewriting system. For this case some extra considerations are necessary; in proofs we have to make sure that we reach all computation paths through a program.

Acknowledgements

I would like to thank the ProCoS group in Kiel, especially Bettina Buth and Yassine Lakhneche, for their help in clarifying my ideas, and Ursula Martin for drawing my attention to the $\lambda\sigma$-calculus. Bettina also carefully read several draft version of this paper.

References

[ACCL90] M. Abadi, L. Cardelli, P.-L. Curien, and J.-J. Lévy. Explicit substitutions. In *Proceedings of the 17th ACM Symposium on Principles of Programming Languages*, pages 31–46, 1990.

[BHB+89] Dines Bjørner, C. A. R. Hoare, Jonathan Bowen, et al. A ProCoS project description - ESPRIT BRA 3014. *Bulletin of the EATCS*, 39:60–73, 1989.

[Bru72] N. De Bruijn. Lambda-calculus notation with nameless dummies. *Indag. Mat.*, 34:381–392, 1972.

[But92a] Karl-Heinz Buth. Simulation of transition systems with term rewriting systems. Bericht 9212, Institut für Informatik und Praktische Mathematik, Christian-Albrechts-Universität Kiel, 1992.

[But92b] Karl-Heinz Buth. Using SOS definitions in term rewriting proofs. Bericht 9214, Institut für Informatik und Praktische Mathematik, Christian-Albrechts-Universität Kiel, 1992.

[Daw91] John Dawes. *The VDM-SL reference guide*. Pitman, 1991.

[Frä92] Martin Fränzle. Operational failure approximation. In Dines Bjørner, editor, *ESPRIT BRA 3104, Provably Correct Systems ProCoS, Draft Final Deliverable, Vol. III: Compiler Development*, pages

165–206. Department of Computer Science, Technical University of Denmark, 1992.

[GG89] Stephen J. Garland and John V. Guttag. An overview of LP, the larch prover. In Nachum Dershowitz, editor, *Proceedings of the Third International Conference on Rewriting Techniques and Applications*, pages 137–155. Springer, 1989. LNCS 355.

[GG91] Stephen J. Garland and John V. Guttag. *A Guide to LP, The Larch Prover*. Massachussetts Institute of Technology, November 1991. Release 2.2.

[Jon90] Cliff B. Jones. *Systematic Software Development using VDM*. Prentice Hall, 2nd edition, 1990.

[Kah91] Stefan Kahrs. *λ-rewriting*. PhD thesis, Fachbereich Mathematik und Informatik, Universität Bremen, January 1991.

[Lak91] Yassine Lakhneche. Equivalence of denotational and structural operational semantics of PL_0^R. ProCoS Technical Report Kiel YL1, Christian-Albrechts-Universität Kiel, 1991.

[MO90] Markus Müller-Olm. Correctness proof for SubLisp to PL_0^R translation. ProCoS Technical Report Kiel MMO3, Christian-Albrechts-Universität Kiel, 1990.

[Plo83] Gordon D. Plotkin. An operational semantics for CSP. In Dines Bjørner, editor, *Formal Description of Programming Concepts - II*, pages 199–225. North-Holland, 1983.

An exercise in LP:
The Proof of a Non Restoring Division circuit

Boutheina Chetali

&

Pierre Lescanne

CRIN(CNRS) and INRIA-lorraine,University of Nancy I
Nancy, France

Abstract

This paper describes our experience in using the Larch Prover to verify correctness of a digital circuit. We took as an example the proof made by Verkest & al. of the correctness of the Cathedral-II ALU and we tried to make a similar proof with LP. The proof consists in checking the correctness of the non restoring division algorithm with respect to an abstract specification, and then proving that this algorithm was correctly implemented on the Cathedral-II ALU.

1 Introduction

The proof presented here is based on the studies of Verkest & al. on the Cathedral-II system. They developed a methodology to prove the correctness of an ALU within the Boyer & Moore system [1]. We were interested in one of these proofs, i.e., the proof of the *non restoring division* algorithm described in [2].

The circuit under consideration is sequential and is supposed to implement an iterative arithmetic function, i.e. a division. It seems that the Boyer & Moore (B&M) theorem prover is well-suited for this kind of circuit because its logic is essentially based on recursion. We have chosen a proof of a circuit already made with the B&M prover since it was somewhat different from other proofs of circuits that use LP in the literature, and we wanted to show that LP can compete with the B&M theorem prover on this kind of problem.

In the first part of the proof, we prove that the non restoring division algorithm is correct with respect to its abstract specification, and in the second part, we prove that the division operation of the Cathedral ALU is an implementation of this algorithm.

The approach made by Verkest & al. is a kind of reverse engineering: the algorithm (ANRD), which is implemented on the Cathedral ALU differs from the classical *non restoring division algorithm* on the post processing of the result which is incorporated in the process. The authors explain that the result of the algorithm found by simulation at *the logic gate level* was not the one returned by simulation at *the register transfer level*. So, they had to figure out what the ANRD algorithm effectively computes, which results in a complex specification. Since we wished to redo a similar proof, we had to prove that the ANRD algorithm is correct with respect to this abstract specification. Before starting, let us remind the reader of the methodological aspects of LP [3]. In order to do a large proof within LP, it is recommended (but not mandatory) to first make the full proof by hand. We have done this proof by following the main lines of the Boyer & Moore proof, basically, the structures of the proof are the same. Actually it is worthwhile noticing that since our only source is the list of papers cited in the bibliography, we did not know the detail of the B&M proof. The second step, where LP is actually used, is when the manual proof is reproduced in LP. In this part, steps that are implicit or very brief in the manual proof have to be made explicit.

2 The input to the proof

In hardware verification, there are three main steps: description of the circuit in a high level language, translation into a functional description and translation of this description into the logic of the theorem prover used. In our case, we dealt only with the final step. We started with the functional descriptions given in [2] and we expressed them in the LP logic. Then we performed manually an LP_like proof which we run afterwards in LP.

The formalization of the proof requires an adequate data representation which fits the one used by the prover. When we deal with an iterative arithmetic circuit, most of the time the specification is given as a classical recursive function but this is not the case for the specification of the ANRD algorithm. Indeed as mentioned previously, it does not have the expected behavior, and this specification specifies the result of the algorithm for all values of cycle count, dividend and divisor.

The input of the proof is the non restoring division algorithm (ANRD), its specification, and the functional description of its implementation. The specification involves naturals and integers as arguments and result. The ANRD algorithm takes a natural and two integer arguments and returns a bit vector. So the sorts used are *naturals, integers* and *bit vectors*.

Bit vectors are defined recursively and each bit vector constructor function takes a bit and a bit vector as argument. Our representation of bit vectors is inspired from the shell principle of B&M system:

The bottom   : **bvnil**.
The constructor: **bitvec**.
The accessors   : **bit, vec**.

Example: **bitvec**(*false*,**bitvec**(*true*,**bitvec**(*true*,**bvnil**))) represents the number 3.

The specification corresponds to a higher level function which takes only natural and integer parameters, whereas the implementation involves bit vectors. Therefore, we need functions (*vec_to_nat* and *vec_to_int*) to convert bit vectors into naturals or integers.

The **ANRD** algorithm is:

$q_n := sign(divisor) \oplus (1 - sign(dividend))$
$R_n := dividend$
$For \ \ i = n - 1 \ \ to \ \ 0$
$\quad R_i := if(q_{i+1} = 0, R_{i+1} + (2^i * divisor)$
$\qquad\qquad\qquad R_{i+1} - (2^i * divisor))$
$\quad q_i := sign(divisor) \oplus (1 - sign(R_i))$

and its functional description in the logic of LP is:

anrd(0,x,y) == bvnil
anrd(s(i),x,y)==bitvec((not($y < 0$)=not((new_R(s(i),x,y) < 0))),
$\qquad\qquad\qquad$ **anrd(i,new_R(s(i),x,y),y))**

new_R(s(i),x,y) == if((($y < 0$) = ($x < 0$)),
$\qquad\qquad\qquad$ (x + m($y*$p2(i))),
$\qquad\qquad\qquad$ (x + ($y*$p2(i))))

where

- $p2$ is a linear representation of *power two*, i.e., $p2(x) = 2^x$.

- m is a unary operator that returns the opposite of an integer, i.e., m(3)=-3

- s is the successor.

The function **anrd** takes two integers x,y and computes a bit vector which is the 2's complement notation of the quotient x/y, after i iteration steps. Initially x is equal to the dividend and during the execution, it holds the consecutive partial remainder. In every recursion step, one quotient bit is computed. The function **new_R** computes the new remainder from the old one, the divisor and the cycle.

Examples:
$anrd(3, 8, 2) = bitvec(true, bitvec(false, bitvec(false, bvnil)))$, which is the 2's complement notation of the integer (-4). The result is not (4) as expected because the number (4) could not be represented on three bits.
$anrd(4, -17, 2) = bitvec(false, bitvec(true, bitvec(true, bitvec(true, bvnil))))$, represents the integer (7), so the result is not (-8) but $(-17/2) + 16 - 1$.

The specification of the ANRD is:

$\forall X \in Z, \forall Y \in Z^*, \forall i \in N^* : anrd(i, X, Y)$		$Y > 0$	$Y < 0$
$0 \le X < |Y| * 2^{i-1}$		X/Y	$X/Y - 1$
$|Y| * 2^{i-1} \le X < |Y| * 2^i$		$X/Y - 2^i$	$X/Y + 2^i - 1$
$|Y| * 2^i \le X$		-1	0
$- \ \ |Y| * 2^{i-1} \le X < 0$	$\wedge X\%Y = 0$	X/Y	$X/Y - 1$
$- \ \ |Y| * 2^{i-1} \le X < 0$	$\wedge X\%Y \ne 0$	$X/Y - 1$	X/Y
$- \ \ |Y| * 2^i \ \ \le X < -|Y| * 2^{i-1}$	$\wedge X\%Y = 0$	$X/Y + 2^i$	$X/Y - 2^i - 1$
$- \ \ |Y| * 2^i \ \ \le X < -|Y| * 2^{i-1}$	$\wedge X\%Y \ne 0$	$X/Y + 2^i - 1$	$X/Y - 2^i$
$X < -|Y| * 2^i$		0	-1

where X/Y stands to the sign-magnitude division and $X\%Y$ is the corresponding remainder.

3 The proof of the ANRD

The theorem that asserts the correctness of the ANRD algorithm states that for any value of the dividend X, divisor Y and i, the bit vector obtained after i cycles of the algorithm represent the 2's complement notation of the result given by the specification for X,Y and i.

This theorem expressed in the logic of LP is:

$$\text{vec\_to\_nat}(\text{anrd}(i,X,Y),i) == \text{nrd\_spec}(i,X,Y) + C(i)$$

where C is a natural to be added in order to get the correct result with respect to the 2's complement notation.

Example:

$anrd(3,5,-2) = 101$

$nrd\_spec(3,5,-2) = (-2) - 1 = -3$

The bit vector 101 represent the integer (-3) on three bits, and

$vec\_to\_nat(anrd(3,5,-2),3) = 5$ so $c(i) = 2^i = 8$.

This theorem is proved by induction on the number of cycles. Here, an induction based on a divide and conquer approach cannot be used because the sign of the operands can change arbitrary during the execution. For example, if $0 \leq X < |Y| * 2^i$ and $Y > 0$, then the partial remainder is $X - (Y * 2^i)$ which is negative ($-|Y| * 2^i \leq X - (Y * 2^i) < 0$). So at each step of the proof, we have to check the corresponding case of the specification in order to apply the induction hypothesis. Therefore, the proof must be planned carefully before proving the induction step. We have indeed to consider all possible combinations of tests in the induction hypotheses and in the induction conclusion [4].

A computer proof is not a manual proof run on a computer !

The axiomatization of the specification is a critical point in our proof. Due to its complexity, we can not represent it by a recursive function. However, several deduction rules were required, where each deduction rule represents one case of the specification:

> **assert**
>   **when** not($x < 0$),
>   ($x < (abs(y) * p2(i + m(1))))$)
>   **yield** nrd_spec(i,x,y) == if(not($y < 0$),q(x,y),(q(x,y)+m(1)))
>   c(i)==if(not($y < 0$),0,p2(i))

In another hand, the specification used in the automatic proof differs from the one used in the manual proof. The reason is that there are aspects which are implicit for the user but which must be made explicit for the theorem prover. For example, mathematical properties about division or equalities, as

if $X \geq 0$ then $0 \leq X < |Y| * 2^{i-1}$
or $|Y| * 2^{i-1} \leq X < |Y| * 2^i$
or $|Y| * 2^i \leq X$

which we express in the LP logic :

assert
   when not$(x < 0)$
   yield $((0 <= x)$ & $(x < (abs(y) * p2(i+m(1)))))$
      $|(((abs(y)*p2(i+m(1)))) <= x)$ & $(x < (abs(y)*p2(i))))$
      $| ((abs(y) * p2(i)) <= x)$

Even simple properties like $((0 \leq X < |Y| * 2^i)$ & $(Y > 0)) \Rightarrow -|Y| * 2^i \leq X - (Y * 2^i) < 0$ must to be explicited to the prover:

assert
   when $(0 <= x),$
      $(x < (abs(y) * p2(pred(s(i))))),$
      not$(y < 0)$
   yield $(m((abs(y) * p2(i))) <= (x + m(y * p2(i)))),$
      $((x + m(y * p2(i))) < 0)$

Making all the assumptions and properties explicit prevents the use of erroneous hypotheses and makes the user more confident with his proof. Thus the specification given to the prover is more detailed than the one used in our manual proof. Other properties are added to the specification, about the quotient and remainder of division with integer arguments.

4 The proof of the implementation

The first part of the correctness proof asserts that the ANRD algorithm is correct w.r.t. its specification; it remains to prove that the division operation of the Catheral-II ALU is an implementation of this algorithm.

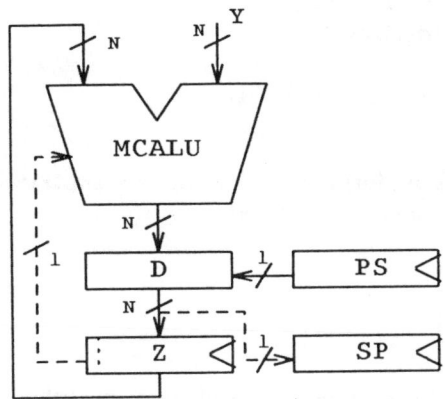

Figure 1: A simplified version of the ALU

Figure 1 is a simplified version of the ALU with only the components that are used in the algorithm; namely a Mead & Conway core ALU (MCALU), a parallel-serial register PS, a serial-parallel register SP, a register Z and a shifter. All these components process signals of length N and return a result of the same length. The correctness of all these components have been proved by Verkest & al. and we rely on these proofs in our own proof.

The division process is: initially the Z and PS register are loaded with some parts of the dividend [2]. During the computations, the Z register holds the partial remainders and at the end of the computations the SP register holds the quotient bit vectors. At each step, the MSB of the register Z controls the add/sub operation of the next cycle. By comparing the sign of the divisor Y with the sign of the shifter output the quotient bit is determined and shifted-in into the SP register.

The functional description which corresponds to this implementation is:

```
hard_anrd_it(i,Y,PS,Z,sign)==
   if((size(Y)=size(PS)) & (size(Y) = size(Z)),
      if(i=0,bvnil,
            bitvec(next_q(bit(next_Z(Z,Y,sign))),Y),
                  hard_anrd_it(i − 1,
                              Y,
                              left_shift(PS,false),
                              left_shift(next_Z(Z,Y,sign),bit(PS)),
                              bit(next_Z(Z,Y,sign)))))),
      bvnil)


next_Z(Z,Y,sign)
   == if((sign=bit(Y)),
            alu_sub(size(Z),Z,Y),
            alu_add(size(Z),Z,Y))

next_q(sign,Y)==(sign=bit(Y))
```

The function next_Z performs an addition or a subtraction depending on the sign of the divisor Y and the parameter *sign*.

4.1   The proof

We take the same approach as in [2] and the same refinement steps in order to prove the correctness of the implementation of the ANRD algorithm. Verkest & al. propose several versions of the algorithm, the first one is close to the algorithm and the last one is very to the actual implementation.

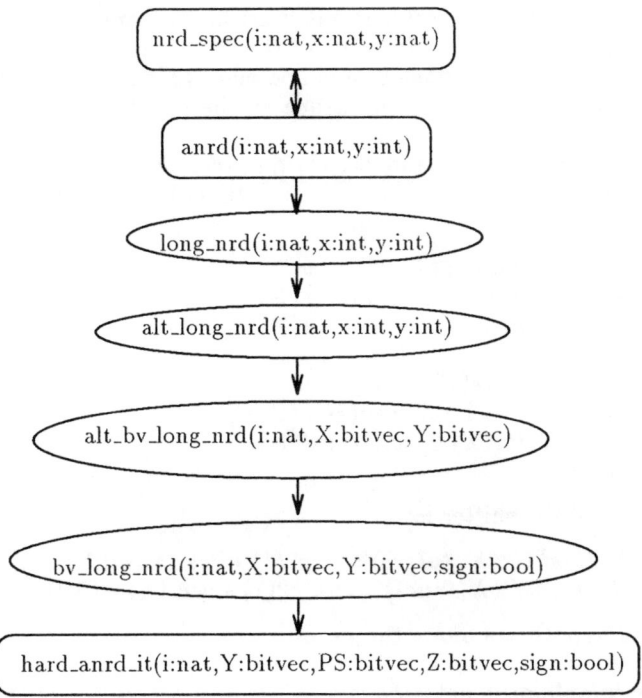

We start with these functional descriptions, and we prove that all these implementations are equivalent. So, we had five theorems to prove, and each one corresponds to a refinement.

Example: The third theorem states the equivalence between *alt_long_nrd* and its implementation:

If $(size(X)=size(Y))$ & even$(size(X))$ & not$(Y=$bvnil$)$

⊢ alt_long_nrd$(i,$vec_to_int$(X),$vec_to_int$(Y))$
$==$
alt_bv_long_nrd(i,X,Y)

4.2 Comments

• The function new_Z used in our proof differs from the one given by Verkest & al.: To represent addition or subtraction performed by the MCALU, we use two simple functions *alu_add* and *alu_sub*. These functions take a natural s and two bit vectors X,Y and return a bit vector of size s, which represents the addition (or subtraction) of the corresponding integers.
Verkest & al. represent the subtraction as:

csobv_bitvec(
   $mcalu(size(Z), F, Z, Y, (nat\_bv(12, 4)), (nat\_bv(5, 4)), (nat\_bv(10, 4)), F))$

The function *mcalu* takes 8 arguments and returns a bit vector representing the result of the add/sub operation together with flags and the function *csobv_bitvec* selects the correct output. Since in the proof, we are concerned only by the fact that the size of the bit vector result must be the same as the size of the input parameter Z, the other arguments of the function $mcalu$ are irrelevant and we combine these two functions in a single one. This simplification is possible because these functions have no influence on the proof implementation.

- Correction of the MCALU and *the shifter.* In several steps of the proof, we need hypotheses on the correctness of the MCALU. Its representation in the LP logic is:

$$vec\_to\_int(alu\_sub(size(Z), Z, Y)) ==$$
$$if(((size(Z) = size(Y))\&even(size(Z))),$$
$$(vec\_to\_int(Z) + vec\_to\_int(Y)),$$
$$error)$$
$$vec\_to\_int(alu\_add(size(Z), Z, Y)) ==$$
$$if(((size(Z) = size(Y))\&even(size(Z))),$$
$$(vec\_to\_int(Z) + vec\_to\_int(Y),$$
$$error)$$

The correction of the shifter is:

$$vec\_to\_int(left\_shift(X, false)) == p2(1) * vec\_to\_int(X)$$
$$vec\_to\_int(left\_shift(X, true)) == s(p2(1) * vec\_to\_int(X))$$

We use other hypotheses along the proof:

- In the 2's complement notation, the MSB of a bit vector is the sign of the corresponding integer.

$$(vec\_to\_int(X) < 0) = bit(X)$$

We define a function to append two bit vectors and we state that the MSB of a vector X is the MSB of the bit vector obtained by appending X and a bit vector Y on the LSB side:

$$bit(bv\_app(X, Y)) == bit(X)$$

- The addition (or subtraction) of a bit vector obtained by appending two bit vectors X and Y, and a bit vector of the same length obtained by extending a vector Z to an all zero bit vector on the LSB side, is equivalent to the bit vector obtained by appending the bit vector result of the addition (or subtraction) of X and Z, with the vector Y:

$$alu\_add(size(bv\_app(X, Z)),$$
$$bv\_app(X, Z),$$
$$bv\_app(Y, zerovec(size(X))))$$
$$== bv\_app(alu\_add(size(X), X, Y), Z)$$

- Let V, W be two bit vectors, b be a boolean. Let V_d, be the bit vector that results of shifting up V while shifting in the MSB of W, let W_d, be the result of shifting up W while shifting in the value b. Then the bit vector formed by appending V_d and W_d is equal to the one formed by appending V and W and shifting up the result while shifting in the value b:

$$bv\_app(left\_shift(V, bit(W)), left\_shift(W, b))$$
$$== left\_shift(bv\_app(V, W), b)$$

Comments on the use of LP

We did not use the completion facility of LP, because all theorems proved are of equivalence between functions. Therefore, we were not concerned with the problem of rewriting systems.

Along our experiments, most of the time we used the predefined ordering, i.e., **noeq-dsmpos**, and all the equations of the original specification were oriented in the desired direction. However, in some places we used the facility to modify the *registry* that contains information about the operators [3]. For instance in the proof of the correction of ANRD, we assigned specific *height* between operators in order to get the correct orientation. This requires to trace the proof in order to understand why equations have been oriented in unexpected directions and what modifications of the registry are necessary.

We had some problems with the proofs of Theorem 3 and 5 due to the fact that LP does not offer the possibility of proving deduction rules by induction. We circumvent this problem by using the if-construct to express a condition that should be true at the induction step $(size(N) = size(Z)$ & $size(Z) = size(PS)$ & $even(size(Z)))$.

5 Conclusion

Our experiment have shown that LP seems well-suited for this kind of proof. Unlike the B&M system which uses extensively predefined functions, LP requires to reconstruct all basic functions. But this point could be an advantage because it gives the user more freedom for choosing the functions and designing the proof. This complete mastering of the proof is a tremendous advantage for debugging proofs of wrong specifications which is after all the main activity of the computer scientist faced with a computer proof of correctness.

Many authors use the B&M system when the hardware is defined recursively but we think that the verification of such circuits could be done using LP. Our further work will be the verification of the correctness of similar but more complex circuits using LP.

Acknowledgements

We are grateful to Ursula Martin and Jeannette Wing for organizing the workshop where we had stimulating discussions. Thus, we thank all the participants collectively. Moreover, we are especially indebted to Steve Garland and Jim Saxe for communicating us part of their LP expertise on the delicate problem of proving deduction rules.

References

[1] R.S.Boyer,J.S.Moore,*A Computational Logic Handbook*,Perspectives in Computing,Vol.23,Academic Press Inc.,1988.

[2] D.Verkest, L.Claesen, H.De Man, *A proof of the non restoring division algorithm and its implementation on the Cathedral-II ALU*, Proceedings of the IFIP Conference on Designing Correct circuits, J.Staunstrup and R.Sharp, Elsevier Science Publishers B.V. (North Holland), 1992, p173-192.

[3] S.J. Garland and J.V. Guttag. *A Guide to LP, The Larch Prover.*TR 82, DEC SRC, Dec. 1991.

[4] B.Chetali, *Preuve automatisée de circuits digitaux: Utilisation de LP pour prouver l'algorithme de division sans restauration et son implementation* , DEA report 1992, CRIN,University of Nancy I, France.

A The rewriting rules for the implementation proofs

Induction rules:

```
nat.2: nat generated by zero, s:nat->nat
nrd.3: vector generated by bvnil, bitvec
```

Operator theories:

```
nat.1: ac +:nat,nat->nat
nrd.1: ac *
nrd.2: ac +:ent,ent->ent
```

Rewrite rules:
```
nat.3:      zero + i -> i
nat.4:      s(i) + j -> s(i + j)
nat.5:      pred(i) + j -> pred(i + j)
nrd.4 :   bit(bvnil) -> false
nrd.5 :   vec(bvnil) -> bvnil
nrd.6 :   bit(bitvec(a, v)) -> a
nrd.7 :   vec(bitvec(a, v)) -> v
nrd.8 :   p2(zero) -> 1
nrd.9 :   p2(i) + p2(i) -> p2(s(i))
nrd.10 :  0 + x -> x
nrd.11 :  m(x) + x -> 0
nrd.12 :  x <= y -> not(y < x)
nrd.13 :  c(zero) -> 0
nrd.14 :  m(x) < 0 -> true
nrd.15 :  p2(s(i)) -> p2(1) * p2(i)
nrd.16 :  p2(i) < 0 -> false
nrd.17 :  not(p2(i) < 0) -> true
nrd.18 :  not((p2(i) * x) < 0) -> not(x < 0)
nrd.19 :  (p2(i) * x) < 0 -> x < 0
nrd.20 :  (x * y) + (x * z) -> (y + z) * x
nrd.21 :  m(x * y) -> m(y) * x
nrd.22 :  size(bvnil) -> zero
```

```
nrd.23 :   size(bitvec(a, v)) -> s(size(v))
nrd.24 :   size(left_shift(v, a)) -> size(v)
nrd.25 :   size(alu_sub(s, xv, yv)) -> s
nrd.26 :   size(alu_add(s, xv, yv)) -> s
nrd.27 :   bit(bv_app(xv, yv)) -> bit(xv)
nrd.28 :   bv_app(left_shift(xv, bit(yv)), left_shift(yv, b))
               -> left_shift(bv_app(xv, yv), b)
nrd.29 :   vec_to_int(if(a, v, zv))
               -> if(a, vec_to_int(v), vec_to_int(zv))
nrd.30 :   not(a) = not(b) -> a = b
nrd.31 :   vec_to_int(xv) < 0 -> bit(xv)
nrd.32 :   bit(alu_sub(size(xv), zv, yv))
               ->
               if((size(yv) = size(zv)) & even(size(zv)),
                  (m(vec_to_int(yv)) + vec_to_int(zv)) < 0,
                  errbool)
nrd.33 :   bit(alu_add(size(xv), zv, yv))
               ->
               if((size(yv) = size(zv)) & even(size(zv)),
                  (vec_to_int(yv) + vec_to_int(zv)) < 0,
                  errbool)
nrd.34 :   if(a, x, y) < 0 -> if(a, x < 0, y < 0)
nrd.35 :   vec_to_int(left_shift(bvnil, b)) -> error
nrd.36 :   vec_to_int(left_shift(xv, true))
               -> (p2(1) * vec_to_int(xv)) + 1
nrd.37 :   vec_to_int(left_shift(xv, false))
               -> p2(1) * vec_to_int(xv)
nrd.38 :   vec_to_int(alu_sub(size(xv), zv, yv))
               ->
               if((size(yv) = size(zv)) & even(size(zv)),
                  m(vec_to_int(yv)) + vec_to_int(zv),
                  error)
nrd.39 :   vec_to_int(alu_add(size(xv), zv, yv))
               ->
               if((size(yv) = size(zv)) & even(size(zv)),
                  vec_to_int(yv) + vec_to_int(zv),
                  error)
nrd.40 :   alu_sub(size(bv_app(xv, zv)),
               bv_app(xv, zv),
               bv_app(yv, zerovec(size(xv))))
               -> bv_app(alu_sub(size(xv), xv, yv), zv)
nrd.41 :   alu_add(size(bv_app(xv, zv)),
               bv_app(xv, zv),
               bv_app(yv, zerovec(size(xv))))
               -> bv_app(alu_add(size(xv), xv, yv), zv)
nrd.42 :   vec_to_nat(bvnil, i) -> 0
nrd.43 :   vec_to_nat(bitvec(false, v), s(i)) -> vec_to_nat(v, i)
nrd.44 :   vec_to_nat(bitvec(true, v), s(i))
               -> p2(i) + vec_to_nat(v, i)
nrd.45 :   new_Z(zv, yv, prev)
```

```
                     ->if(bit(yv) = prev,
                         alu_sub(size(zv), zv, yv),
                         alu_add(size(zv), zv, yv))
nrd.46 :  new_q(prev, yv) -> bit(yv) = prev
nrd.47 :  anrd(zero, x, y) -> bvnil
nrd.48 :  anrd(s(i), x, y)
              ->
              bitvec(not(new_R(s(i), x, y) < 0) = not(y < 0),
                anrd(i, new_R(s(i), x, y), y))
nrd.49 :  new_R(s(i), x, y)
              -> if((x < 0) = (y < 0),
                    m(p2(i) * y) + x,
                    (p2(i) * y) + x)
nrd.50 :  long_nrd(zero, x, y) -> bvnil
nrd.51 :  long_nrd(s(i), x, y)
              ->
              bitvec(not(long_new_R(x, y) < 0) = not(y < 0),
                long_nrd(i, long_new_R(x, y) * p2(1), y))
nrd.52 :  long_new_R(x, y)
              -> if((x < 0) = (y < 0), m(y) + x, x + y)
nrd.53 :  alt_long_nrd(zero, x, y) -> bvnil
nrd.54 :  alt_long_nrd(s(i), x, y)
              ->
              bitvec(not(alt_long_new_R(x, y) < 0) = not(y < 0),
                alt_long_nrd(i, alt_long_new_R(x, y), y))
nrd.55 :  alt_long_new_R(x, y)
            -> if((x < 0) = (y < 0),
                  (p2(1) * x) + m(y),
                  (p2(1) * x) + y)
nrd.56 :  bv_long_nrd(zero, xv, yv, prev) -> bvnil
nrd.57 :  bv_long_nrd(s(i), xv, yv, prev)
              ->
              bitvec(bit(bv_long_new_R(xv, yv, prev)) = bit(yv),
                bv_long_nrd(i,
                  left_shift(bv_long_new_R(xv, yv, prev), false),
                  yv,
                  bit(bv_long_new_R(xv, yv, prev)))))
nrd.58 :  bv_long_new_R(xv, yv, prev)
              ->
              if(bit(yv) = prev,
                  alu_sub(size(xv), xv, yv),
                  alu_add(size(xv), xv, yv))
nrd.59 :  alt_bv_long_nrd(zero, xv, yv) -> bvnil
nrd.60 :  alt_bv_long_nrd(s(i), xv, yv)
              ->
              bitvec(bit(alt_bv_long_new_R(xv, yv)) = bit(yv),
                alt_bv_long_nrd(i, alt_bv_long_new_R(xv, yv), yv))
nrd.61 :  alt_bv_long_new_R(xv, yv)
              ->
              if(bit(xv) = bit(yv),
```

```
                    alu_sub(size(xv), left_shift(xv, false), yv),
                    alu_add(size(xv), left_shift(xv, false), yv))
nrd.62 :   hard_anrd_it(zero, yv, ps, zv, prev) -> bvnil
nrd.63 :   hard_anrd_it(s(i), yv, ps, zv, prev)
              ->
           if((size(ps) = size(yv)) & (size(yv) = size(zv)),
               bitvec(new_q(bit(new_Z(zv, yv, prev)), yv),
                  hard_anrd_it(i,
                      yv,
                      left_shift(ps, false),
                      left_shift(new_Z(zv, yv, prev), bit(ps)),
                      bit(new_Z(zv, yv, prev)))),
               bvnil)
theo5.1:   hard_anrd_it(i, n, ps, zv, prev)
              ->
           if((size(n) = size(ps)) & (size(n) = size(zv)),
               bv_long_nrd(i,
                  bv_app(zv, ps),
                  bv_app(n, zerovec(size(zv))),
                  prev),
               bvnil)
```

B   Benchmarks

Here are the benchmarks for the proof of the correctness of the non restoring division. The corresponding script file is 450 lines long. The script file for the proof of the implementation is 200 lines long. (Times are for a SUN Sparcstation2)

	Success		Failure		Total
	count	time	count	time	time
Ordering	316	37:24.13	230	3.19	37:27.32
Rewriting	2746	30.35	34428	1:44.78	2:15.13
Deductions	616	46.51	32333	2:04.11	2:50.62
Unification	0	0.00	0	0.00	0.00
Prover					10.99
GCs	187				
total time					43:49.00

Figure 1: Proof of the correction of the ANRD

	Success		Failure		Total
	count	time	count	time	time
Ordering	115	8:08.25	1061	8.11	8:16.36
Rewriting	588	5.83	985	3.61	9.44
Deductions	25	0.45	54	0.01	0.46
Unification	0	0.00	0	0.00	0.00
Prover					13.26
GCs	33				
total time					8.54.55

Figure 2: Proof of the implementation of the ANRD

Integrating ASSPEGIQUE and LP

Christine Choppy

LRI, C.N.R.S. U.R.A. 410 & Université Paris-Sud
91405 Orsay Cedex, France

Michel Bidoit

LIENS, C.N.R.S. U.R.A. 1327 & Ecole Normale Supérieure
75230 Paris Cedex, France

Abstract

In this paper, we present various issues w.r.t. proving properties of
PLUSS specifications with LP, and building an integrated interface between ASSPEGIQUE (the environment that supports PLUSS) and LP.
We investigate how general properties can be proved using an adequate
presentation of the specification that may be understood by LP. We address the issue of interfacing the two environments in a way that would
be as "transparent" to the user as possible.

1 Introduction

In order to make use of algebraic specifications the essential ingredients are a
specification language and an environment where tools to design, verify and
use specifications are integrated.

While developing the ASSPEGIQUE environment [9, 6, 5] that supports the
PLUSS specification language [10, 3, 4], there has been a strong motivation
for developing interfaces with tools and/or environments developed by other
research groups, such as REVE [1] and SLOG.

LP (the *Larch Prover*) [19, 20] has been developed both as a "debugging tool"
for LSL (*Larch Shared Language*) specifications [24, 23, 21, 22], and with the
intent of interfacing it to specific application front-ends.

In this paper, we present various issues w.r.t. proving properties of PLUSS specifications with LP, and building an integrated interface between ASSPEGIQUE
and LP.

We first provide a brief overview of the PLUSS specification language syntax
and semantics. The PLUSS building primitives that will be considered in this
work are: enrichment, parameterization, instantiation and renaming. The semantics of a PLUSS specification is defined as a class of models that satisfy the
axioms of the specification, that are finitely generated w.r.t. the generators, and
that comply with constraints relative to both hierarchy and modular construction. The ASSPEGIQUE environment is then shortly presented; it comprises
tools for browsing, editing, analyzing and prototyping specifications. We then

---

[1]REVE is the "ancestor" of LP, although it was not related to any particular specification
language.

examine what kind of properties of PLUSS specifications can be proved with the LP theorem prover. Since it is not possible to provide a finite first-order axiomatization that reflects the semantics of a PLUSS specification, the only point that may be checked w.r.t. the consistency of a PLUSS specification is the consistency of the axioms. Although sufficient completeness is insured by the finitely generated property, it may be worth to provide the specifier with means to check the relative completeness of an operation axiomatization. We then examine how general properties can be proved using an adequate presentation of the specification that may be understood by LP. Finally we address the issue of interfacing the two environments in a way that would be as "transparent" to the user as possible.

2 The PLUSS algebraic specification language

In this section we provide a brief overview of the PLUSS specification language syntax and semantics. However, we shall restrict ourselves to presenting those characteristics of PLUSS that will be used in the work reported here (for more details see e.g. [10, 3, 4]). Moreover, we assume that the reader is familiar with both the *Larch Shared Language* (LSL) [24, 23, 21, 22] and the *Larch Prover* (LP) [19, 20].

The design of the PLUSS specification language is the result of numerous experiments in writing large specifications, some of them being done in cooperation with industry [11, 10, 28, 5, 14]. The experience gained from these experiments led to put strong emphasis on modularization facilities. Moreover, these experiments have proved the need to state a careful distinction between "implementable" ("achieved") specification modules, and "not yet implementable" ("under development") specification modules.

2.1 The PLUSS specification building primitives

In all specification modules, the axioms are expressed by first order logic formulas. In achieved specification modules (**spec**) the distinguished subset of generators is specified apart from the other operations of the signature and is introduced by the keyword **generated by**.

The *enrichment* primitive, denoted by the keyword **use**, provides a straightforward way to add new domains, objects, properties, to a specification, as e.g. shown in the SYSTEM specification below. In LSL the enrichment primitive is denoted by **includes**.

```
Spec : SYSTEM;
    use : DIRECTORY;
  sort : System;
  generated by:
    ...
End SYSTEM.
```

Parameterization saves the writing of many instances of the same specification. In the example below, ELEM is a *formal parameter* specification (**Par**), LIST

(ELEM) is a *parameterised specification* (**Generic spec**), and L-IDENT is an *instance* of LIST (ELEM) where ELEM is instanciated by IDENT through a "fitting morphism m" that maps "Elem" to "Ident"; in addition, a *renaming* of the sort "List" into "L-ident" and of the operation "Empty" into "none" is performed in order to customize names for this particular instance. It should be noted that, when dealing with PLUSS achieved specifications, the "meaning" of renaming is aliasing [8] (while renaming in LSL rather means copying). In LSL there is no explicit parameterization mechanism. However, "the **includes** and **assumes** clauses, together with renamings, make possible much of the reuse for which parameterization is advocated" [23].

```
Par : ELEM;
  sort : Elem;          ''this is a comment''
End ELEM.

Generic spec : LIST (ELEM);
  sort : List;
  generated by :
    Empty :              -> List;
    _ :    Elem          -> List;
      ''this is a coercion : any Elem is a one element List''
    _ _ : Elem * List -> List;
      ''this is an anonymous operation to add an Elem to a List''
  operation :
    _ union _ : List * List -> List;
      ''the _'s indicate the argument locations''
  predicates :
    _ is in _ :  Elem * List;
    _ all in _ : List * List;
  axioms :
    ''omitted here due to lack of space''
End LIST (ELEM).

Spec : L-IDENT
    use : LIST (ELEM => IDENT by m);
    where : m : Elem => Ident;
    renaming : List into L-ident, Empty into none;
End L-IDENT.
```

As a means to improve readability of specifications, and to allow a maximum flexibility in the choice of identifiers, the specification signature may contain (as in LIST (ELEM) above) coercions, anonymous operations, overloaded operator symbols, etc. The price to pay is that the resulting term language may be ambiguous, and cannot be parsed using classical techniques: a tool called CIGALE has been designed to generate for each specification the corresponding grammar and the appropriate parser [30, 31].

As mentioned above, the main originality of PLUSS is to state a careful distinction between "implementable" specification modules (**Spec**), and "not yet implementable" ones. The specification modules under development are intro-

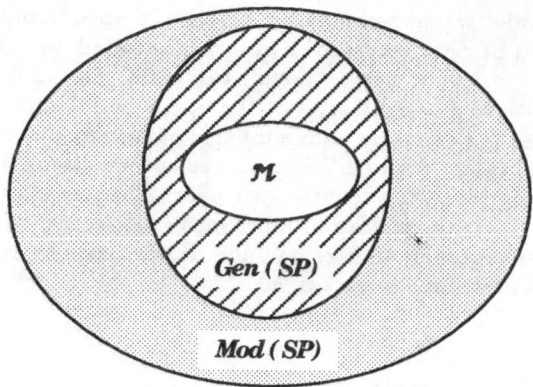

Figure 1: Models associated to a specification

duced by the keywords **Draft** or **Sketch**. They have a more flexible semantics than **Specs**, since the signature and the axioms are not fully fixed and may be further refined by means of appropriate combination of enrichments and instanciations. A draft may enrich another draft (**with**) or a specification (**use**):

```
Draft : STATE
    use : L-IDENT;
    with : COND-LIST (ELEM => spec ATTRIBUTE by m);
      where : m : Elem => Attribute;
      renaming : C-List into State
                 ''a State is a conditional list of attributes'',
                 Empty into no-attribute;
  ...
End STATE.
```

where COND-LIST is a generic draft. In the case of specifications under development, the meaning of renaming is copying (as in LSL).

After this short overview of the PLUSS syntax and specification-building primitives, we will now focus on its semantics.

2.2 The stratified loose semantics of PLUSS

Several choices have to be taken when designing the semantics of an algebraic specification language. A first issue is the approach chosen to describe the semantics [29]: the semantics of a PLUSS specification is defined as some class of *models* (Σ-algebras) (while the semantics of an LSL specification is defined as the *theory* induced by the axioms). Another point is the choice of a *loose* semantics (in this case the semantics of a specification is a class of models) as opposed to an initial [16, 15] or final [33] approach where only one model is allowed. Obviously the models of a specification should satisfy the axioms. It is usual to add a further condition by only considering finitely generated models w.r.t the signature of the specification. In the case of PLUSS, only models that are finitely generated w.r.t. the operations declared as generators are considered (it is possible to state a similar condition in LSL): this guaranties that for any model, all values will be denotable as some composition of these generators (an important consequence of this constraint is that *structural induction restricted to the generators* is a correct proof principle). Finally, the semantics of PLUSS introduces some hierarchical constraints (cf. the so called "no junk" and "no confusion" properties) as well as constraints to reflect the modular structure of the specification. As a consequence, the class of models of a PLUSS specification is, in general, strictly included into the class of finitely generated models (w.r.t. the generators) that satisfy the axioms (cf. Fig. 1). A more precise definition of the PLUSS semantics is given below.

An algebraic (flat) specification SP is a tuple $(S, \Sigma, \mathcal{A}x)$ where (S, Σ) is a signature, $\Omega \subset \Sigma$ is the distinguished subset of generators, and $\mathcal{A}x$ is a finite set of Σ-formulas. We denote by $Mod(\Sigma)$ the category of all Σ-algebras, by $Mod(SP)$ the full sub-category of all Σ-algebras for which $\mathcal{A}x$ is satisfied, and by $Gen(SP)$ the full sub-category of all Σ-algebras that are finitely generated w.r.t the generators Ω and for which $\mathcal{A}x$ is satisfied.

Let us assume that the PLUSS modular specification SP_2 is made of one specification module ΔSP that enriches only one modular specification SP_1.

According to the loose approach of PLUSS, the semantics of the specification SP_1 will be defined as some class $\mathcal{M}_1$ of Σ_1-algebras (where Σ_1 denotes the signature associated to SP_1). Similar notations hold for SP_2. Since we assume that SP_2 is defined as an enrichment of SP_1 by the specification module ΔSP, we have $\Sigma_1 \subseteq \Sigma_2$. Let $\mathcal{U}$ denote the usual forgetful functor from Σ_2-algebras to Σ_1-algebras.

With the help of this simple context, our intuition about the adequate models of a PLUSS modular specification can be summarized as follows [4]:

1. Any model of the "large" specification SP_2 must also provide, through the forgetful functor $\mathcal{U}$, a correct model of the sub-specification SP_1, i.e. we should have: $\mathcal{U}(\mathcal{M}_2) \subseteq \mathcal{M}_1$.

2. Any model of the sub-specification SP_1 should be extensible to a model of the larger specification SP_2, i.e. we should have: either $\mathcal{M}_2 = \emptyset$, or $\mathcal{U}(\mathcal{M}_2) \supseteq \mathcal{M}_1$.

3. It should be possible to implement the specification module ΔSP without knowing which specific realization of the sub-specification SP_1 has been (or will be) chosen. Thus, the various specification modules should be implementable **independently** of each other.

The first two requirements can be easily achieved by embedding some appropriate *hierarchical constraints* into the semantics of the use enrichment specification-building primitive. Roughly speaking, it is sufficient to require the following property:

Either $\mathcal{M}_2 = \emptyset$ (in that case the specification module ΔSP will be said to be hierarchically inconsistent) or $\mathcal{U}(\mathcal{M}_2) = \mathcal{M}_1$.

The third requirement, however, cannot be achieved without providing a suitable (loose) semantics to **specification modules** themselves (and not only to specifications as a whole).

Definition (Stratified loose semantics) [3]: Given a modular specification SP_2 defined as the enrichment of some modular specification SP_1 by a specification module ΔSP, the semantics of the specification module ΔSP and of the modular specification SP_2 are defined as follows:

Basic case: If the sub-specification SP_1 is empty (hence the specification SP_2 is reduced to the specification module ΔSP), then:

- The semantics of the specification SP_2 is by definition the initial model of $Gen(SP_2)$, if any; if $Gen(SP_2)$ has no initial model, then SP_2 is said to be *inconsistent*.
- The semantics of the specification module ΔSP is defined as being the functor $\mathcal{F}$ from the category **1** to $Gen(SP_2)$, which maps the object of **1** to the initial model of $Gen(SP_2)$.[2]

General case: Let us denote by $\mathcal{M}_1$ the class of models associated to the modular specification SP_1, according to the current definition.

- The semantics of the specification module ΔSP is defined as being the class $\mathcal{F}_1^2$ of all the mappings $\mathcal{F}$ such that:
  1. $\mathcal{F}$ is a (**total**) functor from $\mathcal{M}_1$ to $Gen(SP_2)$.
  2. $\mathcal{F}$ is a right inverse of the forgetful functor $\mathcal{U}$, i.e.:
  $$\forall M_1 \in \mathcal{M}_1 : \mathcal{U}(\mathcal{F}(M_1)) = M_1.$$
  If the class $\mathcal{F}_1^2$ is empty, then the enrichment is said to be *hierarchically inconsistent*.
- The semantics of the whole specification SP_2 is defined as being the class of all the models in the image of the functors $\mathcal{F}$:
  $$\mathcal{M}_2 = \bigcup_{\mathcal{F} \in \mathcal{F}_1^2} \mathcal{F}(\mathcal{M}_1).$$

The class $\mathcal{M}_2$ of the models of the specification SP_2 is said to be **stratified** by the functors $\mathcal{F}$.

It is important to note that with this PLUSS loose stratified semantics, the *hierarchical constraints* mentioned above are satisfied. More precisely, as soon as the specification module ΔSP is hierarchically consistent, then we have $\mathcal{U}(\mathcal{M}_2) = \mathcal{M}_1$. As a consequence, both the so-called *"no junk"* and *"no confusion"* properties are guaranteed. In other words, we know that the "old" carrier sets (i.e. the carrier sets of sorts defined in SP_1) will contain no "new" value, and that "old" values who may be distinct before (in at least one model of SP_1) should not be forced to be equal by the new specification module ΔSP.

As a consequence of the "hierarchical constraints" required by modularity, it is desirable to state a careful distinction between *implementable* and *not yet implementable* specification modules:

---

[2] As usual, the category **1** denotes the category containing only one object, which can be interpreted as a Σ_1-algebra for an empty signature Σ_1.

- *Implementable specification modules* will have a semantics defined accordingly to the stratified loose framework, in order to allow for a **modular** software development and verification process.

- *Not yet implementable specification modules* will have a more flexible semantics, in order to allow for a specification development process by stepwise refinements.

Hence, the semantics of a PLUSS achieved specification results from both *explicit* and *implicit* features. The *explicit part* of the semantics is that the models of the specification should satisfy its axioms. The *implicit part* of the semantics result from the following constraints:

1. Only finitely generated models w.r.t the generators are considered.

2. Only models that comply with the hierarchical constraints are considered ("no junk", "no confusion").

3. Only models that are in the image of the functors are considered.

The first constraint has an equivalent counterpart in LSL, but not the two other ones (the second has no more counterpart since the **imports** and **constrains** constructs have been removed from LSL [23]).

3 The ASSPEGIQUE/ASSPEGIQUE+ specification environment

ASSPEGIQUE [9, 6, 5] is an integrated environment for the development of large algebraic specifications and the management of a specification data base (cf. Fig. 2).

One of our goals in the design of ASSPEGIQUE is that this environment should allow the design and management of large specifications; this point is especially important as far as one is concerned with bridging the gap between research prototypes and industrial use of specifications.

The main issues addressed in the design of ASSPEGIQUE are: dealing with modularity and reusability, and providing ease of use, flexibility of the environment and user-friendly interfaces.

ASSPEGIQUE is intended to be a flexible structure where new tools may be easily integrated; its components are browsing tools, specification editing tools, parsing tools, semantics analysis tools, rapid prototyping tools (through symbolic evaluation [26, 25] and code generation [12, 13]), theorem proving tools (initially, a theorem prover that makes explicit use of induction w.r.t. the generators; then interfaces with the REVE system [27, 17] and with the SLOG system [18, 1] were implemented), and a tool for assistance to Ada implementation. Special care was taken to provide an homogeneous, user-friendly interface. ASSPEGIQUE has been distributed in many research laboratories (both academic and industrial ones), and has been used by students for projects in algebraic specification courses.

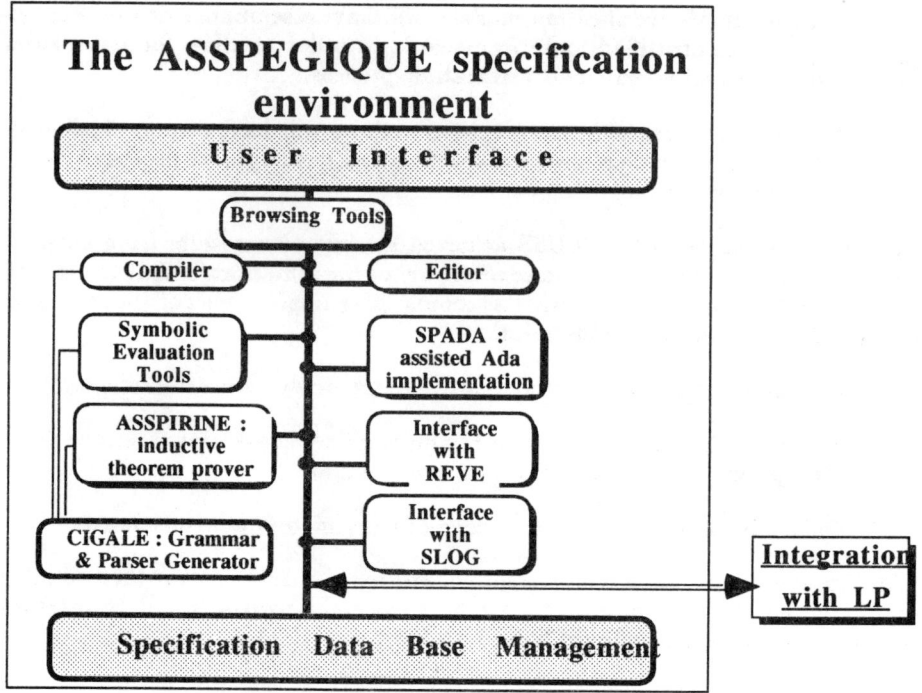

Figure 2: Integrating ASSPEGIQUE and LP

ASSPEGIQUE was designed to support a strongly modular (and "middle-out") approach: when using ASSPEGIQUE, the user deals with specification modules, that may be introduced independently (and with no required bottom-up - or top-down - order). As a consequence, there is no flattening in the internal representation of the specifications: there is one internal representaion per specification module, and ASSPEGIQUE keep track of the global modular structure of the specification.

Up to recently, ASSPEGIQUE only supported a subset of the PLUSS language restricted to the enrichment primitive. The new version ASSPEGIQUE+ [7] also supports the parameterization and instanciation primitives, as well as the renaming primitive. ASSPEGIQUE+ was demonstrated this year, running symbolic evaluations on a transit-node specification adapted from [28].

While developing this environment, there has been a strong motivation for developing its integration with other tools and/or environments developed by other research groups. In particular, limited effort was put on developing theorem proving tools within ASSPEGIQUE, while interfaces where built with the REVE and SLOG systems. Building these interfaces without requiring any participation from the other system developers was possible, but led to some limitations (these design issues will be discussed in section 5).

LP (the Larch Prover) [19, 21, 20] was initially designed as a "debugging tool" for specifications, that allows the user to use theorem proving tools to check her specifications. While the main goal was to provide a debugging tool for specifications written in Larch (LSL), LP was also explicitely designed with the intent of interfacing it to other specific application front-ends.

The aim of the work presented here is to build an integrated interface between ASSPEGIQUE+ and LP (cf. Fig. 2). This will provide both a powerful theorem prover for ASSPEGIQUE+ and a PLUSS front-end for LP.

4 Interfacing ASSPEGIQUE and LP: Motivations and Issues

Most of the issues raised by the integration of ASSPEGIQUE and LP are similar to those raised by the interface between LSL and LP. The *Larch Shared Language Checker* [21] analyzes a given LSL specification to produce, in a suitable format:

- A signature and some equations.

- Some deduction rules (e.g. *generated by...*, *partitioned by...*).

- Three categories of proof obligations: consistency, theory containment, relative completeness.

We will have to achieve a similar task for PLUSS specifications, even if PLUSS does not yet include the proof related constructs of LSL, such as e.g. *implies* and *converts*. In the following, we focus on three categories of proof obligations that one may wish to discharge w.r.t. PLUSS specifications: consistency, relative completeness (that a set of operators is adequately defined), and consequences (that a formula is valid for all models of a specification). We do not consider explicitly here theory containment, since the semantics of parameterization in PLUSS is quite different from the one of the **assumes** construct of LSL.[3]

4.1 Semantic checks

A crucial issue is obviously to know when some given PLUSS specification module is *hierarchically consistent*. From a general point of view, it is well-known that this is an undecidable problem. However, we would like to point out that, in the PLUSS stratified loose framework, there are distinct grounds for hierarchical inconsistency:

- As usual, hierarchical inconsistency may result from the axioms introduced by the specification module. While the consistency of a set of axioms is undecidable in general, it is well-known that, in the case of equations or positive conditional equations, a semi-decision procedure is obtained through completion. The LP *complete* command is available to perform such a completion on a system of equations and its extension to positive conditional equations is under study. LP designers stress

---

[3] We believe that, in PLUSS, to prove that an actual parameter specification is correct w.r.t. the corresponding formal parameter specification does not raise other issues than the three categories of proof obligations studied here. This point obviously requires further investigation.

that, while LP has proved useful in debugging specifications (here in showing evidence for inconsistency), it may not succeed in proving consistency because the completion process either is not applicable or cannot be completed in an acceptable amount of time and space [21].

- It is well-known that there exist consistent theories with no finitely generated model (w.r.t. the full signature) [34]. It is very easy as well to exhibit some cases where the theory is consistent, has finitely generated models (w.r.t. the full signature) but no finitely generated models w.r.t. the declared generators. There is, to our knowledge, no obvious way to check the existence of a finitely generated model (either w.r.t. Σ or w.r.t. Ω).

- Moreover, in PLUSS, hierarchical inconsistency may result from an improper structure of the specification. In some cases, there may be no **total** mapping from $\mathcal{M}_1$ to $Gen(SP_2)$, since some model M_1 of SP_1 cannot be extended to a model of SP_2. A typical example of such a situation is the following one: if we assume that SP_1 specifies natural numbers (with $\mathcal{M}_1 \supseteq \{\mathbf{N}, \mathbf{Z}/n\mathbf{Z}\}$), specifying a "$<$" operation in ΔSP will result in an hierarchically inconsistent specification module ($\mathbf{Z}/n\mathbf{Z}$ cannot be extended to a model of $Gen(SP_2)$ and the requirement $\mathcal{U}(\mathcal{M}_2) \supseteq \mathcal{M}_1$ is not satisfied). Thus, this "$<$" operation should rather have been defined in the appropriate specification module, i.e. in the module where the natural numbers are defined. It is worth noting that the "flat" version of this specification (e.g. with only one module) is consistent. As a consequence, there is no way to detect the former inconsistency through mere analysis of the axioms. The only way to prevent these inconsistencies from arising is to enforce some structuration rules that can be syntactically checked.

- A further ground for inconsistency is the functorial semantics provided to specification modules. In some cases, even if the hierarchical constraints are satisfied, and even if there exist some total mappings from $\mathcal{M}_1$ to $Gen(SP_2)$, it may happen that none of these mappings is a functor (i.e. morphisms are not preserved). In such a case the specification module is inconsistent [4].

It is clearly not possible in general to find a finite first order axiomatization that would present the theory associated to a Pluss specification. While the *explicit part* of the semantics (the axioms) may be checked (w.r.t. consistency), this is not the case for the *implicit part*.

4.2   Checking "relative completeness" of operations

While the sufficient completeness property of a specification is usually worth checking, this issue when dealing with a PLUSS specification is meaningless since only models that are finitely generated w.r.t the generators are considered (hence, by definition, they have no junk values).

One motivation for the restriction to finitely generated models w.r.t. the generators is to avoid overspecification of some operations [4, 2]. For instance, in the specification given in Fig. 3, it is more adequate to leave some flexibility w.r.t. the Msg-Window and Menu-Window positions, etc. The same preoccupation is shared in LSL to let the user have "intentionally incomplete"

```
spec : WINDOW ;
    use : WINDOW-ATTRIBUTES ;
  sort : Window ;
  generated by :
      Create : Coordinates * Dimension * Dimension ⟶ Window ;
  operations :
      Msg-Window, Menu-Window : ⟶ Window ;
      the position of : Window ⟶ Coordinates ;
      the height of, the width of : Window ⟶ Dimension ;
      Move : Window * Coordinates ⟶ Window ;
      Resize : Window * Dimension * Dimension ⟶ Window ;
  axioms :
      position : the position of Create(c, d1, d2) = c ;
      height : the height of Create(c, d1, d2) = d1 ;
      width : the width of Create(c, d1, d2) = d2 ;
      move : Move(w, c) = Create(c, the height of w, the width of w) ;
      resize : Resize(w, d1, d2) = Create(the position of w, d1, d2) ;
      where :  w : Window ;  c : Coordinates ;  d1, d2 : Dimension ;
end WINDOW .
```

Figure 3: Window specification.

specifications [21]. Hence, the situation here is quite similar for PLUSS and LSL.

However, in some cases, "incompleteness" might result from a specification error (for instance, when the axiom $x+s(y) = s(x+y)$ is given and the axiom $x+0=0$ is forgotten). Since, in most cases, the intent of the specifier is to provide a complete definition of the operation, it is of practical interest to provide means to check it. In our example, one way to check the "relative completeness" of the operation $+$ would be to prove that *generated by 0,s,+ implies generated by 0,s.*

As a matter of fact, LSL provides another way to state that some operation is, in the intent of the specifier, completely "defined": the **converts** (and **exempting**) clauses. In our example, one would like to check that *converts +* is true.

While the practical interest of the **converts** clause is obvious, is is rather difficult to understand whether *converts +* is equivalent to or stronger than *generated by 0,s,+ implies generated by 0,s.*[4]

---

[4]In [21], the meaning of the **converts** clause is explained as follows: "given any fixed interpretations for the other operators, all interpretations of f that satisfy the specification axioms are the same."

4.3 Proving consequences

The class of models $\mathcal{M}$ of a PLUSS specification SP is, in general, strictly included in the class $Gen(SP)$ of Σ-algebras that are finitely generated w.r.t. the generators and that satisfy the axioms. In section 4.1, it was noted that there is usually no finite first order presentation of the theory associated to a PLUSS specification. However, if it is possible to produce a sensible presentation $\mathcal{P}res$ for a PLUSS specification that has a larger class of models than $\mathcal{M}$, then any property proved correct for all models of $\mathcal{P}res$ will be correct for all models in $\mathcal{M}$. This presentation $\mathcal{P}res$ may correspond to a "flattened" version of the PLUSS specification.

The issues raised here are mostly similar to those raised by the computation of a suitable term rewriting system in the symbolic evaluation tools of AS-SPEGIQUE+. Hence, we believe that the solutions adopted for these symbolic evaluation tools will prove convenient as well for LP, namely the way we are dealing with the **renaming, parameterization** and **instanciation** primitives of PLUSS.

Nevertheless, there is still a strong requirement that must be fulfilled for this computation of $\mathcal{P}res$ to make sense: the formulas allowed to express the axioms should be "almost equivalent" in both PLUSS and LP (The issues raised by the differences between authorized identifiers in both PLUSS and LP, and more generally syntax issues, will be addressed in the next section.)

LP is based on a fragment of first-order logic in which equations play a prominent role. Some of LP's inference mechanisms work directly with equations, but most require that equations are oriented into (terminating) rewrite rules.

Even if arbitrary first order formulas are allowed in PLUSS, in most cases only conditional equations are used. Hence, it is not a major difficulty to assume that the PLUSS specifications under consideration only contain (positive) conditional equations.

Unfortunately, a (naive and direct) translation of these conditional equations into either *if-then-else formulas* or *deduction rules* is not adequate: even when the semantical meaning of the axiom can be preserved, the operational content is quite different. This was a main motivation (among others) to introduce conditional equations into LP, as done in the last experimental release.

5 Interface issues

In the previous section, the issue of finding a sensible presentation $\mathcal{P}res$ of a PLUSS specification was addressed, in particular with the aim of producing a set of LP formulas so that proofs about the PLUSS specification could be achieved with LP. Another aspect in developing an interface between AS-SPEGIQUE and LP is to be able to transfer appropriate information between the two systems, in particular how to produce a text of $\mathcal{P}res$ with the appropriate LP syntax. We have to distinguish three different levels of language (cf. Figure 4): the *term language* (obtained through the signature), the *formula language* (language for expressing the axioms), and the *LP command language* (key-words to *declare* sorts, operators, and variables, to *assert* axioms or e.g. *generated by* clauses, to *prove* e.g. some formula, etc.).

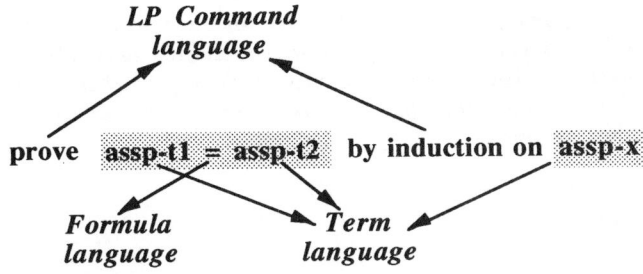

Figure 4: Writing an LP command with some ASSPEGIQUE syntax

In section 3 it was mentioned that when building previous interfaces with the REVE and SLOG systems, some limitations were encountered. What could be achieved in these interfaces was to produce the text of a presentation that respects the other system syntax. Since ASSPEGIQUE supports the PLUSS facility to declare operators with a mixfixed syntax (e.g. push _ onto _ : Elem Stack →Stack), as well as coercions and anonymous operators (e.g. _ _ : Elem List →List) which are not always supported in other systems, this implied a translation of some identifiers. Other identifiers had to be translated because of some key-words or some conventions (e.g. + has in the REVE system a built-in theory, that may be different from the theory of some + operator in a PLUSS specification). This was not very satisfactory, since there is no straightforward translation definition that insures that all names should be as close as possible to the original ones, and that there would be no collapsing of names. Another point is that, while the translation at the formula language level (e.g. $a = b$ becomes $a == b$) may be easier to adapt oneself to, the translation of the operation names is a bigger change (e.g. $0 + x$ was translated to $plus(0,x)$). Therefore, in order to address commands to the other system, or to read output produced by the other system, the ASSPEGIQUE user had to learn a new (and probably rather different) term language.

When designing this interface between ASSPEGIQUE and LP, our goal is to obtain an integrated interface that would save the user the learning of a new term language, and even the learning of a new formula language. The user should be able to type a sentence as in Figure 4, where the formula "assp-t1 = assp-t2" is written using the ASSPEGIQUE/PLUSS formula language and the specification term language. In this situation, it is still needed to produce the presentation $\mathcal{P}res$ in an LP form, but the user does not need to be aware of it. Therefore syntax issues (authorized identifiers, term language, ...) are much simpler, since the result of the translation does not need to be polished. However, this framework involves that some additional features enable LP to accept such a "mixed" sentence as an input and to be able to translate it into a form adequate for LP. Conversely, this framework involves some mechanism that filters LP output to produce an output with ASSPEGIQUE/PLUSS term and formula language syntax.

As in [32] other aspects addressed in this design are the communication protocol between the two systems, and the user interface. Technical solutions to these problems are being designed in collaboration with S. Garland, J. Guttag and F. Voisin. It is quite interesting that, while we are mainly interested in interfacing two specific systems, the technical solutions may probably be applied when interfacing other systems together (at least, when interfacing ASSPEGIQUE or LP with other systems).

6 Conclusion

In this paper, we presented various issues w.r.t. proving properties of PLUSS specifications with LP, and building an integrated interface between ASSPE-GIQUE and LP. While it is not possible to provide a finite first-order LP axiomatization that fully reflects the semantics of a PLUSS specification, some properties of the specification can be proved using an adequate presentation of the specification. We also presented a preliminary design for interfacing the two environments in a way that would be as "transparent" to the user as possible.

A first step towards a better understanding of how LP can be used to efficiently check PLUSS specifications is to implement the interface mechanisms outlined in the last section and to perform various experiments, from which experience will be gained. The carefully detailed design and implementation of this interface are made in strong cooperation between Steve Garland, John Guttag, Frédéric Voisin and the authors.

Acknowledgements

This work is partially supported by a joint CNRS-NSF grant, and the E.E.C. ESPRIT Working Group COMPASS. Special thanks are due to Steve Garland, John Guttag, and Frédéric Voisin for many fruitful discussions.

References

[1] Slog 1.1, User's Manual, 1986. C.G.E. Report, Route de Nozay, 91460 Marcoussis, France.

[2] G. Bernot and M. Bidoit. Proving the correctness of algebraically specified software: Modularity and Observability issues. In *Proc. of the 2nd International Conference on Algebraic Methodology and Software Technology (AMAST)*, 1991.

[3] M. Bidoit. The stratified loose approach: A generalization of initial and loose semantics. In *Recent Trends in Data Type Specification, Selected Papers of the 5th Workshop on Specifications of Abstract Data Types*, pages 1–22. Springer-Verlag L.N.C.S. 332, 1987.

[4] M. Bidoit. Pluss, un langage pour le développement de spécifications algébriques modulaires. Thèse d'Etat, Université Paris-Sud, 1989.

[5] M. Bidoit, F. Capy, and C. Choppy. The design and specification of the ASSPEGIQUE data base. In *Proc. of the Int. Symp. on Design and Implementation of Symbolic Computation Systems (DISCO)*, pages 205–214. Springer-Verlag L.N.C.S. 429, 1990.

[6] M. Bidoit and C. Choppy. Asspegique: an integrated environment for algebraic specifications. In *Proc. of the 1st International Joint Conference on Theory and Practice of Software Development (TAPSOFT)*, pages 246–260. Springer-Verlag L.N.C.S. 186, 1985.

[7] M. Bidoit, C. Choppy, C. Roques, and F. Voisin. Prototyping algebraic specifications with ASSPEGIQUE+, 1992. In preparation.

[8] M. Bidoit, C. Choppy, C. Roques, and F. Voisin. About the semantics of renaming in PLUSS, 1993. In preparation.

[9] M. Bidoit, C. Choppy, and F. Voisin. The Asspegique specification environment: Motivations and Design. In *Proc. of the 3rd Workshop on Theory and Applications of Abstract Data Types*, pages 54–72. Springer-Verlag I.F.B. 116, 1984.

[10] M. Bidoit, M.-C. Gaudel, and A. Mauboussin. How to make algebraic specifications more understandable? An experiment with the Pluss specification language. *Science of Computer Programming*, 12(1), 1989.

[11] B. Biebow and J. Hagelstein. Algebraic specification of synchronization and errors: A telephonic example. In *Proc. of the 1st International Joint Conference on Theory and Practice of Software Development (TAPSOFT)*, pages 294–308. Springer-Verlag L.N.C.S. 186, 1985.

[12] C. Choppy. Formal specifications, prototyping and integration tests. In *Proc. of the 1st European Software Engineering Conference*, pages 185–192, 1987.

[13] C. Choppy and S. Kaplan. Mixing abstract and concrete modules : specification, development and prototyping. In *Proc. of the 12th International Conference on Software Engineering*, pages 173–184, 1990.

[14] P. Dauchy and B. Marre. Test data selection from algebraic specifications : application to an automatic subway module. In *Proc. of the 3rd European Software Engineering Conference (ESEC'91)*. Springer-Verlag L.N.C.S. 550, 1991.

[15] H. Ehrig, W. Fey, and H. Hansen. ACT ONE: an algebraic specification language with two levels of semantics. Technical Report 83–03, TU Berlin FB 20, 1983.

[16] H. Ehrig and B. Mahr. *Fundamentals of algebraic specification 1. Equations and initial semantics*, volume 6 of *EATCS Monographs on Theoretical Computer Science*. Springer-Verlag, 1985.

[17] R. Forgaard and J. Guttag. REVE: a term rewriting system generator with failure-resistant Knuth-Bendix, 1984. Proc. of an NSF workshop on the rewrite rule laboratory, and Report n° 84GEN008, General Electric.

[18] L. Fribourg. SLOG: a logic programming language interpreter based on clausal superposition and rewriting. In *Proc. of the International Symposium on Logic Programming*, 1985.

[19] S. Garland and J. Guttag. An overview of LP, the Larch Prover. In *Proc. of the Third International Conference on Rewriting Techniques and Applications*, pages 137–151. Springer-Verlag L.N.C.S. 355, 1989.

[20] S. Garland and J. Guttag. A Guide to LP, The Larch Prover. Technical Report 82, DEC-SRC, 1991.

[21] S. Garland, J. Guttag, and J. Horning. Debugging Larch Shared Language Specifications. *IEEE Transactions on Software Engineering*, 16(9):1044–1057, 1990.

[22] S. Garland, J. Guttag, K. Jones, A. Modet, and J. Wing. Larch: languages and tools for formal specification, 1992. Draft book.

[23] J. Guttag, J. Horning, and A. Modet. Report on the Larch Shared Language: Version 2.3. Technical Report 58, DEC-SRC, 1990.

[24] J.V. Guttag and J.J. Horning. Report on the Larch shared language. *Science of Computer Programming*, 6(2):103–134, 1986.

[25] S. Kaplan. A compiler for conditional term rewriting systems. In *Proc. of the 2nd Conference on Rewrite Techniques and Applications*. Springer-Verlag L.N.C.S. 256, 1987.

[26] S. Kaplan. Simplifying conditional term rewriting systems. *Journal of Symbolic Computation*, 4:295–334, 1987.

[27] P. Lescanne. Computer experiments with the REVE term rewriting systems generator. In *Proc. of the 10th ACM Symposium on Principles of Programming Languages (POPL)*, 1983.

[28] A. Mauboussin, H. Perdrix, M. Bidoit, M.-C. Gaudel, and J. Hagelstein. From an ERAE requirements specification to a PLUSS algebraic specification: a case study. In *Proc. of the Meteor workshop, Algebraic methods II, Mierlo, L.N.C.S. 490, Springer Verlag*, 1989.

[29] D.T. Sannella and A. Tarlecki. Building specifications in an arbitrary institution. In *Proc. of the International Symposium on Semantics of Data Types*. Springer-Verlag L.N.C.S. 173, 1984.

[30] F. Voisin. CIGALE: a tool for interactive grammar construction and expression parsing. *Science of Computer Programming*, 7(1):61–86, 1986.

[31] F. Voisin. A bottom-up adaptation of Earley parsing algorithm. In *Proc. of the Int. Workshop on programming language implementation and logic programming*, pages 146–160. Springer-Verlag L.N.C.S. 348, 1988.

[32] F. Voisin. A new front-end for the Larch Prover. In *Proceedings of the First International Workshop on Larch, (U. Martin and J. Wing, editors), Workshops in Computing Science Series this volume*. Springer-Verlag, 1992.

[33] M. Wand. Final algebra semantics and data type extensions. *Journal of Computer and System Sciences*, 19:27–44, 1979.

[34] M. Wirsing, M. Broy, W. Dosch, H. Partsch, and P. Pepper. On hierarchies of abstract data types. *Acta Informatica*, 20:1–33, 1983.

Mechanical Verification
of Concurrent Systems with TLA*

Urban Engberg
Computer Science Department, Aarhus University
DK-8000 Aarhus C, Denmark

Peter Grønning
Department of Computer Science, Technical University of Denmark
DK-2800 Lyngby, Denmark

Leslie Lamport
Digital Equipment Corporation, Systems Research Center
Palo Alto, CA 94301 USA

Abstract

We describe an initial version of a system for mechanically checking the correctness proof of a concurrent system. Input to the system consists of the correctness properties, expressed in TLA (the temporal logic of actions), and their proofs, written in a humanly readable, hierarchically structured form. The system uses a mechanical verifier to check each step of the proof, translating the step's assertion into a theorem in the verifier's logic and its proof into instructions for the verifier. Checking is now done by LP (the Larch Prover), using two different translations—one for action reasoning and one for temporal reasoning. The use of additional mechanical verifiers is planned. Our immediate goal is a practical system for mechanically checking proofs of behavioral properties of a concurrent system; we assume ordinary properties of the data structures used by the system.

1 Introduction

TLA, the Temporal Logic of Actions, is a logic for specifying and reasoning about concurrent systems. Systems and their properties are described by logical formulas; the TLA formula $\Pi \Rightarrow \Phi$ asserts that the system represented by Π satisfies the property, or implements the system, represented by Φ. TLA is a linear-time temporal logic [4] that can express liveness (eventuality) as well as safety (invariance) properties. Although TLA is a formal logic, the TLA specification of a concurrent system is no more difficult to write than the system's description in a conventional programming language.

Since TLA is a formal logic, it allows completely rigorous reasoning. It is clear that TLA proofs can, in principle, be checked mechanically. In 1991,

---

*This article appeared in *Proceedings of the Fourth International Workshop on Computer-Aided Verification*.

we began a one-year effort to determine if mechanical verification with TLA is practical. We decided to use the LP verification system [1, 2], initially planning to write proofs directly in LP. However, we found the LP encoding to be distracting, making large proofs difficult. We therefore decided to write a TLA to LP translator, so specifications, theorems, and proof steps could be written in TLA. Writing specifications and theorems directly in TLA avoids the errors that can be introduced when hand translating what one wants to prove into the language of a verifier. The translator also allows mechanically checked proofs to have the same structure as hand proofs, making them easier to write and understand.

Working on the translator has thus far allowed us time to verify only a few simple examples, including an algorithm to compute a spanning tree on an arbitrary graph. Experience with more realistic examples is needed to determine if mechanical verification of TLA formulas can be a practical tool for concurrent-system design. It will never be easy to write rigorous proofs. However, we find it very encouraging that mechanically checkable proofs written in the translator seem to be only two to three times longer than careful hand proofs.

TLA, its LP encoding, and the translator are described in the following three sections, using the spanning-tree algorithm as an example. In this example, we prove that a system satisfies a property. An important feature of TLA is the ability to prove that one system implements (is a refinement of) another. However, space does not permit an example of such a proof.

2 TLA

For the purposes of this paper, we can consider TLA to be ordinary predicate logic, except with two classes of variables called *rigid variables* and *flexible variables*, extended with the two operators ′ (prime) and □. Quantification is over rigid variables only. (Full TLA also includes quantification over flexible variables, which serves as a hiding operator.) We often refer to flexible variables simply as variables.

The semantics of TLA is based on the concept of a *state*, which is an assignment of values to (flexible) variables. The meaning of a TLA formula is a set of *behaviors*, where a behavior is a sequence of states. The operator □ is the standard temporal-logic "always" operator [7]; the prime is a "next-state" operator. The complete semantics of TLA can be found elsewhere [6]; here we explain TLA informally through simple examples.

As a first example, we write a TLA formula specifying a program that starts with the variable x equal to any natural number, and keeps incrementing x by 1 forever. Letting Nat denote the set of natural numbers, the obvious way to express this with the prime and □ operators is

$$(x \in Nat) \land \Box(x' = x + 1) \tag{1}$$

The predicate $x \in Nat$ asserts that the value of x in the initial state is an element of Nat; the action $x' = x + 1$ asserts that the value of x in the next state is always 1 greater than its value in the current state, and the temporal formula $\Box(x' = x + 1)$ asserts that this is true for all steps—that is, for all pairs of successive states.

Formula (1) asserts that the value of x is incremented in each step of a behavior. For reasons explained in [5], we want also to allow steps that leave x unchanged. Letting $[\mathcal{A}]_f$ denote $\mathcal{A} \vee (f' = f)$, this is expressed by the TLA formula

$$(x \in Nat) \;\wedge\; \Box[x' = x + 1]_x \;\wedge\; \text{WF}_x(x' = x + 1) \tag{2}$$

The conjunct $\Box[x' = x + 1]_x$ asserts that every step of the program either increments x by 1 or leaves it unchanged. It allows behaviors in which x remains unchanged forever. The conjunct $\text{WF}_x(x' = x + 1)$ expresses the liveness property that infinitely many $x' = x + 1$ steps (ones that do increment x) occur. The reader is referred to [6] for an explanation of the WF operator and its definition in terms of $'$ and $\Box$.

In general, the canonical form of a TLA formula describing an algorithm is

$$Init \;\wedge\; \Box[\mathcal{N}]_v \;\wedge\; F \tag{3}$$

where $Init$ is a predicate describing the initial state, $\mathcal{N}$ is an action describing how the variables may change, v is the tuple of all program variables, and F is a liveness condition. The conjunct $\Box[\mathcal{N}]_v$ asserts that every step is either an $\mathcal{N}$ step or else leaves all variables unchanged (since a tuple is unchanged iff every component is unchanged).

Our major example is a simple algorithm that, given a finite connected graph and a root, constructs a spanning tree. For each node n, the algorithm computes the distance $d[n]$ from n to the root and, if n is not the root, its father $f[n]$ in the spanning tree.

When the algorithm is expressed formally, d and f are variables whose values are functions with domain equal to the set of nodes. Before describing the algorithm, we introduce some notation for expressing functions. The expression $\lambda x \in S : e(x)$ denotes a function f whose domain is S, such that $f[x]$ equals $e(x)$ for all x in S. If f is a function, then $f[s := v]$ is the function that is the same as f except with $f[s] = v$. This is defined formally as follows, where $dom\ f$ denotes the domain of f, and $\triangleq$ means *equals by definition*.

$$f[s := v] \;\triangleq\; \lambda x \in dom\ f : \textbf{if } x = s \textbf{ then } v \textbf{ else } f[x]$$

(Thus, $s \notin dom\ f$ implies $f[s := v] = f$.) If f is a function and T a set, then $f[s :\in T]$ is the set of all functions $f[s := v]$ with $v \in T$. Finally, $[S \rightarrow T]$ denotes the set of all functions f with domain S such that $f[x] \in T$ for all $x \in S$.

We now describe the spanning-tree algorithm. Initially, $d[n]$ equals 0 for the root and equals ∞ for all other nodes. For each node n, there is a process that repeatedly executes *improvement steps* that choose a neighbor m with $d[m] + 1 < d[n]$, decrease $d[n]$, and set $f[n]$ to m. The improvement step could simply decrease $d[n]$ to $d[m] + 1$, but for reasons that are irrelevant to

$$Init \quad \triangleq \quad \wedge \; d = \lambda n \in Node : \textbf{if} \;\; n = Root \;\; \textbf{then} \;\; 0 \;\; \textbf{else} \;\; \infty$$
$$\wedge \; f \in [Node \rightarrow Node]$$

$$\mathcal{N}_2(n, m) \quad \triangleq \quad \wedge \; d[m] \neq \infty$$
$$\wedge \; d' \in d[n :\in [d[m] + 1, \; d[n])]$$
$$\wedge \; f' = f[n := m]$$

$$\mathcal{N} \quad \triangleq \quad \exists n \in Node : \exists m \in Nbrs(n) : \mathcal{N}_2(n, m)$$

$$v \quad \triangleq \quad (d, f)$$

$$\Pi \quad \triangleq \quad Init \; \wedge \; \Box[\mathcal{N}]_v \; \wedge \; \mathrm{WF}_v(\mathcal{N})$$

Figure 1: The spanning-tree algorithm.

this discussion, we consider a more general algorithm in which $d[n]$ is set to a nondeterministically chosen number between its old value and $d[m]$. The algorithm terminates when no more improvement steps are possible.

The TLA formula Π describing this algorithm is defined in Figure 1, where *Node* is the set of nodes, *Root* is the root, $Nbrs(n)$ is the set of neighbors of node n in the graph, and $[a, b)$ is the set of natural numbers c such that $a \leq c < b$. We adopt the convention that a list bulleted with $\wedge$'s denotes the conjunction of the items, and we use indentation to eliminate parentheses. We have found this convention extremely helpful in making large formulas easier to read.

The initial condition is described by the predicate *Init*. It asserts that $d[n]$ has the appropriate value (0 or ∞) and that $f[n]$ is a node, for each $n \in Node$.

Action $\mathcal{N}_2(n, m)$ describes an improvement step, in which $d[n]$ is decreased and $f[n]$ set equal to m. However, it does not assert that m is a neighbor of n. The action is enabled only if $d[m] + 1 < d[n]$. (In this formula, d and f are flexible variables, while m and n are rigid variables.)

Action $\mathcal{N}$ is the disjunction of the actions $\mathcal{N}_2(n, m)$ for every node n and neighbor m of n. It is the next-state relation of the algorithm, describing how the variables d and f may change. We define v to be the pair (d, f) of variables, and Π to be the canonical formula describing the algorithm. The weak fairness condition $\mathrm{WF}_v(\mathcal{N})$ asserts that $\mathcal{N}$ steps are eventually taken as long as they remain possible—that is, as long as the action $\mathcal{N}$ remains enabled. Concurrency is represented by the nondeterministic interleaving of the different processes' (atomic) improvement steps.

The correctness property to be proved is that, for every node n, the values of $d[n]$ and $f[n]$ eventually become and remain correct. Letting $Dist(n, m)$ denote the distance in the graph between nodes n and m, the correctness of these values is expressed by the predicate *Done*, defined to equal

$$\forall n \in Node : \; \wedge \; d[n] = Dist(Root, n)$$
$$\wedge \; 0 < d[n] < \infty \; \Rightarrow \; \wedge \; f[n] \in Nbrs(n)$$
$$\wedge \; Dist(Root, f[n]) = Dist(Root, n) - 1$$

(If the graph is not connected, then for every node n not in the root's connected component, *Done* asserts only that $d[n] = \infty$.) The assertion that

Done eventually becomes and remains true is expressed by the TLA formula $\Diamond\Box Done$, where $\Diamond F$, read *eventually F*, is defined to equal $\neg\Box\neg F$. Correctness of the algorithm is expressed by the formula $\Pi \Rightarrow \Diamond\Box Done$, which asserts that $\Diamond\Box Done$ holds for every behavior satisfying Π.

The usual first step in reasoning about a concurrent algorithm is to prove an invariant. The appropriate invariant *Inv* for our algorithm is the following, where $\backslash$ denotes set difference.

$$
\begin{aligned}
&\wedge\ d \in [Node \rightarrow Nat \cup \{\infty\}] \\
&\wedge\ f \in [Node \rightarrow Node] \\
&\wedge\ d[Root] = 0 \\
&\wedge\ \forall n \in Node \backslash \{Root\}\ :\ d[n] < \infty\ \Rightarrow\ \wedge\ Dist(Root, n) \leq d[n] \\
&\qquad\qquad\qquad\qquad\qquad\qquad\qquad\qquad \wedge\ f[n] \in Nbrs(n) \\
&\qquad\qquad\qquad\qquad\qquad\qquad\qquad\qquad \wedge\ d[f[n]] < d[n]
\end{aligned}
$$

The invariance of *Inv* is asserted by the formula $\Pi \Rightarrow \Box Inv$. For brevity, we prove the invariance only of the first two conjuncts of *Inv*, which we call *TC*. A careful hand proof of the TLA formula $\Pi \Rightarrow \Box TC$ expressing the invariance of *TC* appears in Figure 2 and is discussed below. A similar proof for the complete invariant *Inv* takes about two pages, but has the same basic structure.

The proof in Figure 2 uses a structured format that we find quite helpful for managing the complexity of proofs. Step 1 proves that *TC* holds in the initial state. Step 2 proves that any single step starting in a state with *TC* true leaves it true. Step 3 applies the following standard TLA proof rule [6], where I' denotes the formula obtained from I by replacing x with x', for each flexible variable x.

$$
\text{INV1}: \quad \frac{I \wedge [\mathcal{N}]_v \Rightarrow I'}{I \wedge \Box[\mathcal{N}]_v \Rightarrow \Box I}
$$

The theorem follows trivially from steps 1 and 3. Step 2, the "induction step", is the major part of an invariance proof. For this simple invariant, its proof is easy.

The proof that $\Pi \Rightarrow \Box Inv$ is like the invariance proof for *TC*, except step 2 is more difficult. The proof of the correctness property $\Pi \Rightarrow \Diamond\Box Done$ then uses ordinary temporal-logic reasoning and the TLA proof rule WF1 [6]; space does not permit its description.

3 Encoding TLA in LP

LP is based on a fragment of multisorted first-order logic. To reason about TLA with LP, one must encode TLA formulas in LP's logic. Our initial plan was to have a single encoding. However, as Figure 2 shows, two different kinds of reasoning are used in TLA proofs: steps 1 and 2 illustrate *action reasoning*, not involving temporal operators; step 3 illustrates *temporal reasoning*. Since it is formally a special case, action reasoning is possible in any encoding that

Theorem $\Pi \Rightarrow \Box TC$

1. $Init \Rightarrow TC$
   Proof We assume $Init$ and prove TC.
   1.1. $d \in [Node \rightarrow Nat \cup \{\infty\}]$
      Proof By definition of $Init$, considering separately the cases $n = Root$ and $n \neq Root$.
   1.2. $f \in [Node \rightarrow Node]$
      Proof By definition of $Init$.
   qed Step 1 follows from 1.1, 1.2, and the definition of TC.

2. $TC \wedge [\mathcal{N}]_v \Rightarrow TC'$
   Proof We assume TC and $[\mathcal{N}]_v$ and prove TC'.
   2.1. $\mathcal{N} \Rightarrow TC'$
      Proof Since $\mathcal{N} = \exists n \in Node, m \in Nbrs(n) : \mathcal{N}_2(n, m)$, it suffices to assume $n \in Node$, $m \in Nbrs(n)$, and $\mathcal{N}_2(n, m)$, and to prove TC'.
      2.1.1. $d' \in [Node \rightarrow Nat \cup \{\infty\}]$
         Proof By definition of TC and $\mathcal{N}_2$, since $[d[m] + 1, d[n]) \subseteq Nat \cup \{\infty\}$.
      2.1.2. $f' \in [Node \rightarrow Node]$
         Proof By definition of TC and $\mathcal{N}_2$, since $Nbrs(n) \subseteq Node$, for all nodes n.
      qed Step 2.1 follows from 2.1.1, 2.1.2, and the definition of TC.
   2.2. $(v' = v) \Rightarrow TC'$
      Proof Follows trivially from the definitions.
   qed Step 2 follows from 2.1 and 2.2, since $[\mathcal{N}]_v = \mathcal{N} \vee (v' = v)$.

3. $TC \wedge \Box[\mathcal{N}]_v \Rightarrow \Box TC$
   Proof By step 2 and rule INV1.
qed The theorem follows from 1, 3, and the definition of Π.

Figure 2: The proof of invariance of TC.

allows temporal reasoning. However, such reasoning can be made easier with a special encoding for formulas not containing the temporal operator $\Box$. Action reasoning is almost always the longest and most difficult part of a proof, so we decided to use separate encodings for the action and temporal reasoning. We have found the resulting simplification of action reasoning to be worth the inconvenience of having two different encodings.

The encoding of action reasoning in LP is straightforward. TLA's rigid variables become LP variables. For each TLA flexible variable x, we encode x and x' as two distinct LP constants. Thus, the TLA action $(x' = x+1) \wedge (y' = y)$ is encoded in LP as $(\text{x'=x+1}) \& (\text{y'=y})$.

The encoding of temporal reasoning is more subtle. In TLA, a formula is an assertion that is true or false for a behavior. Let $\sigma \models F$ denote that the behavior σ satisfies the TLA formula F. Formula F is valid iff $\sigma \models F$ is true for all behaviors σ. The validity of F is represented in LP's logic by $\forall \sigma : \sigma \models F$. Neglecting details of the precise ASCII syntax, this formula is written in LP as $\sigma \models F$, universal quantification over the free variable σ being implicit. The semantic operator $\models$, which cannot appear in a TLA formula, becomes part of the formula's LP translation.

TLA's (temporal) proof rules have straightforward translations into LP. For example, the proof rule INV1 asserts

$$\frac{\forall \sigma : \sigma \models (I \wedge [N]_f \Rightarrow I')}{\forall \sigma : \sigma \models (I \wedge \Box[N]_f \Rightarrow \Box I)}$$

In this rule, $\wedge$, $\Rightarrow$, and $'$ are operators declared in LP to represent the corresponding TLA operators. In particular, $\wedge$ and $\Rightarrow$ are different from LP's built-in conjunction (&) and implication (=>) operators. Propositional reasoning about temporal formulas is done in LP using such axioms as

$$\sigma \models (F \wedge G) \;=\; (\sigma \models F) \,\&\, (\sigma \models G)$$

4 The Translator

The TLA translator is a program written in Standard ML [3] that translates "humanly readable" TLA specifications and proofs into LP proof scripts. Their readability makes proofs easier to maintain when the specifications change than they would be if written directly in LP. The different encodings for action reasoning and temporal reasoning are translated into two separate LP input files. Formulas proved in the action encoding are asserted in the temporal encoding. The proof succeeds if LP successfully processes both files.

4.1 Specifications

Figure 3 is the input to the TLA translator corresponding to the spanning-tree algorithm of Figure 1. (All translator input is shown exactly as typed by the user, except that multiple fonts have been used for clarity.) It begins with a declaration of *Span* as the name of the specification, followed by a directive to read the file *frame*, which contains declarations of all constants such as 0, $+$, *Nbrs*, and *Node*. The next two lines declare d and f to be (flexible) variables. (In TLA's typeless logic, the only sorts are Boolean and Any.) The rest of the specification is a direct transliteration of Figure 3, except for two differences: the action $N1(n)$ is defined for use in the proofs, and $*$ is used instead of comma to denote ordered pairs. The translation of these definitions into LP rewrite rules is straightforward, except for quantified expressions and the lambda-construct. LP does not now support full first-order quantification, so we have defined LP operators and associated proof rules for quantification and lambda abstraction. Each occurrence of a quantifier or "lambda" requires the definition of an auxiliary function, which is named for reference in proofs by a term in brackets [* ... *].

In TLA, prime ($'$) is an operator that can be applied to predicates like *Init* and to state functions like v, where priming an expression replaces all variables by their primed versions. In the LP action encoding, primed and unprimed variables become distinct constants, so the prime operator cannot be

Name *Span*
Use *frame*
Variables
    d, f   : **Any**
Predicates
    Init   == $/\backslash$ *d* = **Lambda** *n* **in** *Node* :
                          If *n* = *Root* **Then** 0 **Else** *infty* [* dist : **Any** *]
              $/\backslash$ *f* **in** [*Node* -> *Node*]
Actions
    N2(n, m) == $/\backslash$ *d*[*m*] $\tilde{}$= *infty*
                    $/\backslash$ *d'* **in** *d*[*n* :**in** *openInter*(*d*[*m*] + 1, *d*[*n*])]
                    $/\backslash$ *f'* = *f*[*n* := *m*]
    N1(n)   == **Exists** *m* **in** *Nbrs(n)* : *N2(n, m)* [* n1(n) *]
    N   == **Exists** *n* **in** *Node* : *N1(n)* [* n *]
Statefunctions
    v   == (*d* * *f*)
Formulas
    Pi   == *Init* $/\backslash$ $\square$ [*N*]_*v* $/\backslash$ **WF**(*v, N*)

Figure 3: The spanning-tree algorithm, in the translator's input language.

expressed. The "bar operator" used in refinement [6, Section 9.3.2] and TLA's *Enabled* operator [6, Section 3.7] are similarly inexpressible. The translator must therefore add to the LP encoding rewrite rules explicitly defining such expressions as *Init'*, $\overline{v}$, and *Enabled* $\mathcal{N}$. Definitions for the primed and barred expressions are generated automatically by the translator. Definitions for the *Enabled* predicates must now be provided by the user; future versions of the translator will generate them as well.

4.2 Proofs

The invariant *TC* of our spanning-tree algorithm is specified in the translator's language as

    TC == *d* **in** [*Node* -> *NatInf*] $/\backslash$ *f* **in** [*Node* -> *Node*]

where *NatInf* denotes *Nat* $\cup$ {∞}. The hand proof of invariance of *TC* was based on certain tacit assumptions about *Root*, *Node*, and *Nbrs*. The formal statement of these assumptions is the assertion *Assump*, defined in the translator input to be the conjunction of the following two assertions. (Since the set construct has a bound variable, it requires the same kind of auxiliary function used for quantifiers and "lambda".)

    Assump1 == *Root* **in** *Node*
    Assump2 == **Forall** n **in** *Node* :
                  Nbrs(n) = {*m* **in** *Node* :
                                  NbrRel(n, m) [* a22(n) *]} [* a21 *]

where *NbrRel* denotes the neighbor relation on the graph. Further assumptions about *NbrRel* are needed for the complete correctness proof of the algorithm.

Figure 4 contains the translator version of the invariance proof of Figure 2. It has the same structure as the hand proof in Figure 2. Steps are numbered in the more compact fashion ⟨*level*⟩*step*, with **Step**⟨2⟩3 denoting the third substep of level two and **Hyp**⟨1⟩.2 denoting the second hypothesis of level one of the current proof.

The proof is written in a natural deduction style, the translator input **Assume** *A* **Prove** *B* denoting that $A \Rightarrow B$ is to be proved by assuming *A* and proving *B*. The goal *B* can be omitted if it is the same as the current goal. (In the temporal encoding, assuming *A* and proving *B* means assuming $\sigma \models A$ and proving $\sigma \models B$, for an arbitrary constant σ.) The construct **Reduce by** *A* **To** *B* expresses an argument of the form "By *A* it suffices to prove *B*." It is converted into LP's style of direct reasoning by rearranging the proof steps. **Normalize**, **Apply**, and **Crit** are LP commands. The applied rules, such as BoxElim1, are defined in LP for reasoning about the translator output. In step ⟨1⟩3, INV1 applies the INV1-rule and **Crit**'s the current hypotheses with the resulting fact.

Figure 5 shows the LP input in the action-reasoning file generated from step ⟨3⟩1 in the proof of step ⟨1⟩2. Additional translator constructs allow arbitrary LP input to be inserted into the output, making the full power of LP available through the translator. (Soundness is maintained if no LP **assert** commands are inserted.) Such direct use of LP was not needed in this proof; our ultimate goal is to make it unnecessary in general.

The predicate *TC* is just one part of the entire invariant *Inv*. About three more pages of translator input completes the proof of invariance of *Inv*. The rest of the correctness proof takes about six more pages. These proofs required additional properties of numbers (elements of *NatInf*), functions, and the distance function *Dist*—including the well-foundedness of the ordering on $[Node \rightarrow Nat \cup \{\infty\}]$ defined by $f \leq g$ iff $f[n] \leq g[n]$ for all $n \in Node$. Properties of the natural numbers (associativity of addition etc.) were expressed directly in LP. Properties of the distance function needed for the proof were asserted in the translator input. Although these properties can be proved from more primitive definitions, we have ignored such conventional verification in order to concentrate on the novel aspects of TLA.

5 Future Directions

It is obviously easier to write a TLA proof in TLA than in an LP encoding of TLA. It was not obvious to us how much easier it would be. Our initial experience indicates that writing a proof with the translator can be an order of magnitude faster than doing the proof directly in LP. Such a speed-up is possible only if the proof can be written in the translator with no direct use of LP. We are planning to enhance the translator to eliminate all direct LP reasoning.

Theorem TC
    Assume [] *Assump* **Prove** *Pi* => [] *TC*

Proof
    ⟨1⟩1 **Assume** *Assump, Init* **Prove** *TC*

        ⟨2⟩1 *d* **in** [*Node* -> *NatInf*]
        Reduce by Normalize **Hyp**⟨1⟩.2 with *Init*,
                  Apply ProveFuncSpaceLambda to **Red**
        To **Assume** *n* **in** *Node* **Prove** *d*[*n*]**in** *NatInf*

            ⟨3⟩1 **Case** *n* = *Root*
            Qed by Normalize **Hyp**⟨1⟩.2 with *Init*

            ⟨3⟩2 **Case** *n* ˜= *Root*
            Qed by Normalize **Hyp**⟨1⟩.2 with *Init*

        Qed by Cases

        ⟨2⟩2 *f* **in** [*Node* -> *Node*]
        Qed by Normalize **Hyp**⟨1⟩.2 with *Init*

    Qed by Normalize **Goal** with *TC*

    ⟨1⟩2 **Assume** *Assump, TC,* [*N*]_*v* **Prove** *TC'*

        ⟨2⟩1 **Case** *N*
        Reduce by Normalize **Hyp** with *N*
        To **Assume** *n* **in** *Node* /\ *N*1(*n*)
        Reduce by Normalize **Hyp** with *N*1
        To **Assume** *m* **in** *Nbrs*(*n*) /\ *N*2(*n, m*)

            ⟨3⟩1 *d'* **in** [*Node* -> *NatInf*]

                ⟨4⟩1 **Assume** *k* **in** *openInter*(*d*[*m*] + 1, *d*[*n*]) **Prove** *k* **in** *NatInf*
                Qed by Normalize **Hyp** with UseOpenInterval

            Qed by Normalize **Hyp**⟨1⟩.2 with *TC*,
                Normalize **Hyp**⟨2⟩ with *N*2,
                Apply ProveFuncSpaceUpdateIn to **Hyp**⟨1⟩.2 **Hyp**⟨2⟩ **Step**⟨4⟩1

            ⟨3⟩2 *f'* **in** [*Node* -> *Node*]

                ⟨4⟩1 *m* **in** *Node*
                Qed by Normalize **Hyp**⟨1⟩.1 with *Assump Assump2*

            Qed by Normalize **Hyp**⟨1⟩.2 with *TC*,
                Normalize **Hyp**⟨2⟩ with *N*2,
                Apply ProveFuncSpaceUpdateEq to **Hyp**⟨1⟩.2 **Hyp**⟨2⟩ **Step**⟨4⟩1

        Qed by Normalize **Goal** with *TC*

        ⟨2⟩2 **Case** Unchanged(*v*)
        Qed by Normalize **Hyp** with *v*,
             Normalize **Hyp**⟨1⟩.2 with *TC*,
             Normalize **Goal** with *TC*

    Qed by Cases

    ⟨1⟩3 **Assume** [] *Assump, TC,* [][*N*]_*v* **Prove** [] *TC*
    Qed by INV1 on **Step**⟨1⟩2

Qed by Normalize **Hyp** with Pi,
     Apply BoxElim1 to **Hyp**,
     Crit **Hyp** with **Step**1 **Step**3

Figure 4: Proof of invariance of *TC*, in the translator's input language.

```
set name Theorem_Tc1_2_1_1
prove in(d', funcSpace(Node, NatInf))
  set name Theorem_TC_2_1_1_1
  prove (in(v_k_, openInter(((d@v_m_c)+1), (d@v_n_c))) => in(v_k_,NatInf))
    resume by =>
    <> 1 subgoal for proof of =>
      normalize Theorem_TC_2_1_1_1ImpliesHyp with UseOpenInterval
      [] => subgoal
    [] conjecture
  set name Theorem_TC_2_1_1
  normalize Theorem_TC_2ImpliesHyp.2 with TC
  normalize Theorem_TC_2_1ImpliesHyp with N12
  apply ProveFuncSpaceUpdateIn to Theorem_TC_2ImpliesHyp.2 Theorem...
  [] conjecture
```

Figure 5: Translator output for step ⟨3⟩1 in the proof of step ⟨1⟩2 of Figure 4.

Translating the steps of a proof rather than just the property to be proved permits the use of multiple verification methods. The translator now generates separate LP input for action and temporal reasoning. We plan to generate input to other verification systems as well. Steps that are provable by simple temporal reasoning will be verified automatically by a decision procedure for propositional temporal logic. Some steps might be proved with a model checker by enumerating all possibilities. We may also investigate the use of theorem provers other than LP as "back ends" for the translator.

References

[1] Stephen J. Garland and John V. Guttag. An overview of LP, the Larch Prover. In N. Dershowitz, editor, *Proceedings of the Third International Conference on Rewriting Techniques and Applications*, volume 355 of *Lecture Notes on Computer Science*, pages 137–151. Springer-Verlag, April 1989.

[2] Stephen J. Garland and John V. Guttag. A guide to LP, the Larch Prover. Technical Report 82, Digital Equipment Corporation Systems Research Center, December 1991.

[3] Robert Harper, David MacQueen, and Christopher Wadsworth. Standard ML. Internal Report ECS–LFCS–86–2, Edingburgh University, March 1986.

[4] Leslie Lamport. 'Sometime' is sometimes 'not never': A tutorial on the temporal logic of programs. In *Proceedings of the Seventh Annual Symposium on Principles of Programming Languages*, pages 174–185. ACM SIGACT-SIGPLAN, January 1980.

[5] Leslie Lamport. What good is temporal logic? In R. E. A. Mason, editor, *Information Processing 83: Proceedings of the IFIP 9th World Congress*, pages 657–668, Paris, September 1983. IFIP, North-Holland.

[6] Leslie Lamport. The temporal logic of actions. Technical Report 79, Digital Equipment Corporation, Systems Research Center, December 1991.

[7] Amir Pnueli. The temporal logic of programs. In *Proceedings of the 18th Annual Symposium on the Foundations of Computer Science*, pages 46–57. IEEE, November 1977.

The DECspec Project: Tools for Larch/C

Gary Feldman and Joseph Wild

Software Development Technologies Group

Digital Equipment Corporation

Nashua, NH, USA

Abstract

This paper describes our experiences providing support for the *Larch Formal Specification Method*. We are transferring this technology to make it useful in our software development environment and elsewhere. We describe the extensions we made to Larch, the tools we needed to develop, and what we learned along the way.

Abstract

1   Introduction

In current environments, where applications running on many platforms must communicate with other separately developed applications, the design of interfaces between applications is more crucial than the design of the applications themselves. Such interfaces are destined to become long-lived, widely implemented, and widely used. Users of the interface will require consistent behavior across multiple platforms, implementations, and versions. Implementors of the interfaces need to know precisely what is required of them. New versions of the interfaces must inter-operate with existing clients of previous versions.

We have identified formal specification as an approach that could help our group address the above problem. Our group, Software Development Technologies (SDT), produces many of Digital's compilers and CASE tools. SDT's products are becoming bigger and more complicated, in response to continual demands for more functionality, inter-operability across platforms and vendors, and inter-product integration. We need a better technology for the precise specification of interfaces. A formal specification is likely to be more complete, and the process of developing it will tend to expose the areas in which it is (deliberately or accidentally) incomplete. We also needed tools for the mechanical analysis of program interfaces, to help in understanding and debugging them.

In mid-1990 we launched the DECspec Project, with the support of Digital's Systems Research Center, to explore the application of formal methods in a production environment. The goal was to take an existing method and provide support tools suitable for use in our environment and similar environments elsewhere. We selected the Larch formal specification method [3,4], with C as the target programming language. This paper presents the experiences of the first year of that project.

2 Current specification practice

One traditional approach to interface definitions is letting the users of an interface read the implementation code. This effectively destroys the notion of an interface, which should be independent of any particular implementation. There is no way for implementors of the interface to know what properties of previous implementations, or previous versions of an implementation, users of the interface may have relied on. This creates unexpected and uncontrollable dependencies between separately developed programs.

A somewhat more modern approach is supplying function headers in a common language (e.g., C prototypes) along with prose descriptions. This helps, but is not adequate. Headers do not contain enough information to safely use the function. Even strongly typed languages, such as Ada, limit the scope of globally available data only roughly, and only partially specify constraints upon the values of parameters. Such information is frequently provided in prose descriptions accompanying the function headers, but they may be incomplete, ambiguous, and unclear.

3 Current formal methods

A number of formal specification methods are now available, including *Z* [10], *VDM* [9], *LOTOS* [7], *Estelle* [8], and *Larch*. Z has been researched for many years at Oxford University, and was used for one of the largest commercial applications of formal methods to date, the IBM CICS project [13]. LOTOS and Estelle are widely used in telecommunications.

Larch is a formal method that has been researched for over fifteen years, primarily by Jim Horning and John Guttag. Before our involvement, Larch had been largely confined to the research community. Interface languages had been defined for Pascal [11], CLU [12], and Ada [2].

4 The Larch method

A major reason for choosing Larch as a specification tool was the availability of researchers to act as consultants to our work. Larch also has the distinct advantage of having been explicitly designed with the specifications of interfaces in mind.

The distinguishing feature of the Larch method is its two-tiered approach. One tier is explicitly tied to programming-language-specific notations and semantics. This tier consists of a family of *Larch interface languages*, with an interface language designed for each programming language. The second tier has a single language, the *Larch Shared Language* (LSL), which is independent of any programming language.

An interface is specified in the interface language, using a syntax that parallels the programming language. The usual function header information is augmented with a variety of semantic information, such as preconditions that must be met by clients using the function, information about potential side effects on parameters and global variables, and properties of the state resulting from calling the function.

The semantic information is expressed in first-order logic, using both concepts defined within the interface language and concepts defined in the LSL. The shared language is useful for describing the abstract building blocks of a system. Abstract definitions for underlying concepts have the advantage of being more likely to be reusable. LSL is accompanied by a library of specifications and specification components, defining many basic concepts, such as stacks and sets [5].

5 Making Larch fit in our environment

We needed an interface language for a programming language used in our environment and tools to support it. We chose Standard C as a widespread, stable, not-too-complicated language that we're currently using for most of our new development. To get started we designed a Larch/C Interface Language (LCL), and built:

- syntax and type checkers for LSL and LCL,

- prettyprinters (automatic formatters).

The Larch/C interface language needed to be designed from scratch. The foundation is a subset of C, suitable for expressing many of the features of a programming interface. This was augmented first to allow a greater degree of information hiding, and then to include the semantic information we wanted.

Prior specification writing experience had shown we could get significant benefit at low cost by having syntax and type checkers for both the interface and shared language specifications. This benefit is similar to benefits provided by compilers in checking programming languages; undeclared constructs, incorrectly called functions, syntax errors, etc. are all caught. This is particularly important because a specification is usually made of many pieces (in different files). The checkers are able to check all the pieces together, which is difficult to do manually.

A theorem prover is required to check the completeness and implications of specifications. The Larch Prover (LP) [1], available from MIT, is capable of these checks. We have not yet explored this area due to time constraints, and our concern that theorem proving may be too time consuming and complicated for use in the average software development group. Our experience writing specifications, without verifying them with a prover, indicates that significant benefit can be derived from writing specifications alone.

Because of the reliance on mathematical notation and the need to machine process the specifications, we needed to provide two different language formats. The interchange format is an ASCII representation that is used to write and check specifications. The presentation format is used to produce more readable specifications. For example, the forall symbol would appear as the ASCII string \forall in the interchange format and as ∀ in the presentation format. The prettyprinters are used to convert the checked specifications from the interchange format to the presentation format.

6 Results of our experience

As a result of this project, we gained valuable experience in several directions. We discovered how the act of formally specifying an interface could improve the design of the interface, and help uncover previously unknown bugs. We gained a deeper understanding of the tactics available in C for supporting information hiding and abstract data types. An indirect, yet very important result, was learning how to speed up the transfer of technology from the research community to actual practice.

Throughout the design of LCL, we relied heavily on a few small examples, most notably a dynamic string package, to help drive the design of the language. We were pleasantly surprised when we realized that this was a two-way street, as the specification helped focus on features of the string package that could be improved. A concrete benefit is that the specification revealed a serious flaw in the package, namely the volatility of the string objects being returned. These benefits are the result of the more rigorous approach to interface design required by a formal specification.

An important benefit of the LCL design was the ability to automatically generate header files from the formal specifications. We cannot generate a complete .h file, since C requires that users of an interface see the actual implementations of types. Instead, we generate .lh files, which are included into a .h file supplied by the implementor. The .lh files contain the information that may be safely derived from the specification, thus saving the implementor from having to maintain two copies of that information.

The most difficult, yet most rewarding part of our effort was designing LCL so that it could support information hiding and abstract data types while still allowing the inherent flexibility of C. After much work, we settled on two concepts, which we called *exposed* types and *abstract* types. Exposed types use the traditional C syntax and mechanisms, providing the user with most of the power of C. Abstract types hide the details of the data structure within the implementation module, leading to cleaner specifications and more reliable interfaces. The semantics of abstract types allow the underlying implementation data structures to change without changing the interface or breaking client code that observes the specifications. By providing both mechanisms, designers are encouraged to consider the tradeoffs early in their process.

It was the difficulty of the above design that taught us the most about technology transfer. When we started, part of the team knew Larch well and part of the team knew C well. It wasn't until the whole team knew both pieces that we made real progress designing LCL. In retrospect, we concluded that it would have been worthwhile to invest time at the start, immersing ourselves in each other's culture.

We feel that we now have enough basics in place to begin using and evaluating formal methods in general and Larch in particular. Our tools are still at the prototype level, but they are sufficiently stable to be useful. At this point, we need to test the current state of the method by using it to develop some production-size programs. Our experience so far indicates that writing formal specifications (before or during) development leads to better designs, and more reliable implementations. We are beginning to write Larch/C specifications ourselves and are planning to enlist an external (to Digital) group or two to do a cooperative case study.

7   Availability of toolset

Our toolset is available to the public under a no-cost license. It contains:

- LSL Syntax and Type Checker

- LSL to LATEX Translator/Pretty Printer

- LCL Syntax and Type Checker

- Library of Common LSL Specifications

- LSL and LCL Research Reports

The toolset is available by anonymous FTP from the pub/DEC/Larch/toolset directory on node gatekeeper.dec.com. This directory contains the complete toolset as a compressed tar file (larch_0_1_4.tar.Z), a copy of the license (license.txt), and a README file. The license describes the terms under which this toolset may be used. The README file contains detailed instructions for fetching and installing the toolset.

A description of the Larch/C interface language is available as a research report [6] from Digital's System Research Center.

8   Acknowledgements

We are thankful to Jim Horning and Kevin Jones, for guidance in writing this paper and throughout the project. John Guttag and Steve Garland were major contributors to our east coast team. Jeannette Wing contributed throughout the project. Bill McKeeman was invaluable as the catalyst for making this project happen; he provided intensive consulting and help.

References

[1] S. J. Garland and J. V. Guttag, "An Overview of **LP**, The Larch Prover," *Proceedings 3rd International Conference on Rewriting Techniques and Applications*, 1989, pp. 137-151.

[2] D. Guaspari, C. Marceau, and W. Polak, "Formal Verification of Ada Programs," *IEEE Transactions on Software Engineering*, Vol. 16, No. 9, September 1990, pp. 1058-1075.

[3] J.V. Guttag, J.J. Horning and J.M. Wing, "The Larch Family of Specification Languages," *IEEE Software*, September 1985, pp. 24-36.

[4] J.V. Guttag, J.J. Horning, and A. Modet, "Report on the Larch Shared Language: Version 2.3," *Digital Equipment Corporation Systems Research Center Research Report*, DEC/SRC SRC-58, April 1990.

[5] J.V. Guttag and J.J. Horning, "An LSL Handbook," *DEC Systems Research Center Research Report, to be published.*

[6] J.V. Guttag and J.J. Horning "Introduction to LCL, A Larch/C Interface Language," *Digital Equipment Corporation Systems Research Center Research Report*, DEC/SRC SRC-74, July 24, 1991.

[7] ISO, Information Processing Systems–Open Systems Interconnection, *LOTOS-A Formal Description Technique Based on the Temporal Ordering of Observational Behavior*, IS8807, 1989.

[8] ISO, DIS ISO/OSI 9074–*ESTELLE: A Formal Description Technique Based on an Extended State Transition Model*, 1989.

[9] C. B. Jones, *Systematic Software Development Using VDM*, Prentice-Hall, 1990.

[10] J. M. Spivey, *The Z Notation: A Reference Manual*, Prentice-Hall, 1989.

[11] J. M. Wing, *A Two-Tiered Approach to Specifying Programs*, Ph.D. Thesis, Laboratory for Computer Science, Massachusetts Institute of Technology, May 1983, Report MIT/LCS TR-299.

[12] J.M. Wing, "Writing Larch Interface Language Specifications," *ACM TOPLAS*, January 1987, pp. 1-24.

[13] J. C. P. Woodcock, "Calculating Properties of Z Specifications," *ACM SIGSOFT Software Engineering Notes*, Vol. 14, no. 5, July 1989, pp. 43-45.

Formal Verification of Ada Programs

David Guaspari
Odyssey Research Associates
Ithaca, NY 14850-1313

Carla Marceau
Odyssey Research Associates
Ithaca, NY 14850-1313

Wolfgang Polak
Consultant
Sunnyvale, CA 94087

Abstract

This paper describes the Penelope verification editor and its formal basis. Penelope is a prototype system for the interactive development and verification of programs that are written in a rich subset of sequential Ada.

Because it generates verification conditions incrementally, Penelope can be used to develop a program and its correctness proof in concert. If an already-verified program is modified, one can attempt to prove the modified version by replaying and modifying the original sequence of proof steps.

Verification conditions are generated by predicate transformers whose logical soundness can be proven by establishing a precise formal connection between predicate transformation and denotational definitions in the style of continuation semantics. Penelope's specification language, Larch/Ada, belongs to the family of Larch interface languages. It scales up properly, in the sense that we can demonstrate the soundness of decomposing an implementation hierarchically and reasoning locally about the implementation of each node in the hierarchy.

Index-terms— Ada, formal specification, formal verification, Larch, software development environments.

1   Introduction

A formal program verification is a (mathematical) proof that a program executed according to its intended model of execution meets some specification[1]. It proves that the algorithm defined by the program is *correct* in the precise technical sense of being consistent with a particular specification. A program correct in this sense is free from a large and important class of errors, even though its behavior may still produce unintended results—either because the actual implementation does not match the model of program execution, or because the specification does not correctly express the user's intentions.

This work was supported by DARPA and RADC under Contract BOA 3695.STARS-043 and is part of the STARS program. ©1992 IEEE. Reprinted, with permisssion, from IEEE transactions on Software Engineering vol 16, no 9, Sept 1990 pp 1058-1075.

[1]Throughout this paper we use "specification" in its ordinary sense of "statement of requirements." The Ada Language Reference manual uses the word "specification" as a technical term for what might in other languages be called "headers" or "signatures."

Formal verification requires a careful analysis and formulation of the problem to be solved (the construction of an explicit formal specification) and provides a very high degree of confidence that the resulting code is correct. Such verifications involve an enormous amount of clerical detail, whose manipulation must, insofar as possible, be automated. Work by Floyd [8] and Hoare [15] provided the formal basis for building automatic verification systems.

A program is annotated with formal statements (annotations) expressing the specification of the program as well as internal assertions that serve as induction hypotheses for iteration and recursion. A formal definition of the programming language, e.g., given in Hoare's axiomatic formalism, relates the semantics of the program to first-order sentences (*verification conditions*)[2]. A set of verification conditions is a set of first-order formulas which, collectively, imply that the program meets its specification. Proving that the verification conditions are true is sufficient to prove that the program is correct.

The first generation of program verification systems, dating from the mid-1970's (e.g. [11, 19, 23]), were based on this theory. The typical verification system of the time was a batch tool that accepted annotated programs, performed syntactic and semantic analysis of the input, and generated verification conditions that were subsequently submitted to a theorem prover. While this process is rather straightforward in principle, experience with early systems has revealed a large number of practical problems.

Specifications for nontrivial programs can become very complex and unmanageable. Their consistency and adequacy are difficult to determine. Specification languages that provide support for some form of abstraction offer a possible solution. Both Gypsy [11] and Affirm [23] have addressed this issue to some degree.

Verification conditions can be extremely large formulas. For realistic programs the complexity of the formulas quickly reaches the limits of current theorem proving technology. Again, mechanisms for creating abstractions and for defining domain specific theories can reduce the complexity of proofs.

If a verification condition cannot be proved, this may be due to an inadequate theorem prover, an error in the program, or insufficient internal annotations. Unfortunately, it can often be very difficult to determine which of the three possible reasons applies. Worse yet, even if one knows that the problem is in the program, it can be very difficult to relate a failing proof attempt to a particular piece of code.

Finally, if the program is modified, new verification conditions must be generated and information from previous proofs may be lost and may have to be rediscovered.

The experience with early verification systems underlines the importance of abstraction mechanisms in the specification language and suggests that verification should not be a batch process that is applied after the program is written. Instead, a verifier must be viewed as a design tool that aids the programmer in the incremental development of code. Incremental verification addresses many of the previous shortcomings: Proofs need only deal with comparatively small formulas corresponding to incremental changes. Errors are detected early and are therefore easier to locate. Any later program modification is just a special

---

[2]Throughout this paper we are concerned with program verification carried out in the "inductive assertion" style, traceable ultimately to Floyd . That is the style of Penelope, as well as all first-generation and most second-generation verification systems.

case of the incremental mode of operation. Dijkstra [7] and Gries [12] have proposed a development methodology based on formal specifications and proof; a verifier must be seen as a tool to support this methodology.

In addition, typical first-generation systems lacked fully mathematical foundations, and therefore failed to provide a truly mathematical analysis of program behavior.

We are developing Penelope, a prototype verification system, with three principal goals in mind: 1) To accommodate programs written in a rich subset of (sequential) Ada and annotated in a rich specification language. 2) To support incremental development of verified programs, thus making verification more tractable and more practical. 3) To provide a formal mathematical basis for the system. We hope, in addition, to integrate formal methods into a software engineering environment. In support of this goal Penelope became part of the STARS software engineering environment in October 1989.

1.1 The ada subset and its formal basis

The theory underlying Penelope deals with a subset of sequential Ada that includes packages, side effects, access types, exception-raising, and exception-handling[3]. Section 2.1 describes the details of the language and gives the rationale for the choice of our subset.

Program specifications are given in Larch/Ada, a member of the Larch family of "two-tiered" specification languages [14], [34]. Larch/Ada specifications constitute an interface between a world of well-behaved mathematical idealizations and the messier world of computational behavior, in which resources are bounded, and computations might not terminate or might terminate exceptionally.

We use the Larch Shared Language to organize the description of axiomatic theories—e.g., theories of integers, booleans, stacks, domain specific theories, etc. These theories act as reservoirs of mathematical notions that can be drawn on in writing software specifications and in proving verification conditions.

Generation of verification conditions must be based on a formal semantic definition of the programming language. Since there is no official semantic definition for Ada and the unofficial definitions (e.g., [32],[3]) were not devised with verification in mind, it was necessary to develop an appropriate formal definition for our subset of Ada as the basis for Penelope.

Penelope is based on predicate transformers ([7]) rather than the axiomatic proof rules or path analysis that are traditionally used. As is shown later, predicate transformers for our subset of Ada are formulated within a very general framework with intimate ties to denotational semantics. To define the semantics of our subset one could use our predicate transformers (as is done in Penelope), or use a closely related denotational definition constructed from them, but the justification of any formal semantics against the *Ada Reference Manual* must be informal.

The development of Penelope is testimony to the general usefulness of formal methods: the implementation of its verification condition generator is derived

---

[3]The implementation of Penelope is incomplete; details of this implementation are described in section 3.

systematically from the predicate transformers that are formally specified in a version of the typed lambda-calculus.

1.2 The implementation

Special consideration was given to the usability of Penelope. As argued before, it is crucial that a verifier operate incrementally and support the concurrent development of programs and their proofs. In this way programming errors will be detected at the earliest possible time. There is no need to prove large monolithic formulas. Instead, as fragments of a program are written only small incremental simplifications are required to obtain a proof for the modified program.

Penelope is a syntax-directed editor that accepts a nontrivial set of sequential Ada programs, together with specifications expressed in the language Larch/Ada. In addition to performing static semantic checks on the program text[4] and specifications, the editor provides an environment for formal program verification: it incrementally generates *verification conditions* (VC's) by applying *predicate transformers* whose results the user may inspect, reason about, and simplify as program development proceeds.

Penelope is implemented with the Synthesizer Generator [30], which accepts as input an attribute grammar and generates from it a syntax-directed editor. As the Penelope user edits program text and annotations, or carries out proof steps, the system "underneath" creates and edits abstract syntax trees that represent pieces of annotated Ada programs and proofs. The attributes of the nodes of this tree carry information about the static semantics of the program and the generation of verification conditions, and they are computed incrementally.

1.3 Organization of this paper

The remainder of the paper consists of two parts. Section 2 describes the formal foundations of Penelope. This includes the Ada subset and its rationale, the definition of Larch/Ada, and a description of the technique used to define predicate transformers. Section 3 describes the current implementation and illustrates the use of the system with a moderate-size example. The reader primarily interested in the Penelope system may read through section 2.2.4 and then skip directly to the example.

2 Formal foundations

2.1 A verifiable subset of ada

There are a number of reasons for subsetting the language for the purpose of building a program verifier. These reasons range from technical problems such as the definition of concurrency, to the mundane such as the desire to complete the project within the given time limits. This section characterizes our Ada subset, called Ada', by listing the omissions, restrictions, and assumptions

---

[4] Our prototype does not currently enforce full compliance with the *Ada Reference Manual*.

about the model of execution. Even with these restrictions, we believe that Ada' qualifies as a real usable language rather than a toy.

Tasking All tasking constructs and *delay* statements are disallowed. The practical verification of concurrent programs is on the border of current technology. There are a number of techniques available to describe the semantics of concurrent programs and some of these have been applied to Ada (e.g. [9]). Yet, to integrate these techniques into a practical verification system still requires significant work.

Abstraction Ada' does contain packages with their Ada semantics. But the language unfortunately provides numerous way to "break" abstractions, so Ada packages are not true abstract data types. Abstractions can be violated, for example, by calls on the predefined equality operation and by the raising of exceptions. Treating packages as truly abstract types will require additional restrictions on Ada'.

For the purpose of verification, private and limited private types are treated as synonyms for their implementation types. This means that the semantics of objects of private types is defined on the level of the implementation, both inside and outside the scope of the package. Static semantic checks ensure use of private types consistent with Ada rules.

In addition to private types, the local variables of a package may be considered an abstraction. As with private types, there are several possibilities to violate the abstraction. Local variables of a package are simply treated as global variables of package subprograms. Again, the semantics is defined on the implementation level.

The use of abstraction in specifications is independent of the abstraction mechanisms provided by the programming language. Even in the absence of packages it is possible and desirable to describe data structures in terms of the abstract objects they represent. This can be done by explicitly defining an appropriate *abstraction function* that maps the concrete data representation to the intended abstraction. Clearly, packages can be annotated in this way even if they are not a secure abstraction mechanism. For instance, the subprograms of a package, a stack for example, can be annotated in terms of the functions *push* and *pop* of an abstract stack theory (trait of stacks) and a representation function that maps the implementation, an array and a natural number for instance, to abstract stacks. This treatment is similar to the proof of correct data representations described in [16] except that the representation invariant becomes visible.

Generics Generics are omitted for several reasons. First, a systematic approach would treat the generic formal parameters as an abstract data type. As in the case of packages, additional restrictions are required to guarantee abstractness. Secondly, the verifier of a generic faces problems familiar to the compiler writer who attempts to share common code among all instances. For instance, the constraint checks required for parameter passing differ in subtle ways depending on generic type arguments. The compiler writer's simple solution, generating separate code for each instance, is not acceptable for verification[5]. This would amount to reverification of every instance, a very expensive proposition. A comprehensive treatment of generics must address this problem.

Libraries and library units Ada′ does not define the semantics of libraries and library units. An Ada library cannot simply be viewed as a collection of program units characterized by input-output annotations. Rather, the semantics of a program unit depends on the order of elaboration of all units that participate in a main program. For instance, a package p may define a visible constant c whose value depends on a variable x defined in package q. The value of x can be changed by calls to q. Thus, the value of c depends on all calls made to package q before p is elaborated. As a result, a property $P(\mathbf{p}.\mathbf{c})$ cannot be verified locally as part of the proof of p without assumptions about the elaboration order. Such assumptions can only be discharged at the point where a main program is defined.

The semantics of libraries is subject to current investigation and future versions of Penelope will include support for program libraries and *separate verification*.

Runtime environment Ada's predefined IO packages, as well as package calendar, are not defined in Ada′. Once libraries are available, properly annotated IO packages can be defined. Their inclusion requires some model of the operating system environment in which Ada′ programs are executed and depends on the physical environment of the program.

Fixed and floating point types Ada′ has no fixed or floating point types. Formal reasoning about floating point arithmetic is still subject to active research. Inclusion of fixed point types may be possible but tedious; a simple model might use integers with appropriate scaling factors.

Numeric and storage error exceptions The numeric error and storage error exceptions are not supported. More precisely, any property that is proved about an Ada′ program is only true for those executions that do not cause numeric overflow or exhaust available storage.

In the case of storage error the reason for omission is its implementation dependence. The semantics of the exception cannot be defined without regard to the compiler and the target architecture.

The reason for omitting numeric overflow is one of pragmatics. It was felt unacceptable to include clauses in verification conditions for all possible ways in which a numeric error could occur. The resulting explosion in the size of formulas threatens to make their proof intractable.

Optimization The Ada definition allows optimizing compiler to alter the semantics of a program. For obvious reasons, optimizations that change the semantics of a program are disallowed in Ada′.

---

[5]There are few Ada compilers that actually share code among different instance of a generic.

Unchecked conversion and deallocation The semantics of unchecked conversion is highly implementation dependent. Unchecked deallocation, although understood in principle, was omitted because of its complexity.

Dependence on evaluation order Pragmatics and the usability of the system have been major concerns. Even with incremental operation we must be concerned about the size of verification conditions. Consider, for instance, the constraint checks required for a trivial program consisting of the sequential composition of n calls to procedures with m (scalar) arguments. This program involves $n * m$ constraint checks, each of which results in two implications and a conjunction in the resulting verification condition. Assume further, that we wish to prove that the program is correct for all possible evaluation orders. Expressing this fact is a trivial matter; one can simply generate the conjunction of the verification conditions for all possible evaluation orders. Unfortunately, there are $(m!)^n$ possible evaluation orders.

Instead, we choose to ensure the independence of an Ada' program from the evaluation order of expressions by decidable static tests. Such tests are sufficient but not necessary, and Ada programs that do not suffer from an "incorrect order dependence" will be ruled out of Ada' because they fail our test.

If two arguments to a subprogram can raise two different exceptions, then which exception is raised depends on the order of evaluation of the subprogram arguments. The current checks do not rule out order dependencies due to such multiple exceptions. In this case Ada' semantics defines left to right evaluation.

Aliasing The situation for aliasing is similar to that for evaluation order dependencies. It is, in principle, possible to account for all possible aliasing situations. The cost is larger verification conditions. Instead, we opted for sufficient (but not necessary) static tests that ensure the absence of aliasing. But these tests will also reject certain programs that do not have aliasing.

Dependence on parameter passing mechanism A subprogram whose effect depends on the parameter passing mechanism used is *erroneous*, and its effect is undefined. Different parameter passing mechanisms can affect a program's behavior in the case of aliasing (which we rule out) or when exceptions are propagated from a procedure. The semantics of Ada' is such that nothing is provable about the value of an *out* or *in out* argument of nonscalar type if a call terminates exceptionally. Thus, every property provable about any Ada' program will be true regardless of the parameter passing mechanism. This conservative restriction could be relaxed—for example, to permit specifications stating that the values of variables are unchanged upon exceptional exit.

2.2 The Larch/Ada specification language

The constructs of Larch/Ada serve two purposes. One is to determine the *specification* of each subprogram and package—i.e., the implementation-independent description of its behavior that may be assumed by its users. The other is to provide information necessary to the proof of each unit—loop invariants, for example, or directives for organizing its proof. Larch/Ada constructs serving either purpose are called *annotations*.

Larch/Ada is a *two-tiered* language whose *mathematical component* is defined in the Larch Shared Language. A brief introduction to two-tiered specifications is given below. For more information about the Larch Shared Language see [34], and the papers by Wing and by Guttag and Horning in this issue.

2.2.1 Two-tiered annotations

The basic idea of two-tiered annotations is to model the set of values of each programming language type as a *subset* of some domain that is mathematically tractable. For example, the (finite) set of values of type integer is modeled as a subset of the infinite set of mathematical integers, a decision that is expressed by saying that type integer is "based on" sort *Int*—where the carrier of sort *Int* is the collection of mathematical integers.

Because of this, the logical formulas expressing embedded assertions, entry and exit conditions, verification conditions, etc., take their meanings in (well-behaved) mathematical domains. They nonetheless express constraints on program behavior, because they are true relative to some states and false relative to others. For example, if x and y are program variables of type integer, the assertion that $(x + y < 2^{64})$ holds in some computation state is understood as follows: The symbols $+$ and $<$, and the exponentiation operation, denote the usual "mathematical" operations over the infinite domain of mathematical integers, not the executable operations of Ada. This assertion says that (in the given state) the values of x and y, which are modeled as values of sort *Int*, have a (mathematical) sum less than 2^{64}—whether or not evaluation of the Ada expression x+y in that state would overflow, and whether or not the integer value 2^{64} is representable in the implementation executing the program.

The only Ada entities that may occur in the logical formulas of Larch/Ada or in the verification conditions generated by Penelope are program variables or constants, and formal parameters; all the other symbols denote mathematical entities. These formulas and their subexpressions are never undefined; and such computational notions as nontermination, exception-raising, and side-effects do not apply to them. In particular, if x is an integer variable, then from the point of view of Larch/Ada it always denotes a value—but in all those states preceding the initialization of x that value is left unspecified. Composites are modeled similarly: Let a be an array variable and i a variable of its index type. Then the Larch/Ada term a[i], an application of the two-place mathematical operation#[#] to arguments a and i, always denotes a value (whether or not i is "in range"); the value it denotes is the value of the Ada object a(i), when that object has a defined value, and is otherwise irrelevant.

Larch/Ada specifies subprograms that raise exceptions, or cause side-effects, by describing the circumstances under which such behavior occurs and by describing the states that result. Predicate transformation, by computing a corresponding case analysis, maps programs to formulas of ordinary first-order logic rather than some more or less exotic variant logic. That has the important advantage of simplicity.

Larch/Ada has notational similarities to Anna [21], the best-known Ada specification language; and, as both languages provide entry-exit specifications for sequential programs, there inevitably exist analogies of meaning between specifications written in the two styles. Their semantic differences, however, are fundamental. The meaning of an Anna specification is defined operationally— by translating an Ada program containing Anna annotations into another Ada program. The translated program contains code that checks the annotations at run-time. The logic of Anna is therefore quite different from ordinary first-order logic; and for our purposes (mathematical reasoning, rather than run-time checking) seems too complex.

2.2.2 Specifications

The specification of a program is a logical construct computed from its annotations. It consists of two parts, a mathematical component and an interface component.

The Mathematical Component: The mathematical component of a specification defines a collection of mathematical operations (like the $+$ and $<$ of the example above). The interface component may draw on this vocabulary to construct formulas expressing the desired constraints on program behavior. All the types used in the program must be based on sorts from the mathematical component.

The mathematical component of a Larch/Ada specification is a collection of first-order logical axioms—i.e., a theory. Annotations define this theory by referring to a (reusable) library of theories described in the notation of the Larch Shared Language.[6]

This paper uses a simple subset of the Larch Shared Language that is largely self-explanatory, but we note here one important piece of terminology: a *trait* is a Larch construct that denotes a theory; the subexpressions of a trait organize the description of the theory it denotes. For example, subexpressions of a trait may do such things as: include the theories denoted by other traits; introduce (i.e., declare) new mathematical operations; and assert axioms about those operations (and operations included from other traits).

The Interface Component: The interface component of a specification expresses constraints on program execution in terms of the vocabulary defined in its mathematical component. For example, the clause

> `RAISE too_big  =>  IN` $(x + y) > 2^{64}$

where x and y are formal parameters, says that the exception `too_big` cannot be raised unless the (mathematical) sum of the actual parameters to the call is greater than 2^{64}. Specifications may state entry conditions and exit conditions (either normal or exceptional), may describe the return values of functions, and must document any access of the program to global variables.

Without the mathematical component, expressions in the interface component would be meaningless. The vocabulary needed to specify and reason about all the basic Ada operations—e.g., $+$, $<$, and $\#[\#]$—belongs to predefined theories automatically included, as needed, in the mathematical component of each specification.

---

[6] We find it convenient to extend the Larch Shared Language with some special notational conventions.

SortingAndSearching : **trait**
 introduces
   present: Int, array_int_of_int, Int, Int $\longrightarrow$ Bool
   sorted: array_int_of_int, Int, Int $\longrightarrow$ Bool

 asserts for all $[x, lo, hi$: Int, a: array_int_of_int$]$
  present$(x, a, lo, hi) =$
   $lo \leq hi$ & $(a[hi] = x \mid$ present$(x, a, lo, hi - 1))$
  sorted$(a, lo, hi) =$
   $hi \leq lo \mid ($sorted$(a, lo, hi - 1)$ & $a[hi - 1] \leq a[hi])$

Figure 1: The trait *SortingAndSearching*

2.2.3 A simple specification

Section 3 demonstrates the use of Penelope by developing two versions of a simple example, a binary search program, and this section uses its specifications to illustrate some simple features of Larch/Ada specifications. Annotations of implementations are discussed in section 2.2.4 and Penelope's embedded proof directives in section 3.3.

The trait *SortingAndSearching* The specification of procedure **bin_search** will use the trait *SortingAndSearching*, defined in Figure 1, and we assume that this trait belongs to our trait library. Its **introduces** and **asserts** clauses respectively declare and axiomatize the operations relevant to the specification of a search routine.

 Note that arithmetic operations and the selection operation #[#] have been used without being explicitly introduced. A more subtle point arises in the specification of **bin_search** introduced immediately below: type **integer** is based on sort Int and the type **intarray**, to be declared in package **searching**, is based on sort array_int_of_int, yet there is no explicit association of the types with their sorts. The discussion of "types and sorts," below, briefly describes how these associations are effected.

The specification In Ada, the natural way to provide a binary search routine would be to export it from an appropriately parameterized generic package. To stay within the limits of our current formal theory we make the package non-generic, and to stay within the subset accepted by the current Penelope implementation, we search through objects having the somewhat improbable type of integer arrays indexed by all of **integer**.

 Package **searching** (Figure 2) supplies a (nonprivate) type **intarray** and some operations on it. It is the final version of the program developed in section 3. Instead of the "logical" notation previously used, which distinguished between Ada operations and mathematical operations by using a different type face, Figure 2 shows the look of the specification "on the screen." No ambiguity results: the occurrences of <=, =, etc., must denote the mathematical order and

```
--| WITH TRAIT SortingAndSearching
PACKAGE searching

TYPE intarray IS ARRAY(integer) OF integer;

FUNCTION bin_search(a : intarray; m,n,x: integer)
   RETURN integer;
--| WHERE
--|   IN sorted(a,m,n);
--|   RETURN k such that  k >= m and k <= n and a[k] = x;
--|   RAISE not_present <=> IN not present(x,a,m,n);
--| END WHERE;

   -- ... Rest of package omitted ...

END searching;
```

Figure 2: Specification of package **searching**

equality operations, not the executable ones.

Each line of the annotations is preceded by --|, a notational device taken from Anna. Since -- is the Ada comment sign, it follows that an Ada compiler will ignore the rest of the line and will therefore compile a specified program as is.

The mathematical component of the specification of any compilation unit is determined by its Larch/Ada *context clause*: the (library) traits named in its WITH TRAIT clause; the specifications of those compilation units named in its Ada WITH clause. In the case of package **searching**, that recipe simplifies to: the theory denoted by trait *SortingAndSearching*, which automatically includes definitions of the appropriate predefined operations. The specification of **bin_search** inherits its mathematical component from that of **searching**.

The clauses of the interface component express entry-exit conditions that are almost self-explanatory. An IN clause expresses an entry condition.[7] The RETURN clause constrains the value returned by the function (and can also describe any side-effects on the state) if execution terminates without raising an exception. Specifications of both procedures and functions may use OUT clauses to specify the effects of normal termination. RAISE clauses are used to describe the initial conditions that give rise to exceptions and the states resulting from exceptional termination. Larch/Ada specifications are partial correctness specifications, and cannot require that a subprogram terminate. The given RAISE annotation therefore means: If **val** is not present and if program execution terminates, then it terminates by raising **not_present**; and if execution terminates by raising **not_present** then **val** must not be present. As noted in section 2.1, the "underdetermination" of parameter passing mechanisms obliges

---

[7]The IN condition of **bin_search** should also require that all the components of **a** between **m** and **n** have defined values. That part of predicate transformation dealing with definedness has not yet been implemented in Penelope.

us to restrict what can be asserted of a state that arises as a result of exceptional termination.

Since no other exceptions are mentioned, this specification makes the positive assertion that the only exception that can be raised by this function is the exception **not_present**. (This is subject to the hypotheses on storage and numeric overflow mentioned in section 2.1.)

Logically, a specification also contains a GLOBALS clause. A global variable not qualified as an IN global may not be read, and one not qualified as an OUT global may not be written. Since this specification lacks an explicit GLOBALS annotation, then—by default—it stipulates that no globals are either read or written.

Types and sorts As noted above, type **integer** is based on sort Int and type **intarray** on sort array_int_of_int. The definition of trait *SortingAndSearching* is independent of the declaration of the type **intarray**, so the question arises how the association of type and sort takes place.

The answer is that, whereas Ada types obey a discipline of name equivalence, Larch/Ada bases "structurally equivalent" types on the same sort. So, for example, after

```
type T is range 1..10;
type S is new integer;
x : T;
y : S;
```

the types T, S, and **integer** are all based on sort *Int*, even though they are mutually incompatible: an Ada expression like "y = x" (executable equality) is illegal and must be rejected by a compiler, but the Larch/Ada logical formula "y = x" is well-formed and legal. Similarly, any array type whose index and component types are structurally equivalent to **integer** is based on sort array_int_of_int. There is nothing contradictory or paradoxical about such a modeling decision; hardware, after all, models all Ada types in the same domain, the domain of bit strings.

Larch/Ada provides a set of conventions (suggested by the mnemonic character of array_int_of_int) for naming the sorts associated with all the "type structures" of Ada'.

2.2.4 Annotating implementations

The Ada structure of a program largely determines the organization of its Larch/Ada annotations. For example, when the declaration and implementation of a program are distinct (like the declaration and implementation of package **searching**), we can effect a complete logical separation between them: annotations of the declaration determine the specification (visible to users) and all proof details are hidden in the annotations of the body.

Local interface The body of **bin_search** may be associated with entry-exit conditions different from those of its specification. For example, the implementor of **bin_search** may strengthen the RETURN annotation to:

```
--|    RETURN k such that
--|         k >= m and k <= n and a[k] = val and
--|         forall j :: m <= j and j < k -> a[j] /= val;
```

and would then be obliged to prove that the implementation satisfies these entry-exit conditions, and that these conditions imply those of the specification of **bin_search**.

The proving theory The theory from which the verification conditions of a program are to be proven, which we will call *VCProve*, is determined by the annotations of its body. *VCProve* includes the theory denoted by the mathematical part of the program's specification, and also includes the axioms obtained from its Larch/Ada context clause—i.e., from the specification of any Ada units imported by WITH and from any library traits named in its WITH TRAIT clause. These extra library traits might be used, for example, to define the concepts needed to formulate loop invariants.

In general, therefore, *VCProve* will contain a larger vocabulary and more axioms than the "visible" theory constituting the mathematical component of the specification. The problem of keeping the extra information in *VCProve* safely hidden will be discussed in section 2.2.5.

Assertions In the usual fashion of assertion-based formalisms the user must supply loop invariants, and may supply other embedded assertions along the way. The user may choose how to partition the program proof by choosing whether any particular loop invariant or embedded assertion should be a cut-point.

The syntax of cut-point assertions is

```
--| ASSERT <logical_formula>
```

A cut-point assertion acts like a logical interface between the code that precedes it and the code that follows; and code between two cut-points is encapsulated like the body of a procedure having those cut-points as its entry and exit conditions. The syntax of a non-cut-point assertion is simply

```
--| <logical_formula>
```

Non-cut-point assertions are typically used to indicate "milestones" in the algorithm and to supply information resulting in simpler and more readable intermediate preconditions. For examples of their use, see section 3.

Loop invariants have the usual meaning—even if a while-loop terminates not by failing its loop guard, but by executing an **exit**, or because an exception is raised in its body, or because an exception is raised while evaluating the loop guard. If these more complicated possibilities actually come into play, of course, devising an appropriate invariant becomes more difficult. The development of section 3 chooses to make the loop invariant a cut-point.

2.2.5 Formalities

The paradigm example in the Larch literature has been the specification and implementation of an abstract data type (or, in Ada terms, of a private type).

To apply the ideas of two-tiered semantics to the rest of a programming language and its proof formalism requires a certain amount of care.

This paper, and the initial implementation of Penelope, has been concerned with programming in terms of an already given collection of abstract data types, including abstract data types like **integer** and **intarray** that are supplied by Ada itself. We briefly consider some of the mathematical, or "foundational," problems that arise.

This section shows, in particular, why the divide-and-conquer strategies of modular programming and information hiding require justification, and outlines the proof discipline that must be followed in Larch/Ada (or any two-tiered specification language) in order to use those strategies correctly. Full mathematical details can be found in [13]. Finally, it indicates what remains to be done in order to have a formalism for proving Ada programs that includes abstraction as well.

Satisfaction and consistency The fundamental notion in any specification language is the notion of *satisfaction*—of what it means for a program P to satisfy a specification of *Spec*. For simplicity's sake we will assume, below, that P uses only the types supplied by Ada (although the discussion applies to any program written over a given collection of abstract data types).

Intuitively, to say that P satisfies *Spec* is to say that: assuming nothing about the predefined symbols (like $+$, $\#[\#]$, etc.) except what follows from their defining axioms, and assuming nothing about the symbols introduced by *Spec* other that what's given in the mathematical part of *Spec*, we can prove that P is consistent with its interface component.[8]

The demonstration that a specification is satisfied consists of two parts: proof of the program's verification conditions (from the axioms of *VCProve*), and a demonstration that the proof of those verification conditions is "coherent." The "coherence" test, described below, is a very strong one—and implies, among other things, that both *VCProve* and the mathematical component of the program's specification are consistent. The full significance of this test is that it makes possible modular programming, as we now show.

Modular programming We have already noted that the proof of a program's verification conditions typically requires definitions and axioms in addition to those of its (visible) specification. That raises problems for the user of the program, who sees only its visible specification, and needs some assurance that the hidden assumptions on which its verification depends do not constitute a logical time-bomb that will explode when the program is called on or reasoned about in an environment in which those assumptions (of which he is unaware) are not satisfied.

Here is an example. Let the traits *HiddenTrait*, *LibTrait*, and *ApplixTrait* consist of just one axiom each (in addition to the predefined axioms):

---

[8]Those familiar with Larch will note that this definition of the meaning of a specification that *uses* a abstract data types differs from the standard definition of the meaning of a specification that *defines* an abstract data type.

Trait	Axiom
Hidden Trait	$lo = 10$
Lib Trait	$lo > 0 \ \wedge \ hi = lo + 1$
Applix Trait	$lo = 5$

We then specify three programs as follows:

```
--| WITH TRAIT HiddenTrait
function hidden return integer;
--| WHERE
--|   RETURN lo;
--| END WHERE;

--| WITH TRAIT LibTrait
procedure lib(x : out integer);
--| WHERE
--|   OUT x <= hi-1;
--| END WHERE;

--| WITH TRAIT ApplixTrait
procedure applix(y : out integer);
--| WHERE
--|   OUT y <= 5;
--| END WHERE;
```

These specifications are independent of one another, and the fact that their interface components have the identifiers hi and lo in common has no logical significance. Let us implement them as follows:

Subprogram	Body
`hidden`	`return 10`
`lib(x)`	`x := hidden`
`applix(y)`	`lib(y)`

The verification conditions of all these programs are provable—more precisely, the verification condition for each is provable in the appropriate version of *VCProve*:

Program	VC	VCProve
`hidden`	$lo = 10$	$lo = 10$
`lib`	$lo \leq hi - 1$	$lo = 10 \ \wedge \ lo > 0 \ \wedge \ hi = lo + 1$
`applix`	$\forall z \ z \leq hi - 1 \longrightarrow z \leq 5$	$lo > 0 \ \wedge \ hi = lo + 1 \ \wedge \ lo = 5$

One might regard this as a proof of the correctness of `applix` but for the unfortunate fact that `applix` plainly fails to satisfy its specification.

The fallacy could be discovered by a global analysis of the proof of `applix`, including the proofs of all the units ultimately involved in its implementation. What we see is that, globally, the various uses of the symbols lo and hi have in fact been identified and the totality of assumptions made about them is inconsistent. To require such a global analysis is to forego modular, or hierarchical, design altogether. In particular, a change to any program at all, however deeply "hidden" in an implementation hierarchy, would require reanalysis of the whole.

The alternative is to discover some local discipline which suffices to guarantee that the correctness of each node in a hierarchy entails the correctness of the whole. That is the point of the "coherence" test.

The diligent reader will notice that `lib` does not satisfy its specification either—since it does not obey its return annotation for *all* the instantiations of *hi* and *lo* consistent with the axioms of *LibTrait*. We were able to prove the verification condition of `lib` only by introducing a hidden hypothesis, going beyond the properties defined in *LibTrait*: the hypothesis that $lo = 10$. Because of this, the proof of `lib` fails its coherence test. In the jargon of formal logic, the coherence test fails because *VCProve* fails to be a conservative extension of *LibTrait*.

Coherence   The coherence test provides a formal guarantee that information that ought to be hidden, remains so. It justifies regarding each individual element of a hierarchical implementation as a separate module, which can be reasoned about and implemented independently of the rest of the hierarchy.

To give a concrete illustration, we indicate why the above verification of `applix` in terms of `lib` passes its coherence test, and is therefore valid. *VCProve* for `applix` must be a conservative extension of two things:

- *ApplixTrait*—that is, the mathematical component of the specification being implemented.

- The predefined theory of the specifications of type `integer`—that is, the mathematical component of the abstract data types used by the implementation.

We do *not* require *VCProve* to be a conservative extension of *LibTrait*, even though `lib` is used in the implementation of `applix`.[9]

The property of "being a conservative extension" is stronger than the property of "being consistent"; and the current Penelope system provides the user no way of attempting to establish it. For now, coherence assumptions are explicit hypotheses on the validity of Penelope verifications.

There do exist disciplines for extending theories in ways that are guaranteed to be conservative. For example, we can prove that the trait *Sorting-AndSearching* is a conservative extension of Penelope's predefined theories by showing that the recursively defined operations it introduces can also be defined explicitly (using quantification), or by showing that they can be defined by primitive recursion. The more difficult case is the extension of a theory by adding new sorts and operations. The shell principle of the Boyer-Moore theorem prover [6] is one example of a discipline sufficient to guarantee that such extensions are conservative.

General theory of two-tiered semantics   The discussion of this section has been conducted, for convenience, in terms of proof and provability—the mathematical world described in first order logic and the programming language described by predicate transformation—but the basic ideas of two-tiered

---

[9]Experts should note: the coherence test for the *implementation* of abstract data types differs from—and is, in a sense, dual to—the one presented above for the *use* of abstract data types.

semantics are much more general. The descriptions of the mathematical world might instead be formulated in equational logic with initial algebra semantics, temporal logic, higher-order logic, etc. Similarly, the programming language semantics might be denotational semantics, labeled transition graphs, Hoare-style proof rules, process algebra, etc.

Satisfaction and coherence can be defined in a general setting in which all logical bookkeeping, such as the formal justification of modular programming, can be done once and for all. The details of [13] are worked out in a setting in which the mathematical world forms an institution (in the sense of Goguen-Burstall [10]) and the programming language semantics is an institution in the sense of Schoett [31].

2.3 Predicate transformers

The basis for a verification system is, of course, a formal semantic definition of Ada'. For such a definition we need a framework general enough to describe features such as side-effects during expression evaluation and declaration elaboration, exceptions, and so on. Hoare logic is often used as the formal basis for verification systems. Indeed, there are proof rules that, individually, deal with all the language features we were interested in. For example, see [4, 5, 20, 33, 35]. Yet, given the complexity of Ada, we were concerned about the size, consistency, and soundness of an axiom system that integrates these different approaches.

Instead, the verification condition generator of Penelope is based on predicate transformers for Ada'. In principle, a predicate transformer [7] is a function that, given a program fragment S and a postcondition q, returns a precondition p.

Predicate transformers are closely related to sentences in Hoare logic. If pt is a predicate transformer, then the intuitive meaning of the first-order formula $p \Rightarrow \text{pt}(S, q)$ is very close to that of the Hoare triple $\{p\}S\{q\}$.

In our case preconditions given by predicate transformers do not imply the termination of the program and they are not the *weakest* possible preconditions. Rather, the generated preconditions depend on annotations of the given program. While annotations affect the preconditions, they do not affect the soundness of the predicate transformers. Improper annotations will merely lead to preconditions that are too strong (e.g., *false*) and are useless.

Termination is not directly expressible in our formalism; Penelope deals only with partial correctness. There are, however, well-known techniques for proving termination in a partial correctness framework (see, e.g., [17]). Such techniques can in principle be added to Penelope.

The formalism used in the Ada' definition is closely related to and uses many of the idioms of continuation semantics. As we will show, this style of defining predicate transformer has the great advantage that the definition of many complex language features is completely systematic. Such a definition, all by itself, has a plausibility that Hoare-style definitions lack.

The predicate transformer definition does not express the *static semantics* of Ada', but assumes an abstract syntax representation in which overloading and use clauses have been resolved. Originally, we hoped to build upon existing compiler technology and reuse an existing compiler front-end. As it turned out, Penelope currently contains its own semantic checking (see Section 3).

In the remainder of this section we present a very brief exposition of the kind of predicate transformers used in Penelope. A more comprehensive treatment and formal justification of this technique are beyond the scope of this paper (see [25, 27]).

2.3.1 Environments and control flow

To take care of context dependencies, a precondition depends on an *environment e* that describes bindings of global identifiers. The environment contains the following information[10]:

1. For each label identifier the environment contains the precondition that is assumed at the point of the label definition.

2. Each loop name is bound to the postcondition of the loop.

3. Each subprogram name is bound to a function which, given a postcondition and a set of arguments, will return the precondition of the call.

4. Each exception name is bound to the precondition of the appropriate hander.

If S is a statement we write

$$prec_S [\![S]\!] e\; q$$

for the precondition of S in environment e with postcondition q. In general, we use double brackets ($[\![\ldots]\!]$) to indicate syntactic arguments, i.e., terms of the Ada' abstract syntax. As in the lambda calculus, function application is written as juxtaposition.

As an example, consider the definition of various statements that transfer control:

$$prec_S [\![\text{goto I}]\!] e\; q = e[\![I]\!]$$
$$prec_S [\![\text{exit I}]\!] e\; q = e[\![I]\!]$$
$$prec_S [\![\text{raise I}]\!] e\; q = e[\![I]\!]$$

These definitions say that the precondition of the statement goto I is the precondition of the label I as given in the current environment. Similarly, the precondition of an exit statement is the postcondition of the loop; again, this information is given by the current environment. The precondition of the raise statement is the precondition of the appropriate exception handler, which is found in the environment. In these cases, the precondition is independent of the given postcondition q. The definition of sequential composition has a different flavor:

$$prec_S [\![\text{S1; S2;}]\!] e\; q = prec_S [\![\text{S1;}]\!] e(prec_S [\![\text{S2;}]\!] e\; q)$$

---

[10]This presentation is simplified; the actual environment contains other information about objects, types, etc.

2.3.2 Iteration

In Penelope, as in other assertion based verification systems, loops must be annotated with a loop invariant. This invariant forms the induction hypothesis for the proof of the loop's correctness.

Let us abbreviate the annotated Ada loop

```
--| invariant p
I:loop
    S;
end loop I;
```

as `I:loop (p, S)`. Here `I` is the name of the loop, `S` is a sequence of statements, and `p` is a Larch/Ada formula. The loop predicate transformer is defined as

$$\text{prec}_S[\![\text{I:loop (p, S)}]\!]e\; q = p \wedge \forall \vec{x}.(p \rightarrow \text{prec}_S[\![\text{S}]\!]e'\; p)$$

where e' is an environment that differs from e in that the loop name I is bound to the loop postcondition q. The quantification ranges over all variables $\vec{x}$ that could possibly be changed by the loop body S.

In this definition the conjunct $\forall \vec{x}.(p \rightarrow \text{prec}_S[\![\text{S}]\!]e'\; p)$ corresponds to the traditional verification condition for the loop. One can strengthen the loop precondition by including in $\vec{x}$ all variables that are free in $p \rightarrow \text{prec}_S[\![\text{S}]\!]e'\; p$. This case corresponds to the traditional way of verifying loops: the (closed) loop verification condition can be proved separately and, given this proof, the precondition simplifies to p.

Using our definition with a more restrictive quantification simplifies the required loop invariants. For example, assume that the correctness of a loop depends on the fact that $y > 0$ throughout the loop, where y is some variable that is not changed by the loop body S. This means that the verification condition $\forall \vec{x}.(p \rightarrow \text{prec}_S[\![\text{S}]\!]e'\; p)$ contains y free and the fact $y > 0$ can be deduced from the context. If one constructs the universal closure instead, the fact $y > 0$ must be added to the loop invariant.

Penelope provides the option of generating either form of precondition and verification condition. This option can be selected independently for each loop.

In connection with the definition of the *exit* statement, the above definition of the loop semantics uniformly applies to all loops with arbitrary forms of exits. Only *for* loops require a separate definition. For instance, a while loop

```
--| invariant p
I:while E loop
    S;
end loop I;
```

corresponds to

```
--| invariant p
I:loop
    if E then S; else exit I; end if;
end loop I;
```

2.3.3 Side-effects

The traditional way to define the meaning of an assignment is

$$\text{prec}_S[\![\mathbf{x} := \mathbf{E}]\!]e\ q = q[\mathbf{E}/\mathbf{x}]$$

where $q[\mathbf{E}/\mathbf{x}]$ denotes the substitution of E for $\mathbf{x}$ in q. There are a number of things wrong with this approach. First, it requires that the expression E be a legal term of the logic. In our case, that is not true. Even if it were, this approach assumes that the term E is semantically equivalent to the evaluation of the program expression E. That is untrue because the evaluation of E may cause side-effects or may cause a change in the flow of control by raising an exception.

To address these problems we introduce the notion of *expression conditions*; these are the postconditions of expressions. Using expression conditions, we can define the semantics of expression evaluation by a new predicate transformer prec_E for expressions. Intuitively, an expression condition is a function that, given a term t, returns a predicate. Such a function defines the *disposition* of an expression result once it is computed. We use k to range over expression conditions. The assignment, for example, is defined as follows.[11]

$$\text{prec}_S[\![\mathbf{x} := \mathbf{E}]\!]e\ q = \text{prec}_E[\![\mathbf{E}]\!]e(\lambda t.q[t/\mathbf{x}])$$

Here $\text{prec}_E[\![\mathbf{E}]\!]e(\lambda t.q[t/\mathbf{x}])$ computes the precondition of the evaluation of E with a postcondition that depends on the value computed by E. If the value is t, then the postcondition will be $q[t/\mathbf{x}]$. First, consider the trivial case of numeric literals:

$$\text{prec}_E[\![\mathbf{N}]\!]e\ k = k\mathbf{N}$$

For a numeral N, the precondition is the expression condition applied to N. The predicate transformer for the trivial assignment

$$\begin{aligned}
\text{prec}_S[\![\mathbf{x} := 3]\!]e\ q\ &= \text{prec}_E[\![3]\!]e(\lambda t.q[t/\mathbf{x}])\\
&= (\lambda t.q[t/\mathbf{x}])3\\
&= q[3/\mathbf{x}]
\end{aligned}$$

gives the expected result.

If F is a (single argument) function, then the environment binds F to the predicate transformer for a call to F, i.e., a (mathematical) function that maps the expression postcondition to an expression precondition, which in turn is the expression postcondition of the evaluation of the argument. The predicate transformer for a call to a single argument function is then defined as

$$\text{prec}_E[\![\mathbf{F(E)}]\!]e\ k = \text{prec}_E[\![\mathbf{E}]\!]e(e[\![\mathbf{F}]\!]k)$$

For example, a function f that doubles its argument has the denotation $\lambda k.(\lambda v.k(v+v))$. In $\lambda v.k(v+v)$ the variable v ranges over terms and the notation $v_1 + v_2$ is a constructor that, given two terms v_1 and v_2, constructs a term that denotes the sum of v_1 and v_2.

---

[11] This presentation is simplified. The actual definition has to describe potential constraint checks that are required for assignments. A failing constraint check will cause a change of control flow to the handler for constraint error.

Let **g** be a function with a side-effect, assigning its argument to the global variable **y** and returning 0. This situation corresponds to the denotation $\lambda k.(\lambda v.(k0)[v/\mathbf{y}])$.

Finally, a function h that always raises the exception **w** is given by $\lambda k.(\lambda v.r)$, where the precondition of the handler for **w** is the predicate r.

A scope where function **f**, **g**, and **h** and exception **w** are defined as above corresponds to an environment e such that

$$
\begin{aligned}
e[\![\mathbf{w}]\!] &= r \\
e[\![\mathbf{f}]\!] &= \lambda k.(\lambda v.k(v + v)) \\
e[\![\mathbf{g}]\!] &= \lambda k.(\lambda v.(k0)[v/\mathbf{y}]) \\
e[\![\mathbf{h}]\!] &= \lambda k.(\lambda v.r)
\end{aligned}
$$

The following three examples demonstrate how the denotations of **f**, **g**, and **h** are used to compute predicate transformers for their calls.

$$
\begin{aligned}
\mathrm{prec}_S[\![\mathbf{x} := \mathbf{f}\ (1);]\!] e\,q\ &= \mathrm{prec}_E[\![\mathbf{f}\ (1)]\!] e(\lambda t.q[t/\mathbf{x}]) \\
&= \mathrm{prec}_E[\![1]\!] e(e[\![\mathbf{f}]\!](\lambda t.q[t/\mathbf{x}])) \\
&= \mathrm{prec}_E[\![1]\!] e(\lambda k.(\lambda v.k(v + v))(\lambda t.q[t/\mathbf{x}])) \\
&= \mathrm{prec}_E[\![1]\!] e(\lambda v.(\lambda t.q[t/\mathbf{x}])(v + v)) \\
&= \mathrm{prec}_E[\![1]\!] e(\lambda v.q[(v + v)/\mathbf{x}]) \\
&= (\lambda v.q[(v + v)/\mathbf{x}])1 \\
&= q[1 + 1/\mathbf{x}]
\end{aligned}
$$

$$
\begin{aligned}
\mathrm{prec}_S[\![\mathbf{x} := \mathbf{g}\ (1);]\!] e\,q\ &= \mathrm{prec}_E[\![\mathbf{g}\ (1)]\!] e(\lambda t.q[t/\mathbf{x}]) \\
&= \mathrm{prec}_E[\![1]\!] e(e[\![\mathbf{g}]\!](\lambda t.q[t/\mathbf{x}])) \\
&= \mathrm{prec}_E[\![1]\!] e(\lambda k.(\lambda v.(k0)[v/\mathbf{y}])(\lambda t.q[t/\mathbf{x}])) \\
&= \mathrm{prec}_E[\![1]\!] e(\lambda v.((\lambda t.q[t/\mathbf{x}])0)[v/\mathbf{y}]) \\
&= \mathrm{prec}_E[\![1]\!] e(\lambda v.(q[0/\mathbf{x}])[v/\mathbf{y}]) \\
&= q[0/\mathbf{x}][1/\mathbf{y}]
\end{aligned}
$$

$$
\begin{aligned}
\mathrm{prec}_S[\![\mathbf{x} := \mathbf{h}\ (1);]\!] e\,q\ &= \mathrm{prec}_E[\![\mathbf{h}\ (1)]\!] e(\lambda t\ q[t/\mathbf{x}]) \\
&= \mathrm{prec}_E[\![1]\!] e(e[\![\mathbf{h}]\!](\lambda t.q[t/\mathbf{x}])) \\
&= \mathrm{prec}_E[\![1]\!] e(\lambda k.(\lambda v.r)(\lambda t.q[t/\mathbf{x}])) \\
&= \mathrm{prec}_E[\![1]\!] e(\lambda v.r) \\
&= r.
\end{aligned}
$$

We leave it as an exercise to determine the predicate transformer for

$$\mathbf{x} := \mathbf{h}\ (\mathbf{g}\ (\mathbf{f}\ (1))).$$

2.3.4 Continuation semantics

The observant reader will notice that the predicate transformer definition looks like a continuation semantics: postconditions correspond to continuations and expression conditions correspond to expression continuations. In fact, the Ada' definition uses declaration conditions that correspond to declaration continuations in a similar way.

This correspondence between predicate transformers and continuation semantics has been observed in [25]. We have developed necessary extensions to cover the language constructs of interest. As a result, the Ada' definition is written in a style very similar to continuation semantics and it uses a large number of definitional idioms developed there.

In places where a continuation semantics uses fixed points, the predicate transformer definition requires suitable program annotations. The loop example is a simple instance of this. But other required annotations such as input/output conditions for subprograms, exception annotations, and label annotations, are also formally justified as "approximations" to fixed points.

We feel this style of definition offered a number of benefits. First, there was rarely a question of how to express the often subtle semantics of Ada; the necessary mechanisms are well understood. Second, the resulting definition is rather well structured and readable and might serve as a primary language definition. Third, the soundness of a definition written in this style can be proven straightforwardly with respect to a corresponding denotational semantics (see [25]).

3 The Penelope editor

Based on the predicate transformers for Ada' and the Larch/Ada specification language, we have developed Penelope, a prototype verification editor for Ada programs. The user of Penelope enters a specification and program, Penelope generates verification conditions, and the user proves them correct within Penelope. In a typical Penelope session, however, the user does not proceed in the strict sequence of specification, programming and proof; rather he may input a specification, implement a fragment of a program, inspect the verification condition, edit the program, and so on. Users often modify either the subprogram or the specification (for example to restate a lemma, to document global variables used in the subprogram or to modify the handling of unexpected input). Penelope immediately performs static semantic checking and with each change made by the user and generates verification conditions. The user constructs a proof within the context of Penelope, so that the activities of specifying, coding and proving are interleaved. In this section we will first describe the subset of Ada' implemented in Penelope and then describe interactive verification. We will conclude with some details about the implementation.

3.1 The implemented subset

To test our approach to verification we wanted Penelope to implement a real subset of Ada' that is recognizably Ada (hence the inclusion of packages, side-effects and exceptions) without becoming overwhelmed by a massive programming effort. We excluded some features because they would not teach us anything new: for example, we do not support Ada's **case** statement or **for** loops. Others, such as constraint checking and checks for definedness, seem likely to greatly increase the combinatorial complexity of the verification conditions generated, and we decided to postpone a study of how to attack them until we had first dealt with more traditional programming features.

Penelope supports a limited subset (integer, boolean, constrained array, record) of the data types of Ada'. The implementation does not support enumeration types (except boolean), access (pointer) types, strings, or variant records. Subtypes and constraint checking were omitted, as noted above. The

```
FUNCTION bin_search(a : IN intarray; n, x : IN integer)
         RETURN integer
IS
   hi : integer := n;
   lo : integer := 1;
   k : integer := (lo+hi)/2;
BEGIN
   WHILE (lo<=hi) LOOP
     --| INVARIANT
     --     (present(x, a, lo, hi) = present(x, a, 1, n))
     --     AND k=(lo+hi)/2 AND lo>=1 AND hi<=n;
     IF  a(k)=x
        THEN RETURN k;
     ELSIF (a(k)<x) THEN
        lo:=(k+1);
     ELSE
        --! PRECONDITION =
        --   (present(x,a,lo,k-1) = present(x,a,1,n))
        --   AND lo>=1 AND k-1<=n;
        hi:=k-1;
     END IF;
     k:=((lo+hi)/2);
   END LOOP;
   RETURN  0;
   END IF;
END bin_search;
```

Figure 3: An initial implementation of binary search

penalty is that verification with Penelope works only under the assumption that *constraint_error* is never raised and no uninitialized scalar is ever read. Since constraint error and uninitialized variables are common manifestation of errors in programs, this is a serious limitation on Penelope's current usefulness in practical examples.

The basic control structures are supported, including subprogram calls, which may be recursive.

Penelope implements some Ada static semantic checking, including type checking and overload resolution. No attempt is made to include all of Ada's static semantics.

3.2   Program Proving

In the remainder of this paper we will discuss interactive verification with Penelope. We will use an implementation of binary search (see Figure 4) as an example, showing how a user might develop parts of the program and proof.[12] An initial version of code for the binary search program is shown in Figure 3

---

[12]This version differs somewhat from that of Figure 2 of Section 2.2.

```
FUNCTION bin_search(a : IN intarray; n, x : IN integer)
RETURN integer
    --| WHERE
    --|     IN sorted(a, 1, n);
    --|     RETURN k SUCH THAT (k>=1 AND k<=n AND a[k]=x)
    --|             OR (k=0 AND NOT present(x, a, 1, n));
    --| END WHERE;
```

Figure 4: Specification for a binary search function

and a more general version with full verification is shown in the Appendix. The code and verification shown in this paper are of course only the results of an interactive process and we will try to give some indication of the way in which some of the verification steps could have come about.

The work of proving verification conditions naturally factors into "program proving" and "theorem proving." Program proving consists of providing specifications, code, and the necessary invariants, and deciding what simplifications to apply to intermediate stages of verification condition generation and when to apply them. It manages the complexities introduced into verification conditions by the program's control flow and by the basic operations of the programming language. The goal of program proving is to construct a (reusable) proof sketch that reduces the proof of the program to a set of conceptually significant—and, one hopes, "obvious"—lemmas. Theorem proving is the activity of proving the lemmas. Penelope's incrementality makes the effort devoted to program proving more productive.

For each subprogram Penelope generates a verification condition of the form: given the entry condition, show that the weakest precondition of the exit condition holds. Penelope computes and displays intermediate stages of the predicate transformation that results in the verification condition. The user can prove the verification condition as in a traditional batch system, but he also has the option of simplifying the intermediate conditions by inserting *simplification directives* into the text of the program. Thus there is a tradeoff in Penelope between simplification of preconditions and more traditional proving techniques. While the user is free to chose whichever style he prefers, simplification directives make the proof not only easier to complete but also more apt to replay when changes are made to the program.

Simplification directives Every piece of code has a purpose and is justified by some property of the problem domain or its data representation. Simplification directives associate such justifications with a piece of code and are reusable even if major changes are made to other parts of the program. Embedded simplification directives are "replayed" whenever changes are made to the code, providing a significant level of incrementality in verification.

Penelope's simplification directives are of two kinds: the user can request that the current precondition be simplified using built-in knowledge about Ada data types, notably predicate calculus and integer arithmetic. Penelope's current simplifier [28] is based on the Nelson-Oppen algorithm for cooperating

```
--| TRAIT SortingAndSearching
--|   . . .
--| LEMMAS:
--| present: present(t, a, m, n)
       = EXISTS i::i>=m AND i<=n AND a[i]=t;
--| narrow_right: sorted(a, m, n) AND i>=m AND i<=n AND a[i]>t
       -> present(t, a, m, i-1) = present(t, a, m, n);
--| narrow_left: sorted(a, m, n) AND i>=m AND i<=n AND a[i]<t
       -> present(t, a, (i+1), n) = present(t, a, m, n);
--| empty_range: m>n -> present(t, a, m, n) = FALSE;
--| sorted_subrange:  m<=i AND l<=n AND sorted(a,m,n)
       -> sorted(a,i,l);
--| END LEMMAS;
```

Figure 5: Lemmas for binary search

decision procedures [24].

When more specialized knowledge is needed, such as is found in the traits described in Section 2.2, a second form of simplification directive enables the user to appeal to axioms or lemmas of the theory as rewrite rules. Penelope enables the user to list and name consequences of traits in LEMMAS clauses. For example, some lemmas needed for our binary search subprogram are shown in Figure 5. Following Larch style, most "interesting" mathematics is pushed into the lemmas, so that proofs of verification conditions consist largely of appeals to lemmas followed by simplification. To apply a lemma as a rewrite rule the user inserts into the program a simplification directive such as

```
--! USE LEMMA narrow_right IN trait SortingAndSearching
--       WITH x, a, lo ,k, hi FOR t, a, m, i, n;
```

The directive begins with --!, a notation that tells Penelope that this is part of a proof but that is treated as a comment by Ada compilers. It acts on the current precondition. The effect of the directive is first to instantiate the lemma as indicated (x for t, etc.). Then the right hand side of the instantiated equality ($present$ (x, a, lo, hi)) is substituted for any terms in the current precondition that match the left hand side of the equality, on condition that the antecedent of the equality holds.[13] Thus an occurrence of $present(x, a, lo, hi)$ would be replaced by

if $sorted(a, lo, hi) \land k \geq m \land k \leq hi \land a[k] < x$
   then $present(x, a, lo, k-1)$
   else $present(x, a, lo, hi)$

This form of lemma is usually invoked when the antecedent of the equality is known to be true and further simplification immediately yields the desired result.

---

[13]Note that this "rewriting" capability is not a general term rewriting system; it simply enables the user to replace the left hand side of an (explicitly instantiated) equality with the right hand side.

The proof editor   In addition to the simplification directives, Penelope offers an interactive proof editing capability. The proof editor is integrated into Penelope so that proving a verification condition can actually occur concurrently with developing the program. The abtract syntax of Penelope includes *proofs* in the form of trees of proof steps in a sequent calculus; possible proof steps include not only invocations of the simplifier and appeals to axioms and lemmas, but also general theorem proving steps such as analysis by cases and proof steps based on the syntax of the verification condition itself.

Proof steps applied by the user take their place in the syntax tree of the program, and the user can cut and paste them just as he would pieces of Ada syntax. For example, if P is a verification condition and a change in the program results in the new verification condition **if** B **then** P **else** Q, the new proof may begin by considering two cases, B and $\neg B$. The old proof of P can be moved to the subproof for case B.

The binary search example   Let us now consider the binary search program of Figure 3. The program works by repeatedly narrowing the range of indexes to be searched. Binary search relies on the fact that if we are searching for x in a sorted array, knowing that $a[k] > x$ allows us to rule out searching indexes greater than k. This general property of ordered sequences is expressed by the lemma *narrow_right*, and a symmetric property is expressed by *narrow_left*. In the case of $a[i] > x$ the range can be narrowed to $[lo..k - 1]$. This fact, expressed logically by the lemma *narrow_right*, is expressed operationally by the statement **hi:=k-1**. If, during the narrowing process, the desired value x is found, the corresponding index value k is returned. When the array is empty, we know that the desired value, whatever it is, is not present, a fact that is expressed by the lemma *empty_range*. If the range being searched is empty, or becomes empty, control leaves the loop and the value 0 is returned.

Most of the subprogram consists of a loop that narrows the range. Figure 3 shows that the user has annotated it with an invariant generalizing the exit condition of the subprogram. We assume that the user has decided to prove the loop verification condition separately. Penelope generates two verification conditions for the subprogram **bin_search**, one for the loop and one for the initialization statements.

3.3   Use of simplification directives

We now look in some detail at how the user goes about verifying binary search. Figure 6 represents a situation in which the user is attempting to simplify the precondition of Figure 3, with the goal of proving that the invariant is preserved.

In Figure 6 the precondition of Figure 3 has been simplified by an appeal to lemma *narrow_right*. To justify the appeal to the lemma, the user includes an *embedded assertion*, stating that the antecedent of the lemma is satisfied:

```
--| sorted(a,lo,hi) AND k>=lo AND k<=hi AND a[k]>x
```

The result of applying the lemma and embedding the assertion is syntactically a rather complicated precondition, which the user then simplifies with the command:

```
--! SIMPLIFY PRECONDITION;
```

```
IF
   . . .
ELSE
   --! PRECONDITION = sorted(a,lo,hi) AND lo<=k AND k<=hi
       AND x<a[k]
       AND present(x,a,lo,hi)= present(x,a,1,n)
       AND 0<lo AND k<=1+n
   --! SIMPLIFY PRECONDITION;
   --| sorted(a,lo,hi) AND k>=lo and k<=hi and a[k]>x
   --! USE LEMMA narrow_right IN trait SortingAndSearching
       WITH x, a, lo ,k, hi FOR t, a, m, i, n;
   --! PRECONDITION =
       (present(x,a,lo,k-1) = present(x,a,1,n))
       AND lo>=1 AND k-1<=n;
  hi:=k-1;
END IF;
```

Figure 6: Simplification of the precondition

Although the result does not immediately look simpler than the original precondition, we note that the term **present(x, a, lo, k-1)** has been effectively reduced to **present(x, a, lo, hi)**, which is given in the invariant of Figure 3.

The resulting precondition does not follow from the invariant, however, since it requires the user to prove $sorted(a, lo, hi)$. Of course, we know that $sorted(a, lo, hi)$ must hold, since the array was sorted to begin with, the subprogram does not change the array and any slice of the array must necessarily be sorted. The user will therefore need to reformulate the invariant to include $sorted(a, lo, hi)$.

```
--| INVARIANT
    (present(x, a, lo, hi) = present(x, a, 1, n))
   AND sorted(a, lo, hi)
   AND k=(lo+hi)/2 AND lo>=1 AND hi<=n;
```

After he does so, predicate transformation is replayed, and then the term $sorted(a, lo, k-1)$ appears in the precondition of hi:=k-1.

But this must hold by the same argument, which is captured in the lemma $sorted\_subrange$. The user therefore associates this lemma too with the program text, as shown in Figure 7. We note that syntactically the result of this simplification has been to effectively replace the conjunct $sorted(a, lo, k-1)$ with $sorted(a, lo, hi)$.

We can see that the precondition of this simplification follows immediately from the invariant and $a[k] > x$, and indeed this branch of the IF statement is taken just when $a[k] > x$. Thus no further information from trait **SearchingAndSorting** is required to simplify this precondition.

```
IF
   . . .
ELSE
   --! PRECONDITION = sorted(a,lo,hi)
         AND lo<=k and k<=hi
         AND x<a[k]
         AND present(x,a,lo,hi)=present(x,a,1,n)
         AND 0<lo and k<=1+n
   --! SIMPLIFY PRECONDITION;
   --! USE LEMMA sorted_subrange IN trait SortingAndSearching
         WITH a, lo, k-1, lo, hi FOR a, i, l, m, n;
   --| sorted(a,lo,hi) AND k>=lo and k<=hi and a[k]>x
   --! USE LEMMA narrow_right IN trait SortingAndSearching
         WITH x, a, lo ,k, hi FOR t, a, m, i, n;
   --! PRECONDITION =
         (present(x,a,lo,k-1) = present(x,a,1,n))
         AND sorted(a,lo,k-1)
         AND lo>=1 AND k-1<=n;
   hi:=k-1;
END IF;
```

Figure 7: Further simplification of the precondition

3.4 Use of the proof editor

Penelope encourages a style of verification in which as much simplification as possible is accomplished by means of embedded simplification directives. In general, however, some trivial verification condition is generated and the user is required to prove it.

Figure 8 shows the verification condition for the loop of bin_search. In the display of sequents the hypotheses of verification conditions are numbered (for reference in proving) and the conclusion is marked by >>. The verification condition ensures that if the loop test is met the invariant holds, but if control exits the loop then the loop's postcondition holds.[14]

The proof of this verification condition is shown in Figure 9. The proof first treats the case in which the invariant must be preserved and then the case of exiting from the loop. In the former case the user needs to show that k lies between lo and hi. The claim follows from an appeal to lemma

$$div2: a \leq b \rightarrow (a \leq (a+b)/2 \wedge (a+b)/2 \leq b),$$

which is a direct consequence of the theory underlying Ada's binary division, but must be stated by the user since it is not currently encoded in the system and is not within the capabilities of the simplifier. To prove that exit from the loop establishes the loop postcondition (x not in the array), appeal must be

---

[14] The verification condition does not ensure loop termination, but in this case we can argue informally that each execution of the loop decreases $hi - lo$ and that therefore execution will eventually terminate.

```
--! 1. present(x, a, lo, hi) = present(x, a, 1, n)
--! 2. sorted(a, lo, hi)
--! 3. k= (lo+hi)/2
--! 4. lo>=1
--! 5. hi<=n
--! >> IF lo<=hi
        THEN IF a[k]=x
          THEN IF 0<k THEN k<=n
                      ELSE (k=0 and NOT present(x,a,lo,hi))
          ELSE lo<=k and k<=hi
        ELSE NOT present(x,a,lo,hi)
```

Figure 8: Verification condition for the loop

```
--! VC Status: proved
--! BY cases, using lo<=hi
--! CASE TRUE
--!     BY CLAIM lo<=k AND k<=hi
--!         BY lemma div2 in trait Arithmetic
--!                 WITH lo, hi FOR a, b
--!         BY simplification
--!         BY synthesis of TRUE
--!     AND THEN
--!         BY simplification
--!         BY synthesis of TRUE
--! CASE FALSE
--!     BY lemma empty_range in trait SortingAndSearching
--!                 WITH x, a, lo, hi FOR t, a, m, n
--!     BY simplification
--!     BY synthesis of TRUE
--! □
```

Figure 9: Proof of the loop

```
FUNCTION bin_search(a : IN intarray; m, n, x : IN integer)
RETURN integer
    --| WHERE
    --|        IN sorted(a, m, n);
    --|        RETURN k SUCH THAT (((k>=m) AND (k<=n))
                                       AND ((a[k])=x));
    --|        RAISE not_present <=> IN (NOT present(x, a, m, n));
    --| END WHERE;
```

Figure 10: bin_search with variable array bounds

made to the lemma *empty_range*, which states that no values are present in an empty range of an array.

The simple capabilities of Penelope's theorem prover are not adequate in general to prove the lemmas or to prove logical properties of the traits such as coherence (cf. Section 2.2.5). Currently our approach is to hand-prove the necessary lemmas and properties of the theory, and use Penelope's theorem-proving capability for the syntactically complex but mathematically shallow component of the verification conditions that results from mechanical implementation of predicate transformation. In principle Penelope can be linked to a mathematical theorem prover if machine-checked proof of the lemmas or of properties of the traits is desired.

3.5 Replaying proofs

Penelope's support for incremental changes is useful for developing correct programs, for exploring alternatives, and also for dealing with changes to specifications or implementations. When changes are made to a program Penelope automatically recomputes verification conditions and replays the proofs, marking any inappropriate proof steps. The user can delete such proof steps in order to see the sequent that remains to be proved (an example is shown below).

For example, suppose that, having completed the verification of bin_search, the programmer decides to change the specification, for example to generalize the array bounds to m and n, and thus to make m a parameter to the function. (This example appears somewhat forced, since idiomatic Ada would include neither m nor n as parameters, but rather refer to them as a'first and a'last. The programmer is thus unlikely in Ada to have referred throughout the program to 1 as the first array index. In any case, we trust the reader to accept the revised program as an example of the kind of changes that often occur in any programming language.)

The revised specification is shown in Figure 10. Allowing the lower bound to vary requires rethinking the way that errors are signalled to the caller, and the user is apt to decide on a more general solution. We assume that he modifies the subprogram to raise an exception if the value is not found in the array.

To implement the modified function the programmer needs to change instances of 1 used as a lower bound of the table to m, and to raise an exception instead of returning 0. (The Appendix shows the complete text of the modified

```
--! VC Status: ** not proved **
--! BY cases, using lo<=hi
--! CASE TRUE
--!      BY CLAIM lo<=k AND k<=hi
--!           BY lemma div2 in trait Arithmetic
                    WITH lo, hi FOR a, b
--!           BY simplification
--!           BY synthesis of TRUE
--!      AND THEN
--!           BY simplification
--!           1. present(x,a,lo,hi)=present(x,a,m,n)
--!           2. sorted(a, lo, hi)
--!           3. k=(hi+lo)/2
--!           4. m<=lo
--!           5. hi<=n
--!           6. lo<=hi
--!           7. lo<=k
--!           8. k<=hi
--!           9. a[k]=x
--!           >>present(x,a,lo,hi)
--!           <proof>
--! CASE FALSE
--!      BY lemma empty_range in trait SortingAndSearching
                    WITH x, a, lo, hi FOR t, a, m, n
--!      BY simplification
--!      BY synthesis of TRUE
--! []
```

Figure 11: Incomplete proof of the revised loop VC

program, with its verification.) After the textual modifications to the subprogram, the proof that the loop's postcondition holds on termination of the loop remains valid but simplification is no longer sufficient to show that the invariant is maintained. The now invalid proof is decorated with an error message. When the user displays the sequent to which the inappropriate proof step was applied, and displays the unproved sequent (see Figure 11), the difficulty becomes apparent: when $a[k] = x$—that is, if an exception is not raised— it must be possible to show $present(x, a, m, n)$. This is because of the annotation that not_present is raised *if and only if x* is not present in the array segment. The new proof requirement is satisfied by appeal to the lemma *present*, as shown in Figure 12. Note that all of the in-line simplification remains valid. The user is only required to change that part of the proof that was invalidated by the change in the program.

Thus a significant change to a program—adding a new parameter and modifying the program to raise an exception—results in a very modest change to the proof of the program. This economy results from our factoring the proof and associating part of it closely with the code, and also from integrating the

```
--! VC Status: proved
--!      . . .
--!      AND THEN
--!          BY simplification
--!          BY lemma present in trait SortingAndSearching
--!                  WITH x, a, lo, hi FOR t, a, m, n
--!          BY synthesis of EXISTS exhibiting k
--!          BY simplification
--!          BY synthesis of TRUE
--!      . . .
--! □
```

Figure 12: Proof of the revised loop

proof editor into Penelope so that proofs are automatically replayed whenever a change is made to the program.

3.6   The implementation

Penelope is a mixed-mode (syntax-directed and text) editor compiled from an attribute grammar specification using the Synthesizer Generator [30]. Editors generated by the Synthesizer Generator perform attribute evaluation incrementally; that is, after a change is made to the program or proof, only those attributes are reevaluated whose value may actually have changed. Incremental updating is essential to providing an interactive verification system with acceptable performance. (An earlier implementation of a verification editor for Dikstra's language using the Synthesizer Generator is described in [30].)

We have found it relatively straightforward to translate the predicate transformers defined in [26] into equations of an attribute grammar. The subprogram annotation provides the exit condition of the subprogram. Environments and statement postconditions are represented by *inherited* attributes in the attribute grammar—they are arguments to predicate transformation. Preconditions of statements are implemented as *synthesized* attributes.

As a simple example, consider the predicate transformation of statement composition:

$$\text{prec}_S[\![\texttt{S1; S2;}]\!]e\ q = \text{prec}_S[\![\texttt{S1;}]\!]e(\text{prec}_S[\![\texttt{S2;}]\!]e\ q)$$

This corresponds to an attribute grammar production

```
statement_sequence ::= S1; S2;
```

The predicate transformation of S2 and S1 is described by

$$S2.e = statement\_sequence.e$$
$$S2.post = statement\_sequence.post$$
$$S1.e = statement\_sequence.e$$
$$S1.post = S2.post$$
$$statement\_sequence.pre = S1.pre$$

where e is the environment attribute, and *post* and *pre* are the statement post- and preconditions respectively. (The composition of environments is complicated by the possibility of forward jumps and is not shown here.)

The proof editor is modelled after the interactive proof checker of [29]; proof steps are treated as syntactic objects operating on sequents that are implemented as inherited attributes. The verification condition is a sequent whose hypotheses are the collective input conditions for the subprogram and whose conclusion is the predicate transformation of the exit condition. It is implemented as an attribute of the subprogram; its value is recomputed automatically as the program changes. The sequents of the proof of the verification condition are computed as a function of the verification condition and the syntactic structure of the proof. For example, when case analysis is applied to the sequent $\Gamma \vdash P$, using cases Q and $\neg Q$, we obtain the two subsequents to prove:

$$\Gamma, Q \vdash P$$
$$\Gamma, \neg Q \vdash P$$

The inherited attributes for a proof step, then, are just the hypotheses and conclusion, and the status of the proof is a synthesized attribute; when all subsequents are proved then the entire verification condition has been proved. Replaying a proof consists simply of running a new sequent (the new verification condition) through the syntactic proof structure.

4 Current status

The theory underlying Penelope and the editor itself are still under development. We are currently developing the theory of Ada libraries and approaches to the problems of abstraction, in particular private types and generics. We are also looking at ways to improve the expressiveness of Larch/Ada, for example by adding bounded quantifiers. Current work on the implementation includes static semantic checking of annotations, improving the proof editor interface and studying the implementation of libraries and separate verification.

Our experience in using the current limited implementation and the incremental mode of developing verified programs has been encouraging. To date Penelope has been used to verify a number of examples from the programming literature, including the Dutch National Flag, saddleback search, and Ackermann's function, a circular queue package and a rational number package, and security properties of a portion of the Army Secure Operating System (ASOS). In response to a challenge to the verification community [18], we wrote and verified a software repeater designed to operate in an RS232 data transmission link.

5 Acknowledgment

Many people have contributed to the work presented in this paper. We wish especially to thank N. Ramsey, who led the project in its early days and is responsible for many of the key technical decisions. M. Stillman has provided unflagging leadership and support as our project manager for the past two years. P. Cenciarelli, C. D. Harper, G. Hird, and D. G. Weber have worked on the proof editor and simplification directives, sort checking for Larch/Ada, user documentation, and development of a suite of examples. Penelope is generated in part by the Synthesizer Generator under license from Cornell University. We acknowledge T. Reps and T. Teitelbaum for their role in its development. Aerospace Corporation has provided the SDVS simplifier used by Penelope.

A Verification of bin_search

```
--| TRAIT SearchingAndSorting IS
--| INTRODUCES present: Int, intarray, Int, Int-> Bool;
--| INTRODUCES sorted: intarray, Int, Int-> Bool;
--| AXIOMS:
--| END AXIOMS;
--| LEMMAS:
--| present: (
    present(t, a, m, n)
  =
    (EXISTS i::(((i>=m) AND (i<=n)) AND ((a[i])=t))));
--| narrow_right: (
    present(t, a, m, (i-1))
  =
    (
    IF (((sorted(a, m, n) AND (i>=m)) AND (i<=n)) AND ((a[i])>t))
      THEN present(t, a, m, n)
      ELSE present(t, a, m, (i-1))));
--| narrow_left: (
    present(t, a, (i+1), n)
  =
    (
    IF ((sorted(a, m, n) AND (i>=m)) AND ((i<=n) AND ((a[i])<t)))
      THEN present(t, a, m, n)
      ELSE present(t, a, (i+1), n)));
--| sorted_subrange: (
    sorted(a, i, l)
  =
    (
    IF ((m<=i) AND (l<=n))
      THEN sorted(a, m, n)
      ELSE sorted(a, i, l)));
--| empty_range: (
    present(t, a, m, n)
  =
    (IF (m>n) THEN FALSE ELSE present(t, a, m, n)));
--| END LEMMAS;

--| TRAIT Arithmetic IS
--| AXIOMS:
--| END AXIOMS;
--| LEMMAS:
```

```
--| div2: (
    ((a<=b)->(((((a+b)/2)-1)<b))
  AND
    ((a<=b)->(a<(((a+b)/2)+1))));
--| END LEMMAS;
PROCEDURE main
  --| WHERE
  --| END WHERE;
  --! VC Status: proved
  --! BY synthesis of TRUE

IS
  TYPE intarray IS ARRAY(integer) OF integer;
  FUNCTION bin_search(a : IN intarray;
    m, n, x : IN integer) RETURN integer
    --| WHERE
    --|       IN sorted(a, m, n);
    --|       RETURN k SUCH THAT (((k>=m) AND (k<=n))
                                    AND ((a[k])=x));
    --|       RAISE not_present <=> IN (NOT present(x, a, m, n));
    --| END WHERE;
    --! VC Status: proved
    --! BY synthesis of TRUE


  IS
    hi : integer := n;
    lo : integer := m;
    k : integer := ((lo+hi)/2);
    not_present : exception;


  BEGIN
    --! VC Status: proved
    --! BY cases, using (lo<=hi)
    --! CASE TRUE
    --!    BY CLAIM ((lo<=k) AND (k<=hi))
    --!      BY lemma div2 in trait Arithmetic WITH lo, hi FOR a, b
    --!      BY simplification
    --!      BY synthesis of TRUE
    --!    AND THEN
    --!      BY simplification
    --!      BY lemma present in trait SearchingAndSorting
                 for occurrence 1 in conclusion
    --!      BY synthesis of EXISTS
    --!          exhibiting k
    --!      BY simplification
    --!      BY synthesis of TRUE
    --! CASE FALSE
    --!    BY lemma empty_range in trait SearchingAndSorting
                 WITH x, a, lo, hi FOR t, a, m, n
    --!    BY simplification
```

```
    --!    BY synthesis of TRUE
    --!  []
    WHILE (lo<=hi) LOOP
      --| INVARIANT  (((((present(x, a, lo, hi)=present(x, a, m, n))
             AND sorted(a, lo, hi))
             AND (k=((lo+hi)/2)))
             AND ((lo>=m) AND (hi<=n)));
      IF (a(k)=x) THEN
        RETURN  k;
      ELSIF (a(k)<x) THEN
        --! SIMPLIFY PRECONDITION;
        --! USE LEMMA sorted_subrange IN TRAIT SearchingAndSorting
               WITH a, (k+1), hi, lo, hi FOR a, i, l, m, n;
        --| (((sorted(a, lo, hi) AND (k>=lo)) AND (k<=hi))
               AND ((a[k])<x));
        --! USE LEMMA narrow_left IN TRAIT SearchingAndSorting
               WITH x, a, k, hi, lo FOR t, a, i, n, m ;
        lo:=(k+1);
      ELSE
        --! SIMPLIFY PRECONDITION;
        --! USE LEMMA sorted_subrange IN TRAIT SearchingAndSorting
               WITH a, lo, (k-1), lo, hi FOR a, i, l, m, n;
        --| (((sorted(a, lo, hi) AND (k>=lo)) AND (k<=hi))
               AND ((a[k])>x));
        --! USE LEMMA narrow_right IN TRAIT SearchingAndSorting
               WITH x, a, lo, k, hi FOR t, a, m, i, n;
        hi:=(k-1);
      END IF;
      k:=((lo+hi)/2);
    END LOOP;
    RAISE not_present;
  END binsearch;
BEGIN
  NULL;
END main;
```

References

[1] ANSI. *The Programming Language Ada Reference Manual*, 1983. ANSI/MIL-STD-1815A.

[2] E.R. Anderson, B. Di Vito, and R.M. Hart. ASOS: Information Security for Real-Time Systems. In *AFCEA West Intelligence Symposium*, 1987.

[3] E. Astesiano et al. Draft formal definition of Ada. Technical report, CRAI, DDC, 1987. Deliverable 7 of the CED MAP project.

[4] H. Barringer, J. H. Cheng, and C. B Jones. A logic covering undefinedness in program proofs. *Acta Informatica*, 21, 1984.

[5] Boehm, H.-J. Side-effects and aliasing can have simple axiomatic descriptions. *ACM Transactions on Programming Languages and Systems 7, 4* (October 1985).

[6] Robert S. Boyer and J Strother Moore. *A Computational Logic Handbook.* Academic Press, 1988.

[7] Edsger W. Dijkstra. *A Discipline of Programming.* Prentice Hall, Englewood Cliffs, 1976.

[8] R. Floyd. Assigning meaning to programs. In *Mathematical Aspects of Computer Science XIX*, pages 19–32. American Mathematical Society, 1967.

[9] R. Gerth. A sound and complete Hoare axiomatization of the Ada rendezvous. In *Proc. 9th ICALP*, Lecture Notes in Computer Science 140, Springer Verlag, New York, 1982, pp. 252–264.

[10] Joseph A. Goguen and R. M. Burstall. *Introducing Institutions*, volume 164 of *Lecture Notes in Computer Science*. Springer Verlag, 1984.

[11] Donald Good. Revised report on gypsy 2.1 (draft). Technical report, University of Texas, July 1984.

[12] David Gries. *The Science of Programming.* Springer-Verlag, 1981.

[13] David Guaspari. Formal semantics of two-tiered specifications. Technical Report 89-35, Odyssey Research Associates, September 1989. original number 17-14.

[14] J. V. Guttag, J. J. Horning, and J. M. Wing. Larch in five easy pieces. Technical Report TR 5, DEC/SRC, July 1985.

[15] C. A. R. Hoare. An axiomatic basis for computer programming. *Communications of the ACM*, 12(10):576–580,583, October 1969.

[16] C. A. R. Hoare. Proof of correctness of data representations. *Acta Informatica*, 1(1):271–281, 1972.

[17] S. Katz, Z. Manna. A Closer Look at Termination. Acta Informatica 5, pp 333–352 (1975)

[18] Carl Landwehr. The rs-232 software repeater problem. *Cipher: Newsletter of the IEEE technical committee on security and privacy.*

[19] D. C. Luckham et al. Stanford Pascal Verifier user manual. Technical Report STAN-CS-79-731, Stanford University, March 1979.

[20] Luckham, D.C., and Polak, W. Ada exception handling: An axiomatic approach. *ACM Transactions on Programming Languages and Systems 2*, 2 (April 1980), pp. 225–233.

[21] D. C. Luckham et al. Anna: A language for annotating Ada programs. Technical Report CSL-84-261, Stanford University, 1986. Reference Manual.

[22] C. Marceau and C.D. Harper. An interactive approach to Ada verification. *Proceedings of the 12th NBS/NCSC National Computer Security Conference*, MBS/NCSC, October 1989.

[23] D. R. Musser. Abstract data type specifications in the AFFIRM system. In *Proceedings of the Specifications of Reliable Software*, pages 47–57, April 1979.

[24] Greg Nelson and D. C. Oppen. Simplification by cooperating decision procedures. *ACM Transactions on Programming Languages and Systems*, 1(2):245–257, October 1979.

[25] Wolfgang Polak. Program verification based on denotational semantics. In *Conference Record of the Eighth Annual ACM Symposium on Principles of Programming Languages*, 1981.

[26] Wolfgang Polak. Predicate transformer semantics for Ada. Technical Report 89-39, Odyssey Research Associates, September 1989. original number was 17-12.

[27] Wolfgang Polak. A technique for defining predicate transformers. Technical Report 89-53, Odyssey Research Associates, 1989. original number was 17-4.

[28] T. Redmond. Simplifier description. Technical Report ATR-86A (8554)-2, Aerospace, November 1987.

[29] Thomas Reps and Bowen Alpern. Interactive proof checking. In *Conference Record of the Eleventh Annual ACM Symposium on Principles of Programming Languages*, pages 36–45, January 1984. Salt Lake City, UT.

[30] Thomas W. Reps and Tim Teitelbaum. *The Synthesizer Generator: A System For Constructing Language-Based Editors*. Springer-Verlag, 1988.

[31] Oliver Schoett. *Data abstraction and the correctness of modular programming*. PhD thesis, Edinburgh, 1987. CST-42-87.

[32] Edmond Schonberg and Brian Siritzky. Adasem, Static semantics for Ada. Technical report, Dept. of Computer Science, Courant Institute of Mathematical Science, 1984.

[33] Schwartz, R.L. An Axiomatic Treatment of Algol68 Routines, In *Proc. Sixth Int'l Conf. on Automata, Languages and Programming* (July 1979), Springer Verlag, New York, 1979.

[34] Jeannette M. Wing. Writing Larch interface language specifications. *ACM Transactions on Programming Languages and Systems*, 9(1):1–24, January 1987.

[35] Yemini, S., and Berry, D.M. An axiomatic treatment of exception handling in an expression-oriented language. *ACM Transactions on Programming Languages and Systems 9*, 3 (July 1987).

A Semantics for a Larch/Modula-3 Interface Language

Kevin D. Jones

Digital Equipment Corp.,

Systems Research Center,

Palo Alto, CA 94301, U.S.A.

Abstract

We describe a method for giving a semantics to a Larch interface language specification by a translation of the specification into typed first-order logic. This is illustrated using LM3, a Larch/Modula-3 interface language.

We show that a side effect of this approach to semantics gives an easy way of using existing Larch tools to check the type/sort correctness of a specification in the interface language.

1   Introduction

The Larch approach to formal specification differs from most other methods in two significant ways:

1. interface specifications are given in a language that is very closely tailored to the programming language used to implement the interface, for example, Larch/CLU[9] for CLU or LCL[3] for C;

2. these specifications are dependent on auxiliary specifications written in a separate language, the Larch Shared Language (LSL)[4], which are programming language independent and are often general abstractions used across the spectrum of programming/interface languages.

The justification and benefits of the two tier approach have been discussed elsewhere[2], for the current purpose it is sufficient to realise that this requires any approach to the semantics of a Larch interface language to take the semantics of LSL into account.

We propose to give a semantics to LM3[6], a Larch/Modula-3 interface language, by providing translation rules mapping the language constructs into a well understood semantic domain. We choose a typed first order predicate calculus as our semantic domain. Rather than presenting extra complexity, LSL actually simplifies the problem. This approach has the serendipitous effect of providing a tool for checking the type/sort correctness of LM3 specifications "for free".

We assume assume familiarity with LSL and its semantics and an understanding of the general ideas of Larch interface languages. We do not present a detailed discussion of the Modula-3 programming language, see Greg Nelson's book[8] for the "truth" or Sam Harbison's book[5] for a tutorial. However, to give a flavor of the language so that readers uninterested in Modula-3 itself can understand why the specification language has the features it does, we offer the following paraphrase of the concept of Modula-3 as described by its designers:

> The goal of Modula-3 is to be as simple and safe as it can be while meeting the needs of modern systems programmers. Instead of exploring new features, we studied the features of the Modula family of languages that have proven themselves in practice and tried to simplify them into a harmonious language.
>
> Modula-3 descends from Mesa, Modula-2, Cedar, and Modula-2+. It retains one of Modula-2's most successful features, the provision for explicit interfaces between modules. It adds objects and classes, exception handling, garbage collection, lightweight processes (or threads), and the isolation of unsafe features.

LM3 is a language for giving formal specifications of safe Modula-3 interfaces and supports all of the features of the programming language that can be used in this context. For a tutorial introduction to LM3, see the LM3 chapter of the Larch Book[2].

2 Informal description of an LM3 specification

An LM3 specification defines the functional behaviour of the procedures, variables, and constants exported by an interface.

An LM3 specification has two distinct parts:

the Modula-3 interface declaration — any valid Modula-3 safe interface declaration has a meaning as an LM3 specification;

LM3 specification annotations — LM3 extends a Modula-3 interface declaration by giving additional semantic constraints as specification annotations within pragmas.

The declarations in the Modula-3 interface declaration define:

- sorts used within specification (from the TYPE declarations);

- constants (from the CONST and EXCEPTION declarations);

- state components (from the VAR and PROCEDURE declarations).

The specification annotations give predicates that constrain the values and behaviors of the components of the interface beyond the general constraints enforced by their Modula-3 types. These predicates are written as LSL terms, plus sorts, operators and syntactic sugar provided to correspond to Modula-3 constructors and operations.

2.1 The state

An LM3 specification is based on the notion of a state, which is a repository for mutable values. It can be regarded as a time-dependent mapping from *locs* to *values*. Entities that can be changed (parameters representing designators, global variables, etc.) have values that depend on the state. Each variable is associated with a `loc` and a type. Entities whose value is independent of the state are treated as constants and are not associated with a `loc`. To model assigned storage, the state also contains a number of variables representing the heap, one for each distinct `OBJECT` or `REF` type. Any procedure or method that allocates storage modifies the state component associated with the heap of that type.

The global state of an interface specification is defined by its type, variable, constant and specification variable declarations and by the global states of the interfaces it imports.

The local state of a procedure specification is defined by its argument list, the components of the global state that its specification explicitly allows it to access and a number of implicitly declared variables representing values unnamed by Modula-3, such as the return value of a function.

Within a specification, immutable values (constants) are state independent and are represented directly by name. Mutable values (variables) are state dependent and must be evaluated with respect to a state.

2.1.1 Procedure specifications

For most purposes, we do not distinguish between procedures and methods in LM3. We use the term procedure to mean both unless we specifically indicate otherwise.

Each procedure is specified by a predicate on a pair of states that constrains the state transformation the procedure implements. The two states of interest in a procedure specification are the state at call (denoted by `pre`) and the state on return (denoted by `post`. By convention in LM3, to refer to the value of a mutable state component `x` in the post-state, we write `x'`; (in a context where a value is required) `x` means the value in the pre state. Since there are only a few specific places in an LM3 specification where the `loc` maybe referred to directly, this convention does not cause any ambiguity in practice.

The precondition constrains the acceptable values of `pre`. The postcondition constrains `post` and its relation to `pre`. The other significant component of a procedure specification defines its target variables, which are the subset of the mutable components of the state to which it may assign new values.

This gives enough of the context of LM3 for our current purpose. The rest of this paper is concerned with giving a more formal semantics to an LM3 specification.

3 Semantic translation of LM3

Our approach to giving a semantics to an LM3 specification is to provide a translation into a known semantic framework. Since LM3 specifications are made up of LSL terms, a natural target for our translation would be one for which the meaning of the LSL components are already defined. The semantics of LSL are given in the LSL report[4] in terms of a translation into a kernel language that defines a theory in a typed first-order logic. Our aim for the work reported here is to give a translation of an LM3 specification into the same logic.

Since the LSL semantics provides for a translation from LSL into the predicate calculus, it is sufficient to provide a translation from an LM3 specification into an LSL trait. This allows a significant reduction in the complexity of the translation of LM3, since we can take advantage of the higher level framework provided by LSL.

We should be completely honest and admit that we cannot provide a simple translation into "kosher" LSL. The LM3 predicate language allows arbitrary expressions from the first order calculus, whereas LSL does not permit explicit quantification. These limitations on LSL were largely imposed by the wish to keep the language within the bounds that could be efficiently mated with a theorem prover. At the time of LSL's design, this meant no quantifiers. This restriction is expected to be lifted in future incarnations of LP[1] and, so, in future versions of LSL. Since it is clear that the same semantic mechanisms apply to this more general LSL, we allow ourselves the liberty of a little precognition and translate our quantified predicates as if they were simple LSL terms.

There is a further problem with parameters having procedure types that does not have such a simple solution. This is discussed in Section 3.4.9.

Our translation of an LM3 specification consists of generating an LSL trait that gives the semantics of the specification. This involves including existing traits, introducing new operators and sorts and asserting equations. In the following sections, we describe the translation of LM3 in terms of these actions.

The semantics of the specification is then the theory that this generated trait produces in the predicate calculus using the semantic rules of LSL. We do not have the space here to give a complete description of the translation for LM3. We illustrate the approach, describing the most important features. The full mechanism is described in the LM3 Reference Manual[7] and is also implemented as a Modula-3 program (see Section 4).

3.1 Types, sorts and values

All entities defined in a Modula-3 interface have a type. Entities in LSL, and our logic, have sorts. To each expression in Modula-3, we associate a corresponding sort. Each type has two associated sorts: one that represents the sort of a variable of the type (which by convention will have a postfix of _loc) and one representing a value of the type.

We give rules to generate the equivalent sorts for each base or constructed type in Modula-3. These sorts are given semantics by including library traits.

We discuss the translation of a simple base type and of some of the Modula-3 type constructors. Rules for all base types and all constructors can be found in the LM3 Reference Manual[7].

3.1.1 INTEGER

INTEGER is the Modula-3 type representing Integer values. We associate this type with the sort Int from the trait M3Integer which is includes on the standard handbook trait Integer[10][1].

---

[1]It may often be the case that the sort includes more values than the type. We may

Formally, we stipulate that

- `INTEGER` is associated with the sort `Int` from the trait `Integer(Int)`

- a *variable* of type `INTEGER` has sort `Int_loc`

- a *value* or *constant* of `INTEGER` has sort `Int` and has the operators defined in the `Integer` trait.

The generated trait must therefore include `Integer(Int)`.

The rest of the base types of Modula-3 are similarly associated with sorts from suitable traits. Type constructors are a little more interesting since a sort must be associated with each instance of a constructor.

3.1.2 Enumeration types

An enumerated type is one of the simplest constructors in Modula-3. A sort is associated with each enumeration type and we provide constants of that sort to represent the elements of the enumeration.

We generate a unique name for the sort associated with the type[2] and give semantics to the sort using the LSL shorthand **enumeration of**. This is one place where taking advantage of LSL saves us work in the translation.

For `TYPE E = {a, b, c}`

- type `E` is associated with a sort $\mathcal{E}$ and the LSL shorthand
  $\mathcal{E}$ `enumeration of` $\mathcal{E}$_a, $\mathcal{E}$_b, $\mathcal{E}$_c
  is included in the generated trait,

- a *variable* of type `E` has sort $\mathcal{E}$_loc,

- a *value* or *constant* has sort $\mathcal{E}$,

- a use of `E.a` is represented by the constant $\mathcal{E}$_a which has sort $\mathcal{E}$.

3.1.3 ARRAY

Arrays are a little more complex. In the state model, we have chosen to treat an array as an "entire variable". Assignment to an indexed element is modeled as replacing the whole array value with one that differs from its previous value only at that one index. The state component for an array is a `loc` that maps to an array value.

For `TYPE A = ARRAY Index OF Element`

---

use extra operators and axioms in the trait, such as defining constants like **LAST** which give an upper bound on valid values of the sort, or to add an invariant to the type definition restricting the values of the sort that are valid values of the type. It is always possible to write specifications that are impossible to implement within the Modula-3 type system. Using the trait **M3Integer** rather than the handbook trait `Integer` directly allows us the flexibility to strengthen the trait if we wish. For our current discussion, we'll use the handbook traits, since they are probably more accessible to the reader.

[2] The actual generation of the name is not significant here but we should say that we use a scheme (and program) provided by Mick Jordan of SRC that provides a unique "typecode" for each type. In this paper, we represent such a generated sort using the cal font, as in $\mathcal{S}$.

- type A is associated with a sort $\mathcal{A}$ from the trait $\text{Array1}(\mathcal{E}, \mathcal{I}, \mathcal{A})$. Array1 is the handbook trait representing one dimensional arrays. $\mathcal{E}$ is the sort associated with the type Element and $\mathcal{I}$ is the sort associated with type Index

- a *variable* of type A has sort $\mathcal{A}\_\text{loc}$

- a *value* or a *constant* of type A has sort $\mathcal{A}$ and the operators defined by the trait Array1.

A multi-dimensional array is normalized into a one dimensional array of arrays before it is translated.

3.1.4 OBJECT

As a final illustration of the translation from Modula-3 types to sorts, we look at the translation of an OBJECT type. This is the most complex translation we have to perform.

Objects are somewhat peculiar in that they contain an implicit reference, allowing the modification of their component fields even when they are passed as value parameters. Since objects are normally modified via their method suite, they are not often passed as VAR parameters.

The state representation for an object is a collection of map-valued entire variables, one for each field in the type, that have the sort of the object type as their key and the sorts of the types of the fields as values[3]. Modifying a field of an object means replacing the map representing that field with one that differs from its previous value only at the place indexed by the current object. For example, for an object having two fields, say an integer and a boolean, we represent this type by a pair of maps, the first from the object sort to Int, the second from the object sort to Bool.

For TYPE O = OBJECT f: F, g: G END

- the type O is associated with a sort $\mathcal{O}$

- a *variable* of this type is given sort $\mathcal{O}\_\text{loc}$

- a *value* of this type has sort $\mathcal{O}$ and is used only as the index to a map or to compare object identity

- we introduce

    - the sorts $\mathcal{O}\_\text{F\_Map}$ from the trait $\text{Map}(\mathcal{O}\_\text{FMap}, \mathcal{O}, \mathcal{F})$. $\mathcal{O}\_\text{F\_Map}$ is the sort of the map-valued state component and $\mathcal{F}$ is the sort corresponding to type F

    - a constant $\mathcal{O}\_\text{f}$ of sort $\mathcal{O}\_\mathcal{F}$ to represent the value of the map in a state.

    - similarly for g

---

[3]Part of the motivation for this choice is the desire to use the LM3 language as the specification language within the Sparta project. Sparta involves research into the verification of Modula-3 programs. The "map"-based state allows efficient use of a theorem prover for the reasoning we intend to undertake.

In an LM3 specification, a user would write something that looks very similar to a Modula-3 field access even though the translation involves an application of a map. A claim to modify a field of an object is a shorthand for a claim to modify the map associated with that field, together with a restriction that the value of the map for all other keys is unchanged.

3.2 The state

In Section 2.1, we described the state as a mapping from locs to values. The components of the state are all entire variables. The previous section indicated that the domain of the state is a number of loc sorts based on the types involved. For simple types like INTEGER, the entire variable has sort Int_loc. For more complex entities, like OBJECT types, the state component is a collection of maps.

Formally, we model the state by a collection of functions σ, one for each _loc sort involved.

The types discussed in the previous section cause the following functions to be introduced in our generated trait:

- σ : Int_loc, State $\rightarrow$ Int

- σ : $\mathcal{E}$_loc, State $\rightarrow$ $\mathcal{E}$

- σ : $\mathcal{A}$_loc, State $\rightarrow$ $\mathcal{A}$

- σ : $\mathcal{O}$_$\mathcal{F}$, State $\rightarrow$ $\mathcal{O}$_F_Map

- σ : $\mathcal{O}$_$\mathcal{G}$, State $\rightarrow$ $\mathcal{O}$_G_Map

We introduce constants pre, post of sort State, representing the pre-state and the post-state respectively.

A reference to a variable, v, in the pre-state is therefore translated as $\sigma(\text{v}, \text{pre})$ and a reference to its value in the post-state, denoted in the specification as v', translates to $\sigma(\text{v}, \text{post})$.

3.3 The Modula-3 interface declaration

Any valid safe Modula-3 interface declaration is a valid LM3 specification, although one with very weak constraints. We must therefore attribute meaning to any Modula-3 construct that can be found in such a declaration.

3.3.1 Interface declaration

The declaration of the interface gives us the name of the interface and, by extension, the name for the trait we are generating. Since we want the sorts and operators we generate to be uniquely associated with the current interface, to facilitate inclusion in importing interfaces, we generally prefix all generated names with the name of the interface.

For INTERFACE Id;

- IdSem : **trait**

- *prefix* = Id

Generic interfaces are handled in precisely the same way, although less checking is possible, since we do not have full information about the types in the parameters and cannot find a sort with matching semantics. In practice, we translate and check the instantiations not the generic interface itself.

3.3.2 Import declaration

A Modula-3 Import allows declarations in the imported interface to be used in the importing interface. In LM3, we wish to have the same access to the components of the specification of the imported interface. We again take advantage of the LSL mechanisms and simply include the trait representing the semantics of the imported interface, remembering that our prefixing scheme makes renaming unnecessary.

For IMPORT I;

- **includes** ISem

For an **IMPORT FROM**, we extend the inclusion with a renaming that gives the imported item the name it would have if it were declared locally.

3.3.3 Constant declaration

A constant declaration defines a constant operation of the associated sort that is asserted to have the given value.

For, CONST Id [: T] = E

- **introduces**
  $prefix\_$Id $: \rightarrow T$

- **asserts equations**
  $prefix\_$Id $= e$
  (where T is the sort associated with T — or with the type of E if no type is explicitly given — and e is the translation of E)

The expression is translated into an LSL term that delivers an equivalent value of the sort corresponding to the type of E.

3.3.4 Type declaration

Type declarations introduce new sorts (and traits and constants) into the specification following the rules outlined in Section 3.1.

3.3.5 Exception declaration

Exception declarations introduce new constants of the sort Except. If the exception has an argument, the sort corresponding to the type of the argument will be used as the sort of RAISEARG (see Section 3.3.7) in a procedure that may raise this exception.

LM3 defines CHECKEDRTE of sort Except to represent a checked runtime error.

For EXCEPTION Id (T);

- **introduces** $prefix\_$Id $: \rightarrow$ Except

3.3.6　Variable declaration

Interface level variable declarations extend the global state, i.e. introduce new values of loc sorts corresponding to the types of the variables.

For VAR Id :　T;

- **introduces** $prefix\_Id$: $\rightarrow T\_loc$

We must also ensure that the sort for T is properly defined by including the traits associated with it, if it is not a Modula-3 base type or a type named in a type declaration, and by defining σ (Id, s).

3.3.7　Procedure declaration

A procedure declaration defines the local state for its specification and introduces a constant of sort Proc. Each item in the parameter list introduces a constant, if it is a value, or else a new local state component. In addition, if the procedure has a result type, we introduce a state component RESULT to represent that unnamed value. If the procedure may raise any exceptions, we introduce a state component RAISEVAL to represent the exception. If the exception has an argument, we introduce RAISEARG of the sort corresponding to the type of the exception argument. Since these latter components only have meaning in the post-state, we adopt the convention of always expanding their use in this state and do not require the explicit prime, e.g. RESULT always expands to σRESULT, post. CURRENT is a state component of sort Thread_loc that represents the invoking thread of a procedure.

As with the global state, we decorate operators with a prefix given by the procedure name to ensure uniqueness.

For PROCEDURE Id (a:　T, ...):　RT RAISES Raise

- **introduces**
  $prefix\_Id$: $\rightarrow$ Proc
  $prefix\_procPrefix\_a$: $\rightarrow T$
  $\ldots$
  $prefix\_\ procPrefix\_RESULT$: $\rightarrow \mathcal{RT}$
  $procPrefix\_RAISE$: $\rightarrow$ Except_loc
  $prefix\_procPrefix\_CURRENT$: $\rightarrow$ Thread_loc

3.3.8　Method declaration

Method declarations are exactly the same as procedure declarations except that we must generate one extra state component corresponding to the current value of the object (the implicit parameter in Modula-3 method declarations) that has sort corresponding to the object type. This is referred to as SELF in the specification.

For METHOD Id ... of an object type O, we do exactly as for PROCEDURE Id ... plus

- **introduces** $prefix\_procPrefix\_SELF$: $\rightarrow \mathcal{O}$

3.3.9 Revelation

A revelation adds further detail to a previously opaque type declaration. We translate the fully expanded declaration following the rules given previously for type declarations.

This completes the description of the Modula-3 part of LM3.

3.4 LM3 specification annotations

The other components of an LM3 specification are annotations giving the specification specific information. The use of the Modula-3 declarations discussed in Section 3.3 provide the basic elements for use in a specification, the annotations define the constraints on these elements.

3.4.1 Traits

LM3 uses LSL implicitly to define operators for the elements of its type system. The TRAITS declaration allows explicit reference to named traits to include their operators and sorts in the scope of the current specification. The semantics of this construct are the same as the LSL **include** except that we allow a Modula-3 type name to be given as a target in a renaming. The sort associated with the type is substituted in the translation.

For <* TRAITS Id (T FOR S) *>

- **includes** Id ($\mathcal{T}$ **for** S)
  where $\mathcal{T}$ is the sort associated with T, if T is a type, or T otherwise

3.4.2 Invariant

An invariant may take one of two forms:

1. an invariant on the entire interface — in this case the predicate must be conjoined to the pre-condition and post-condition of every procedure in the interface;

2. a type invariant — in this case the predicate must be conjoined to the pre-condition of any procedure that accesses an element of the type and to the post-condition of any procedure that may modify an element of the type. In this case, we also introduce a new variable bound to the sort of the type. This variable is instantiated to be the variable of the type that is in scope for each procedure the invariant is conjoined to.

In the invariant predicate, all state dependent accesses to a variable, say x are left undecorated and are instantiated to $\sigma(x, pre)$ when the invariant is conjoined to a pre-condition and $\sigma(x, post)$ when the invariant is conjoined to a post-condition.

For <* INVARIANT P *>

- conjoin P to the pre-condition and the post-condition of all procedures in the interface, instantiating variables in the appropriate state in each case.

For <* INVARIANT t: T P *>

- conjoin P to the pre-condition and the post-condition of all procedures in the interface that reference a T, replacing t with the local variable of type T.

3.4.3 Specification variable declaration

Specification variables are analogous to interface variables in the Modula-3 declarations. They may be given a Modula-3 type or associated with a sort directly or given a sort by using the shorthand construct described in Section 3.4.8. Semantically, a specification variable declaration introduces a new state component into the scope.

For <* VAR Id : T *>

- **introduces** prefix_Id : $\rightarrow \mathcal{T}$_loc
  where $\mathcal{T}$ is the sort directly or indirectly associated with T.

3.4.4 Specification field declaration

Specification fields have the same analogy to object field declaration that specification variables do to variable declarations. The effect of a specification field declaration on an object type is the same as if the field had been declared as part of the object, except that it may be associated with a sort directly and it is in scope only in the specification.

For <* FIELDS OF O sf: T *>

- the sorts $\mathcal{O}$_T_Map from the trait Map($\mathcal{O}$_T_Map, $\mathcal{O}$, $\mathcal{T}$) where $\mathcal{O}$_TMap is the sort of the map-valued state component and $\mathcal{T}$ is the sort corresponding to type T

- a constant $\mathcal{O}$_sf of sort $\mathcal{O}$_T to represent the value of the map in the state.

3.4.5 Procedure/Method specification

A procedure or a method is specified in terms of a predicate on the pre-state and the post-state of a call. To aid readability, LM3 provides a number of syntactic conveniences to construct this predicate.

The essential features[4] of a procedure or method specification are:

a precondition which gives a predicate that constrains the pre-state, introduced by REQUIRES;

a modifies list which indicates the state components that may be changed, introduced by MODIFIES;

a postcondition which in LM3 is split into three parts:

    1. the normal post-condition introduced by ENSURES;

---

[4] In LM3 there may be a number of other components in a procedure specification, indicating the parts of the global state a procedure specification refers to, allowing local shorthands to be introduced and allowing the state at the beginning of execution to be separated from the state at call in the presence of concurrent action by the environment. The translation of these features does not illustrate anything new, so they are elided here.

2. the guarded exception conditions indicated by EXCEPT;

3. the unguarded exceptions indicated by UNLESS.

For a specification of the form:

```
<* PROCEDURE P(x)
   REQUIRES R
   MODIFIES x
   ENSURES N
    EXCEPT G => E
    UNLESS U *>
```

we assert a predicate of the form:

$$R \Rightarrow isMod(x) \wedge ((\neg G \wedge N) \vee (g \wedge E) \vee U)$$

where each component of this predicate is generated from the equivalent component of the specification. Any procedure or method that does not have an explicit specification is given a weak default specification:

```
<* REQUIRES true
   MODIFIES ANY
   ENSURES true *>
```

LM3 also allows the specification of non-atomic procedures as sequences of atomic actions. Each action is translated as an atomic procedure. The translation of the composition is not discussed further in this paper, see the LM3 Reference Manual[7] for the full detail.

3.4.6 Method strengthening

The specifications of super-type methods are inherited by the corresponding methods in sub-types. It is often desirable to strengthen this specification with respect to the current type. The STRENGTHEN declaration allows this to be done succinctly.

For $<*$ STRENGTHEN T.m P $*>$, we generate a translation of the inherited specification of T.m, instantiated in the current scope and conjoined with the translation of P.

3.4.7 Predicates

Predicates are terms based on LSL operators. These operators need no translation. The other components of predicates are the LM3 forms allowing access to Modula-3 constructs. These are translated according to the rules for their type. So, for the examples of type given in Section 3.1:

constant c translates to *prefix_c*

variable v translates to $\sigma(prefix\_v, \text{pre})$
        v' translates to $\sigma(prefix\_v, \text{post})$

enumeration T.foo translates to *prefix_T_foo*

array access v'[i] translates to $\sigma(\mathit{prefix\_v}, \text{post})[i]$

object field SELF.f' translates to $\sigma(\mathcal{O}\_f, \text{post})[\text{SELF}]$

RME predicate The syntactic form used for a procedure specification may be used anywhere a predicate is allowed. It translates to the single predicate as defined above.

3.4.8 Shorthands

Shorthands provide a convenient way of generating sorts both for commonly used data structures and for allowing the use of Modula-3 types to specify a sort. In the following the translation rules are applied recursively if necessary.

SET OF S translates to the sort SetOf$\mathcal{S}$ which is produced by including the trait Set(SetOf$\mathcal{S}$ for C, $\mathcal{S}$ for E)

MAP D TO R translates to the sort Map$\mathcal{D}$To$\mathcal{R}$ produced by including the trait Map(Map$\mathcal{D}$To$\mathcal{R}$, $\mathcal{D}$, $\mathcal{R}$)

SEQUENCE OF S translates to the sort SequenceOf$\mathcal{S}$ produced by including the trait Sequence(SequenceOf$\mathcal{S}$ for C, $\mathcal{S}$ for E)

TYPE T translates to the sort corresponding to T.

3.4.9 Procedure types

The translation of LM3 specifications into first-order logic has one problem. Modula-3 has procedure types and, since procedures are characterised within specifications by predicates, the use of procedure types requires second order operations, namely those which return predicates as their results.

For a procedure type, we would like to define the following operators:

.REQUIRES which delivers the predicate giving the precondition of the procedure;

.MODIFIES which gives the predicate obtained from the modifies list of the procedure;

.ENSURES which gives the postcondition of the procedure;

.SPEC which gives the full predicate representing the procedure.

These cannot be expressed in LSL. If we are to use the mechanism we've discussed for giving the semantics to LM3 specifications, then we need to provide a "work-around" for this situation.

In most cases, we can simply avoid the problem. Usually, we have access to the procedure's specification at translation time and so can still translate into a first order logic by syntactically replacing the second order operator by the actual predicate from the procedure's specification during translation, even performing renaming if desired.

This leaves the problem of the use of procedure parameters. In this case, we do not have access to the text of the parameter's specification at translation time. This area is a topic of current research and we do not have a satisfactory solution yet.

The best solution would be to use a shared language based on a higher order logic. This is not currently considered feasible since it introduces a number of technical problems even ignoring the fact that our theorem proving tools are based on first-order logic.

Our current solution is to continue to use LSL and accept some severe restrictions on the reasoning we can do about specifications involving procedure parameters. We introduce the operators listed above, but as uninterpreted boolean functions. This allows a weak first order translation of a specification involving procedure parameters, one which contains no semantic information about them.

For TYPE P = PROCEDURE ..., we generate

- _.REQUIRES: Proc $\rightarrow$ Bool

- _.MODIFIES: Proc $\rightarrow$ Bool

- _.ENSURES: Proc $\rightarrow$ Bool

- _.SPEC: Proc $\rightarrow$ Bool

More encouragingly, we note that this restriction is not as onerous in practice as it may first appear. The restriction is only on reasoning we wish to do in the context of only the formal parameters. Any reasoning we wish to do about a call of the procedure can be done after syntactically instantiating the uninterpreted operators by the corresponding predicates of the actual parameters. Since we believe most interesting reasoning is done in the context of a call, we feel the trade-offs of this approach are still worthwhile.

4 Checking

One of the first tasks of any Larch interface language designer is certain to involve building a tool that performs the equivalent of type checking for the specification language.

The above translation process offers a way of getting a "low-ambition" checking tool very quickly. If one translates the specification into an LSL trait, then one can use the existing LSL checking tools to sort check this generated trait. This checking of the trait will reveal many of the errors that are likely to be present in the original interface specification.

For LM3, we have developed a tool that checks specifications in precisely this manner. The LM3 is parsed into an abstract syntax tree. This AST is walked by a program that implements the translation into LSL and an LSL trait is generated. This trait is checked using the LSL checker and the error messages are passed, after a little reverse translation, to the user. We expect to gradually move more and more of the checking into the LM3-specific tool to give stronger checking and better error reporting, but this is a useful way of both validating the semantics and getting a "quick-and-dirty" checker for LM3. It also permits specifiers to quickly generate LP input from the LM3 specification if they wish to do formal reasoning, using the existing LSL to LP translators.

In practice, to simplify the translation process and to fit within the currently existing LSL, we do not implement the full semantic translation. The following simplifications are made:

1. quantified predicates are translated by introducing a new constant representing the bound variable and the predicate without the quantification is translated in the scope of the new variable.

2. invariants are sort checked by instantiation in a single state and we do not implement their conjunction with procedure specifications.

3. modifies lists are checked only to ensure that the components are in scope and are of loc sorts. We do not generate the predicate requiring that the rest of the state remains unchanged, for the post-condition.

4. procedure parameters are translated as uninterpreted predicates even in the case where the specification is in scope at translation time.

Even with these limitations, this tool still provides useful feedback when writing LM3 specifications and indicates the feasibility of the approach.

As an example, the simplest interface taken from the LM3 example in the Larch Book[2] is

```
INTERFACE EmployeeData;
  CONST MaxSal = 1000000;
  TYPE
    Gender = {Male, Female};
    Job = {NonMgr, Manager};
    Salary = [1 .. MaxSal];
    SSnum = INTEGER;
END EmployeeData.
```

This translates to the trait shown in Figure 1, illustrating the semantic interpretation of a Modula-3 interface declaration as an LM3 specification..

5 Conclusions

We have shown how an interface specification language can be given a formal semantics via a translation into typed predicate calculus. This task can be simplified by taking advantage of the existing semantics of the LSL. We have illustrated this method by showing the translation process for LM3.

Further, we have shown that an implementation of this process can provide a simple "type checker" for the interface language by taking advantage of the existing tools for LSL.

Since LM3 is at least as complex as any other currently existing interface language, we believe that this method is generally applicable to any Larch interface language and offers a good "standard" approach to giving a semantics to a Larch interface language.

6 Acknowledgements

Special thanks to Jim Horning for valuable comments on a draft of this paper. Many of the ideas described here came out of discussions with, joint work with or borrowing from a number of people. It is not reasonable to try to name them all individually but they are: the members of the Sparta project at SRC; the Larch group at MIT; the Larch-interested folk at CMU; the DECspec team at Digital; other attendees at the first Larch workshop. Some of these people provided ideas, some provided code, all helped. All mistakes are almost certainly my own.

References

[1] S.J. Garland and J.V. Guttag. " An Overview of LP, The Larch Prover", *Proceedings of the Third International Conference on Rewriting. Techniques and Applications*, Chapel Hill, N.C. *Lecture Notes in Computer Science* **355**, Springer-Verlag, 1989, 137–151.

[2] J .V. Guttag, J.J. Horning (eds.). **Larch: Languages and Tools for Formal Specification**. Springer-Verlag, 1993 (forthcoming)

[3] J.V. Guttag and J.J. Horning. *LCL: A Larch Interface Language for C.* Report 74, DEC Systems Research Center, Palo Alto, CA, Jul. 1991.

[4] J .V. Guttag, J.J. Horning, and Andrés Modet. *Report on the Larch Shared Language: Version 2.3.* Report 58, DEC Systems Research Center, Palo Alto, CA, Apr. 14, 1990.

[5] Samuel P. Harbison. **Modula-3**. Prentice Hall, 1992

[6] Kevin D. Jones. *LM3: A Larch Interface Language for Modula-3: Version 1.0.* Report 72, DEC Systems Research Center, Palo Alto, CA, Jun. 1991.

[7] Kevin D. Jones, *LM3 Reference Manual*, in preparation.

[8] Greg Nelson (ed.). **Systems Programming with Modula-3**. Prentice Hall, Englewood Cliffs, 1991.

[9] J.M. Wing. *A Two-Tiered Approach to Specifying Programs.* Technical Report MIT/LCS/TR-299, MIT, 1983. Ph.D. thesis, MIT EECS, May 1983.

[10] *A Larch Shared Language Handbook.* in [2]

EmployeeDataSem : **trait**

> **includes** *M3Integer*(*Int*)
> **includes** *M3FloatingPoint*(*Float*)
> **includes** *M3Character*(*Char*)
> **includes** *M3Text*(*Text*)
> **includes** *M3Mutex*(*Mutex*)

> *EmployeeData_Gender* **enumeration of** *Male*, *Female*
> *EmployeeData_Job* **enumeration of** *NonMgr*, *Manager*

> **introduces**
> $\quad$ *CHECKEDRTE* :$\rightarrow$ *Except*
> $\quad$ *RETURNS* :$\rightarrow$ *Except*
> $\quad$ *PRE* :$\rightarrow$ *State*
> $\quad$ *POST* :$\rightarrow$ *State*
> $\quad$ *sigma* : *Except_loc*, *State* $\rightarrow$ *Except*
> $\quad$ *sigma* : *Bool_loc*, *State* $\rightarrow$ *Bool*
> $\quad$ *sigma* : *Int_loc*, *State* $\rightarrow$ *Int*
> $\quad$ *sigma* : *Float_loc*, *State* $\rightarrow$ *Float*
> $\quad$ *sigma* : *Char_loc*, *State* $\rightarrow$ *Char*
> $\quad$ *sigma* : *Text_loc*, *State* $\rightarrow$ *Text*
> $\quad$ *sigma* : *Mutex_loc*, *State* $\rightarrow$ *Mutex*
> $\quad$ *sigma* : *Thread_loc*, *State* $\rightarrow$ *Thread*
> $\quad$ *EmployeeData_MaxSal* :$\rightarrow$ *Int*
> $\quad$ *sigma* : *EmployeeData_Gender_loc*, *State* $\rightarrow$ *EmployeeData_Gender*
> $\quad$ *isMod* : *EmployeeData_Gender_loc* $\rightarrow$ *Bool*
> $\quad$ *fresh* : *EmployeeData_Gender_loc* $\rightarrow$ *Bool*
> $\quad$ *unchanged* : *EmployeeData_Gender_loc* $\rightarrow$ *Bool*
> $\quad$ *sigma* : *EmployeeData_Job_loc*, *State* $\rightarrow$ *EmployeeData_Job*
> $\quad$ *isMod* : *EmployeeData_Job_loc* $\rightarrow$ *Bool*
> $\quad$ *fresh* : *EmployeeData_Job_loc* $\rightarrow$ *Bool*
> $\quad$ *unchanged* : *EmployeeData_Job_loc* $\rightarrow$ *Bool*
> $\quad$ *sigma* : *Int_loc*, *State* $\rightarrow$ *Int*
> $\quad$ *isMod* : *Int_loc* $\rightarrow$ *Bool*
> $\quad$ *fresh* : *Int_loc* $\rightarrow$ *Bool*
> $\quad$ *unchanged* : *Int_loc* $\rightarrow$ *Bool*
> $\quad$ *sigma* : *Int_loc*, *State* $\rightarrow$ *Int*
> $\quad$ *isMod* : *Int_loc* $\rightarrow$ *Bool*
> $\quad$ *fresh* : *Int_loc* $\rightarrow$ *Bool*
> $\quad$ *unchanged* : *Int_loc* $\rightarrow$ *Bool*

> **asserts equations**
> $\quad$ *EmployeeData_MaxSal* $= 1000000$

Figure 1: EmployeeDataSem.lsl

Preliminary Design of Larch/C++

Gary T. Leavens*
Department of Computer Science, 229 Atanasoff Hall
Iowa State University, Ames, Iowa 50011-1040 USA
leavens@cs.iastate.edu

Yoonsik Cheon
Department of Computer Science, 226 Atanasoff Hall
Iowa State University, Ames, Iowa 50011-1040 USA
cheon@cs.iastate.edu

Abstract

We describe the problems encountered in the design of Larch/C++, especially its object-oriented features. We discuss a range of possible solutions to these problems, and give the rationale for our particular solutions. We also present examples of Larch/C++ specifications and discuss differences from Larch/C.

1 Introduction

A pre-condition for reading this paper is that you understand the basics of object-oriented programming (see [Cox86] otherwise), have some familiarity with C or C++ [Str91], and have a good understanding of model-oriented interface specifications using Larch [GHW85]. The post-condition of this paper is that you should understand the rationale for our design of Larch/C++.

1.1 Challenges of C++

The programming language C++ [ES90] [Str91] is an object-oriented extension to C. Although it is difficult to find hard data about language usage, anecdotal evidence, such as the amount of junk mail concerning C++, makes it clear that in the US C++ is the most widely used object-oriented language. Wide use of C++ in industry and growing use in academia is the motivation for the Larch/C++ design.

C++ offers some interesting challenges for interface language design. The major challenge is the size and complexity of the language. One reason for this complexity is the desire to support old C programs, but the main reason is concern for run-time efficiency. Because of this concern for efficiency, C++ is not a "pure" object-oriented language, but a hybrid language. For example, C++ has both static and dynamic overloading (i.e., message passing), as well

---

*This work was supported in part by the National Science Foundation under Grant CCR-9108654.

as values that are not objects in the sense that they cannot be sent messages. Objects in C++ can either by dynamically allocated on the heap or can be allocated on the run-time stack.

Another complexity in C++ is related to inheritance. C++ allows one to declare inheritance relationships as either public, private, or protected. Public inheritance relationships are used by the C++ type system to allow subtype polymorphism; that is, if `BorderedWindow` is a public subclass[1] of `Window`, then a pointer to a `BorderedWindow` object may be assigned to a variable of type `Window*` (i.e., a variable of type "pointer to `Window`") or passed as an actual argument to a procedure that expects an argument of type `Window*`. Similar remarks hold when `Window*` is replaced by `Window&` — a reference instead of a pointer type. Declaring a private or protected inheritance relationship does not permit such subtying. Similarly, members of a class (instance variables and methods) can be declared as public, protected, or private. Public members are available to clients, protected members are only available to subclasses, and private members are hidden from both clients and subclasses. Since C++ can describe two interfaces for each class, one for clients and one for subclasses, Larch/C++ must also be able to specify these two interfaces.

The desire to support old C programs in C++ gives the interface language designer two additional challenges: whether to support old style C interfaces, and compatibility with Larch/C interface specifications. We have chosen to make LarchC++ compatible with Larch/C whenever possible. We have not worried about supporting old style C interfaces, since Larch/C++ also ignores them.

1.2 Goals

Our overall goal for Larch/C++ is to have Larch/C++ in use in academia and industry in the next several years. Thus we aim to make Larch/C++ a practical language, not just an academic curiosity. To this end, our more specific goals for Larch/C++ are as follows.

- To have a syntax that is intuitive for C++ programmers. That is, the syntax used to specify interfaces should match that of C++ declarations in detail and in spirit.

- To aid the specification of modules that use common C++ idioms. For example, one should be able to specify modules that use subtype polymorphism and message passing (virtual functions). Also one should be able to specify modules that use mutation and aliasing, modules that use either references or pointers, and classes that use different kinds of inheritance.

- To promote inheritance of specifications. That is, one should be able to specify a class's interface by stating how it differs from another class's interface. Because of this goal, automated support for browsing class interface specifications and their relationships is needed.

---

[1] In the C++ jargon, a subclass is called a derived class, and a superclass is called a base class. However, we will use the more familiar terms subclass and superclass in this paper.

- To allow the specification of two interfaces for each class: an interface for clients and an interface for subclasses.

- To have no unmotivated differences from Larch/C. This applies both to language details, such as syntax and semantics, and to programming environment issues.

The above goals are directed at making Larch/C++ practical. In addition, we have some other goals which should help make Larch/C++ useful, but which are motivated by a particular view of object-oriented programming [Ame87] [Mey88] [LW90] [Lea90] [Lea91]. This view centers around *supertype abstraction*, which is the ability to reason about a program based on nominal (i.e., static) type information by letting supertypes stand for all their subtypes. Informally, a *subtype* is an abstract data type such that each object of the subtype acts like some object of its supertypes. The idea is that one reasons about a program while thinking of these hypothetical supertype objects, and thereby abstracts away the details of the exact specifications of the subtype objects. This view of object-oriented programming leads us to the following additional goals.

- To help designers use supertype abstraction in the sense that when subtypes of existing types are specified, already specified types and functions do not need to be respecified.

- To be able to specify properties needed for the modular verification of C++ programs (so that when new modules are added to a program, unchanged modules should not have to be reverified). For example, one must be able to specify enough information about the relationships between subtypes and supertypes so that one can verify programs using static type information [LW90]. Another example: one must be able to verify a subclass using the specification of the public and protected interfaces of its superclasses, independent of the implementation of the superclasses.

1.3   Related Work

The most closely related work are other interface specification languages in the Larch family [Win83] [Win87] [Che89] [Win90] [GMP90] [Jon91] [GH91] [Che91]. The greatest influence has been from Larch/C and Larch/Smalltalk. From Larch/C we have adopted much syntax and the basic semantics of such common types as pointers. From Larch/Smalltalk we have taken much of the approach to inheritance and subtyping. Larch/C, however, does not deal with the object-oriented parts of C++. Larch/Smalltalk has a completely different syntax, and does not deal with the different kinds of inheritance possible in C++.

Outside the Larch family, Meyer's work on the programming language Eiffel has advanced the cause of applying formal methods to object-oriented programs [Mey88]. In Eiffel, one can specify pre- and post-conditions for operations of abstract data types using boolean expressions written in Eiffel. That is, unlike a Larch-style interface specification language, program expressions are used in pre- and post-conditions. In post-conditions one can also refer to the old value of an instance variable, **v**, with the expression "**old v**". Assertions can also be written using operations that are not implemented, called deferred operations; such assertions constrain the implementation of the deferred operations when they are implemented in a subclass in much the same way that the operations of an equational-algebraic specification mutually constrain each other. This leads to a style of specification that is more terse than a typical model-based specification language, because the users do not have to specify both a trait (the abstract model) and an interface. However, there are several technical problems with Eiffel's specification sublanguage.

1. There is no way to express universally or existentially quantified assertions.

2. One is sometimes forced to export more operations than one would like in order to specify some types. For example, to specify a statistical database with instance operations **insert**, **mean**, and **variance**, one would also need to export operations that enumerate the elements to state the post-condition of **insert**.[2] However, a designer may wish to hide such operations for other reasons.

3. The meaning of an assertion is unclear if the operations involved fail to terminate normally or use non-portable parts of the language.

A refinement of the Eiffel specification language is found in the specification language Annotated C++, or A++ [CL90]. Assertions in A++ may use universal and existential quantification, and hence are not generally executable, although they are still expressed using the expressions of C++. A difference from Eiffel is that the assertions must be expressed in a pure subset of C++, which makes them more amenable to formal manipulation. Furthermore, besides pre- and post-conditions for operations, in A++ one can give pre- and post-conditions for blocks of C++ code, which allows one to specify that if **s** is a pointer to a stack object, then the two statements

```
s->push(x); s->pop();
```

do not change the object to which **s** points. While A++ is more expressive than Eiffel's specification sublanguage, it still suffers from all but the first of the problems with Eiffel's specification language described above.

The specification languages Larch/Smalltalk, Larch/Modula-3 (LM3), and Larch/C++ are object-oriented in the sense that they specify program modules for object-oriented programming languages.

A different sense of object-oriented specification language is one which is not tailored to specifying the interfaces of programs written in a particular programming language, but one that uses ideas from object-oriented programming to aid in writing specifications. For example, the specification language Object-Z [CDD+89] [DD90] [Cus91] extends the specification language Z with inheritance of specifications. Larch/Smalltalk, LM3, and Larch/C++ also use inheritance of specifications to define subtypes.

---

[2]Suppose such operations were hidden. Then how would a client understand the specification of **insert**? That is, a client cannot test whether **insert** satisfies its specification, because it cannot call **insert** and evaluate its post-condition.

1.4 Outline

In the rest of this paper we discuss some specific problems we have faced in the design of Larch/C++, describe future work, and end with discussion and conclusions.

2 Specific Problems and Solutions

As of summer 1992 we have confronted three kinds of problems in designing Larch/C++: how much to make Larch/C++ look like C++, what to do about subtypes and inheritance, and what, if any, style of C++ programming to favor.

2.1 Integration and Connection with C++

Many of our problems in integrating Larch/C++ with C++ notations were solved by taking ideas from Larch/C. For example, we have adopted without change the distinction between basic values and locs (locations) made in section 2.3 of [GH91]. Basic values, called *abstract values* below, are the abstraction of an object's state used in specifications [Hoa72]. Abstract values are specified by traits written in the Larch Shared Language. Locations are abstractions of computer memory cells. In Larch/C++ locations are thought of as containers for abstract values.

We have also adopted the Larch/C distinction between pointers and arrays, the idea that an array a has an upper bound maxIndex(a), and the idea that a pointer p contains both an upper and lower bound for the contiguous locations to which it can point.

There is one horrible incompatibility between Larch/C and C that is inherited by the current version of Larch/C++. The equals sign (=), means assignment in C and C++, but means equality in Larch/C and Larch/C++ specifications, whereas == in C++ means equality and is used in the Larch Shared Language to separate sides of an equation [GHM90]. Since a common bug in C and C++ programs is using the wrong symbol, it may be wise to use == for equality in assertions in Larch/C++ specifications. For the time being we are following Larch/C and using = for equality in assertions. (If only we could change C and C++ instead!)

2.1.1 Const

In C++ the keyword **const** can be used to declare that the contents of a location should not be changed. A **const** qualifier can also be used to state that a pointer variable cannot be changed, or that the location pointed to by a pointer cannot be changed, or both. For example, the C++ declaration

```
bool stripes(const zebra * z1, zebra * const z2);
```

says that the object pointed at by z1 cannot be changed, and the pointer z2 cannot be changed. The first of these is useful to the caller, but because C++ uses call by value, the second only constrains the implementation. That is, the caller should not care whether the implementation of **stripes** is able to assign to its local variable z2, although the caller does care whether the object pointed to by z1 can be changed. C++ distinguishes the interface

```
bool stripes(const zebra * z1, zebra * z2);
```

from the one given above, but we want to investigate a semantics for Larch/C++ that would allow the first interface for **stripes** to be an implementation of a specification that used the second.

In C++ an operation (member function) of a class can be declared to be **const**, meaning that the member function cannot change the bits of the object of which it is a member. (However, this protection is not absolute [ES90].) Since such declarations are enforced by C++, we had the idea of replacing the typical Larch **modifies** clause in a function specification with the use of **const**. Since the same mechanism is available in ANSI C, the designers of Larch/C also had the same thought.

However, there is a difference between changing the bits in an object's representation and changing the object's abstract value. More precisely, if the bits do not change, then the abstract value does not change, but the converse is not true. A classic example is a rational number object, where one may want to reduce the representation of numerator and denominator to lowest common terms, without changing the object's abstract value.

Even recognizing the distinction between changing bits and abstract values, one could try to use **const** to eliminate redundancy in specifications. The idea would be that the **modifies** clause could be omitted if it could be unambiguously reconstructed from the declarations of the formal parameters. For example, consider the following function specification.

```
void foo(blob x, const zebra y) {
    ensures P(x,y);
}
```

The idea would be that the default **modifies** clause would be **modifies x**, meaning that **y** cannot be changed, nor can any other global object. However, this default would not be what is intended for examples like reducing a rational number to lowest terms; in such an example, the arguments cannot be declared as const, but the intended modifies clause is **modifies nothing**. So like the designers of Larch/C, we decided to follow the Larch tradition of making the default for an omitted modifies clause be **modifies nothing**.

To achieve the effect of the rejected alternative, the user must write:

```
void foo(blob x, const zebra y) {
    modifies x;
    ensures P(x,y);
}
```

At least here the redundancy buys something, because it highlights what is being changed. This is especially welcome for the implicit argument to the operations of a class.

2.1.2 Variations on Formal Arguments

In C all arguments are passed by value, although one can pass a pointer and the value of an array is a pointer to its first location. C++ also has call by reference. For example, if **swap** is specified as follows,

```
void swap(int& i, int& j) {
    modifies i, j;
    ensures (i' = j^) /\ (j' = i^);
}
```

then one may make the call **swap(a,b)**, where **a** and **b** are **int** variables.

What kind of thing is **i** in the above specification? We take the position that it denotes a location, not an abstract value. Thus to get an abstract value from **i** one must use the notation **i'**, which means the abstract value of **i** in the post-state (the state after the function returns). The notation **i^** means the abstract value of **i** in the pre-state (the state before the function is invoked).

We plan to adopt defaults for the ' and ^ annotations. As in LM3, the convention will be that in pre- and post-conditions an unannotated variable of an appropriate type is implicitly annotated with ^. However, as we have not yet implemented this syntactic sugar, in this paper we use ' and ^ as needed.

2.1.3 Default Arguments

C++ permits the declaration of a function to specify defaults for actual arguments to a function. Certainly such information needs to be part of the specification of a function. One might argue that default arguments should be specified using the full range of C++ expression, as this would allow the specifications that use default arguments to express the full range of declarations allowed in C++ programs. However, the C++ grammar for expressions is sufficiently complex that this would cause significant complications to the Larch/C++ grammar, and there is no other place in Larch/C++ where the full range of C++ expressions is needed. Instead we decided to limit what can be written as a default argument to terms of the Larch Shared Language. Since these terms already include the C++ literals for integers, floating point numbers, characters, and strings, our decision will only be a disadvantage for default arguments of more complex types. But one can write operators in the Larch Shared Language to describe the abstract values of more complex C++ expressions.

2.1.4 Classes

In Larch/C++, class interface specifications replace the abstract data type specifications of Larch/C. An example of a Larch/C++ class interface specification is given in Figure 1. The implementation must be a class template, **SymbolTable**, with two type parameters **Key** and **Value**. (These type parameters do not have to be classes; **<class T>** is just the C++ syntax for declaring **T** as a type parameter in a template.)

The notation following **uses** says that the abstract model used to specify symbol tables is given by the trait **SymbolTableTrait**. (That trait is presented in Figure 2 using the syntactic conventions of the Larch Shared Language checker as tailored for Larch/C.) Following the trait name in the uses clause is a parenthesized list that gives the type to sort mapping used in the specification. The type to sort mapping associates to each type name in the interface a sort name. Unlike Larch/C, the uses clause does not allow arbitrary renamings—in Larch/C++ such renamings must be handled by traits. This

```
template <class Key, class Value>
class SymbolTable {

    uses SymbolTableTrait (SymbolTable for ST, Key for S,
                           Value for T);

    public:
     // a constructor    ... and this line is a comment
      SymbolTable() {
         modifies self;
         ensures self' \eq empty;
      }

      // a destructor
      ~SymbolTable() {
         modifies self;
         ensures trashed(self);
      }

      void add(const Key k, const Value v) {
         requires not(v^ \in self^);
         modifies self;
         ensures self' \eq add(self^, k^, v^);
      }

      bool includes(const Key k) const {
         ensures result = include(self^, k^);
      }

      Value retrieve(const Key k) const {
         requires include(self^, k^);
         ensures result = retrieve(self^, k^);
      }
};
```

Figure 1: Specification of a symbol table class.

changes allows the type to sort mapping to be more easily extracted from an interface specification.

A class interface specification, like a class declaration in C++, can specify the access that clients and subclasses are allowed to various parts of the implementation. In Figure 1, the line **public:** specifies that all the lines that follow it are to be implemented as public members. One can also write **protected:**, which says that the following member specifications (down to the next such access specifier) are only visible to subclasses. In this way one can specify interfaces for both clients and subclasses. While obvious, this way of specifying interfaces for subclasses is not entirely satisfactory. The (protected)

```
SymbolTableTrait (S, T, ST): trait
  introduces
    empty: -> ST
    add: ST, S, T -> ST
    retrieve: ST, S -> T
    include: ST, S -> Bool
    __ \eq __: ST, ST -> Bool
  asserts
    forall st, st1: ST, s, s1: S, t: T
      ~include(empty, s);
      include(add(st, s, t), s1) == s = s1 \/ include(st, s1);
      retrieve(add(st, s, t), s1) ==
          if s = s1 then t else retrieve(st, s);
      (st \eq st1) == (st = st1);
```

Figure 2: A trait for symbol tables, in LSL.

interface for subclasses should be a property of a particular implementation of
the (public) class specification, and different implementations should be able to
specify different interfaces for subclasses while sharing the same public interface. Therefore it might be better, if more complex, to allow a more thorough
separation of the specification of these interfaces.

We have debated about whether to allow the specification of private members of a class. Of course, private parts of a class are solely the domain of
an implementation, and are of no interest to clients. However, we would also
like to support the same kind of automatic generation of "include files" that
is done in Larch/C. In Larch/C, the .lcl file is used to generate a .lh file,
which is included in the normal header (.h) file. In the normal header file,
the user can add other implementation specific details. This scheme cannot
work for Larch/C++, because the private part of a class definition must be in
the header included by clients and the private part must be defined lexically
within the class definition. One alternative is to have another file, the .pri
file, to define the private parts of a class, and to have the .lh file automatically
include it, which would then be included in the .h file. But since such a scheme
is unwieldly, we are exploring the ramifications of letting users specify private
parts.

Returning to Figure 1, the next line following public: is a comment, as
all the characters on the line after // are ignored. Following the comment is
the specification of a constructor for the SymbolTable type. In C++ the call of
a constructor determines whether the newly created object is allocated on the
heap or on the run-time stack. The only job of a constructor is to initialize the
state of the newly created object, which in the specification is referred to as
self. (This is similar to the way empset is initialized in [GH91, Section 3.3].)
The specification of this constructor says that in the post-state the abstract
value of the constructed object should be an empty symbol table.

The special specification variable self is an abbreviation for *this. This
abbreviation is useful because one would otherwise have to write (*this)' to

refer to the post-state of the receiving object, which is error prone because of the ambiguity in (a human reader's) parsing of *this' as (*this)' or *(this'). Wing's paper on Avalon/C++ [Win90] uses this as if it were a location containing the abstract value of the object receiving a message, but in C++ this is a pointer to that location, not the location itself. We thought it would be too confusing to have the type of this be different in C++ and in Larch/C++, so instead we use self to abbreviate *this.

Following the constructor in Figure 1 is the specification of a destructor ~SymbolTable. A destructor is called by a C++ statement of the form delete st, where st is an object of type SymbolTable. The job of a destructor is to deallocate any component objects stored in the instance variables (data members) of the object. But since clients have no knowledge of any component objects, it seems impossible to talk about them in the specification. Certainly delete st changes the abstract value of st, and the modifies clause modifies self says that. The ensures clause says that the object itself is "trashed", so that any further access to it will be an error; the notation trashed is borrowed from Larch/C. The intention is that this should also mean that the implementation should also deallocate component objects, but how to say that formally is problematic.

The other specifications of member functions in Figure 1 are fairly standard. For example, an implementation of add must be such that if st is a symbol table such that the abstract value of val is not in the mapping defined by the abstract value of st, then the call st.add(ky, val) terminates normally, modifies nothing but the state of st, and changes the state of st by associating ky to val.

As in Larch/C, result denotes the formal result parameter for a function. (To be precise, result denotes the abstract value returned, not a location containing the abstract value.) An example is in the specification of includes in Figure 1. The use of const just before the { in the specification of includes means that the implementation is not allowed to change the bits in the representation of the object st in a call such as st.includes(ky). An omitted modifies clause means the same as modifies nothing, but that only prohibits the abstract value of st from changing. As usual, an omitted requires clause stands for requires true.

2.2 Subtypes and Subclasses

The features that most distinguish object-oriented programming languages from languages that only support data abstraction (such as CLU and Ada) are inheritance and message passing. The inheritance mechanism of C++ is in many ways more complex than that of Smalltalk and Modula-3. Since message passing causes special difficulties in program verification it is worth taking extra trouble in specification if that will make the job of verification easier. One way to make such verification easier is by the use of legal subtype relationships [LW90] [Lea90] [Lea91].

2.2.1 Distinguish Subtypes and Subclasses?

In software engineering it is important to distinguish between the notions of type and class and the relationships of subtype and subclass. A type (i.e., an abstract data type) is a behavioral notion, and may be implemented by many different classes. A class is a program module that implements an abstract data type. Similarly, a subtype is an abstract data type, each of whose objects behave in a way that is similar to some objects of its supertypes. A subclass is an implementation that is derived by inheritance from its superclasses. A subtype relationship is a behavioral relationship, which could be proven by examining the specifications of the types involved, while a subclass relationship is a purely implementation relationship. In Larch/Smalltalk we were able to completely separate these two notions [Che91], since Smalltalk-80 has no static type system.

Unfortunately, the C++ type system does not distinguish completely between subtypes and subclasses. For type checking each class name is the name of a type; furthermore, the only way to tell the type system that S is to be a subtype of T is to declare the class S as a public subclass of T. One can have purely implementation relationships between classes by declaring that C2 is a private or protected subclass of C1, but one cannot have a subtype relationship without a subclass relationship.

So the question arises as to whether Larch/C++ should distinguish classes from types and subclasses from subtypes. In the end, we decided to make Larch/C++ match C++[3]. It would be pointless to artificially separate subtyping from subclassing in Larch/C++. Thus our syntax for class interface specifications uses the keyword **class** instead of **type**, and for declaring subtypes of a given type we use the C++ syntax for declaring public subclasses. Indeed, we also currently allow the declaration of protected and even private subclass relationships.

As an example of the specification of subtypes and subclasses, consider first Figure 3, which specifies a class **BankAccount**. This class will be the superclass of other classes to follow. It specifies objects that can be asked for their balance and to pay interest. The trait **BankAccountTrait** used in the specification of **BankAccount** is presented in Figure 4. The trait **Rational** which is included by **BankAccountTrait**, is found in the Larch Shared Language Handbook [GH86]. The two member functions are both specified as **virtual**, which means that the code executed in a call such as **ba->pay_interest()** will execute code determined by the dynamic class of the object pointed to by **ba**.

2.2.2 Abstract Classes

In Figure 3 the notation **abstract class** means that **BankAccount** should not be used to create objects.[4]

Since **BankAccount** is specified as an abstract class, the usual rule that all specified operations must be implemented is relaxed. For example, an implementation of **SymbolTable** must have definitions of all the specified operations that satisfy their specifications in the usual way. However, an implementation of **BankAccount**, while it must have a definition of **pay_interest**, may have a definition of the form:

---

[3] Although having written much about the importance of distinguishing subtyping from subclassing we debated not distinguishing them in Larch/C++ for a long while.

[4] Although the term "abstract class" is confusing, it seems firmly entrenched in the literature; furthermore, the next best alternative "virtual class" would be confusing when used with certain forms of inheritance in C++.

```
abstract class BankAccount {

    uses BankAcccuntTrait (BankAccount for Acct);

    public:
    virtual double balance() const {
        ensures approximates(result, balance(self^), (1/100));
    }

    virtual void pay_interest(const double rate) {
        requires (0/1) <= rate /\ rate <= (1/1);
        modifies self;
        ensures approximates(toDouble(balance(self')),
                             ((1/1) + rational(rate))
                                 \times balance(self^),
                             1/1);  // intentionally sloppy
    }
};
```

Figure 3: Specification of a bank account type.

```
BankAccountTrait (Acct): trait
  includes
    Rational
  introduces
    createAcct: Q -> Acct
    balance: Acct -> Q
  asserts
    forall q: Q
    balance(createAcct(q)) == q;
```

Figure 4: Trait for bank accounts.

```
virtual void pay_interest(const double rate) = 0;
```

In C++ jargon, such an implementation is called a *pure virtual function*. Although a pure virtual function is not usable, it serves as a place-holder for C++, and thus we allow a pure virtual functions as correct implementations of virtual function specifications in abstract classes. However, the catch is that any object of a non-abstract subclass of **BankAccount** must have a working member function **pay_interest** that satisfies the specification.

Currently there is no way that the Larch/C++ user can specify whether a particular function must or must not be implemented in subclasses. But while such information is important for subclasses, it seems too closely associated with a particular implementation of **BankAccount** to be included in the public interface. It more properly belongs in the protected interface specification, even if it is a property of the implementation of a public operation.

Even though one should not create objects of type **BankAccount**, the specification clearly defines the set of abstract values. In a specification language like A++ or Eiffel, one would have no way of describing **balance** without introducing additional operations.

2.2.3 Specifying the Abstract Values of a Subtype

Since **BankAccount** is specified as an abstract class, the main use for the specification is to constrain the implementation of subtypes. That is, we wish to have subtypes inherit the specification of the virtual functions. But what does the specification of **balance** or **pay_interest** mean when invoked on an object of a subtype? The assertions in the pre- and post-conditions of those operations are expressed in the language defined by the trait **BankAccountTrait**, and would be meaningless if **self^** and **self'** had some sort other than **Acct**.

We see two kinds of solutions to this problem:

- Bring the trait functions of the supertypes down to the subtype's abstract values, or

- Bring the values of the subtypes up to the supertypes.

Bringing the trait functions down means defining the meaning of each trait function that takes supertype arguments for subtype arguments. This allows the assertion to be interpreted by a kind of dynamic overloading of trait functions [Lea90] [Lea91]. One must specify a simulation relation that relates each abstract value of the supertype to one or more abstract values of the subtype in a way that is preserved by the trait functions; this ensures that the trait functions are redefined in the subtypes in a consistent way.

To bring the values of the subtype up one uses a coercion function (not a relation) that maps each subtype abstract value to a single supertype abstract value [BW90] [GM87] [Ame91] [Rey80]. This allows assertions to be interpreted by mapping all values to the nominal type of the variables used in the assertion. With this approach, assertions may use equality (=) freely for all types, but with the approach of bringing the trait functions down equality cannot be used in assertions between terms of visible type. The reason for this is easy to see if one imagines the "bringing the values up" approach with coercion relationships instead of functions; one would be hard-pressed to define the meaning of "x = y" when both x and y could denote sets of abstract values instead of single values. It is also clear that when the simulation relation is a function, the approach of bringing the trait functions down can simulate the approach of bringing the values up — by defining the trait functions of the subtype using the coercions.

As an example, we specify a subtype **SavingsAccount** by overloading the trait function **balance** in the trait **SavingsAccountTrait** (Figure 5). This is done in a stylized way by using the trait **CoercionTrait** (found in the same figure). The trait **SavingsAccountSubTrait** includes **BankAccountTrait** and uses the assumed coercion operation, **toAcct**, to define an overloading of the trait function **balance**. This ensures that the coercion function homomorphically maps **SavingsAccount** abstract values to **BankAccount** abstract values.

```
CoercionTrait (Sub, Super, coerce): trait
  introduces coerce: Sub -> Super

SavingsAccountSubTrait: trait
  assumes CoercionTrait(SA, Acct, toAcct)
  includes
    BankAccountTrait
  introduces
    balance: SA -> Q
  asserts
    forall sa: SA
    balance(sa) == balance(toAcct(sa));

SavingsAccountTrait: trait
  includes
    SavingsAccountSubTrait
  introduces
    savings: Q -> SA
    toAcct: SA -> Acct
  asserts
    forall q: Q, sa: SA
    toAcct(savings(q)) == createAcct(q);
```

Figure 5: The CoercionTrait and traits for savings accounts.

That **toAcct** commutes with the overloaded **balance** trait function, is important for verification of programs using supertype abstraction [Lea90] [Lea91]. Its importance is similar to Hoare's requirement that the abstraction map from the representation of a data abstraction to the abstract values, used to verify the correctness of an implementation of a data abstraction [Hoa72], commute with all the type's operations.

By including the **SavingsAccountSubTrait**, all that is left for the trait **SavingsAccountTrait** is to define a way to create abstract values of the sort **SA**, and the actual coercion function.

In this example of defining a trait for a subtype, **SavingsAccountSubTrait** is small. However, a trait like **SavingsAccountSubTrait** must define one trait function for each unary trait function in the supertype's trait that takes the supertype's sort as an argument, three trait functions for each binary trait function in the supertype's trait that takes the supertype's sort as an argument, and so on. Since defining so many overloaded trait functions quickly becomes tedious, we would like to augment the Larch Shared Language with some special syntax for defining such traits as **SavingsAccountTrait** without explicitly writing the **SavingsAccountSubTrait** with the overloaded trait functions.

The proposed short-hand notation for defining traits with coerced operations (from [LW]) is given in Figure 6. The idea is that the parameters of **CoercionTrait**, namely **toAcct**, **SA**, and **Acct** are described following the keywords **by**, **subsort**, and **Acct**. The meaning of the trait in Figure 6 should be

```
SavingsAccountTrait: trait
  subtrait of BankAccountTrait
    by toAcct subsort SA supersort Acct
  introduces
    savings: Q -> SA
    toAcct: SA -> Acct
  asserts
    forall q: Q, sa: SA
    toAcct(savings(q)) == createAcct(q);
```

Figure 6: Short-hand version for savings accounts.

exactly the same as in Figure 5. If a trait is specified as a subtrait of more than
one other trait, then it is possible to inherit conflicting definitions of the same
trait function; this problem would be solved by requiring the user to explicitly
define any such trait functions.

2.2.4 Syntactic and Semantic Constraints on Subtypes

The class interface specification **SavingsAccount** is given in Figure 7. In the
first line, after the colon (:), the words **public BankAccount** specify that
SavingsAccount is to be a public subclass of **BankAccount**, and hence a subtype of **BankAccount**. A correct implementation of **SavingsAccount** must also
be a public subclass of **BankAccount**.

Ideally the user of Larch/C++ should prove that the subtype relationship
is legal according to some accepted definition [Ame87] [Lea90] [Lea91] [Dha92].
However, it is undecidable whether an arbitrary claimed subtype relationship
is legal, and so for the time being Larch/C++ only requires that certain syntactic conditions be satisfied. First, the used trait must provide overloaded
trait functions that will accept arguments of the supertype's sort; the technical
statement of this condition is described in [Lea90]. Second, the interface must
satisfy the C++ type checker. Satisfying the C++ type checker is not what a
type theorist would expect [Car88]; according to Doug Lea[5], it is impossible
to change the type of the result or of any of the explicitly specified arguments
(i.e., other than **this**) of a member function.

The interface specified in Figure 7 also has an invariant clause. This invariant constrains the abstract values of sort **SA**, and thus restricts the abstract
values of **SavingsAccount** objects to have positive balances.

The members of **SavingsAccount** are specified using the trait function
approximates from the latest version of the Larch Shared Language Handbook trait for Floating Point numbers. The idea is that **approximates(res,
exact, slop)** is true if **res** is an approximation to **exact** within an interval
defined by **slop** and some characteristics of C++ double precision floating point
numbers. The trait function **rational** converts double precision floating point
numbers to rational numbers. The trait function **toDouble** converts rational

---

[5]Private communication.

```
class SavingsAccount : public BankAccount {

    uses SavingsAccountTrait (SavingsAccount for SA,
                              BankAccount for Acct);

    invariant forall sa:SA (balance(sa) > (0/1));

    public:
    // constructor
    SavingsAccount(const double initial_balance) {
        requires (1/100) <= rational(initial_balance);
        modifies self;
        ensures approximates(initial_balance, balance(self'),
                             1/100);
    }

    virtual void deposit(const double amt) {
        requires (0/1) <= rational(amt);
        modifies self;
        ensures approximates(toDouble(balance(self')),
                             rational(amt) + balance(self^),
                             1/100);
    }

    virtual void withdraw(const double amt) {
        requires 0.0 <= amt /\ rational(amt) <= balance(self^);
        modifies self;
        ensures approximates(toDouble(balance(self')),
                             rational(amt) - balance(self^),
                             1/100);
    }
};
```

Figure 7: Specification of a savings account type.

numbers to double precision floating point numbers. Traits for **double** and other built-in C++ types are automatically included by Larch/C++.

2.2.5 Inheritance of Specifications

The type **SavingsAccount** is specified as a subclass of **BankAccount**. Even if it were not specified as a public subclass, one might still wish to inherit specifications from **BankAccount**. The specifications inherited are those of the virtual member functions **balance** and **pay_interest**.

There are several possible ways to interpret what inheritance of specifications means for a class specification. It is not even clear what should be the goal of a semantics of inheritance for specifications. Possible goals include:

- Describing the interface of a class that implements the specification, and describing the effect of each defined message sent to objects of that type or its subtypes.

- Constructing a specification for a class that does not use specification inheritance, thus reducing the specification problem to an already solved problem. This is what is done in Object-Z [CDD+89] [DD90] [Cus91].

One way to satisfy the first goal above is to use overloading of the trait functions to interpret the specifications of **balance** and **pay_interest** sent to objects of type **SavingsAccount**. In this interpretation, for example, if **sav** is an object of type **SavingsAccount** with abstract value **sa**, then the abstract value of the C++ expression **sav.balance()**, call it **result**, must satisfy the post-condition of **balance**, with **sa** substituted for **self^**:

approximates(result, balance(sa), (1/100)).

Note however, that this kind of interpretation of function specifications is only sensible when the trait functions are overloaded as described above, and that such overloading may only be meaningful for subtypes, that is for public subclasses. If one wants to inherit specifications from private superclasses, this alternative is less attractive.

There are at least two ways to satisfy the second goal. The idea is to create a specification of the subclass that no longer needs inheritance by "copying" the specification of an inherited member function to the subclass specification. Of course, such a copy would be done by the semantics, instead of by the specifier. Since the specification of an inherited function is written using the traits of the supertype, there is a problem of how to interpret the copied specification. Two ways of interpreting the copying are as follows.

- To "close" the meaning of the specification by first obtaining its "meaning" relative to the traits used in the superclass specification, and then copying the "meaning." This resembles programming language parameter mechanisms such as call-by-name.

- To make a copy of the text of the specification, and then reinterpret the trait functions in the specification by the used traits of the subclass. This resembles call-by-text.

The call-by-name approach seems not to work, for reasons that we do not have space to go into here. The call-by-text interpretation seems to match the overloading interpretation of inheritance given above to satisfy the first goal. It also seems to suffer from the problem of only being well defined if the used trait in the subclass defines the proper trait functions. We are hoping that experience and theoretical investigation will help pick a good semantics for inheritance, or prove some of them equivalent.

None of the semantics advanced so far for inheritance of specifications resolves the conflicts that can arise when a function specification is inherited from more than one superclass. The alternatives for dealing with multiple specifications seem to be as follows.

- Force the user to give an explicit specification, overriding all the others.

- Pick one of the specifications that would be inherited. Ideally there would be one best or most specific specification, but it is easy to imagine situations where there is no one best specification.

- Combine the specifications in some manner. The obvious idea is to take the disjunction of the pre-conditions, the intersection of the modifies clauses, and the conjunction of all the post-conditions. Eiffel takes this approach.

It is not clear whether we will be able to follow Eiffel in taking the third approach until we have settled on a semantics for inheriting specifications when there are no conflicts. The idea of picking one specification is easily dismissed, and thus we are left, for the time being, with forcing the user to override the specification whenever there is a conflict.

2.2.6 Subtype Constraining Assertions

When specifying functions in a language with subtypes, one has to be careful in the use of equality. For example, consider the specification of a member function **choose** in a class template **Set** with type parameter **aType**. Suppose that this function were specified as follows.

```
virtual aType choose() const {
    requires not(self^ = emptySet);
    ensures  result \in self^;
}
```

Suppose this specification of **choose** is inherited by **ColoredSet**, which is specified using abstract values such as **empty(Red)** and **empty(Yellow)**. In particular, suppose that **emptySet** is *not* an abstract value of **ColoredSet**. Then the precondition of **choose** will be trivially satisfied if the argument to **choose** is a **ColoredSet**, because its abstract value cannot be **emptySet**. To prevent this kind of error, we have to reinterpret equality (=) in assertions. If we are bringing the values of subtype up by a coercion function, then one can interpret = as equality of the coerced abstract values, where the values are coerced to the nominal type used in the assertion. If we are bringing the trait functions down, there may be no coercion function (only a relation), and so one way to proceed is to prohibit the use of = between abstract values of terms of any sort other than the sorts associated with built-in primitive types such as **int**, and **char**. Assertions that use user-defined trait functions, such as \eq, instead of = have the advantage that \eq can always be redefined in the traits used by a subclass, and thus give better constraints on subtypes. Such assertions are called *subtype constraining* [Lea90, Section 3.5.3]. An alternative that we would like to investigate is to interpret = as a behavioral equality (at the nominal type used in the assertion). In this paper we use \eq instead of = for the user-defined trait function that plays the role of =.

3 Future Work

There are many questions still to be answered in our design of Larch/C++.

3.1 Integration with C++

One set of questions for future work involves more integration with C++. Exception handling is a feature that is described in the latest reference manuals for C++ and will be arriving in compilers eventually. We have not designed syntax and semantics for specifying exceptions yet.

We have not yet worked on the interaction of templates (generic polymorphism), subtyping, and inheritance. Some ideas on subtyping and polymorphism were explored in the design of Larch/Smalltalk, but the C++ type system adds complications.

There are a few pragmatic aspects of C++ programming that one might conceivably want a specification language to express. For example, that certain function calls should be expanded in-line or that some variables may change under outside influence (**volatile**). Both of these ideas have static and declarative aspects to them, but seem hard to reconcile to the idea of interface specification. Another practical feature would be a way to intermix Larch/C specifications with Larch/C++ specifications in the same environment. C++ has a feature for declaring that certain external functions are written in C, so this is not terribly far fetched.

In Larch/C, type checking is by name, except that calls to the standard library are structurally type checked. It is unclear whether by-name type checking is or should be applied to function types. Also it is unclear whether Larch/C++ should adopt by-name type checking, since C++ only does type checking by name for classes (and structs).

3.2 Subtyping and Subclassing

Another set of questions for future work involves details of subtyping and inheritance.

A pressing question is how to constrain subtypes effectively without saying too much. For example, often a subtype object has more information (more instance variables) than the supertype specification considers. Thus a specification inherited from the supertype that allows the object to be modified does not constrain the implementation to leave the extra information in the subtype object alone. Perhaps we can augment the modifies clause, which already provides a way to specify what objects cannot be modified by an operation, to say that no other parts of the object can change.

Another question is how we can provide tools that support browsing and reorganizing type specifications.

The implementation of a C++ class must match its declaration (and thus implicitly its specification) in many aspects that are not observable by clients. The most prominent of these is the declaration of private members of a class, but some kinds of **const** declarations in interfaces are also not the concern of clients. We would like to try to weaken such restrictions.

3.3 Verification

A big question for us is how to prove that one type is a subtype of another, based on their specifications. This question will be critical for modular verification.

We plan to investigate C++ coding styles and restrictions that will help avoid difficulties in program verification. We are also interested in how the verification of the implementation of a class is aided or hurt by certain coding styles.

4 Discussion and Conclusions

The Larch/C++ project worked with syntactic issues for several months during the summer of 1992. This effort produced a fairly stable grammar and a parser. (A human-readable grammar appears in the appendix.) We plan to build static semantic checkers and eventually support for proving various properties using the Larch Prover. We need to decide what tools to build and how to integrate them with the Larch/C tools. We would also like to build browsers similar to the prototype browser for Larch/Smalltalk [Che91].

The main effort in the summer of 1992 has been in writing examples, refining the language, and starting on a formal semantics for Larch/C++. We are now working on the semantics and tools.

We hope eventually to specify large portions of various C++ libraries. This should help make Larch/C++ attractive to programmers, and will enable users of Larch/C++ to start from a high level. It will also give us many examples of "real" programs to specify.

A general issue for interface specification language designers that emerges from our work on Larch/C++ is what level of specification is appropriate. That is, should an interface specification be allowed to state properties that are not observable by clients? For example, should the specification of private parts of a class be allowed in Larch/C++? It is not difficult to give meaning to such specifications, one simply requires that the specified private parts be present in the implementation. This blending of program and specification may be a good thing, as it allows the specifier to design some of the program. It is a point of view we are currently experimenting with, by letting the user specify protected and private parts in a class specification. This point of view also has the advantage of simplicity, both in the specification language and in the specification language's notion of a correct implementation. However, the price of this simplicity is reduced flexibility in implementations, because by ignoring the private and protected parts of a specification one could implement a class with the same observable behavior.

Although Larch/C++ takes much from Larch/C, Larch/C++ is not upward compatible with Larch/C. For example, the abstract data type specifications in Larch/C are replaced by class interface specifications in Larch/C++. Another incompatibility is that type checking for Larch/C++ is not by-name, except for classes (and structs). Finally, we do not allow arbitrary renamings in the uses clause, but only allow the specification of the type to sort mapping. Despite these differences, it should not be too difficult for the Larch/C user to use Larch/C++, as many details are the same.

Our goal is to have Larch/C++ in practical use within a few years. This goal is important, because despite its flaws C++ will be around for at least a few years, and possibly forever. If formal methods are to have an impact on the software industry, they will have to be applied to real problems by real programmers using the tools chosen by the programmers. Larch/C++ is a step

Notation	Description
[e]	optional e
e*	zero or more e's
e_s^*	zero or more e's, separated by symbol s
e^+	one or more e's
e_s^+	one or more e's, separated by symbol s
alpha	nonterminal symbol alpha
alpha	keyword alpha
{ e }	grouping
{ x | y }	alternatives within groups

Table 1: Notational conventions

in that direction.

Acknowledgements

Thanks to Albert Baker and Robert Bourdeau for reading a draft of this paper. Thanks to Krishna Kishore Dhara, Kari Lyle, Joe Reynolds, Jim Horning, and Kevin Jones for discussions about Larch/C++ and other Larch family specification languages. Thanks to Jeannette Wing for suggesting this research project. Thanks to Doug Lea and Marshall Cline for discussions about C++ and their A++ specification language. And thanks to the participants at the workshop, especially David Guaspari for discussions.

Appendix: Reference Grammar

The following grammar will certainly change in detail as we gain more experience with Larch/C++.

In the reference grammar an extended BNF is used with conventions shown in Table 1. Nonterminal symbols are in *italic*. Keywords are in **bold** face. Curry braces ({...}) are used to group grammar symbols; these and other meta-notations become terminal symbols when quoted ('{'). Square brackets ([...]) surround optional text. Superscript + and * have their usual meanings, and may be combined with a subscripted separator.

Interface Specifications

interface ::= { *import* | *trait-use* }* { *export-decl* | *private-decl* | *trait-use* }*
import ::= **imports** *interface-name*$_,^+$;
trait-use ::= **uses** *trait-ref*$^+$;
trait-ref ::= { *trait-name* | (*trait-name*$^+$) } [(*tsmapping*)]
tsmapping ::= { { *typedef-name* | *templ-or-class-name*$_:^+$ } **for** *sort-name* }$_,^+$
export-decl ::= *declaration*
private-decl ::= **private** *declaration*
declaration ::= *decl-specifier*$^+$ { *declarator* [= *const-expression*] }$_,^*$;

```
                    | fun-specification | template-declaration
decl-specifier ::= type-specifier
                  | static | extern | virtual | friend | typedef
type-specifier ::= simple-type-name | enum-specifier | class-specifier
                 | elaborated-type-specifier | :: templ-or-class-name
                 | const | volatile
simple-type-name ::= typedef-name | templ-or-class-name⁺̣ [ typedef-name ]
                   | char | short | int | long | signed | unsigned | float
                   | double | void
elaborated-type-specifier ::= class-key { templ-or-class-name | identifier }
                            | enum enum-name
class-key ::= [ abstract ] class | struct | union
enum-specifier ::= enum enum-name '{'
                { identifier [ = const-expression ] }* '}'
templ-or-class-name ::= template-class-name | class-name
const-expression ::= term
```

The Larch/C++ *identifier* is syntactically the same as that of C++, i.e., it is a sequence of letters and digits. The nonterminals *interface-name*, *trait-name*, *sort-name*, *typedef-name*, *class-name*, and *enum-name* are identifiers.

Class Specifications

```
class-specifier ::= class-header '{'
                [ trait-use ] [ invariant-pred ] [ member-list ] '}'
class-header ::= class-key [ identifier | class-name ] [ base-spec ]
base-spec ::= : { [ base-specifier ] templ-or-class-name }⁺
base-specifier ::= virtual [ access-specifier ] | access-specifier [ virtual ]
access-specifier ::= public | protected | private
invariant-pred ::= invariant predicate ;
member-list ::= { member-declaration | access-specifier : }⁺
member-declaration ::= decl-specifier* member-declaration*, ;
                | fun-specification [ ; ] | template-class-name :: name ;
member-declarator ::= declarator | [ identifier ] : const-expression
name ::= identifier | ~ class-name | oprfunc-name | convfunc-name
oprfunc-name ::= operator operator
convfunc-name ::= operator type-specifier⁺ [ pointer-operator ]
declarator ::= decl-name | pointer-operator declarator | ( declarator )
            | declarator ( argument-decls ) { const | volatile }*
            | declarator '[' [ const-expression ] ']'
pointer-operator ::= { '*' | & } { const | volatile }*
                  | templ-or-class-name⁺̣ :: '*' { const | volatile }*
argument-decls ::= { decl-specifier⁺ declarator [ = const-expression ] }*, [ ... ]
decl-name ::= templ-or-class-name | typedef-name
           | [ templ-or-class-name⁺̣ :: ] name
```

The nonterminal *operator* denotes C++ operators which can be overloaded; e.g., **new**, **delete**, +, -, *, and so on.

Function Specifications

fun-specification ::= *decl-specifier* declarator fun-body*
fun-body ::= '{' [*globals*] [*pre-cond*] [*modifies-pred*] *post-cond* '}'
globals ::= { *decl-specifier*$^+$ *declarator*$^+$; }$^+$
pre-cond ::= **requires** *predicate* ;
modifies-pred ::= **modifies** { **nothing** | **anything** | *store-ref*$^+$ } ;
store-ref ::= *term* | **reach** (*term*)
post-cond ::= **ensures** *predicate* [**except** *guarded-exceptions*]
        [**unless** *unguarded-exceptions*] ;
guarded-exceptions ::= { *predicate* => *predicate* }$^+_|$
unguarded-exceptions ::= *predicate*$^+_|$

Templates

template-declaration ::= **template** < *template-argument*$^+$ > *declaration*
template-argument ::= **class** *identifier*
        | *decl-specifier*$^+$ *declarator* [= *const-expression*]
template-class-name ::= *template-name*
        < { *type-specifier*$^+$ | *const-expression*}$^+$ >

The nonterminal *template-name* is an identifier.

Predicates

predicate ::= *term*
term ::= **if** *term* **then** *term* **else** *term* | *logical-term*
logical-term ::= *equality-term* { *logical-opr equality-term* }*
equality-term ::= *simple-opr-term* [= *simple-opr-term*]
        | *quantifier*$^+$ (*term*)
simple-opr-term ::= *simple-opr*$^+$ *secondary* | *secondary simple-opr*$^+$
        | *secondary* { *simple-opr secondary* }*
secondary ::= *primary* | [*primary*] *bracketed* [: *sort-name*] [*primary*]
bracketed ::= '[' *term* { , *term* }* ']'
primary ::= { (*term*) | *varId* | *fcnId* (*term*$^+$) | *lcpp-primary* }
        { *selection* | : *sort-name* | *state-fcn* | '[' *term** ']' }*
selection ::= . *varId* | -> *varId*
lcpp-primary ::= *literal* | **this** | **self** | **result** | **fresh** (*term*$^+$)
        | **trashed** (*store-ref*$^+$) | **unchanged** ({ **all** | *store-ref*$^+$ })
        | **sizeof** (*simple-type-name*)
literal ::= *integer-constant* | *floating-constant* | *character-constant*
        | *string-literal*
store-ref ::= *term* | **reach** (*term*)
quantifier ::= *quantifier-sym* { *varId* : *sort-name* }$^+$
quantifier-sym ::= **forall** | **exists**
state-fcn ::= *pre-sym* | *post-sym*
pre-sym ::= ^

post-sym ::= '

The nonterminal *logical-opr* denotes LSL logical connectives. The nonterminal *quantifier* denotes LSL quantifier symbols. The nonterminal *simple-opr* denotes LSL operators such as <, >=, and user defined operators such as \eq in our examples. Both *varId* and *fcnId* are *identifiers*. The nonterminals *integer-constant*, *floating-constant*, *character-constant*, and *string-literal* denote C++ integers, floating numbers, characters, and strings respectively.

References

[Ame87]   Pierre America. Inheritance and Subtyping in a Parallel Object-Oriented Language. In Jean Bezivin et al., editors, *ECOOP '87, European Conference on Object-Oriented Programming, Paris, France*, pages 234–242, New York, N.Y., June 1987. Springer-Verlag. Lecture Notes in Computer Science, Volume 276.

[Ame91]   Pierre America. Designing an Object-Oriented Programming Language with Behavioural Subtyping. In J. W. de Bakker, W. P. de Roever, and G. Rozenberg, editors, *Foundations of Object-Oriented Languages, REX School/Workshop, Noordwijkerhout, The Netherlands, May/June 1990*, volume 489 of *Lecture Notes in Computer Science*, pages 60–90. Springer-Verlag, New York, N.Y., 1991.

[BW90]   Kim B. Bruce and Peter Wegner. An Algebraic Model of Subtype and Inheritance. In Francois Bançilhon and Peter Buneman, editors, *Advances in Database Programming Languages*, pages 75–96. Addison-Wesley, Reading, Mass., August 1990.

[Car88]   Luca Cardelli. A Semantics of Multiple Inheritance. *Information and Computation*, 76(2/3):138–164, February/March 1988. A revised version of the paper that appeared in the 1984 Semantics of Data Types Symposium, LNCS 173, pages 51–66.

[CDD+89] D. Carrington, D. Duke, R. Duke, P. King, G. Rose, and G. Smith. Object-Z: An object-oriented extension to Z. In *Formal Description Techniques (FORTE '89), Vancouver*, pages 281–296. North-Holland Publishing Co., December 1989.

[Che89]   Jolly Chen. The Larch/Generic Interface Language. Technical report, Massachusetts Institute of Technology, EECS department, May 1989. The author's Bachelor's thesis.

[Che91]   Yoonsik Cheon. Larch/Smalltalk: A Specification Language for Smalltalk. Technical Report 91-15, Department of Computer Science; Iowa State University, Ames, IA, June 1991.

[CL90]   Marshall P. Cline and Doug Lea. The Behavior of C++ Classes. In *Proceedings of the Symposium on Object Oriented Programming Emphasizing Practical Applications, Marist College, 1990*, 1990. To appear.

[Cox86]   Brad J. Cox. *Object Oriented Programming: an Evolutionary Approach.* Addison-Wesley Publishing Co., Reading, Mass., 1986.

[Cus91]   Elspeth Cusack. Object Oriented Modelling in Z. Obtained from the Author., February 1991.

[DD90]   D. Duke and R. Duke. Towards a Semantics for Object-Z. In D. Bjorner, C. A. R. Hoare, and H. Langmaack, editors, *VDM '90: VDM and Z — Formal Methods in Software Development, Third International Symposium of VDM Europe, Kiel, FRG,* volume 428 of *Lecture Notes in Computer Science,* pages 244–261. Springer-Verlag, April 1990.

[Dha92]   Krishna Kishore Dhara. Subtyping among Mutable Types in Object-Oriented Programming Languages. Master's thesis, Iowa State University, Department of Computer Science, Ames, Iowa, May 1992.

[ES90]   Margaret A. Ellis and Bjarne Stroustrup. *The Annotated C++ Reference Manual.* Addison-Wesley Publishing Co., Reading, Mass., 1990.

[GH86]   J. V. Guttag and J. J. Horning. A Larch Shared Language Handbook. *Science of Computer Programming,* 6(2):135–157, March 1986.

[GH91]   J. V. Guttag and J. J. Horning. Introduction to LCL, A Larch/C Interface Language. Technical Report 74, Digital Equipment Corporation, Systems Research Center, July 1991.

[GHM90]   John V. Guttag, James J. Horning, and Andrés Modet. Report on the Larch Shared Language: Version 2.3. Technical Report 58, Digital Equipment Corporation, Systems Research Center, Palo Alto, Calif., April 1990.

[GHW85]   John V. Guttag, James J. Horning, and Jeannette M. Wing. The Larch Family of Specification Languages. *IEEE Software,* 2(4), September 1985.

[GM87]   Joseph A. Goguen and Jose Meseguer. Order-Sorted Algebra Solves the Constructor-Selector, Multiple Representation and Coercion Problems. In *Symposium on Logic in Computer Science, Ithaca, NY,* pages 18–29. IEEE, June 1987.

[GMP90]   David Guaspari, Carla Marceau, and Wolfgang Polak. Formal Verification of Ada Programs. *IEEE Transactions on Software Engineering,* 16(9):1058–1075, September 1990.

[Hoa72]   C. A. R. Hoare. Proof of correctness of data representations. *Acta Informatica,* 1(4):271–281, 1972.

[Jon91]   Kevin D. Jones. LM3: A Larch Interface Language for Modula-3 A Definition and Introduction Version 1.0. Technical Report 72, Digital Equipment Corporation, Systems Research Center, 130 Lytton Avenue Palo Alto, CA 94301, June 1991.

[Lea90]   Gary T. Leavens. Modular Verification of Object-Oriented Programs with Subtypes. Technical Report 90-09, Department of Computer Science, Iowa State University, Ames, Iowa, 50011, July 1990.

[Lea91]   Gary T. Leavens. Modular Specification and Verification of Object-Oriented Programs. *IEEE Software*, 8(4):72–80, July 1991.

[LW]   Gary T. Leavens and William E. Weihl. Subtyping, Modular Specification, and Modular Verification for Applicative Object-Oriented Programs. Forthcoming.

[LW90]   Gary T. Leavens and William E. Weihl. Reasoning about Object-oriented Programs that use Subtypes (extended abstract). *ACM SIGPLAN Notices*, 25(10):212–223, October 1990. *OOPSLA ECOOP '90 Proceedings*, N. Meyrowitz (editor).

[Mey88]   Bertrand Meyer. *Object-oriented Software Construction*. Prentice Hall, New York, N.Y., 1988.

[Rey80]   John C. Reynolds. Using Category Theory to Design Implicit Conversions and Generic Operators. In Neil D. Jones, editor, *Semantics-Directed Compiler Generation, Proceedings of a Workshop, Aarhus, Denmark*, volume 94 of *Lecture Notes in Computer Science*, pages 211–258. Springer-Verlag, January 1980.

[Str91]   Bjarne Stroustrup. *The C++ Programming Language: Second Edition*. Addison-Wesley Publishing Co., Reading, Mass., 1991.

[Win83]   Jeannette Marie Wing. A Two-Tiered Approach to Specifying Programs. Technical Report TR-299, Massachusetts Institute of Technology, Laboratory for Computer Science, 1983.

[Win87]   Jeannette M. Wing. Writing Larch Interface Language Specifications. *ACM Transactions on Programming Languages and Systems*, 9(1):1–24, January 1987.

[Win90]   Jeannette M. Wing. Using Larch to Specify Avalon/C++ Objects. *IEEE Transactions on Software Engineering*, 16(9):1076–1088, September 1990.

Generating Proof Obligations for Circuits

Niels Mellergaard and Jørgen Staunstrup
Department of Computer Science
Technical University of Denmark
DK–2800 Lyngby, Denmark

Abstract

This paper describes an attempt to automate part of the process of circuit verification. Several aspects of the tool-assisted process of verification are discussed. A scheme for automatic translation of an abstract circuit description to a theory in first order logic is presented. The scheme is evaluated with respect to several criteria, including complexity and generality.

1 Introduction

Different languages are often used to specify different aspects of a circuit, e.g., the functional behavior and the structure. While the use of multiple languages may facilitate the process of describing the circuit, it raises problems related to establishing correspondences between the different descriptions.

The philosophy behind SYNCHRONIZED TRANSITIONS is to use the same circuit description as the basis of simulation, synthesis, verification etc. Compilers are used to automatically translate between the general SYNCHRONIZED TRANSITIONS descriptions and the special purpose descriptions each of which emphasize different aspects of the design process.

In this paper, we concentrate on circuit verification. Several aspects of the verification cycle are discussed, but the emphasis is on the translation of circuit descriptions into a notation suitable for reasoning using a mechanical theorem prover, LARCH PROVER (LP). In the section about the translation (section 4) we will presume some basic LP knowledge.

The translation could be done in many ways. Issues as robustness and generality of the generated scripts have to be considered, while at the same time extracting sufficient information from the program text.

2 Synchronized Transitions

We use the circuit design language SYNCHRONIZED TRANSITIONS to describe circuits. This language facilitates behavioral descriptions at different levels of abstraction. The same circuit description in SYNCHRONIZED TRANSITIONS (called a program) is used as the basis of simulation, synthesis, verification,

and other types of analysis. A broad introduction to SYNCHRONIZED TRANSI-
TIONS is contained in [3]. There are strong similarities between SYNCHRONIZED
TRANSITIONS and UNITY, as developed by Chandy and Misra [1].

A program in SYNCHRONIZED TRANSITIONS describes a computation as a
set of independent, concurrently executing transitions. The transitions communicate via shared variables. The physical equivalent of a shared variable is
a wire, transitions are sub-circuits without explicit internal state.

With the cell construct, SYNCHRONIZED TRANSITIONS facilitates a hierarchical description. A cell is a generic sub-circuit possibly with internal state
(i.e. local variables). It contains local declarations and a body that describes
the structure of the circuit. The body may contain transitions and instantiations of other cells. Transitions and cells are composed with the asynchronous
combinator, ||, which means that execution is concurrent and independent. The
internal structure of a cell is hidden from the rest of the circuit.

Each cell can have an invariant and a protocol describing properties of
the cell. Invariants must hold between executions of transitions. Protocols
put restrictions on allowable changes in time. They are boolean expressions
introducing the proof obligations and the measure of correctness. They are not
part of the physical circuit.

3   The example

In this section we will introduce an example of a SYNCHRONIZED TRANSI-
TIONS program. This example is used to illustrate the translation from SYN-
CHRONIZED TRANSITIONS into a logic theory for the circuit and a set of proof
obligations for correctness.

The example is the carry computation in an asynchronous version of the
fast $(\log n)$ n-bit addition circuit described in [1]. The SYNCHRONIZED TRAN-
SITIONS description of the circuit is shown in figure 1.

The two addend words, a and b, are only read initially when the carry word
estimate, d, is initialized. During the computation d will be a partial result
where some bits are the correct carry, 0 or 1, and others are uncomputed, U.
Repeated execution of the transitions will eventually lead to a state where d
is the correct carry-word. t is an auxiliary variable expressing the progress of
the computation. The individual transitions are very simple; they essentially
just perform copying between the d-bits. It is a bit surprising that the circuit
actually computes the carry. In [1] the adder is discussed in further detail,
furthermore an invariant is stated.

For the purposes of this paper it is not important to understand the algorithm or invariant in detail. The following invariant is used to illustrate our
approach (C is the correct carry, which should eventually be computed in d):

$$\forall i \in [\,0\,..\,N\,]\;:$$
$$i \geq t[i] \Rightarrow d[i] = \quad if\;(\forall j \in [\,i - t[i]\,..\,i\,[\,:\,a[j] \neq b[j]\,])\;then\;U\;else\;C[i]\quad \wedge$$
$$t[i] > i \Rightarrow d[i] = C[i]\quad \wedge$$
$$t[i] > 0\quad \wedge$$
$$a[i] \neq U \wedge b[i] \neq U$$

```
STATIC
  N = ...; (* word size *)
  U = 2;   (* uncomputed *)
TYPE
  wordrange = [0..N];
  wordval   = [0..2];   (* "FALSE", "TRUE", uncomputed *)
  word      = ARRAY wordrange OF wordval;
  tarray    = ARRAY wordrange OF INTEGER;

CELL carry(a, b, d: word);
  STATE
    t: tarray;
  INITIALLY
    { i: [0..N-1] | d[i+1] = IF a[i]=b[i] THEN a[i] ELSE U };
    d[0] = 0;
    { i: [0..N] | t[i] = 1 };
  TRANSITION copy(STATIC i, ti: INTEGER)
    ≪ ti=t[i] ∧ d[i]=U → d[i], t[i] := d[i-ti], t[i]+t[i-ti] ≫
BEGIN
  {|| i: wordrange | {|| ti: [0..i] | copy(i, ti) }}
END carry;
```

Figure 1: The asynchronous carry cell

A richer notation is allowed for expressing invariants than for other boolean expressions appearing in the program because they do not have to be executable. The expressive power of the invariant notation is crucial for our ability to state useful invariants. We are still experimenting with this notation, currently the expressive power is roughly similar to LP's, i.e. a somewhat restricted first-order language.

The invariant is formulated in the notation for invariants and added as a part of the program text in SYNCHRONIZED TRANSITIONS. Running the SYNCHRONIZED TRANSITIONS to LP translator will result in a logic description of the circuit with proof obligations for maintenance of the invariant.

In the next section we will describe the translation of some of the constructs in the example, including invariants, types, transitions and the different kinds of quantification, and we will describe the proof obligations for correctness.

4 Translation

This section introduces the general translation scheme of circuit descriptions in SYNCHRONIZED TRANSITIONS into logic descriptions of the circuits and proof obligations for invariance. This translation is done by a compiler. The output from the compiler (called a script) serves as input for the theorem prover, LP. The compiler should extract all the information from the program needed to prove the invariants.

Soundness of the translation is a non-negotiable requirement. The main purpose of this section is make plausible to the reader that the translation is sound. There are other criteria that influence the choice of a translation. We will return to that discussion in a later section.

The generated script can be divided into two parts: A program *independent* and a program *dependent* part. The program independent part contains general definitions, including a theory for integers and declarations of a number of sorts, predicates, etc. used in most generated scripts. The program dependent part is an extraction of information from the specific program.

The following sections will describe the general definitions mentioned above, and illustrate the translation scheme (the program dependent part) for various constructs in the adder example. In these sections we will presume some basic LP knowledge.

4.1   General definitions

The general definitions part is independent of the program to be translated. It is stored as a frozen LP-theory and thawed as the first thing in the script. (So this part only takes up one line in the script.)

The general definitions defines a theory for integers (which is a basic type in SYNCHRONIZED TRANSITIONS but not in LP). This theory is defined in a way which makes it useful with generated scripts. We will not go into more technical details about the integer theory in this text.

The general definitions part also declares various sorts, variables and predicates used in all translations, e.g. sorts for state variable identifiers, predicates defining invariants and transitions, and auxiliary predicates for various hypotheses of the invariance proofs. These predicates which are used in most scripts are *declared* in the general definitions part. However, their actual *definitions* (i.e. the axioms) are dependent of the actual program to be translated, and are therefore not part of the general definitions.

The general definitions part also includes hints to the theorem prover how to order equations into rewrite rules (even before the axioms are stated!) using LP's registry facility.

The next sections deal with the translation of various constructs from SYNCHRONIZED TRANSITIONS programs. In particular, the translation of the addition circuit will be discussed. The overall translation scheme is the same for all programs but the actual details of the output depends on the specific program.

4.2   State variables

Each cell in a SYNCHRONIZED TRANSITIONS program declares a number of state variables. The circuit equivalent of a state variable is a wire. State variables are typed. The carry cell declares four state variables (three of them are formal parameters):

```
a, b, d: word;
t: tarray;
```

A first attempt of a translation would be to define an operator with arity 0 (a constant) for each state variable denoting the value of the state variable. But this is not sufficient to express the proof obligations. When reasoning about invariants it is necessary to refer to the value of a state variable at different times (in our terminology: in different *states*), i.e. the state before and the state after a transition has executed. If a transition is executed in a state s_1 leading to a state s_2 we refer to the value of a state variable, x, before the transition has executed as $x.s_1$ and the value of the state variable after the execution as $x.s_2$. Another transition might then execute leading to the state s_3 in which x would have the value $x.s_3$.

It turns out that this representation of state variables is not sufficient either. The same cell can be instantiated several times introducing several distinct instances of the same state variable (distinct wires in the circuit). x above is really just a *name* that does not refer to a unique instance of the state variable. Similar to the need of a state differentiation it is necessary to distinguish different instances of a state variable.

We therefore view a state variable in three different ways.

o At the syntactic level we need an *identifier* to refer to the state variable name in the program text.

o On the structural level we need a decoration of the identifier to refer to the actual instance of the state variable (the actual wire in the circuit). Such a reference to a state variable in a particular cell instance we call a *variable* because it is allowed to change value independently of other instances of the same state variable.

o On the third level, the *value* level, we need to decorate a variable with a particular state. In this way we can refer to a value held by a state variable in a particular cell instance at a particular time.

(The word *variable* is heavily overloaded. In SYNCHRONIZED TRANSITIONS programs we have the notion of *state variables*, declared in a **STATE** statement. LP also has a notion of *variables* used for implicit universal quantification in logic terms. Finally the translation from SYNCHRONIZED TRANSITIONS to LP introduces a *variable sort* in the logic (one of the three views of a state variable, as explained above).)

The different views of a state variable lead to the following translation. We need three sorts for each type T: sorts **TID** for identifiers, **TVar** for variables and **TVal** for values. For each state variable in the program an operator (with the same name as the state variable) is introduced, denoting the state variable *identifier*:

```
a, b, d:  -> wordID
t:        -> tarrayID
```

For each cell instance `ci` a state variable identifier, e.g. `b`, introduces a *variable* (of sort `wordVar`), written as

```
ci.b
```

and to each such variable corresponds a *value* (of sort `wordVal`) in every state `s`, written:

```
(ci.b).s
```

The auxiliary infix dot-operators above map `ID`-entifiers to `Var`-iables and `Val`-ues:

```
.: Instance, wordID -> wordVar
.: wordVar, State -> wordVal
```

Similar operators are introduced for the type **tarray**. The sorts **Instance** and **State** are part of the standard definitions, as they are used in all scripts. Using instances and states to qualify variables corresponds to the environment and store in the classical denotational semantics for programming languages. What we call state variable identifiers (or wires) correspond to addresses or loc's. To emphasize that we are working with circuits and to preserve the intuition the instance/state terminology introduced above is used.

4.3 Types

Types are used to classify state variables. SYNCHRONIZED TRANSITIONS has two simple build-in types, integer and boolean. These types are defined in the standard definitions part of the translation.

It is possible to define new types in SYNCHRONIZED TRANSITIONS. In the example two subrange types (**wordrange** and **wordval**) and two array types (**word** and **tarray**) are defined.

Pascal-like records are also allowed. The translation of record types is in many ways very similar to that of arrays. Elements of an array correspond to fields of a record, indices correspond to field names. There is the restriction on arrays that all elements must have the same type. On the other hand there is a restriction on records that it is not possible to quantify over field names. We will concentrate on the translation of array types here.

A type definition in the example looks like this:

```
word     = ARRAY wordrange OF wordval;
```

As for all other types three sorts are introduced in the script: In this case the sort **wordID** of word identifiers, the sort **wordVar** of word variables, and the sort **wordVal** of word values. **wordrange** and **wordval** should already be defined introducing sorts in a similar manner.

We always use the integer sort for subrange *values*. This is done because we do not have a subtyping facility in LP, and we want to have the properties of integers for subrange values also. As an example, we do not declare the *value* sorts **wordrangeVal** and **wordvalVal** for the subranges **wordrange** and **wordval** but use the integer sort **Int** instead. As a consequence we have to consider not only *proper* indices (within the bounds of the array) but also *illegal* indices (outside the array bounds) when stating axioms involving arrays.

For each array type a predicate is defined expressing that an integer is a proper index[1] (**i**, **x**, **y**, **z**, **env** are free LP variables):

---

[1] The question of type checking programs — in particular for proper indexing of arrays — is not discussed here.

```
word_Index(i, env) == In_wordrange(i, env)
In_wordrange(i, env) ==
  InRange(i, env.wordrange_low, env.wordrange_high)
InRange(x, y, z) == not((x < y) | (z < x))
```

The first equation above is a result of the array type translation. The equation defining In_wordrange is a result of the translation of the subrange type wordrange. So is the two named bounds of the subrange: wordrange_low and wordrange_high. The last equation defining InRange is from the general definitions part. env is varying over the possible environments in which the types are used.

The essential part of the array type translation is the definition of an index operator. LP does not support mix-fixing, so we define an infix operator, @, for indexing arrays (we write b@i instead of b[i]).

$$@ : \text{wordVar}, \text{Int} \rightarrow \text{wordvalVar}$$

The index operator @ takes an array variable (wordVar) and an index (Int) and returns an element variable (wordvalVar). In a cell instance ci and a state s the value of the i'th element of the word b would be written:

$$((\text{ci.b})@\text{i}).\text{s}$$

We want to define equality on arrays in terms of equality on elements of the arrays. This is complicated by the fact that indices are (arbitrary) integers. Equality on arrays should be immune of illegal indexing (using non-proper indices). It follows immediately that if two arrays are equal, w1 = w2, then their elements are pairwise equal, w1@i = w2@i, no matter if the index, i, is a proper index or not. We also need to express this the opposite way: If all element pairs of two arrays are equal, w1@i = w2@i, where i is a proper index, then the arrays are equal, w1 = w2. This is expressed in the following LP deduction rule (where sc, ci, w1, w2, s1, s2 are free LP variables):

```
when (forall i)
   word_Index(i, sc#ci) => (((ci.w1)@i).s1 = ((ci.w2)@i).s2)
yield
   (ci.w1).s1 = (ci.w2).s2
```

The infix operator # defines the environment in which the type is used from a cell scope (sc) and an instance of a cell (ci).

4.4   Invariants

Invariants introduce the proof obligations for the circuit. An invariant is a boolean expression describing a property that must hold for the circuit. The invariant is not part of the physical circuit (although the presence of an invariant may influence the actual implementation, e.g., by suggesting possible optimizations because of bindings between state variables).

The invariant in the example is translated in a straight forward manner to a predicate in the script. This also illustrates the translation of state variables and array types (we are only showing part of the invariant):

```
Inv(carry, ci, ss, i:Int) ==
  In_wordrange(i, carry#ci) =>
     ... &
     ((ci.t)@i).ss>i => ((ci.d)@i).ss = ((ci.C)@i).ss &
  ...
```

As there may be several instances of, e.g. the same state variable in the program text, each holding different values in different states, the invariant is a different expression in different instances and states. Therefore, the invariant has three arguments `carry`, `ci` and `ss` to uniquely identify the invariant in the cell instance `ci` of the cell `carry` in the state `ss`.

In this example the invariant has one further argument. By adding this argument to the predicate we are able to express the universal quantification in LP. This is explained next.

Ideally we would define the invariant something like this:

$$Inv(carry, ci, ss) == \forall i. \cdots (ci.d)[i].ss = \cdots$$

and try to prove

$$Inv(carry, ci, ss)$$

The explicit universal quantification above is not possible in LP. Instead we define a *specialized* invariant predicate:

$$Inv(carry, ci, ss, i) == \cdots (ci.d)[i].ss = \cdots$$

and try to prove

$$Inv(carry, ci, ss, i)$$

where i is a free LP variable (implicit universal quantification).

4.5   Transitions

Transitions are the core of a SYNCHRONIZED TRANSITIONS program. The transitions correspond to gates in the circuit. Transitions can *execute* thereby changing the state of the program. This is done by assigning new values to state variables. The sample transition

$$\ll \texttt{t<N} \rightarrow \texttt{t := 2*t} \gg$$

has the precondition `t<N` and the action `t := 2*t`. Whenever the precondition holds the transition can execute assigning a new value to `t` as described by the action.

An execution of a transition defines two states `pre` and `post` as the states just before an right after the execution. `pre` can be any state of the program, and `post` is the state determined deterministically by the given transition execution (and `pre`). Executing a transition has three kinds of consequences:

o The precondition of the transition holds in the state `pre` (`t.pre<N`),

o the action binds the values of some state variables in the state `post` (`t.post = 2*t.pre`), and o other variables than those on the left hand side of the assignment are unchanged (e.g. `x.post = x.pre`).

For each transition a predicate is defined stating the consequences of executing the transition. The third kind of consequences, the unchanged state variables, is not part of the transition predicate. This is because the *unchanged-expressions* has a non-monotonic nature. If we wanted to state that two transitions had executed simultaneously the conjunction of the preconditions and the conjunction of the actions would hold. But the conjunction of the unchanged-expressions would be invalid: If, for instance, the sample transition was executed simultaneously with another transition, that other transition might change `x` hence invalidating the unchanged-expression (`x.post = x.pre`) for the sample transition. Therefore the unchanged-expressions are not stated before the actual instantiations in the cell body are known. We will return to the unchanged-expressions in a later section.

4.5.1 The `pre`/`post` notation

A number of other predicates are defined in terms of `pre` and `post`. Conjectures to be proved are always of the form "if some relationship between `pre`/`post` holds, then another relationship holds". To give an example, if the invariant in the `pre`-state holds and a transition has executed (defining a relationship between `pre`/`post`), then the invariant holds in the `post`-state.

`pre` and `post` are declared as constants in the script. This does not mean that the verification results only hold for a specific shift between these two particular states. As long as we make sure not to make any "global" assertions about `pre`/`post` they will simulate free variables. An invariance proof using `pre`/`post` will then be valid for all states and not only for the state change from `pre` to `post`. This is a *meta level* argument (usually called ∀-introduction) which is not a proof obligation on the concrete level, i.e. in the generated script. An advantage is that we do not have to introduce a notion of *traces* on the state space and do induction on these.

We are using the notation with `pre` and `post` for verifying invariants. Other work is being done on refinement reasoning where this notation is also used. Here we are stating, e.g., abstraction functions mapping the concrete states, e.g. pre_c, to corresponding abstract states. The `pre`/`post` notation has also here shown to be very useful.

4.5.2 The `copy` transition

Now that we have explained the general translation of transitions, and introduced the `pre`/`post` notation we will return to the example. The adder has a transition which is a little more complicated than the sample transition above:

```
TRANSITION copy(STATIC i, ti: INTEGER)
  ≪ ti=t[i] ∧ d[i]=U → d[i], t[i] := d[i-ti], t[i]+t[i-ti] ≫
```

The translation may look hairy, but it is very straight forward and follows the same translation scheme as suggested for the sample transition. It is translated to the following transition predicate:

```
when copy(ci, i:Int, ti:Int) yield
  (ti = ((ci.t)@i).pre &
    ((ci.d)@i).pre = (carry#ci).U)        % precondition
  ((ci.d)@i).post = ((ci.d)@(i-ti)).pre   % action 1
  ((ci.t)@i).post =
    ((ci.t)@i).pre + ((ci.t)@(i-ti)).pre  % action 2
```

The transition predicate, copy, is defined by an implication instead of an equation, as the transition may not have executed although the right-hand-side expression holds. Also, we are not trying to reason about whether transitions have executed; we are only concerned about the consequences of a transition, should it execute.

In the next sections we will see a use of this predicate and we will also see the third kind of consequences of transition executions: the unchanged-expressions.

4.6 Quantifiers

Often circuits have repetitions of similar constructs. The number of replications is, off course, always bounded in physical circuits, usually by a word length, as N in the example. Therefore SYNCHRONIZED TRANSITIONS has ways for doing bounded quantifications. In the example, a quantified initialization is used to initialize the arrays d and t. To express the invariant from section 3 in SYNCHRONIZED TRANSITIONS it is necessary to use a quantified expression. We will not illustrate the translation of quantified initializations and quantified expressions.

Instead we will illustrate a third kind of quantification, the quantified instantiation of the copy transition from the example:

$$\{\| \; i: \; \text{wordrange} \; | \; \{ \; \| \; \text{ti: wordrange} \; | \; \text{copy(i, ti)} \; \}\}$$

This quantified instantiation denotes a number of asynchronously composed transitions. When stating that a transition has executed special care has to be taken with quantified instantiations. It must be stated that there *exists* a value of the index variable in the quantification range for which the corresponding transition has executed. This kind of existential quantification is not possible to express directly in LP. Instead a skolem constant for each index variable is introduced. It is asserted that the skolem constant is within the quantification range. Nothing else must be asserted about the constant. The skolem constants are introduced by the predicate InstanceQuant:

```
when InstanceQuant(cnt1, carry, ci) yield
  In_wordrange(i_skolem, carry#ci)
when InstanceQuant(cnt2, carry, ci) yield
  InRange(ti_skolem, 0, i_skolem)
```

The translation above using skolem constants is used to reduce the invariance proof for a number transitions to one proof, as we shall see in the next sections.

4.7   Actions

Each instance of a transition is described by the predicate `Action`. The `Action` predicate states what transition has executed (`copy`), possible instantiation conditions (not present here), possible quantifiers (`InstanceQuant`), and expressions for unchanged state variables:

```
when Action(cnt1, carry, ci) yield
  copy(ci, i_skolem:Int, ti_skolem:Int)          % Transition
  InstanceQuant(cnt1, carry, ci) &
    InstanceQuant(cnt2, carry, ci)               % Quantifiers
  word_Index(i, carry#ci) =>
    ((not(i=i_skolem)) => U((ci.d)@i))           % U(d[i])
  tarray_Index(i, carry#ci) =>
    ((not(i=i_skolem)) => U((ci.t)@i))           % U(t[i])
```

The constants `cnt1` and `cnt2` are counters that the "user" should not be concerned about. It is only used to distinguish between different instances (`Action`) and different quantifiers (`InstanceQuant`). The predicate `InstanceQuant` put bounds on the skolem constants, as explained in the previous section. The expressions for unchanged variables need a little explanation. U is a (overloaded) predicate expressing that a variable is unchanged:

$$U(x) == x.pre = x.post$$

Executing the transition `copy` leaves part of the arrays d and t unchanged. This is expressed in the unchanged-expressions: Elements of d and t are unchanged except for the i'th element which is assigned a new value.

4.8   Proof obligations

This far the logic description of circuits has been illustrated. This describes all the things that the circuit can do. The proof obligations describe some properties we (at least) want the circuit to have. This is an essential part of the translation.

It must be proved that the invariant in the carry cell is preserved by the transitions. This can be done by considering one transition at a time. When this is done *local* invariance has been proved for the carry circuit.

The hypotheses for the proof of local invariance are defined by the predicate `ActionTaken`:

```
when ActionTaken(carry, ci) yield
  inCell(carry, ci)
  Inv(carry, ci, pre, i:Int)
  Action(cnt1, carry, ci)
```

In the proof of local invariance, it can be assumed that the invariant holds in the pre-state (`Inv(..., pre, ...)`), that one of the actions of the cell has executed (`Action(...)`) and that the scope rules etc. for the cell are obeyed (`inCell(...)`). Just by asserting that `Action` holds we have asserted that one of the (possibly many) copy transitions has executed. With this translation of the quantified instantiation of the **copy** transition we have reduced the proof for a number of transitions to one proof. In general (not using quantifications) the **ActionTaken** predicate will contain a disjunction of transitions:

```
Action(cnt1,...) | Action(cnt2,...) | ...
```

The proof obligation is to prove that the invariant holds after executing any transition:

```
when ActionTaken(carry, ci) yield PostObl(carry, ci, i:Int)
```

where **Postobl** in general is a conjunction of the invariant in the **post**-state and the protocol (see section 5). The carry does not have a protocol so **PostObl(...)** is just the invariant in the **post** state, **Inv(..., post,...)**.

If the hypotheses (**ActionTaken**) contain a disjunction of actions, as in the general case explained above, we will do the proof as a case-proof. This is a suggestion to LP that the translator generates in the script.

Local invariance is the only proof obligation for the carry example. In general, when circuits consist of more cells, proof obligations for *non-interference* (as described in [2]) are generated ensuring *global* invariance. We will briefly discuss this in the next section.

5   Localized verification

We want to prove, that execution of any transition maintains the invariants and protocols in all cells. This is done using a method for localized verification of asynchronous circuits presented in [2]. Using this method, the verification of the circuit is divided into smaller localized proof obligations. For each cell local invariance is proved, and for each cell instantiation non-interference is proved. Local invariance and non-interference together ensure what we call *global* invariance: Execution of any transition in any cell will maintain (the conjunction of) all invariants in all cells.

In the local invariance proofs we only use local information from one cell, and we only prove that the cell maintains it's own invariant. This was the case for the carry cell. The proof obligation is independent of the composition of the circuit,i.e. how the cells are instantiated.

In the non-interference proofs, we have to make up for the incompleteness of the local invariance proofs. Each cell instantiation represents a communication path between two parts of the circuit. Non-interference ensures that consequences of actions in one part of the circuit are not propagated in a way that interfere with invariants in the other part of the circuit, and vice versa.

The main point of the method is to break the global invariance proof into smaller, independent and more manageable pieces. It is not possible to describes this in details here.

6   Choice of a translation

The translation of a circuit description to a logic axiomatization serving as input to a theorem prover can be done in many different ways, depending on what issues are given high priority. In this section different criteria that could be relevant and the priorities of these for the translator from SYNCHRONIZED TRANSITIONS programs to LP input are discussed.

6.1   Generality

The translator accepts the full SYNCHRONIZED TRANSITIONS syntax with a very few exceptions. The exceptions are caused by the lack of useful translations of these constructs. The translator is not extracting all information from the program, only what is believed to be relevant using the localized method.

The localized verification method which is the basis of the translation is not logically complete. We are not too concerned about incompleteness in the translation, because we know we have to live with incompleteness, both at the verification level and when we are implementing real circuits. Also, what we verify is invariants expressing only some interesting properties of a circuit (it is not a *complete* specification). Our attitude is to use methods which are adequate for our purposes, in this case to investigate methods to produce circuits that works.

6.2   Proof complexity

A main concern has been to break down the verification in a number of smaller localized proofs. This is in accordance with the localized method described in [2]. This approach has several advantages, proofs tend to be smaller and to be less complex. Another advantage is caused by the experience that proofs often fail. By localizing proofs, it is easier to localize an error in a design (or alternatively, an error in an invariant). We will elaborate more on this in section 7. All proofs are totally independent: No proof relies on another proof to succeed. This means that the proofs can be done in any order, a useful option while debugging critical parts of a circuit.

The carry alone does not illustrate much localization of proofs. But recall that the carry is part of a bigger circuit, an adder, which in turn may be part of an even more complex circuit. The local invariance proof for the carry will then be one of many localized proofs for the more complex design. Furthermore it will be independent of these other proofs.

6.3   Robustness

As mentioned above, proofs often fail because of an error in the program (either the circuit design or the invariants). This means that the program has to be corrected and a new script generated. The translation is done in a way that preserves the overall structure of the script. Localized changes in the program cause localized changes in the script. Only sub-circuits that are affected by the changes may need new proofs. Facts and defined operators and variables in the script are intended to be named robustly. Moving things around in the program text only changes the order of things in the script, not the naming. Names from the program are used in translator generated names. Un-robust names, e.g. names with counters, are avoided wherever possible.

6.4 Readability

The scripts generated by the translator are mainly intended for **LP**. At times it is necessary to look in the scripts. Therefore, the overall structure of the script is made as readable as possible. There is a correspondence between most constructs in the SYNCHRONIZED TRANSITIONS program and (groups of) axioms and operators in the script. Names from the program are used in the script to clarify the correspondence between program and script.

There is a systematic naming of **LP** facts in the script. This makes it possible for the user to utilize the display facility in **LP** instead of reading the script. E.g. the definition of the invariant predicate in the carry cell can be pretty-printed in **LP** with the command: `display Icarry`.

In contrast to the structure of the scripts, it has not been possible to make the individual axioms very readable. As an example, a state variable **x** will usually appear as `((cic.x:<somesort>).pre)` inside a proof. This seems like a lot of excess syntax.

7 Verification cycle

When building circuits, **LP** is used actively as a design tool. It is used in the constructive, iterative process of verification. This process is briefly discussed below.

The basis of the verification is a circuit description in SYNCHRONIZED TRANSITIONS. Such a program describes the structure and functional behavior of the circuit as well as the invariants that must hold.

From the program a description (called a script) of a logical theory for the circuit and a set of proof obligations for the invariance proofs are generated by the SYNCHRONIZED TRANSITIONS to **LP** translator. This translation phase is completely automatic.

The next phase is the proof phase using **LP** with the generated script as input. For simple examples (i.e. mostly small programs or programs with simple invariants) **LP** does the proofs automatically. For most examples, however, user interaction with **LP** is needed.

The user interaction phase is the most critical, in the sense that it requires creativity from the user. It is also the most time consuming. Sometimes this phase results in succeeding proofs. At other times it is realized that the invariants cannot be proved, for the simple reason that they are not preserved by the circuit. In that case it is concluded that the program is erroneous, and the constructive phase of modifying the program is (re-)entered. Another iteration in the verification cycle can start. This is illustrated in figure 2.

When all the proofs are done using **LP** the verification cycle is completed, i.e. it is formally proved that the program preserves the invariants. Another translator can now be used to generate low-level code suitable for synthesis. The basis for this translation is exactly the same circuit description as was used by the SYNCHRONIZED TRANSITIONS to **LP** translator. This gives a high degree of confidence that the properties proved for the program also hold for the physical circuit.

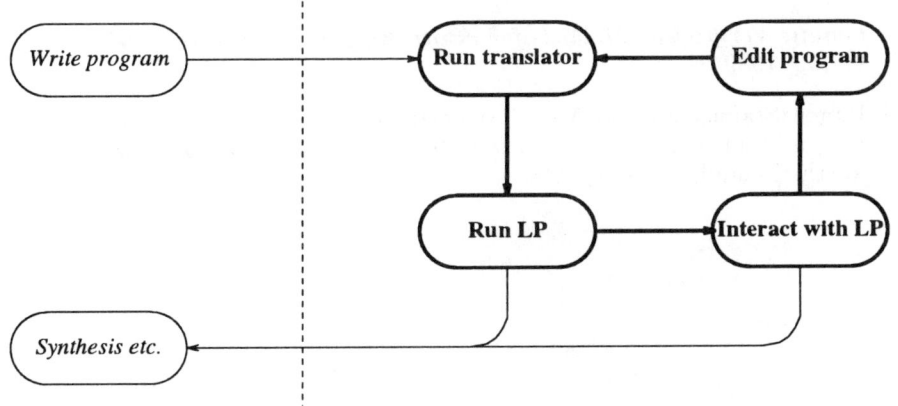

Figure 2: Process graph for the verification cycle.

8 Conclusion

This paper describes a tool-supported method for verifying circuits. The tool described here is a translator from the circuit design language SYNCHRONIZED TRANSITIONS to a notation suitable for reasoning using the LARCH PROVER.

We have discussed some criteria that have influenced the translation. We have also given a detailed (but yet incomplete) description of the translation exemplified with an addition circuit, and we have illustrated the typical verification cycle when verifying circuits.

The example, the fast addition circuit by Chandy and Misra [1], has been verified using the method described. The proof in LP is quite big. The main reason is that LP does not handle integer intervals very well (used in bounded quantifications). Also the general translation of quantified expressions is not very useful. A third reason is the high complexity of the invariant. The proof consists of about 100 lines user supplied LP commands. The proof takes about 10 minutes on a DEC Station 5000 with 64 Mb memory.

We have used this method for verifying invariants for some time. We often need to modify a SYNCHRONIZED TRANSITIONS design, either because we find out it has a bug, or because we find out the invariant is wrong. Each time the design is modified a new script is needed. This is generated easily using the translator. The robustness of the translation ensures that minor changes in the design cause minor changes in the script.

References

[1] K. M. Chandy and J. Misra. *Parallel Program Design, A Foundation.* Addison-Wesley, 1988.

[2] Jørgen Staunstrup, Stephen J. Garland, and John V. Guttag. Localized verification of circuit descriptions. In *Proceedings of the Workshop on Au-*

tomatic Verification Methods for Finite State Systems, LNCS 407. Springer Verlag, 1989.

[3] Jørgen Staunstrup and Mark Greenstreet. Synchronized Transitions. In Jørgen Staunstrup, editor, *Formal Methods for VLSI Design*, pages 71–128. North-Holland/Elsevier, 1990.

Using Transformations and Verification in Circuit Design[1]

James B. Saxe

James J. Horning

Systems Research Center

Digital Equipment Corporation

Palo Alto, CA, U.S.A.

John V. Guttag[2]

Stephen J. Garland[2]

Laboratory for Computer Science

Massachusetts Institute of Technology

Cambridge, MA, U.S.A.

Abstract

We show how machine-checked verification can support an approach to circuit design based on transformations. This approach starts with a conceptually simple (but inefficient) initial design and uses a combination of *ad hoc* and algorithmic transformations to produce a design that is more efficient (but more complex).

We present an example in which we start with a simplified CPU design and derive an efficient pipelined form, including circuitry for reverting the effects of partially executed instructions when a successful branch is detected late in the pipeline. The algorithmic stage of our derivation applies a transformation, retiming, that has been proven to preserve functional behavior in the general case. The *ad hoc* stage requires special justification, which we supply in the form of a machine-checked formal verification.

1   Introduction

This paper presents an integrated approach to designing and verifying circuits. In this approach one starts with a straightforward circuit design, whose semantics are easily understood. This design is then improved—under some measure such as cost, efficiency, or functionality—by a series of transformations. Each transformation may serve either to effect an improvement directly or to enable further transformations.

The transformations used are of two kinds: algorithmic and *ad hoc*. An algorithmic transformation is one that can be mechanically applied to any circuit satisfying some mechanically-checkable preconditions, and that is guaranteed to have a specific effect—or, more commonly, lack of effect—on the functional behavior of any circuit to which it is applicable. When we apply an *ad hoc* transformation, on the other hand, we must produce a specific proof that the

---

[1] This paper is a preliminary draft of a paper scheduled to appear in *Formal Methods in System Design*. It is based upon work originally presented at the Second IFIP WG10.2/WG10.5 Workshop on Designing Correct Circuits, and is published here by permission of Kluwer Academic Publishers, Elsevier Science Publishers B.V., and the International Federation for Information Processing.

[2] John Guttag and Stephen Garland were supported in part by the Advanced Research Projects Agency of the Department of Defense, monitored by the Office of Naval Research under contract N00014-89-J-1988, and by the National Science Foundation under grant CCR-8910848.

behavior of the transformed circuit has some desired relation to that of the original circuit. Doing this is often difficult, and is the main subject of this paper.

Three main issues must be considered when doing such proofs:

1. *The cost of performing the proof.* The primary cost of verification is people time, not machine time. Often, the most important factor in determining the cost is how much and what kind of work must be redone when changes are made to the circuit design or to the properties to be proved.

2. *The soundness of the proof.* A proof can increase one's confidence that some property holds; it cannot provide a guarantee. Proofs, like circuits, can have bugs in them.

3. *The relevance of the proof.* For a proof to be relevant it must be based upon axioms that accurately model the circuit about which properties are being proved. Furthermore, the theorem that is proved must accurately model some property that it is desirable for the circuit to have.

We approach the first issue in two ways. First, by making use of algorithmic transformations, we reduce the difficulty of the proofs to be done. Second, we provide a theorem prover called the Larch Prover (LP) [4], that provides assistance in finding proofs. Nevertheless, the cost is still high, in part because it requires someone who understands both the circuit design and the proof technology to develop the proof.

LP also plays a major part in our approach to the soundness issue. In verifying circuits (or programs) the mass of detail that must be managed increases the likelihood of error. Experience indicates that when a proof is not machine checked, it is highly likely that cases are omitted, undocumented assumptions are relied upon, and clerical errors are made [5, 6, 10]. Even machine-checked proofs may not be sound; there is always the chance that the program doing the checking is flawed.

The relevance issue is the hardest to deal with.[3] We cannot prove theorems about physical devices such as circuits, only about formal abstractions of such devices. The relevance of our proofs rests in part on how accurately the abstractions model the circuits. Of course, this problem is not limited to verification. The same problem arises in other kinds of analysis, such as simulation. One way to increase the likely relevance is to develop a suite of tools for specification, simulation, verification, and fabrication, all using a common source language. Driving all tools off the same source files, would increase the likelihood that results from tools such as simulators and verifiers will be about the circuit that actually gets built.[4]

A key technical question to resolve in building such tools is exactly what proof obligation is entailed when verifying an *ad hoc* transformation. This question is particularly complicated in our setting. While using the same language for expressing specifications and implementations facilitates hierarchical

---

[3] Our comments on relevance are necessarily brief. Cohn [1] addresses the issue at greater length.

[4] The work presented in [12] has similar goals. However, it starts from a different design method, one in which specifications and implementations are written in distinct languages. This leads to significant technical differences.

decomposition, it raises several questions about defining what it means for an implementation to satisfy its specification. In particular,

1. Must the implementation take the same number of clock cycles as the specification to perform each function?

2. Which of the components appearing in the specification must also appear in the implementation? That is, which parts of the specification are part of its interface to the outside world, and which parts are artifacts of our choice of description—virtual components that need not correspond to any localized part of the implementation?

3. Once one has defined the interface of the specification, what aspects of the I/O behavior of the specification must be preserved in the implementation?

In the next section we give an example of circuit design using *ad hoc* and algorithmic transformations. In Section 3 we show how to formalize the claim that one of the transformations is correct, that is, that the transformed circuit description implements the original circuit description. In carrying out this formalization, we address each of the three questions just listed. We also show how the claim of correctness can be proved. In Section 4 we describe the formal verification of the example transformation using the Larch Prover. In Section 5 we discuss some of the lessons we have learned from our experience with machine-checked formal verification.

2 An Example Circuit

This section describes the derivation of an optimized circuit design by the application of both *ad hoc* and algorithmic transformations to a simple initial design. We describe the circuits using (a) informal explanatory text, (b) diagrams, and (c) equations suitable for use in formal verification. We also explain how to get from (b) to (c).

2.1 Specification of a minimal processor

Figure 1 shows an initial ("specification") design for a stripped-down computer. In the diagram, lines represent data paths, rectangles represent *registers* (clocked memory elements), and other shapes represent combinational logic elements.

Registers are presumed to be driven by a global clock, not shown in the diagram. At each tick of the global clock, each register begins to assert at its output whatever value was present at its input just before the clock tick. The changes in the register outputs then propagate through the combinational logic to produce new register inputs, which will be captured at the next tick of the clock.

An *execution history* of a circuit consists of a sequence of values for each data path in the circuit. By convention, we use the label of a data path to denote the sequence of values that appear on it in this history.[5] Similarly, we use the same label for a register and its output data path. We write P.t for the stable value on data path P at the end of time step t.

Each circuit element places a constraint on execution histories, which can be expressed as an equation relating values on the data paths it connects. Combinational elements constrain values at the same time step, while registers constrain values at consecutive time steps.

In each clock cycle, our example computer executes one instruction of the form "destination register becomes function of source register; branch on zero to target instruction." The next few paragraphs follow the instruction execution process in detail, giving both informal commentary and equations. We use here a subset of the notations used by the Larch Prover (LP) [4], but systematically elide details needed by LP, such as declarations. These details will be discussed in Section 4.

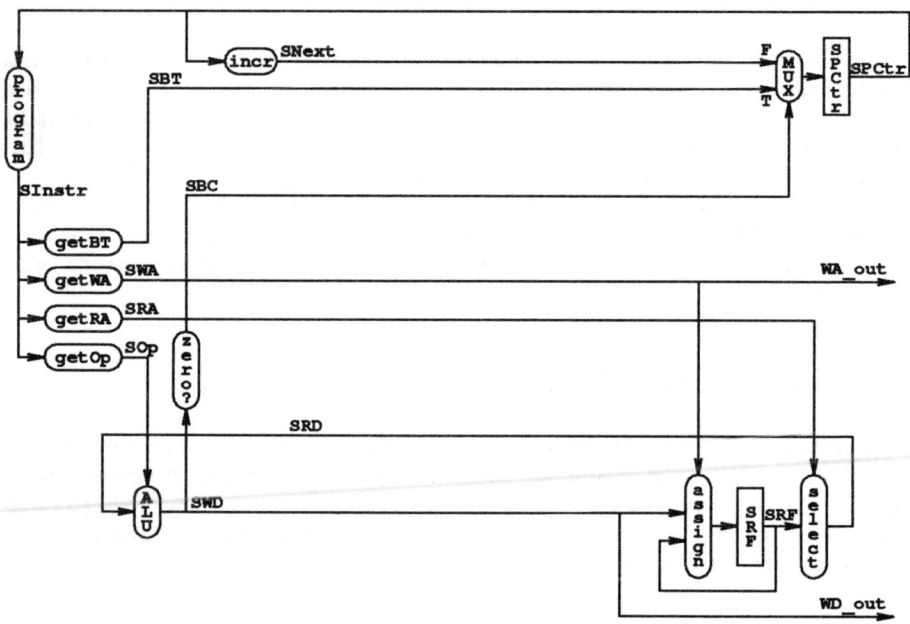

Figure 1: The initial, simple processor design.

At the beginning of time step t, an instruction address, SPCtr.t (the "S" is for specification) is clocked out of the program counter (the rectangle in the upper right hand corner of the diagram). We model the program itself as a block of combinational logic (think of it as a ROM) that takes addresses as input and produces instructions as output. Thus the instruction fetched in time step t is

$$\text{SInstr.t} == \text{program(SPCtr.t)}$$

---

[5]Since we will not have occasion, in this paper, to reason about two specific execution histories of the same circuit at the same time, this convention introduces no ambiguity.

The instruction is then decoded into its four components, namely the read address, the write address, the ALU operation, and the branch target.

```
SRA.t == getRA(SInstr.t)
SWA.t == getWA(SInstr.t)
SOp.t == getOp(SInstr.t)
SBT.t == getBT(SInstr.t)
```

The read address SRA.t is used to read a data value SRD.t from the register file (modeled as a single large register SRF):

```
SRD.t == select(SRF.t, SRA.t)
```

Using the read data and the operation part SOp.t of the current instruction, the ALU computes result SWD.t (for "write data"):

```
SWD.t == ALU(SOp.t, SRD.t)
```

This result is stored back into the register file at the write address:

```
SRF.(t+1) == assign(SRF.t, SWA.t, SWD.t)
```

Meanwhile, the result is also compared to zero. According to the result SBC.t (for "branch control") of this comparison, the new value of the program counter is either set to the branch target or computed by incrementing the current program counter:

```
SBC.t == (SWD.t) = zero
SNext.t == incr(SPCtr.t)
SPCtr.(t+1) == if(SBC.t, SBT.t, SNext.t)
```

where if(B, E1, E2) is read "if B then E1 else E2." The if and "=" operators are among the few built-in operators of LP. The others are the boolean operators "&" (and), "|" (or), "=>" (implies), "<=>" (iff), not, true, and false. For technical reasons, LP uses two different symbols "=" and "==" to denote comparison for equality. The symbol "==" is used only as the top level connective in equations; syntactically, it binds more loosely than "=" and other infix operators.

The machine communicates to the external world by making all writes to the register file visible at an external interface:

```
WA_out.t == SWA.t
WD_out.t == SWD.t
```

Since these interface signals are common to the "specification" circuit described here and the "implementation" circuit described below, we do not apply the convention of starting their names with S.

The speed at which a circuit such as this can run is bounded by the requirement that all the combinational logic outputs must have time to settle to stable values in the interval between one clock tick and the next. In Figure 1 there is a long combinational path that starts at the program counter and goes through the instruction fetch logic, then through the decode logic to select the read address, then through the register file reading logic, then through the ALU, and then through the register write logic. Another long path starts in the same way, going from the program counter through the instruction fetch and decode logic, the register read logic, and the ALU, and then continues through the zero-tester and the branch selection multiplexer. In a physical implementation based directly on Figure 1, one of these two long paths would probably be the critical path limiting the clock speed.

Circuits containing long combinational paths can sometimes be sped up by retiming [8, 9], a technique by which registers are removed from some points in the circuit and inserted at other points according to rules that guarantee preservation of functional behavior. Intuitively, if there are cyclic paths through the circuit on which the registers are distributed unevenly with respect to the combinational logic, retiming can distribute the registers more evenly, thus reducing the maximal combinational delays in the circuit.

Unfortunately, our example circuit in Figure 1 is not a good candidate for improvement by retiming. One of the long combinational paths mentioned above leads from the output of the program counter back to the input of the program counter. The attempt to "distribute the registers more evenly" around a cycle is not likely to be fruitful when there is only one register to distribute.

In the next section, we will transform Figure 1 by *ad hoc* methods to yield a new CPU, shown in Figure 2, that executes the same instruction set. The new CPU is more complicated (and probably slower) than that in Figure 1, but it has a higher ratio of registers to combinational components along its critical feedback cycles, enabling retiming to produce a machine, shown in Figure 3, that is faster than that in Figure 1.

2.2   An *ad hoc* transformation

Roughly speaking, the design of the pipelined machine in Figure 2 is based on the assumption that branches (times for which SPCtr.(t+1) == SBT.t) are less common than straight line execution (SPCtr.(t+1) == incr(SPCtr.t)). When execution of an instruction results in a branch, the machine doesn't "notice" the branch until several time steps have elapsed, during which it has started executing the next few instructions along the straight line path "in the shadow of the branch." Upon detection of the branch condition, the effects of the shadowed instructions are undone and program execution continues along the branching path. The next few paragraphs describe the derivation of Figure 2 from Figure 1 in more detail.

We begin by introducing four registers IBC3, IBC2, IBC1, and IBC0, ("I" for implementation) between the zero-comparator and the branch multiplexer, thereby delaying for four clock cycles all decisions about whether or not to branch. In order to have the decision about whether to branch and the appropriate destination of the potential branch arrive at the branch multiplexer at the same time, we also introduce four registers IBT3, IBT2, IBT1, and IBT0 on the path by which branch targets are communicated from the instruction decode logic to the branch multiplexer.

If these were the only changes we made, we would have produced a machine whose instruction set differed from that of Figure 1 by having delayed branching. Whenever the machine executed an instruction that should result in a branch, the next four instructions along the straight-line execution path would be executed before control transferred to the branch target. In order to restore the semantics of Figure 1, we must introduce additional logic to insure that no effects of these (shadowed) instructions become permanent.

In order to postpone commitment of potentially shadowed register file writes, we introduce delaying registers IWA3, IWA2, and IWA1 for the write addresses, and IWD3, IWD2, and IWD1 for the write data destined to the register file. Whenever a branch is taken, write suppression logic changes all queued write addresses to a special addresses, null. Writing to null causes no change to the register file.

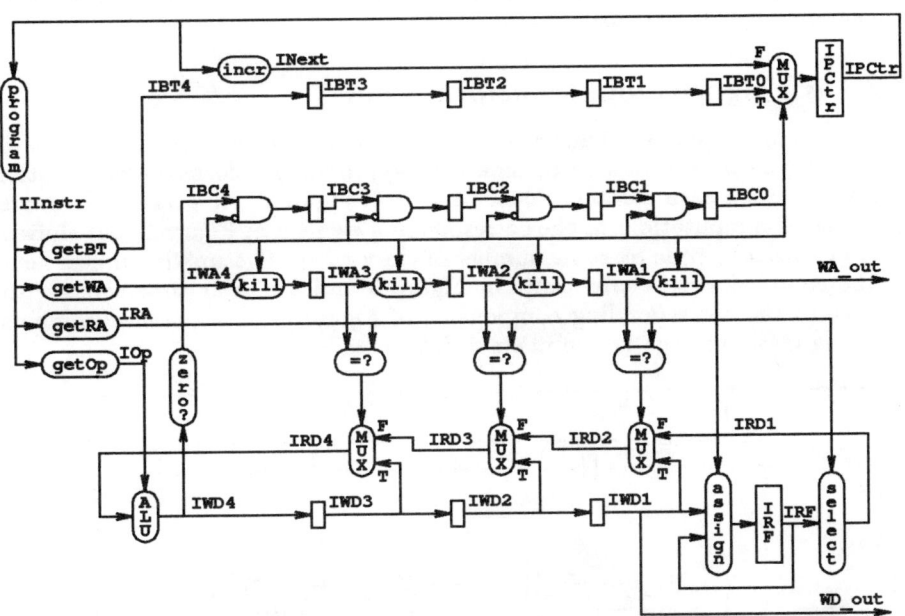

Figure 2: A pipelined processor design, derived from Figure 1 by an *ad hoc* transformation.

Suppose that some instruction writes to a particular address in the register file and the next instruction in the normal execution sequence reads that same address. If both instructions turn out to be permanent (i.e., not shadowed), we want to be sure that the data read by the second instruction is the same as that written by the first, even though that ata has not yet been written to the actual register file. For this purpose, we introduce a series of address-comparitors and read data multiplexers (known as "read-bypass" logic) to allow the results of reading the register file to reflect any pending writes.

Finally, in the case of a branch we must suppress not only the register file writes of shadowed instructions, but also any branches which may have been initiated by shadowed instructions. The gates that drive the inputs of registers IBC3, ... , IBC0 serve this purpose.

The interface signals WA_out and WD_out are supplied from the head of the write queue so that shadowed writes will have had their addresses set to null before they become visible at the interface.

Although the machine in Figure 2 is pipelined, the work done for each instruction is very unevenly distributed among the stages of the pipe. If we look for the longest combinational paths in Figure 2, we will see that the minimal clock period for a circuit based directly on Figure 2 would not be much less (and might well be greater, depending on the relative speeds of register assignment and the read-bypass circuitry) than the minimal clock period of a circuit based directly on Figure 1. Since the Figure 2 circuit also loses four cycles to shadowed instructions on every branch, we seem to have bought worse performance at the price of added complexity. In the next section, we show how retiming can be used to reduce the clock period by changing the distribution of registers in the circuit so as to balance the pipeline.

2.3   An algorithmic transformation

Figure 3 shows a circuit that results from retiming Figure 2. If the circuits of Figures 2 and 3 are run side by side with appropriately corresponding initial conditions, then each combinational element of Figure 3 will execute the same sequence of computations as the corresponding element of Figure 2, but shifted later or earlier in time by some number of clock ticks. The small numbers next to the combinational components in Figure 3 indicate their time shifts with respect to the corresponding components of Figure 2, with positive numbers denoting lags and negative numbers denoting leads.

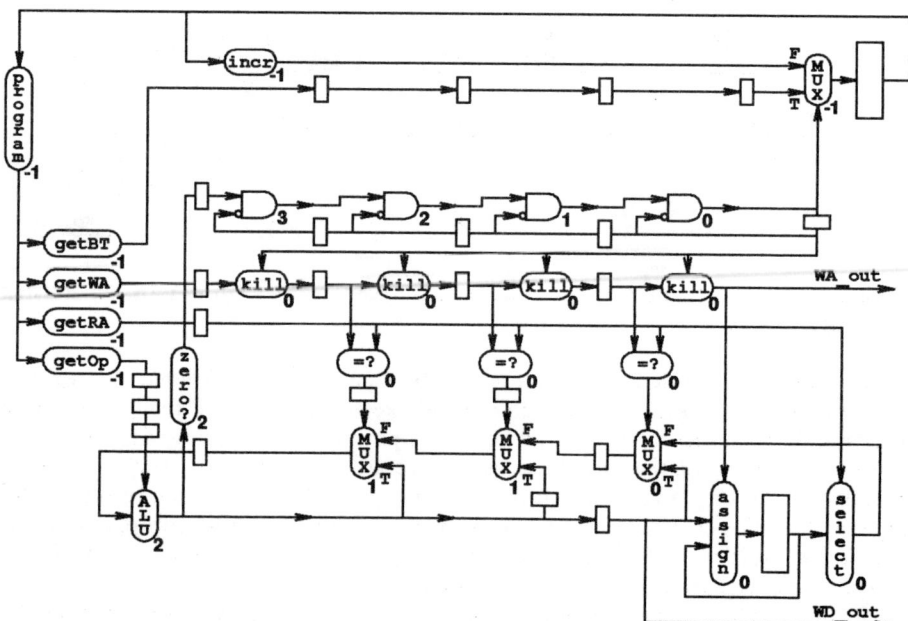

Figure 3: A pipelined processor design, derived from Figure 2 by retiming.

In Figure 3 there is only a relatively small amount of combinational logic on the path from the output of any register to the input of the next register, implying that a circuit built according to Figure 3 can safely run at a much higher clock speed than one based directly on Figure 1. If the frequency of successful branches is sufficiently low, this faster clock speed will more than compensate for the cycles lost to shadowed instructions.

The retiming transformation used to produce Figure 3 from Figure 2 can be performed algorithmically [9] and is guaranteed to preserve circuit behavior [8].[6] The *ad hoc* transformation used to produce Figure 2 from Figure 1 is another matter. Our description in Section 2.1 of the derivation of Figure 2 constitutes an informal argument for its correctness, but is by no means a rigorous proof. A cautious designer would want more convincing evidence that our *ad hoc* transformation is indeed valid. In the next section, we show how the correctness of such a transformation can be proved.

3   A Manual Correctness Proof

Description I *implements* description S if any observable behavior satisfying I also satisfies S. So to demonstrate that our *implementation* (Figure 2) implements our *specification* (approximately given by Figure 1—see Section 3.3) we must demonstrate that for any legal execution history of Figure 2 there exists a corresponding legal execution history of the specification.

3.1   Overview of the proof

We start by presenting the *givens* for the proof: the *implementation equations*, describing the constraints on an arbitrary legal history of the implementation implied by Figure 2, and the *required properties* of various operators such as select, assign, and kill. Then we state the *goals* to be proved. These are the *specification equations* derived from Figure 1, each of which must be satisfied. The proof proper comprises a *level map*, defining a specification history in terms of the implementation history, and a proof of *satisfaction*, showing that each goal is implied by the givens plus the level map.

3.2   Givens

3.2.1   The implementation equations

Each implementation equation describes the behavior of a register and/or some combinational elements. Identifiers starting with I denote the sequences of values that appear on the correspondingly labeled data paths of Figure 2 during some arbitrary execution history; the variable t denotes an arbitrary time step, modeled as a natural number; and the infix operator "." returns the element of its left (sequence) argument indexed by its right (time) argument.

---

[6]Note that guaranteed correctness of transformations is not necessarily linked to algorithmic application. It is often useful to transform a circuit by a series of small steps, where each step consists of applying a simple transformations, already known to preserve behavior, but where the decisions about which transformation to apply at each step are made explicitly by the designer. The Ruby hardware description language supports such a design methodology by providing a linear notation for circuits such that applications of simple transformation steps correspond to algebraic manipulations of circuit expressions. See [11] for a short description of Ruby and a treatment of retiming in the Ruby notation.

```
INext.t        == incr(IPCtr.t)
IInstr.t       == program(IPCtr.t)
IBT4.t         == getBT(IInstr.t)
IBT3.(t+1)     == IBT4.t
IBT2.(t+1)     == IBT3.t
IBT1.(t+1)     == IBT2.t
IBT0.(t+1)     == IBT1.t
IRA.t          == getRA(IInstr.t)
IRD1.t         == select(IRF.t, IRA.t)
IRD2.t         == if((IWA1.t)=(IRA.t), IWD1.t, IRD1.t)
IRD3.t         == if((IWA2.t)=(IRA.t), IWD2.t, IRD2.t)
IRD4.t         == if((IWA3.t)=(IRA.t), IWD3.t, IRD3.t)
IWA4.t         == getWA(IInstr.t)
IWA3.(t+1)     == kill(IWA4.t, IBC0.t)
IWA2.(t+1)     == kill(IWA3.t, IBC0.t)
IWA1.(t+1)     == kill(IWA2.t, IBC0.t)
IRF.(t+1)      == assign(IRF.t, kill(IWA1.t, IBC0.t), IWD1.t)
IOp.t          == getOp(IInstr.t)
IWD4.t         == ALU(IOp.t, IRD4.t)
IWD3.(t+1)     == IWD4.t
IWD2.(t+1)     == IWD3.t
IWD1.(t+1)     == IWD2.t
IBC4.t         == (IWD4.t) = zero
IBC3.(t+1)     == (IBC4.t) & not(IBC0.t)
IBC2.(t+1)     == (IBC3.t) & not(IBC0.t)
IBC1.(t+1)     == (IBC2.t) & not(IBC0.t)
IBC0.(t+1)     == (IBC1.t) & not(IBC0.t)
IPCtr.(t+1)    == if(IBC0.t, IBT0.t, INext.t)
WA_out.t == kill(IWA1.t, IBC0.t)
WD_out.t == IWD1.t
```

3.2.2 Required properties of components

The circuit in Figure 2, relies on certain properties of assign, select, kill, and getRA. We must state them explicitly, since we will use them in the proof. Our proof does not depend on the properties of many other operators, such as ALU and incr, and they can be regarded as parameters, or free variables, of the specification and implementation.

Writing to address null must leave the register file unchanged.

```
assign(x, null, y) == x
```

Writing to an address other than null and then reading from the same address must yield the data last written, and writing to one address must not change the contents of any other address.

```
select(assign(x, y1, z), y2) ==
    if((y1 = y2) & not(y2 = null), z, select(x, y2))
```

The kill function used in the write suppression logic is a simple conditional.

```
kill(x, y) == if(y, null, x)
```

No instruction attempts to read from the address null.

```
getRA(program(x)) = null == false
```

If such a read were attempted, it might retrieve the data word from a suppressed write recently queued by a shadowed instruction. Although this assumption seems obvious in retrospect, we overlooked it in our first attempt at a formal proof.

3.3   The goals: specification equations

The specification equations play a different role than the implementation equations. The implementation equations are assumptions of the verification; the specification equations are the theorems that we must prove to show the correctness of the implementation. More precisely, we would like to show that it is possible to choose an execution history for Figure 1 consisting of sequences SNext, SPCtr, SWA, ... such that these equations hold. Such an execution history would constitute an explanation of how Figure 1 could have produced the behavior produced by Figure 2, as observed on WA_out and WD_out. Unfortunately, such an execution history may not exist.

There are several tedious reasons why there might not be an execution history of Figure 1 to explain an arbitrary execution history of Figure 2. As we modified Figure 1 to produce Figure 2, we loosened the specification in a number of ways that were implicit in the informal derivation of Section 2.1 but must be made explicit if we are to state (and prove) a valid theorem about the possible behaviors of the implementation. Being forced to be explicit is one of the benefits of constructing a formal proof.

If the initial contents of the implementation registers are arbitrary, there can be a startup transient of up to three clock cycles (needed to flush the initial contents of the write queue) during which the behavior of the implementation may not reflect anything allowed by the specification.[7] In a real machine, of course, additional circuitry would be used to initialize the machine state. In the interest of brevity, however, we choose the alternative course of simply not observing the implementation during its first three cycles, by systematically using t+3 rather than t in all the specification equations.

The processor drawn in Figure 1 executes an instruction every clock cycle. The processor in Figure 2, on the other hand, takes five cycles to execute any instruction that actually branches—the four extra cycles being spent on shadowed instructions. In order to allow these extra cycles, we augment the specification by introducing a sequence, Stalled, of booleans indicating cycles on which the system is "stalled," and modify the equations describing the register file and program counter to indicate that the register file's contents are unchanged during such cycles.

```
SRF.(t+4)   == if(Stalled.(t+3),
                  SRF.(t+3),
```

---

[7] The transformation to Figure 3 introduces an additional start-up transient of at most one cycle, arising from the fact that some components have lags of −1 time step with respect to Figure 2, which is one less than the lag (0) of the interface.

```
                               assign(SRF.(t+3), SWA.(t+3), SWD.(t+3)))
      SPCtr.(t+4) == if(Stalled.(t+3),
                        SPCtr.(t+3),
                        if(SBC.(t+3), SBT.(t+3), SNext.(t+3)))
```

The specification of behavior at the interface must also be modified to account for values that may be seen during stalled cycles. Specifically, the write address to the register file is required to be null (so that it won't be seen at the interface as a genuine write), and the write data is irrelevant, leading to the interface equations:

```
      WA_out.(t+3) == if(Stalled.(t+3), null, SWA.(t+3))
      ((WD_out.(t+3)) = (SWD.(t+3))) | (Stalled.(t+3)) == true
```

The remaining specification equations simply describe constraints imposed by registers and combinational elements in Figure 1.

```
      SNext.(t+3)   == incr(SPCtr.(t+3))
      SInstr.(t+3)  == program(SPCtr.(t+3))
      SBT.(t+3)     == getBT(SInstr.(t+3))
      SRA.(t+3)     == getRA(SInstr.(t+3))
      SRD.(t+3)     == select(SRF.(t+3), SRA.(t+3))
      SWA.(t+3)     == getWA(SInstr.(t+3))
      SOp.(t+3)     == getOp(SInstr.(t+3))
      SWD.(t+3)     == ALU(SOp.(t+3), SRD.(t+3))
      SBC.(t+3)     == (SWD.(t+3)) = zero
```

3.4 The proof

3.4.1 The level map

We next construct a specification history to account for the observed behavior of an arbitrary implementation history. Such a history can be given by a *level map*—a set of equations defining a specification history in terms of a given implementation history.

Note that the definitions of the sequences, SRF, SPCtr, etc., comprising the specification history must be just that—definitions. If a "level map" employs multiple or circular definitions of some component of the specification history, then it may implicitly introduce new constraints on the implementation history, or may even be outright inconsistent. Technically speaking, the theory obtained by adding the level map equations to the previously assumed theory (consisting of the implementation equations, the required operator properties, and the standard rules for arithmetic, booleans, and sequences) must be a *conservative extension* of the previously assumed theory. That is, any theorem that doesn't involve the newly introduced symbols, SRF, SPCtr, etc., and that is provable in the new system must be provable in the old system.

```
      SRF.t          == IRF.t
      SPCtr.(t+3)    == if(IBC0.t, IBT0.t,
                           if(IBC1.t, IBT1.t,
                              if(IBC2.t, IBT2.t,
```

```
                          if(IBC3.t, IBT3.t,
                             IPCtr.t
                          )  )  )  )
SNext.t        == incr(SPCtr.t)
SInstr.t       == program(SPCtr.t)
SBT.t          == getBT(SInstr.t)
SWA.t          == getWA(SInstr.t)
SRA.t          == getRA(SInstr.t)
SOp.t          == getOp(SInstr.t)
SRD.t          == select(IRF.t, SRA.t)
SWD.t          == ALU(SOp.t, SRD.t)
SBC.t          == (SWD.t) = zero
Stalled.(t+3)  == (IBC0.t) | (IBC1.t) | (IBC2.t) | (IBC3.t)
```

We insure the conservativeness of our level map by following a certain syntactic style. For each component sequence of the specification history, there is exactly one defining equation, with that component on its left hand side and with only previously defined terms (possibly including previously defined specification history components) on the right hand side. To illustrate these ideas in a simpler context, consider a proof in which we have introduced integers a and b but have not yet used the name c. A legitimate next step would be to say, (1) "Let c == a + b." It would not be legitimate to say (2) "Let c == a + a and also let c == b + b," or (3) "Let c == a + c - b." We know by the syntactic form of (1)—namely, "Let c == ⟨*expression containing neither* c *nor any free variable*⟩"—that it is conservative. Multiple definitions, such as (2), or a circular definition, such as (3), may implicitly introduce unwarranted assumptions about a and b (in these examples, the assumption a == b). As a final example consider (4) "Let a == b + c + 1." While (4) is technically conservative, it does not have the syntactic form of a definition of c. The conservativeness of (4) cannot be deduced by mere examination of its form, but depends on properties of integer addition; if the universe of discourse were the natural numbers rather than the integers, (4) would embody the assumption a > b.[8]

There is no set method for deriving a level map. We arrived at this one by understanding why the system in Figure 2 works and applying brain power. Note that an ill-chosen level map may lead to failure to verify a correct implementation, but, so long as it is conservative, cannot lead to "verification" of an incorrect implementation.

3.4.2 *Validating the specification history*

All that remains is to prove that the execution history given by the level map satisfies the specification equations. There are thirteen specification equations to prove. Nine of them are simply instances of level map equations. The other four do not follow quite so trivially, but can be proved by case analysis on the

---

[8] A fine point: Since the operators "." and "+" appear on the left hand sides of the "definitions" in our level map, the legitimacy of these definitions technically depends on certain properties of sequences and of natural numbers not explicitly stated above. Specifically, (1) every function from indices (natural numbers) to scalars is the characteristic function of some sequence, and (2) addition of the constant 3 to distinct augends gives distinct results.

values of some of the boolean signals in the specification and implementation equations. We give here a sampling of the sort of reasoning used. The non-trivial goals are:

```
SRF.(t+4) == if(Stalled.(t+3),
               SRF.(t+3),
               assign(SRF.(t+3), SWA.(t+3), SWD.(t+3)))
SPCtr.(t+4) == if(Stalled.(t+3),
                  SPCtr.(t+3),
                  if(SBC.(t+3), SBT.(t+3), SNext.(t+3)))
WA_out.(t+3) == if(Stalled.(t+3), null, SWA.(t+3))
(Stalled.(t+3)) | ((WD_out.(t+3)) = (SWD.(t+3))) == true
```

We may proceed by considering first the case in which time step t+3 is a non-stalling cycle and then the case of a stalling cycle.

We consider first the non-stalling case, in which we assume

```
Stalled.(t+3) == false
```

This assumption lets us reduce our four goals to

```
SRF.(t+4) == assign(SRF.(t+3), SWA.(t+3), SWD.(t+3))
SPCtr.(t+4) == if(SBC.(t+3), SBT.(t+3), SNext.(t+3))
WA_out.(t+3) == SWA.(t+3)
WD_out.(t+3) == SWD.(t+3)
```

It also allows us to make some forward inferences. By expanding the definition of Stalled in the level map, we have

```
IBC0.t == false
IBC1.t == false
IBC2.t == false
IBC3.t == false
```

Expanding the definition of SPCtr then gives

```
SPCtr.(t+3) == IPCtr.t
```

from which we obtain[9]

```
SNext.(t+3) == incr(SPCtr.(t+3))
            == incr(IPCtr.t)
            == INext.t
```

and similarly

```
SInstr.(t+3) == IInstr.t
SBT.(t+3)    == IBT4.t
SWA.(t+3)    == IWA4.t
SRA.(t+3)    == IRA.t
```

---

[9] The shorthand used here, in which we write "E1 == E2 == E3 == E4" to indicate the line of reasoning "E1 == E2; E2 == E3; E3 == E4; therefore E1 == E4" is not used by LP, which does not produce—and cannot parse—any "equation" containing more than one "==" sign.

$$\text{SOp.}(t+3) \quad == \text{IOp.}t$$

The rest of the specification state components for time t+3 also map (in this non-stalled case) directly to particular implementation state components for time t, but the calculations necessary to confirm this take a bit more work.

We start by considering the implementation equations for the registers in the branch condition pipeline IBC0, ..., IBC3. Note that

```
IBC0.(t+1) == (IBC1.t) & not(IBC0.t)
           == false & not(false)
           == false
```

Similarly, we obtain

```
IBC0.(t+2) == IBC1.(t+1) == false
IBC0.(t+3) == IBC1.(t+2) == IBC2.(t+1) == false
```

Since IBC0 is false at steps t through t+3, we find that the write addresses in the pipeline at time t propagate to the register file assignment logic without change:

```
WA_out.t       == kill(IWA1.t, IBC0.t)
               == IWA1.t
WA_out.(t+1) == IWA1.(t+1) == IWA2.t
WA_out.(t+2) == IWA1.(t+2) == IWA2.(t+1) == IWA3.t
WA_out.(t+3) == IWA1.(t+3) == IWA2.(t+2) == IWA3.(t+1)
               == IWA4.t
```

Since we already had

```
SWA.(t+3) == IWA4.t
```

we obtain one of our four goals for the not-stalled case:

```
WA_out.(t+3) == IWA4.t == SWA.(t+3)
```

For the remaining three goals, we next consider the level map for the register file and its relation to the read-bypass equations.

If we repeatedly apply the implementation equation for the implementation register file IRF to expand the level map definition for the specification register file SRF, we get

```
SRF.(t+3) == IRF.(t+3)
          == assign(IRF.(t+2),
                    kill(IWA1.(t+2), IBC0.(t+2)),
                    IWD1.(t+2))
          == assign(IRF.(t+2), IWA1.(t+2), IWD2.(t+1))
          == assign(IRF.(t+2), IWA3.t, IWD3.t)
          == ...
          == assign(assign(
                    assign(IRF.t, IWA1.t, IWD1.t),
                    IWA2.t, IWD2.t),
                    IWA3.t, IWD3.t)
```

If we start expanding the definition of SRD for time step t+3, we get

```
SRD.(t+3) == select(SRF.(t+3), SRA.(t+3))
          == select(assign(IRF.(t+2), IWA3.t, IWD3.t),
                    IRA.t)
          == if((IRA.t = IWA3.t) & not((IRA.t) = null),
                IWD3.t, select(IRF.(t+2), IRA.t))
```

Since

```
IRA.t == getRA(IInstr.t) == getRA(program(IPCtr.t))
```

we know

```
(IRA.t) = null == false
```

So the above simplifies further to

```
SRD.(t+3) ==
   if((IRA.t = IWA3.t), IWD3.t, select(IRF.(t+2), IRA.t))
```

Similarly expanding the subexpression select(IRF.(t+2), IRA.t), we eventually get

```
SRD.(t+3) == if((IRA.t = IWA3.t), IWD3.t,
                if((IRA.t = IWA2.t), IWD2.t,
                   if((IRA.t = IWA1.t), IWD1.t,
                      select(IRF.t, IRA.t))))
```

The right hand side of this equation is exactly what we get by applying the implementation equations for the combinational logic that computes IRD4.t. So we have

```
SRD.(t+3) == IRD4.t
```

which we can use to obtain

```
SWD.(t+3) == ALU(SOp.(t+3), SRD.(t+3))
          == ALU(IOp.t, IRD4.t)
          == IWD4.t
```

The equations for the write data pipeline give us

```
IWD1.(t+3) == IWD2.(t+2) == IWD3.(t+1) == IWD4.t
```

So we have

```
WD_out.(t+3) == IWD1.(t+3) == IWD4.t == SWD.(t+3)
```

and another of our four goals is achieved.

The remaining two goals can be proved in a similar fashion. We would then turn to the stalling case, which turns out to need nested case analysis on the position of the first queued branch in the pipeline, but is basically similar. It should be clear by now why such manual proofs are extremely tedious and error-prone. Much of the detailed analysis, formula manipulation, and checking can and should be automated. The next section discusses one way to do that.

4   A Machine-Checked Proof

In this section, we present a slightly abridged script for a formal verification of the Figure 2 circuit using the Larch Prover (LP). While we include brief explanations of the LP commands used in this example, this section is not intended as a tutorial on LP. Readers who want to learn more about LP are referred to [4].

4.1   Declarations

In LP, all user identifiers must be declared, with signatures, before use. Here are some examples of declarations used in our formal verification.

```
declare sort Nat          % The sort of natural numbers
declare variable t: Nat % Used for time steps
declare sorts
   RAddr,                 % The sort of register addresses
   IAddr,                 % Instruction addresses
   Data,                  % Data words
   Instr,                 % Instructions
   RAddr_seq,             % Sequences of register addresses
   IAddr_seq,             % Sequences of instruction addresses
   Data_seq,              % Sequences of data words
   Instr_seq              % Sequences of instructions
   ..                     % ".." ends multi-line LP commands.

declare operators             % "." is overloaded to denote
   .: RAddr_seq, Nat -> RAddr % operators for indexing
   .: IAddr_seq, Nat -> IAddr % sequences of different
   .: Data_seq, Nat -> Data   % sorts.  LP uses the sorts
   .: Instr_seq, Nat -> Instr % of the arguments to disam-
   ..                         % biguate.  LP has no built-
                              % in rules for sequences.

declare variable
   xInstr: Instr              % xInstr is a variable denoting an
   ..                         % arbitrary instruction.

declare operators
   program: IAddr -> Instr % Instruction fetch.  Takes an
                          %    Addr as argument and
                          %    returns an Instr
   incr: IAddr -> IAddr    % Increment.
   ..
declare operators             % Constants in LP are modeled
   IPCtr, INext: -> IAddr_seq % as nullary operators.  Our
```

```
    IInstr: -> Instr_seq          % proof starts by picking an
    ..                             % arbitrary "fixed" execution
                                   % history.
declare operators
    0, 1, 2, 3, 4, 5, 6, 7: -> Nat
    zero: -> Data
    ..
```

It is important to understand the distinction between variables (such as t and xInstr) and constants (modeled as nullary operators, such a IPCtr and zero). An occurrence of a variable in an LP equation indicates that the equation holds for all values of that variable's sort. An occurrence of a constant indicates only that the equation holds for the particular value denoted by the constant.

4.2 Assertions

Having declared the necessary identifiers, we then assert the implementation equations, required operator properties, and level map definition, as described in Section 3.[10] The proof also uses some simple facts about arithmetic. Normally these would come from a standard library but for the sake of completeness, we give here all those that are actually used.

```
    set order left-to-right
    assert          % definitions of numerals
      2 == 1 + 1
      3 == 2 + 1
      4 == 3 + 1
      5 == 4 + 1
      6 == 5 + 1
      7 == 6 + 1
      ..
    assert ac + % "+" is associative and commutative
    assert % implementation equations
      INext.t == incr(IPCtr.t)
      % etc.,  as given in Section 3.2.1
      WD_out.t == IWD1.t
      ..
    assert % required properties of operators (Section 3.2.2)
      assign(xRFile, null, xData) == xRFile
      select(assign(xRFile, xRAddr, xData),yRAddr) ==
        if( (xRAddr = yRAddr) & not(yRAddr = null),
            xData,
            select(xRFile, yRAddr)
          )
      kill(xRAddr, xBool) == if(xBool, null, xRAddr)
```

---

[10] We must admit here that the conservativeness of the level map is not machine-checked. While we know how to remedy this deficiency, to do so with the current version of LP would require a style of proof rather more cumbersome, both to use and to explain, than the one we use in this paper. Instead we have chosen to rely on the syntactic conventions described in Section 3.4.1.

```
      getRA(program(xIAddr)) = null == false
      ..
assert % level map
  SRF.t          == IRF.t
  SPCtr.(t+3)    == if(IBC0.t, IBT0.t,
                         if(IBC1.t, IBT1.t,
                             if(IBC2.t, IBT2.t,
                                 if(IBC3.t, IBT3.t,
                                     IPCtr.t
                         )  )  )  )
  % etc., as given in Section 3.4.1)
  Stalled.(t+3) == (IBC0.t) | (IBC1.t)
                    | (IBC2.t) | (IBC3.t)
  ..
```

Much of LP's deductive system is based upon orienting equations into rewrite rules. The command "set order left-to-right" causes LP to produce rules that rewrite expressions matching the left hand sides of the equations above into corresponding instances of the right hand sides, rather than the other way around. While the left-to-right ordering rule works for our example proof, such user-chosen orderings are potentially dangerous because they may lead to non-terminating rewriting systems. For this reason, LP includes automated strategies for producing rewriting systems that are guaranteed to terminate [2, 4]. One such strategy can be caused to orient all the equations above in the left-to-right direction (thereby certifying the termination of the resulting rewriting system), but only if the user supplies appropriate hints. Further discussion of such ordering hints is beyond the scope of this paper; the reader is referred to [4] for a thorough discussion of LP's ordering facilities and the theory behind them.

4.3 Proving the specification equations

All that remains is to prove the modified specification equations from Section 3.3. LP gets the easy ones without any user guidance:

```
prove SNext.(t+3) == incr(SPCtr.(t+3))
qed
prove SInstr.(t+3) == program(SPCtr.(t+3))
qed
prove SBT.(t+3) == getBT(SInstr.(t+3))
qed
prove SRA.(t+3) == getRA(SInstr.(t+3))
qed
prove SRD.(t+3) == select(SRF.(t+3), SRA.(t+3))
qed
prove ((SWA.(t+3)) = getWA(SInstr.(t+3)))
qed
prove SOp.(t+3) == getOp(SInstr.(t+3))
qed
prove SWD.(t+3) == ALU(SOp.(t+3), SRD.(t+3))
```

```
qed
prove SBC.(t+3) == (SWD.(t+3)) = zero
qed
```

The qed command causes LP to check whether there are any outstanding un-proven conjectures on its stack. If there are, LP displays an error message, and, if the failing qed came from a file, returns to interactive mode.

For some of the proofs LP requires a bit of assistance from the user. There are a variety of ways in which this can be provided. For this example, the only guidance needed is for the user to suggest appropriate uses of case analysis. The necessary commands exhibit several features of LP, which we will explain presently.

```
set box-checking on  % This command is explained on
                     % the next page.
prove
  SPCtr.(t+4) == if(Stalled.(t+3),
                    SPCtr.(t+3),
                    if(SBC.(t+3), SBT.(t+3), SNext.(t+3)))
  ..
  resume by case IBC0.t
  <> 2 subgoals for proof by cases
    [] case IBC0 . tc
    resume by case IBC1.tc
    <> 2 subgoals for proof by cases
      [] case IBC1 . tc
      resume by case IBC2.tc
      <> 2 subgoals for proof by cases
        [] case IBC2 . tc
        [] case not(IBC2 . tc)
      [] case not(IBC1 . tc)
    [] case not(IBC0 . tc)
  [] conjecture
qed
```

The command resume by case E (where the *case expression* E is of sort boolean) causes LP to replace the goal of proving the current conjecture with two subgoals: proving the conjecture under the assumption that the case ex-pression is true and proving the conjecture under the assumption that the case expression is false.[11] These assumptions are known as "case hypotheses" in their respective arms of the proof.

A technical issue arises when the case expression contains a variable. Since variables are implicitly universally quantified, the cases

```
IBC0.t == true   % for all t
```

and

```
IBC0.t == false  % for all t
```

---

[11] LP also supports proofs by multi-way case analyses, where the set of cases examined must be proven to be exhaustive. We do not happen to use this facility in this paper.

do not cover all possible situations. The data path IBC0 might carry the value true on some time steps and false on others. In order to make the case analysis sound, LP replaces each variable in the case expression with a so-far-unused constant (tc in this case). All occurrences of these *case variables* in the conjecture are likewise replaced with the corresponding constants. The soundness of this procedure follows from the observation that, if some property can be proven for a particular time step of tc about which no special information is given, then that property must hold at every time step. Since, within any arm of the case analysis, LP is working on a conjecture in which the variable t has been replaced by the constant tc, nested resume by case commands use case expressions that likewise contain tc in place of t.

The lines beginning with boxes ([]) and diamonds (<>) are annotations to the proof. When LP is run with its "box-checking" mode turned on, and is reading commands from a file, it expects to see a line beginning with a diamond (and an appropriate number) every time it introduces one or more subgoals, and it expects to see a line beginning with a box every time a subgoal is discharged. Otherwise, it displays an error message and returns to interactive mode. This feature, like the qed command described above, is quite useful when one is replaying a slightly modified version of an old command file, since it notifies the user of the first deviation of a proof from its expected course, rather than letting LP proceed to apply additional commands in an inappropriate context. Note that if the box and diamond lines were removed from the proof script above, it would be impossible to tell (even using indentation as a hint) whether the cases analysis on IBC1.tc was intended to be applied within the case IBC0.tc == true or within the case IBC0.tc == false.

The remaining pieces of the proof proceed similarly to those above. Here they are, with the box and diamond lines omitted:

```
set box-checking off
prove
  SRF.(t+4) == if(Stalled.(t+3),
                  SRF.(t+3),
                  assign(SRF.(t+3), SWA.(t+3), SWD.(t+3)))
  ..
  resume by case IBC0.(t)
    resume by case IBC1.tc
      resume by case IBC2.tc
        resume by case IBC3.tc
qed
prove WA_out.(t+3) == if(Stalled.(t+3), null, SWA.(t+3)`
  resume by case IBC0.(t)
    resume by case IBC1.tc
      resume by case IBC2.tc
qed
prove
  (Stalled.(t+3)) | ((WD_out.(t+3)) = (SWD.(t+3)`
  ..                              % "== true" is
  resume by case IBC0.(t)
    resume by case IBC1.tc
      resume by case IBC2.tc
```

```
                    resume by case IBC3.tc
        qed
```

The preceding theorems cover only safety properties of Figure 2, showing
that every step of its execution (after the start-up transient) corresponds either
to a step of Figure 1's execution or to a stall. It would also be useful to
know that the implementation cannot simulate stalling forever. The following
commands suffice to prove that, once the start-up transient is over, the circuit
can never stall for more than four consecutive cycles—the time needed to clear
the pipe of shadowed instructions after a successful branch.

```
        prove
          not( (Stalled.(t+3)) & (Stalled.(t+4)) & (Stalled.(t+5))
               & (Stalled.(t+6)) & (Stalled.(t+7))
             )
            ..
        resume by case IBC0.(t)
          resume by case IBC1.tc
            resume by case IBC2.tc
              resume by case IBC3.tc
        qed
```

5 Discussion

5.1 Distance from a real circuit

The example presented in this paper is at a level of abstraction somewhat
removed from actual circuits. The details we have abstracted away fall into
two broad classes:

1. We have been intentionally silent about some aspects of the circuit design, including

   - The kinds of data carried on internal data paths; for example, how
     big are the instruction and register address spaces?

   - The semantics of the operators; for example, how many ALU op-
     eration codes are there and what does each ALU operation code
     mean?

   - The encodings of the data presented at the interface; for example,
     how is a data word encoded in bits.

2. We have said nothing about the physical realization of the circuit. In
   particular, we have not discussed what design rules must be obeyed in
   order to guarantee that the physical circuit behaves consistently with
   the equations describing it.

We have avoided the first class of details by treating many aspects of the
design as parameters. In effect, we have designed a class of circuits. In a
real application, the specification writer would at some point instantiate the
design parameters by requiring a particular word size, ALU semantics, etc. The

soundness of our algorithmic transformations and our verification of the *ad hoc* transformation do not depend upon how these parameters are instantiated. They are independent not only of the implementation of, say, the ALU, but even of its specification. It is only necessary that Figure 3 be instantiated with the *same* word size, ALU specification, etc. as Figure 1.

In contrast, the second class of details is not easily dealt with within our framework. Recall that each implementation equation in Section 3.2.1 corresponds to one or a few components in the Figure 2 diagram. We assume that if the physical components are properly fabricated and connected to each other in accordance with the diagram, then the resulting system will obey the equations. In general, however, the signals at the inputs and outputs of a physical component (for example, an AND gate) can be guaranteed to satisfy the corresponding equation (out.t == (in1.t) & (in2.t)) only if the system as a whole obeys certain design rules. For example, the outputs of different components must not be shorted together, and the clock period must be long enough to allow all combinational outputs to achieve stable values between successive ticks.

5.2   Debugging and maintaining machine-checked proofs

In our experience with mechanical proof checking, a few things stand out:

- Almost every "theorem" we try to prove isn't.

- If we don't understand why a theorem is valid, there is very little chance of discovering a mechanical proof.

- Even if we *do* understand why a theorem is valid, the first proofs we attempt are likely to be flawed.

Consequently, we want our proof checker to have a number of properties:

- It should assist in the interactive development of proofs.

- It should quickly detect invalid proof steps, and provide feedback that will help the user discover the error.

- To the greatest extent possible, it should "fail fast" on non-theorems, that is, stop and complain rather than automatically indulging in complex or time-consuming heuristics. There's a very good chance that simple proofs aren't working because the conjecture just isn't true.

- It should make it easy to formulate proof scripts that will be robust. It is frequently necessary to replay the proof of a theorem after small changes in axioms, the proofs of previous theorems, or the statement of the theorem itself. These should not require development of a completely new proof script.

- During replay, it should monitor the correspondence between the script and the progress of the proof, and stop as soon as a divergence is detected. This realization led us to the implementation of the <>, [], and qed commands described in Section 4.3.

5.3 Development, debugging, and generalization of our example proof

The circuits in Figures 1, 2, and 3 were originally designed by Jim Saxe to illustrate the application of successive transformations in the systematic design of high-speed digital circuits by deriving Figure 3 from Figure 1 by way of Figure 2. Although he was convinced of the "equivalence" of Figures 1 and 2, because he had carefully derived the latter from the former, he wasn't sure how to prove it formally. So he solicited help from Leslie Lamport, who, in the course of an afternoon, generated both a formal statement of the theorem to be proved and a sketch of a formal proof.[12] Leslie suggested that greater confidence in the proof could be gained by using a term rewriting system some of us had been building, Reve [3, 7], to perform the symbol manipulation needed to complete his proof sketch.

It took us about three man-weeks to come up with our first machine-checked proof based on the sketch we were given. We had to fix a number of small errors that are practically a litany of what goes wrong in hand proofs: there was a missing parenthesis in one of the formulas; there was an off-by-one error in a loop; the restriction that no instruction may attempt to read from the address null was left unstated; one case (branch taken) was ignored in the analysis; the proof used an invariant that we had to strengthen. We also spent time debugging our axiomatization of the circuit. In some places the prover was very helpful in doing this; for example, an inconsistent specification of the assign and select operators was detected by the prover. In other places, it was less helpful.

It is interesting that all the problems we found were errors in the hand proof or in our translation of the hand proof to Reve notation, and not in the machine design. It really was the proof, and not the design, that we debugged. It is important to note, however, that in constructing the proof we were forced to think carefully about the specification of the circuit, making explicit a variety of assumptions upon which the correctness of the design depends. For example, the specification used in our proof included the possibility of a start-up transient and the possibility of occasional stalls. If the circuit described by Figure 1 were to be used in a context where such behaviors were not acceptable, then a physical implementation based on Figure 3 would not be acceptable. Making such assumptions explicit is an important benefit of machine-checked verification.

A key feature of our formalization of start-up transients and stalls was its nondeterminism. For example, the specification equations in Section 3.3 do not, for any given time step t, determine Stalled.(t+1) as a function of SPctr.t and SRF.t. It was by making stalling on any cycle optional, rather than mandatory or forbidden, that we allowed physical implementations based on Figures 2 or 3 without forbidding an implementation based directly on Figure 1.

Figure 2 was produced by adding four stages of pipelining to Figure 1, one of which is partially optimized away. One would expect similar correctness proofs to work for circuits derived by adding more or fewer stages of pipelining. Our experiments in this direction gave precisely the results we expected: It was an entirely straightforward, albeit tedious, task to modify all the circuit

---

[12]Both the original statement of the theorem and the structure of the proof differ significantly from the ones given in this paper, although they are of similar complexity.

descriptions, conjectures, and proofs given above so that they would work with different numbers of stages; but the time and space requirements of such proofs rose exponentially with the number of stages. Under a reformulation of the circuit descriptions using single LP symbols to represent arrays of circuit components, we were able to prove, by induction on the depth, the correctness of versions of Figure 2 with arbitrary-depth pipelines.

When we produced our first machine-checked verification of Figure 2, based on Leslie Lamport's proof sketch, our tools were not as good as they are now. In fact, much of the early evolution of LP from Reve was motivated by the example we have presented here. Also, we had very little experience with mechanical proofs of this nature. However, despite improvements in our tools and our increased experience, it still seems harder to construct machine-checked proofs than hand proofs, not least because the machine has an annoying habit of rejecting plausible but erroneous arguments.

Acknowledgments

We thank Urban Engberg, Cynthia Hibbard, Shankar, and anonymous reviewers for helpful comments on earlier drafts of this paper.

References

[1] Avra Cohn, "The notion of proof in hardware verification," *Journal of Automated Reasoning*, Vol. 5, No. 2, June 1989, pp. 127–139.

[2] David Detlefs and Randy Forgaard, "A procedure for automatically proving the termination of a set of rewrite rules," *Proceedings of the First International Conference on Rewriting Techniques and Applications*, Dijon, France, *Lecture Notes in Computer Science* 202, Springer-Verlag, May 1985, pp. 255–270.

[3] Randy Forgaard and John V. Guttag, "REVE: A term rewriting system generator with a failure-resistant Knuth-Bendix," *Proceedings of a Workshop on Term Rewriting* (ed. by D. Kapur and D. Musser), April 1984, pp. 5–31.

[4] Stephen J. Garland and John V. Guttag, "A guide to LP, the Larch Prover," in preparation.

[5] Stephen J. Garland, John V. Guttag, and James J. Horning, "Debugging Larch Shared Language specifications," *IEEE Transactions on Software Engineering*, Vol. 16, No. 9, September 1990, pp 1044–1057.

[6] Stephen J. Garland, John V. Guttag, and Jørgen Staunstrup, "Verification of VLSI circuits using LP," *Proceedings of the IFIP WG 10.2 Conference on the Fusion of Hardware Design and Verification*, North Holland, 1988, pp. 329–345.

[7] Pierre Lescanne, "REVE: a rewrite rule laboratory," *Proceedings of the 8th International Conference on Automated Deduction*, Oxford, England, *Lecture Notes in Computer Science* 230, Springer-Verlag, July 1986, pp. 695–696.

[8] Charles E. Leiserson and James B. Saxe, "Optimizing synchronous systems," *Journal of VLSI and Computer Systems*, Vol. 1, No. 1, Spring 1983, pp. 41–67.

[9] Charles E. Leiserson and James B. Saxe, "Retiming synchronous circuitry," *Algorithmica*, Vol. 6, No. 1, 1991, pp. 5–35.

[10] John Rushby and Friedrich von Henke, "Formal verification of the interactive convergence clock synchronization algorithm using EHDM," SRI International report SRI-CSL-89-3, February, 1989.

[11] Mary Sheeran, "Retiming and slowdown in Ruby," in George J. Milne, ed., *The Fusion of Hardware Design and Verification*, North-Holland, 1988, pp. 289–308.

[12] Jørgen Staunstrup and Mark Greenstreet, "Synchronized transitions," in Jørgen Staunstrup, ed., *Formal Methods for VLSI Design*, North-Holland/Elsevier, 1990, pp. 71–129.

[13] Jørgen Staunstrup and Robin Sharp, editors, *Proceedings of the Second IFIP WG10.2/WG10.5 Workshop on Designing Correct Circuits*, North-Holland/Elsevier, 1992.

Using LP to Study the Language PL_0^+

E.A. Scott and K.J.Norrie

Department of Computer Science

Royal Holloway, University of London, England

In this paper we use the Larch Prover (LP) [7,8], to study PL_0^+ [15], an occam2 [13] like language. The languages ML_0 [2], which is based on the machine language for the transputer [14], and PL_0 [17], which is subset of PL_0^+, were developed as part of the Esprit funded PROCOS project [1]. One of the aims of that project was to develop provably correct compilers. In [15] there is a specification for a PL_0 to ML_0 compiler and a hand proof that any compiler that satisfies the specification is correct in the sense that original and compiled versions of programs have the same meanings.

Ideally we should like correctness proofs to be automated and carried out by theorem provers. There are two aspects to be considered when automating an existing hand proof. First the system in which the result is expressed has to be specified in the logic of the theorem prover. Then the result has to be proved using the proof techniques that the theorem prover has available. We are presented with some form of specification of the system in which the result is expressed and proved; we shall refer to this as the *original specification*. We have to translate this into an equivalent specification, one with the same fundamental properties, in the logic of the theorem prover we are to use. We call this a *theorem prover specification* of the system. Finally we can use the theorem prover to try to prove the result. Thus, when we ask whether an existing hand proof can be automated, we are really asking two questions:

(i) Can the system in which the proofs are to be carried out be specified in the logic of the theorem prover?

(ii) Are the proof techniques of the theorem prover able to prove the results?

In general the theorem prover specification of a system will not be a direct translation of the original specification, see [4] for a discussion of this in relation to hardware verification. For this reason we have to ask the following question:

In what way is the theorem prover specification equivalent to the original?

It is likely that the theorem prover specification will be more explicit and detailed than the original specification. Indeed, as has been noted in [25], this is a great strength of automated theorem proving. A common reason for undetected errors in hand proofs is that they arise from aspects of the specification which are assumed implicitly rather than specified explicitly. When translating an original specification into a theorem prover specification, we are forced to make implicit aspects explicit. This allows us to identify mistakes that arise from implicit assumptions, and to decide how to modify the original specification to allow a correct proof of the result. Thus theorem provers can be used not only to check proofs, but also to identify the cause and suggest remedies when mistakes are found in hand proofs.

The motivation for this work is to investigate the possibility of giving a machine proof of the correctness of the PL_0 compiler specification given in [15]. We chose to use LP for the investigation because our research group had some expertise in the use of LP, and it was thought that a specification of PL_0^+ and an automation of the proof would be possible using LP. This work is an edited version of [23] in which we gave a specification of PL_0^+ in the logic of LP and discussed the extent to which this specification is equivalent to the original. We have used LP to manipulate our specification in order to help prove that it is equivalent to the original. Both the original and LP specifications of PL_0^+ are given in the Appendix.

In [24] LP is used to check the proofs of compiler correctness given in [15]. It turns out that the proofs given in [15] contain mistakes that arose from the implicit assumptions in the original specification of PL_0^+. Making these assumptions explicit in the specification has indicated how the definition of compiler correctness needed to be modified to allow correct proofs of the theorems, see [24].

As part of a comparative study of theorem provers, Sampaio [22] has implemented a smaller PL_0^+ like language. The theorem provers used in the comparison were OBJ3 [9], B–Tool [6], the Veritas+ Environment [11], and the Occam Transformation System [10]. Part of PL_0^+ has also been specified in an earlier version of LP by Martin, [18].

Compiler proofs have attracted a lot of attention as test cases for automated theorem provers. Most of these have involved essentially the implementation of a "compiler" or at least a compiling function in a theorem prover and then the use of the prover to verify correctness. We mention in particular the early work of Cohn [3] in the LCF system but there have been many others; one noteworthy recent contribution is that of Young [26] as part of the "Stack" project in the Boyer Moore prover. The verification of an add-assign compiler carried out in the Boyer-Moore prover is contained in [25]. Our work differs from these studies in that we start with a detailed hand proof and are attempting to use the prover for the verification of that hand proof. Cohn's paper [4] describing and discussing her work on the Viper chip is particularly interesting in this regard.

The rest of this paper is organized as follows. In Section 1 we given the original specification of PL_0^+. In Section 2 we describe some of the issues addressed when giving an LP specification of PL_0^+. In Section 3 we give some conclusions, both about LP and automated theorem proving in general, that we have drawn from this study.

1 The original specification of PL_0^+

In this section we shall give brief a introduction to the language PL_0^+ which is a relative of occam2. At the end of the section we shall discuss the specification of the languages PL_0 and ML_0. We give the syntax of PL_0^+ in BNF fashion. Its semantics are formally defined by prescribing a partial ordering, $\sqsubseteq$, with a least element, ABORT, on the set of syntactic objects. This is the approach used to give semantics to a subset of occam in [21]. The laws given in [15] to prescribe $\sqsubseteq$ are listed in Appendix 2. In this section we shall just give informal descriptions of the meanings of the syntactic objects.

1.1 Syntax

We begin by naming the syntactic categories and meta-variables that will be used to range over the constructs in each type.

variable	category	
p	process	– the elements of PL_0^+
x	iden	– identifiers; which are strings of letters
n	int	– the integers; which are standard decimals
e	expr	– arithmetic expressions
b	Bexpr	– Boolean expressions

We shall subscript the meta-variables as necessary. The structure of the other constructs is:

$$p ::= \langle x_1, \ldots, x_m \rangle := \langle e_1, \ldots, e_m \rangle \mid \text{SKIP} \mid \text{STOP} \mid \text{ABORT} \mid \text{input?x}$$
$$\mid \text{output!e} \mid \text{INTx:p} \mid \text{SEQ}(p_1, \ldots, p_m) \mid \text{IF}(b_1 \rightarrow p_1, \ldots, b_m \rightarrow p_m)$$
$$\mid \text{WHILE}(b,p) \mid \text{end}(x_1, \ldots, x_m)$$
$$e ::= x \mid n \mid e_1 + e_2 \mid e_1 - e_2 \mid e_1 \times e_2 \mid e_1 \div e_2$$
$$b ::= \text{T} \mid F \mid b_1 \wedge b_2 \mid b_1 \vee b_2 \mid \neg b \mid e_1 < e_2 \mid e_1 \leq e_2 \mid e_1 \neq e_2 \mid e_1 = e_2$$

1.2 Informal semantics

SKIP is the empty process, STOP is a terminated process, and ABORT is thought of as a broken or totally unpredictable process. The instructions *input* and *output* are intended for communication with the environment. There is a list of integers associated with *input* and *input?x* assigns the next integer on the list to the identifier x. There are no semantics given for *output!e* in [15]. The process INT$x : p$ declares the identifier x in the process p. The process $\text{SEQ}(p_1, \ldots, p_m)$ is the concatenation of $p_1, \ldots, p_m$, which are carried out in order, and $\text{WHILE}(b, p)$ repeatedly carries out p until b is false, when it becomes SKIP.

To described the meanings of assignment and the IF constructs we need to consider some denotational semantics. Although this is not mentioned explicitly in [15], we assume the existence of semantic functions in the standard denotational manner, see for example [19]. We have a set of *states* which are functions $s : iden \rightarrow int$ and a semantic function $val : expr \rightarrow (states \rightarrow int)$ defined inductively. So for each expression e, $val[e]$ is a function and we define $val[e] : states \rightarrow int$ by defining its action on a state $s \in states$:

$$val[n](s) = n, \quad val[x](s) = s(x), \quad val[e_1+e_2](s) = val[e_1](s)+val[e_2](s), \quad \text{etc.}$$

Each process, p, determines a function from *states* to *states* denoted by $S[\![p]\!]$. We describe the function determined by the multiple assignment statement $\langle x_1, \ldots, x_m \rangle := \langle e_1, \ldots, e_m \rangle$. For all $s \in states$ we have

$$S[\![\langle x_1, \ldots, x_m \rangle := \langle e_1, \ldots, e_m \rangle]\!](s)(x) = \begin{cases} val[e_i](s) & \text{if } x = x_i \\ s(x) & \text{otherwise.} \end{cases}$$

Thus the assignment is intended to simultaneously assign the current value of each expression e_i to the corresponding identifier x_i. So, for example, if the initial values of x_1, x_2 are 2, 3 respectively, then after the execution of the process $\langle x_1, x_2 \rangle := \langle x_2 + 1, x_1 \rangle$ their values are 4,2, respectively.

We also define a semantic function, $bval : Bexpr \to (state \to \{true, false\})$, for Boolean expressions inductively by the rules

$$bval[T](s) \quad = \quad true \qquad\qquad bval[F](s) = false$$

$$bval[e_1 < e_2](s) \quad = \quad \begin{cases} true, & \text{if } val[e_1](s) < val[e_2](s), \\ false, & \text{otherwise} \end{cases}$$

$$bval[b_1 \wedge b_2](s) \quad = \quad \begin{cases} true, & \text{if } bval[b_1](s) = t \text{ and } bval[b_2](s) = t, \\ false, & \text{otherwise} \end{cases}$$

etc.

For a given state s we call $bval[b](s)$ the (Boolean) value of b.

The intended meaning of an IF construct $\text{IF}(b_1 \to p_1, \ldots, b_m \to p_m)$ is that it should behave like p_i if the value of b_i is true and the values of all b_j to the left are false.

In the original specification of PL_0^+ there is a description of general recursive functions, including WHILE. This description seems to us to be confused and we shall not discuss it here. We also note that since we began this work a modified version of [15] has been produced [16] in which the language PL_0^+ has been replaced by a further extension PL_0^R.

1.3 The semantics of IF via the relation $\sqsubseteq$

We now describe how, in cite14, certain properties of IF were specified without using semantic functions. There is a partial ordering $\sqsubseteq$ defined on PL_0^+. It is thought of as a refinement operator, with $p \sqsubseteq q$ if 'q is a more reliable version of p'. Any process p is a refinement of ABORT, and if $p \sqsubseteq q$ and $P(p)$ is a process containing p as a subprocess then $P(p) \sqsubseteq P(q)$, where $P(q)$ is obtained by replacing p with q in $P(p)$. The set of laws giving the full original definition of $\sqsubseteq$ can be found in Appendix 2. We write $p = q$ for $(p \sqsubseteq q)\&(q \sqsubseteq p)$.

In both the original and the LP specifications, the semantics of PL_0^+ are given by the relation $\sqsubseteq$; there is no mention of integer valued semantic functions. However we have introduced the denotational ideas in Section 1.2 in order to explain the need for certain aspects of the equational specification. For example, it would appear that we should need the function $bval$ in order to replace a process of the form $\text{IF}(b_1 \to p_1, \ldots, b_m \to p_m)$ by the first process p_i for which the value of b_i is $true$. However, we can cope with this situation as follows: There are certain elements $b \in Bexpr$ such that value of b is independent of the state. For example, $e < e + 1$, $1 \neq 2$, etc. In the original specification there are implicit corresponding laws of the form $(e < e + 1) = T$, $(1 = 2) = F$. This allows the evaluation of a process $\text{IF}(b_1 \to p_1, \ldots, b_m \to p_m)$ in the cases where the Boolean expressions have context (state) independent values. There is also a law that allows an assignment to be distributed over an IF construct:

$$\text{SEQ}(\underline{x} := \underline{e}, \text{IF}(b_1 \to p_1, \ldots, b_m \to p_m))$$
$$= \text{IF}(b_1' \to \text{SEQ}(\underline{x} := \underline{e}, p_1), \ldots, b_m' \to \text{SEQ}(\underline{x} := \underline{e}, p_m)),$$

here $\underline{x} = \langle x_1, \ldots, x_n \rangle$, $\underline{e} = \langle e_1, \ldots, e_n \rangle$, and b_j' is obtained by replacing each x_i in b_j by e_i, for $1 \leq i \leq n$. These two properties allow the evaluation of IF constructs in a wide class of situations. For example, we can deduce

$$\text{SEQ}(x := 1, \text{IF}((2 < x) \to p, \neg(2 < x) \to \text{STOP})) = \text{STOP},$$

although we cannot evaluate $\text{IF}((2 < x) \to p, \neg(2 < x) \to \text{STOP})$ itself. The use of constant valued Boolean expressions and substitution of assignments is sufficient to prove all the results that we require in PL_0^+.

1.4 Compiler correctness

We conclude this section by giving a brief description of the way in which the specification of PL_0^+ is used in connection with compiler correctness. Further details can be found in [15] and [24] and the underlying approach is described in detail in [12]. The semantics of the languages PL_0 and ML_0 are defined by inference from the semantics of PL_0^+ as follows. The language PL_0 is a subset of PL_0^+ and its semantics are taken to be directly inherited from PL_0^+. For ML_0 there is a function '$mtrans$' that takes ML_0 processes and translates them into transputer code [14] and a function '$Interp$' that takes transputer code and returns a PL_0^+ process. The functions $mtrans$ and $Interp$ allow the semantics of ML_0 to be defined in terms of the semantics of PL_0^+.

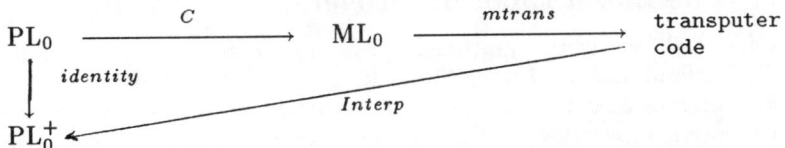

A compiler C is thought of as a map from PL_0 to ML_0, together with an associated family, Ψ, of maps each of which associates a finite set of identifiers in the programming language with addresses in the machine language. A compiler proof requires us to compare p and $C(p)$. Essentially we compare p and $Interp(mtrans(C(p)))$, each suitably modified in ways that we shall indicate.

For technical reasons, the set of identifiers that can be used in PL_0 processes has to be disjoint from the set of identifiers that can appear in processes of the form $Interp(mtrans(m))$. Thus the identifier names in p will be different to the names of corresponding identifiers in $Interp(mtrans(C(p)))$. Furthermore, the compiled version of p will contain references to addresses that do not correspond to identifiers in p. For example a pointer that holds the address of the code currently being executed. So the process p and $Interp(mtrans(C(p)))$ operate on different data spaces and we cannot expect them to be directly comparable. Thus we compare p and $C(p)$ before and after a translation between data spaces: given a compiler C and a PL_0 process, p, a process, $P_\Psi(p)$, is formed by concatenating p with particular multiple assignment and end–of–range processes. Similarly, given an ML_0 process m, we form a PL_0^+ processes $Q_\Psi(Interp(mtrans(m)))$. The processes $Interp(mtrans(m))$ and $Q_\Psi(Interp(mtrans(m)))$, and the processes p and $P_\Psi(p)$, are essentially equivalent except for renaming of identifiers, see [15] and [24] for details. The effect is that we now have two new processes which are essentially equivalent to the originals and which operate on the same data space.

A compiler C is said to be correct if $P_\Psi(p) \sqsubseteq Q_\Psi(Interp(mtrans(C(p))))$, for all PL_0 processes p.

In [15], for each PL_0 process p there is given a set of conditions, $\mathcal{C}_p$, which may be satisfied by ML_0 processes. Furthermore, hand proofs are given, for each process p, of the theorems

'IF m satisfies $\mathcal{C}_p$ THEN $P_\Psi(p) \sqsubseteq Q_\Psi(Interp(mtrans(m)))$',

The theorems show that if for all p, $C(p)$ satisfies $\mathcal{C}_p$, then C is correct in the above sense. In [24] the specification described in this work is used to give automated proofs of these theorems.

2 Specifying PL_0^+ in the logic of LP

In this section we begin with some brief details of LP and then we discuss some of the issues that need to be addressed when attempting to specify PL_0^+ in the logic of LP. The original specification of PL_0^+ is reproduced in Appendix 2. The Laws given there are referred to in the following text using an upper case 'L'. The full specification of PL_0^+ in the logic of LP is described in [23]. Note, in this specification we use the LP notation $==$ to denote the equivalence relation generated by $\sqsubseteq$.

2.1 The Larch theorem prover

The Larch Prover is an equational reasoning theorem prover developed at MIT by S. Garland and J. Guttag [7,8]. It is intended primarily as an interactive proof assistant or debugger, and it is in this capacity that we have used it. LP is a theorem prover for a subset of multisorted first-order logic with equality. Equations are asserted by the user then ordered by LP into a rewrite system which can be used to prove other equations. The logic also contains *deduction rules*, statements of the form

When $[(\text{FORALL } x_1, \ldots, x_n)]$ ⟨hypotheses⟩ Yield ⟨conclusions⟩

where x_i are variables, and where ⟨hypotheses⟩ and ⟨conclusions⟩ are sequences of equations. A specification in the LP logic can be axiomatized with induction rules. The statement

assert *sort* generated by *operators*

ensures that the only elements of *sort* are those that can be constructed using the specified *operators*. Results are proved by term rewriting; the rules are used to simplify both sides of an equation until a known equality is obtained. LP also supports proofs by induction, cases, and contradiction, and equations can be proved by performing critical pair calculations. A detailed description of LP can be found in [8].

2.2 Underlying data structures

As described above, PL_0^+ processes are built up from basic processes such as SKIP, STOP, and assignments, using process constructors such as SEQ. These constructors are specified in the logic of LP as operators on the set of processes. The algebraic system PL_0^+ also involves other types of objects such as identifier expressions, Booleans, integers etc. We declare the sorts *process, iden, int, expr* and *Bexpr* described in Section 1. For the class *expr* of expressions we only specify the operations of addition and subtraction. The other operations from the original specification could be specified in exactly the same way, but we have omitted them to keep the size of this study under control. In the original specification, integers and identifiers are themselves expressions. As the logic of LP does not include subsorts we have to explicitly embed *iden* and *Int* in *expr* using functions l, see Section 3.1.

The original specification of *Bexpr* is as an extension of the set of Booleans. We cannot extend the set *Bool* that is predefined in the logic of LP, thus we have to specify elements T and F that form a Boolean-like subset of *Bexpr*. We specify the usual Boolean-like operators, $\wedge$, $\vee$, $\neg$ on *Bexpr* and two operators $\leq$ and $\neq$. We use the pre-defined equality in LP to correspond to the $=$ of the original specification and we take $\neg(c \leq b)$ to correspond to $b < c$. Four of the laws that specify *Bexpr* are asserted as deduction rules, because they include conditions on the variable involved.

2.3   The IF construct

The nature of some of the original Laws governing the PL_0^+ processes makes their direct translation into the logic of LP impossible. For example, Law 2.2 of [15] involves a list of indefinite length and cannot be handled directly. Thus we specify a sort *glist* of lists of guarded processes, and then define IF^1 as a function from *glist* to *process*. We use the 'generated-by' facility to specify that all elements of type *glist* have the form $(b_1 \rightarrow p_1, \ldots, b_n \rightarrow p_n)$. It is then possible to use LP to prove results about *glist* by induction.

This still leaves problems with the specification of Law 2.2 because it cannot be directly stated using variables of type *glist*. However, a slightly different law, with the permutation that just interchanges two adjacent terms, can be expressed in the logic of LP:

> when $b \wedge c == F$
> yield $IF(gs, b \rightarrow p, c \rightarrow q, hs) == IF(gs, c \rightarrow q, b \rightarrow p, hs).$ $(*)$

Note that $(*)$ is not a law in the sense of universal algebra because it has 'side conditions'; the equality is not true for all instantiations of b and c, only those satisfying certain conditions. Thus this law is specified as a deduction rule in the logic of LP. Law 2.2 is really an infinite set of laws, one for each integer n. Fortunately, all of these laws are consequences of special case of the law for $n = 2$ and an extra law:

> $IF(b_1 \rightarrow p, b_2 \rightarrow q, b_3 \rightarrow r)$
> $== IF((b_1 \vee b_2 \rightarrow IF(b_1 \rightarrow p, b_2 \rightarrow q), b_3 \rightarrow r).$ $(**)$

Furthermore the proof for any given n can be carried out using LP. However, $(**)$ is not a consequence of the laws given in [15]. Since the laws of [15] were a subset of the laws in [21] chosen because they were sufficient for a proof of the correctness of the compiling predicate, we feel that we can choose different laws from [21] if we need to. It is possible to give a formal proof, by hand, that $(**)$ follows from two of the laws from [21], Law 2.1 of [15] and the cases $n = 2, 3$ of Law 2.2 of [15]. The proof that $(*)$ follows from the special case $n = 2$ and the extra law $(**)$ can be carried out using LP. Then, since any permutation is a product of transpositions, it is possible to give a formal hand proof, by induction, that the law

> $IF(gs, b_1 \rightarrow p_1, \ldots, b_n \rightarrow p_n, hs) == IF(gs, b_{\pi 1} \rightarrow p_{\pi 1}, \ldots, b_{\pi n} \rightarrow p_{\pi n}, hs),$

---

[1]In fact we have to call this operator IFF because the name 'if' is reserved in the logic of LP for a special pre-specified operator.

for any permutation π, when $b_i \wedge b_j = F$, for all $i \neq j$, follows from (*).
Note: we could specify, in the logic of LP, the special cases of the laws from
[21] that we require, and then prove (**) using LP. But this is messy, and
unnecessary once we have demonstrated that (**) is a law of [21].

2.4 Assignment

As discussed in Section 1, the assignment that is given in the original specification of PL_0^+ is parallel assignment; all assignments in a list are carried out
simultaneously. Law 3.2 of [15] is the law of the original specification which
guarantees that assignment in PL_0^+ is simultaneous in this sense. We cannot
directly translate Law 3.2 into the logic of LP because it would correspond to
an infinite rewrite rule. Thus it could not be used in a proof system based on
automatic term rewriting. We deal with this problem by using the facility in
the logic of LP that allows an operator to be declared to be associative and
commutative. However, it is not the operation of assignment itself that is commutative but rather that the list of assignments to be carried out is effectively
unordered. It is this view point that is reflected in the specification we now
describe. There is a sort *pairs* that we think of as being lists of pairs of identifiers and expressions. Concatenation of such lists is defined in the normal way,
and this operation is associative and commutative. Thus *pairs* is effectively the
type of unordered lists of pairs of identifiers and expressions. The unordered
property corresponds to Law 3.2 of [15]. Lists of pairs are turned into multiple
assignment statements by defining a function $asn : pairs \rightarrow process$. It can
be formally proved that this aspect of our specification is equivalent to the
original. Furthermore, we can use LP to prove that any specific case of Law 3.2
can be proved in our specification.

It should be noted that we have not included the property that the left-hand
sides of the assignments in a list must all be distinct in our specification, thus
at this point our specification is not equivalent to the original. This is discussed
further in Section 3.

2.5 The concatenation operator SEQ and substitution

The operator SEQ is specified in [15] as a multi–arity function. The logic of
LP does not include such functions. Thus we specify the set *plist* of lists of
processes and define SEQ as an operator from this set to *process*. We specify
concatenation of process lists in the usual way. The Laws 4.1, 4.2, and 4.2 of
[15] translate directly into the logic of LP; however Laws 4.4 and 4.5 involve
IF constructs and hence do not translate directly. We specify the special case
of Law 4.4 where $n = 2$. From this the theorem
  $SEQ(IF(b \rightarrow p, gs), qs) \ == \ IF(b \rightarrow SEQ(p, qs), \neg b \rightarrow SEQ(IF(gs), qs))$
can be proved using LP. It is possible to give a formal hand proof that this
theorem is equivalent to Law 4.4 of the original specification. It is also possible
to use LP to prove Law 4.4 for any particular integer n, and to prove the
corollaries to Law 4.3 and 4.4 (see Appendix 2) that are proved by hand in
[15].

The relationship between the constructors SEQ and IF hinges on the re-
placement of identifiers by expressions in Boolean expressions. This replace-

ment takes place after an identifier is assigned the value of an expression.

We specify substitution inductively on the structure of expressions. We start by defining substitution into an expression which is itself an identifier, then extend this to substitution into general expressions via subexpressions. We write $sub(d, [\underline{x}, \underline{e}])$ for the expression obtained by simultaneously replacing each occurrence, in d, of the identifier x_i in the list of pairs $[\underline{x}, \underline{e}]$ by the corresponding expression e_i. Then, to define substitution into an identifier y we use the pre–defined operators 'if' and '=' of the logic of LP as follows:

$$sub(y, [(x, \underline{x}), (e, \underline{e})]) \quad == \quad \text{if}(y = x, e, sub(y, [\underline{x}, \underline{e}])).$$

(if(b, x, y) returns x if $b = true$ and y if $b = false$.) We can use LP to prove a version of the law

$$\text{SEQ}(\underline{x} := \underline{e}, \text{ IF}(b \to p, \ gs)) \quad ==$$
$$\text{IF}(sub(b, [\underline{x}, \underline{e}]) \to \text{SEQ}(\underline{x} := \underline{e}, p), \ \neg sub(b, [\underline{x}, \underline{e}]) \to \text{SEQ}(\underline{x} := \underline{e}, \text{ IF}(gs))).$$

This can be shown by hand to be equivalent to the general Law 4.5.

In order to specify an equivalent law to Law 4.6 of [15] we need to specify that two lists of multiple assignments have the same left-hand-sides. We achieve this by introducing a function $eqiden$ which is defined inductively on the length of a multiple assignment. Again the specification of the function $eqiden$ uses the operators 'if' and '='. We define

$$eqiden([x, e], [y, d]) \quad == \quad \text{if}(x = y, \text{true}, \text{false}),$$
$$eqiden([(x, \underline{x}), (e, \underline{e})], \ [(x, y), (d, \underline{d})]) \quad == \quad eqiden([\underline{x}, \underline{e}], \ [\underline{y}, \underline{d}]).$$

This does not completely specify the function $eqiden$; it is possible, in our specification, for eqiden$([\underline{x}, \underline{e}], [\underline{y}, \underline{d}])$ to be neither true nor false when $\underline{x}$ and $\underline{y}$ are different. However, if $\underline{x}$ and $\underline{y}$ are equal then this specification does give that eqiden$([\underline{x}, \underline{e}], [\underline{y}, \underline{d}])$ is true. In [23] LP is used to give examples of the behaviour of $eqiden$.

The specification of input in the logic of LP is straightforward, and we shall not discuss it here. There are no laws governing the operator '!' in [15], thus we have given none in our specification. The specification of ABORT is a direct translation of the original specification and the specification of the operators end and INT is straightforward, for details see [23]. We mention here that although Law 5.2(2) corresponds to a non-terminating rewrite rule this does not matter because it is implemented as a deduction rule, and is thus not ordered into a rewrite rule by LP.

2.6 The refinement operator

The laws that ensure that $\sqsubseteq$ is a partial ordering with least element ABORT translate directly into the logic of LP. To specify that by equality ($==$) in the specification we mean the equivalence relation generated by $\sqsubseteq$, we also assert the law

$$p \sqsubseteq q \ \& \ q \sqsubseteq p \quad \Rightarrow \quad p == q.$$

We have not specified the 'substitutive' property of $\sqsubseteq$:

$$\text{if} \quad p \sqsubseteq q \quad \text{then} \quad P(p) \sqsubseteq P(q),$$

where $P(r)$ is a process that contains a specific subprocess r. When we use this specification to prove the correctness of a compiling specification, see [24], we specify this property by adding a deduction rule:

when $p \sqsubseteq q$

yield $\mathrm{SEQ}(r, p, t) \sqsubseteq \mathrm{SEQ}r, q, t)$, $\mathrm{IF}(gs, b \rightarrow p, hs) \sqsubseteq \mathrm{IF}(gs, b \rightarrow q, hs)$.

We note here that we were not able to specify any form of Law 4.11 of [15] in the specification described in Section 2, although we did not try very hard because it contains an operator $\cap$ which is not actually part of the algebraic system declared in [15], and which has infinitely many arguments. Nor did we specify recursively defined processes in PL_0^+. A specification of such processes was attempted in [15] and the Laws 7 represent this. However we feel that this specification is confused and inadequate. A specification of recursively defined processes in the logic of LP is discussed in [20].

3 Discussion

In this section we make some comments drawn from our experience of carrying out the specification described above. We begin with some comments on the difficulties of specifying PL_0^+ in the particular logic of LP. We then discuss, through two examples, how problems in an original specification can be exposed when implicit aspects are made explicit for a theorem prover. Finally we give some general conclusions that we have drawn from this case study.

3.1 Operational aspects of the specification

This section contains the comments on the specification of PL_0^+ in the logic of LP, and on the use of the Larch Prover to manipulate the laws of this specification.

The LP logic is a multisorted logic; there is no sort hierarchy. However, in the specification of PL_0^+ there is a need for a sort hierarchy. We need to be able to identify subsets of some sorts, for example identifiers in the sort of expressions. We have always been able overcome the problem of specifying subsorts in the logic of LP by defining, in each case, a specific operator l that embeds one sort into the other. However, this has made the specification more complex and difficult to read.

We did not use the completion facility of LP. This was partly because we did not need a complete system to be able to prove the results we are interested in. Even had we thought that completion would have been useful the specification is far too large for such an exercise to be attempted. However, to complete many proofs it was necessary to use the critical pair calculating facility. We used critical pair calculations to produce additional rules that are consequences of the equational theory but unobtainable by rewriting in our incomplete set of rewrite rules.

3.2 Making the implicit explicit

In several places in the LP specification of PL_0^+ we have had to make explicit aspects that were only implicit in the original specification. It is necessary not only to decide which implicit axioms were used in the original hand proof, but also to decide which implicit proof techniques were adopted. In this section we discuss both these points using two examples based on the Boolean expressions as illustrations.

In the original specification of PL_0^+ there is an underlying, but unmentioned, notion of a semantic function, $bval$, on Boolean expressions, see Section 1.2. In general the value of a Boolean expression in a process depends on the 'state', s, of the process at the time the value is calculated. However, for certain Boolean expressions the value is independent of the state, i.e. $bval[b](s)$ is constant for all states s. For example, $bval[F](s) = false$, and $bval[e \leq e + 1](s) = true$. In the specification given in [15] this situation is not discussed, because the only Boolean expressions that are ever evaluated are those for which $bval[b](s)$ is constant. Certain laws are implicitly assumed in the original specification, for example $(e \leq e + 1) = T$ and $(0 = 1) = F$. A law of the form $b_1 = b_2$ can only be justified when $bval[b_1](s) = bval[b_2](s)$, for all states s. In a specification in the logic of LP such laws must be made explicit. Since the original specification contains no mention of the function $bval$, or even of the set of Boolean expressions, it is difficult to be sure that a specification in which such laws are explicit is equivalent to the original.

Example: We consider the proof of the correctness theorem for compilation of SKIP given in [15] (see [24] an for automated proof of this). Let as be a list of machine code, so as is thought of as a list of pairs of integers, the first integer is the name of the address and the second is the contents. Define integer valued functions srt and fsh that return the integers that name the first and last addresses in as respectively. Consider also a PL_0^+ identifier denoted by pt that is intended to represent a pointer to the list as. The proof of the theorem requires the law $(srt(as) \leq fsh(as)) = T$. This amounts to making explicit an implicit assumption that $val[srt(as)](s)$ and $val[fsh(as)](s)$ are constant and that $bval[(srt(as) \leq fsh(as)](s)$ is $true$. Because there is no discussion of semantic functions in the original specification, a reader of the original hand proof may find it hard to see that the law $(srt(as) \leq fsh(as)) = T$ holds in the original specification, but that the law $(srt(as) \leq pt) = T$ does not. In fact, adding the 'law' $(srt(as) \leq pt) = T$ to the specification allows a very quick, but invalid, 'proof' of the correctness theorem for SKIP.

As we remarked at the beginning of this section, it necessary to decide which implicit proof techniques have been adopted in a proof. For example, in our study we needed to make a careful distinction between two possible proof methods that involve looking at 'cases' $b = T, b = F$; only one is valid. The following is an illustration of this.

Example: Let $G(pt)$ denote the process:

IF$((2 \leq pt + 1) \rightarrow (pt := 0), \quad (pt + 1 < 2) \rightarrow$
    SEQ$(pt := 4,$ IF$(2 \leq pt + 1 \rightarrow (pt:=3), \quad pt + 1 < 2 \rightarrow (pt:=0))))$

where pt is an identifier. A flawed 'proof-by-cases: b=T, b=F' shows that $G(pt) = (pt:=0)$ as follows:
If $2 \leq pt + 1 = T$ then $G(pt) = (pt := 0)$ by Law 2.6.
If $2 \leq pt + 1 = F$ then
$G(pt) = $ IF$(F \rightarrow (pt:=0), T \rightarrow$ SEQ$(pt:=4,$ IF$(F \rightarrow (pt:=3), T \rightarrow (pt:=0))))$
$\quad = $ SEQ$(pt := 4, pt := 0)$
$\quad = (pt := 0)$.

Thus $G(pt) = (pt := 0)$! The mistake is the assumption that either $(2 \leq pt + 1) = T$ or $(2 \leq pt + 1) = F$; in fact $bval[2 \leq pt + 1](s)$ is not constant.

However it is true that following proof rule is valid:

from   IF$(T \rightarrow p, gs) = r$ and IF$(F \rightarrow p, gs) = r$ deduce   IF$(b \rightarrow p, gs) = r$

The important point here is that when reasoning with Boolean expressions we could not use the 'proof by cases' method built into LP.

Theorem provers vary according to the amount of confidence that one can have in the equivalence of a new specification to the original. For example, it is possible for a user of LP to add the 'law' $(srt(as) \leq pt) = T$ to the new specification. Whereas other theorem provers force one to make consistency checks at all stages. In general the more safeguards of this type that are built in to a theorem prover the more difficult it is to use. Thus there is a trade–off to be considered between the ease of use of a theorem prover against the difficulty of telling whether the final specification is equivalent to the original.

3.3   Conclusions

From a pragmatic point of view the reason for automating existing hand proofs is to check their correctness. We found some problems with the definition of the WHILE construct and were unable to specify the description given in [15]. We also found when we came to specify other aspects of [15], see [24], that we had to change the specification described above and some of the laws of [15]. However, we found no inconsistencies in the aspects of original specification that we have dealt with in this work.

A more general reason for carrying out the specification was to investigate the possible problems involved in automating an existing hand proof. In such cases the new specification will seldom be a direct copy of the original.

In cases where minor changes have to be made to aspects that are explicit in the original specification it may be possible to *prove* that it is equivalent to the original. For example, it is possible to give a formal hand proof that a general law of the following type holds in our specification:

SEQ(IF$(b_1 \rightarrow p_1, \ldots, b_n \rightarrow p_n), q) = $ IF$(b_1 \rightarrow$SEQ$(p_1, q), \ldots, b_n \rightarrow$SEQ$(p_n, q))$

Furthermore, it is possible to use LP to prove specific cases of this law for any fixed integer n; LP cannot be used to prove the general law because this cannot be expressed in our specification.

In cases where major changes are made to aspects that are stated explicitly in an original specification it may only be possible to give an explanation as to why the two specifications are equivalent. For example, we have had to introduce a function *eqiden*, see Section 2.4, whereas in the original specification the condition that the left-hand sides of two multiple assignment statements are equal can be built into the notation. Another example is given by our treatment of Law 2.2, see Section 2.2. We needed to add a new law that does not hold in the original specification. Our justification for this rests on a statement contained in [15, pg 2]:

> "The set of laws is not complete; we restrict ourselves to the laws
> needed in the verification of the compiling specification."

In cases where implicit aspects of a specification have to be made explicit we may be intuitively convinced that the new specification is equivalent to the original, but we cannot expect to be able to give any form of formal proof of our intuition.

We feel that it is worth pointing out that the problems we have discussed only arise when automating an existing hand proof. When a system is originally defined in the logic of the theorem prover it is not, of course, necessary to consider whether the specification is equivalent to an original. This is why it is important to study theorem proving using pre–existing examples.

We have seen that the specification by one person of an algebraic system written by someone else can be a delicate task. This is of practical interest in projects involving collaborating partners one producing hand proofs, and another attempting to check/debug these proofs by producing automated versions. It can be difficult to decide whether a theorem prover specification is equivalent to the original; whether the process of automation has itself introduced or obliterated errors. If the hand proof is very clear and detailed then automation will be easy, but probably unnecessary for such a well written hand proof. If the hand proof is less explicit, with many of the assumptions and proof techniques implicit, then an automation will be much harder but also more valuable. The need for a proof checker increases with the number of implicit aspects of the original proof; it is in these aspects that mistakes are most likely and most difficult to detect.

Acknowledgements We are very grateful to Ursula Martin and to David Cohen for helpful suggestions and discussions during the course of this work.

References

[1] D. Bjørner, C.A.R Hoare, J.P Bowen, et. al., A ProCos project description – ESPRIT BRA 3014, Bulletin of EATCS, **39**, pages 60–73, 1989.

[2] J.P Bowen, Formal specification of the PROCOS/safemos instruction set, Microprocessors and Microsystems, **14** 10, pages 631–643, 1990.

[3] A.Cohn, Machine assisted proofs of recursion implementation, Ph.D. Thesis, Dept. of Comp. Sci., University of Edinburgh, 1979.

[4] A. Cohn, The notion of proof in hardware verification, J. Of Automated Reasoning, **5** pages 127–139, 1989.

[5] P. Dybjer, Using domain algebra to prove the correctness of a compiler, Proc. STACS 1985, Lecture Notes In Computing Science **182** pages 98–108, Springer–Verlag, 1985.

[6] P.Gardiner, T.Vickers, A logic for a theorem proving assistant, Technical Report, Oxford University Computing Laboratory, 1989.

[7] S.J.Garland, J.V.Guttag, An overview of LP, the Larch Prover In: N. Dershowitz, ed, Proc. 3rd International Conf. Rewriting Techniques And Applications, Lecture Notes In Computing Science **355** pages 137–151, Springer–Verlag, 1989.

[8] S.J.Garland, J.V.Guttag, A guide to LP, the Larch Prover Technical Report 28, Digital Equipment Corporation Systems Research Center, 1991.

[9] J.Goguen, OBJ3 as a theorem prover with applications to hardware verification, Technical Report, SRI International, SRI–CSL–88–4R2, 1988.

[10] M.Goldsmith, The Oxford OCCAM transformation system, Technical Report, Oxford University Computing Laboratory, 1988.

[11] K.Hanna, N.Daeche, M.Longley, Schematic definition of the Veritas+ logic, Technical Report, University of Kent, 1989.

[12] C.A.R. Hoare, He Jifeng, Refinement algebra proves correctness of compilation, preprint, 1990.

[13] INMOS Ltd, Occam 2 reference manual, Series In Computing Science, Prentice-Hall, 1988.

[14] INMOS Ltd, Transputer instruction set: a compiler writers guide, Prentice-Hall, 1988.

[15] He Jifeng, P. Pandya, J. Bowen, Compiling specification for ProCos level 0 language, 1990. Procos Technical Report [OU HJF 4].

[16] He Jifeng, J. Bowen, Compiling specification for ProCos language PL_0^R. 1991. Procos Technical Report [OU HJF 6].

[17] H.H. Løvengreen, K.M. Jensen, Definition of the ProCoS programming language level 0, 1989. Procos Technical Report [ID/DTH HHl 2].

[18] U.H. Martin, Case studies in equational reasoning, ERIL Project Report RHBNC, 1990.

[19] N.R. Nielson, F. Nielson, Semantics with applications: A Formal Introduction For Computer Science, Wiley, 1992.

[20] K.J. Norrie, E.A. Scott, On the implementation of recursion and the WHILE construct in an automated theorem prover, in preparation.

[21] A.W. Roscoe, C.A.R. Hoare, The laws of occam programming, Theoretical Computer Science 60, pages 177–229, 1988

[22] A. Sampaio, A comparative study of theorem provers: proving correctness of compiling specifications, Oxford University PRG Tech. Report PRG–TR–20–90, 1990.

[23] E.A. Scott, K.J.Norrie, A study of PL_0^+ using the Larch Prover, RHBNC Technical Report CSD–TR–92–33, 1992.

[24] E.A. Scott, An automated proof of the correctness of a compiling specification, in preparation.

[25] D. Weber–Wulff, Proof movie, Proving the Add–Assign Compiler with the Boyer–Moore Prover, to appear in Formal Aspects Of Computing.

[26] W.D.Young, A mechanically verified code generator, Journal of Automated Reasoning, 5, 1989

Appendix

1. THE LP SPECIFICATION OF PL_0^+

Notation: We will not define all the notation used here, just enough to give
some idea of the meanings of the rules. The notation used here corresponds
exactly to that used in [23] where it is fully defined. Elements bn are variables
ranging over Boolean expressions, p, q, r are variables ranging over PL_0^+ processes, x, y, z are variables ranging over identifiers, e, d, c are variables ranging
over expressions, and $e0, d0, c0$ are variables ranging over integers. A variable
followed by 's' denotes a (finite) sequence of variables of that type, for example
ps denotes a sequence of elements of PL_0^+, and gs denotes a sequence of guarded
processes, $(b_1 \to p_1, \ldots, b_n \to p_n)$. The notation ++ is used for concatenation of
processes, IFF is used instead of IF, b1>>p denotes $b1 \to p$, x@e denotes $x := e$,
|< denotes $\sqsubseteq$, and $e0 >< d0$ denotes $(e0 <= d0)\&(d0 <= e0)$.

Induction rules and operator theories

```
glist generated by nil, COMP          pairs generated by nil, COMP
iden generated by id, nxt             idset generated by embed, union
ac +:expr,expr→expr                   ac ++:  pairs,pairs → pairs
ac +:Int,Int→Int                      commutative eqiden
ac &:Bexpr,Bexpr→Bexpr                ac ++:  inproc,inproc → inproc
ac |:Bexpr,Bexpr→Bexpr                ac union
```

Deduction rules

```
WHEN 1(e0) == 1(d0)  YIELD  e0 == d0

WHEN  not((1(e0)<=1(d0)) = T)  YIELD  (1(e0)<=1(d0)) = F

WHEN 0 <= d == T  YIELD  e <= (d + e) == T, (e - d) <= e == T

WHEN e <= d == T, d <= c == T  YIELD  e <= c == T

WHEN 1(e0) >< 1(d0) == T  YIELD  e0 == d0

WHEN e0 <= d0 == T  YIELD  1(e0) <= 1(d0) == T

WHEN e0 <= d0 == F  YIELD  1(e0) <= 1(d0) == F

WHEN (p |< q) & (q |< p) == true  YIELD  p == q

WHEN b1&b2 == F  YIELD  IFF(COMP(b1,p,b2>>q)) == IFF(COMP(b2,q,b1>>p))

WHEN eqiden(xses, ysds) == true
YIELD SEQ(1(asn(xses)) ++ 1(asn(ysds))) == asn(sub(ysds, xses))

WHEN appear(x, e) | (x=y) == false
YIELD SEQ(1(asn(y@e))++1(end(embed(x))))
                    == SEQ(1(end(embed(x)))++1(asn(y@e)))

WHEN free(x, p) == false
YIELD INT(x,p) == p,  SEQ(1(p)++1(INT(x,q))) == INT(x,SEQ(1(p)++1(q))),
        SEQ(1(INT(x,q)) ++ 1(p)) == INT(x, SEQ(1(q)++1(p)))

WHEN appear(x, e) == false  YIELD  INT(x, asn(x@e)) == SKIP
```

Rewrite rules

```
1.   (nxt(x) = nxt(y))  ⟶   (x=y)
2.   (id = nxt(x))  ⟶   false
```

```
 3.    s(e0) + d0   ⟶   s(e0 + d0)
 4.    l(e0) + l(d0)   ⟶   l(e0 + d0)
 5.    l(e0) - l(d0)   ⟶   l(e0 - d0)
 6.    l(0) + e   ⟶   e
 7.    e - e   ⟶   l(0)
 8.    e - l(0)   ⟶   e
 9.    (d + e) - c   ⟶   (d - c) + e
10.    e - (c + d)   ⟶   (e - d) - c
11.    e - (d - c)   ⟶   (e - d) + c
12.    T & b1   ⟶   b1
13.    F & b1   ⟶   F
14.    T | b1   ⟶   T
15.    F | b1   ⟶   b1
16.    not(T)   ⟶   F
17.    not(not(b1))   ⟶   b1
18.    not(b1) & b1   ⟶   F
19.    not(b1) | b1   ⟶   T
20.    e <= e   ⟶   T
21.    e0 <= s(e0)   ⟶   T
22.    s(e0) <= e0   ⟶   F
23.    e><d   ⟶   (d<=e)&(e<=d)
24.    e0><d0   ⟶   (d0<=e0)&(e0<=d0)
25.    F=T   ⟶   false
26.    (b1≫p) ++ gs   ⟶   COMP(b1, p, gs)
27.    nil ++ gs   ⟶   gs
28.    gs ++ nil   ⟶   gs
29.    gs ++ (hs ++ ks)   ⟶   (gs ++ hs) ++ ks
30.    nil ++ ps   ⟶   ps
31.    ps ++ nil   ⟶   ps
32.    ps ++ (qs ++ rs)   ⟶   (ps ++ qs) ++ rs
33.    nil ++ xses   ⟶   xses
34.    COMP(x, e, ysds)   ⟶   (x @e) ++ ysds
35.    eqval(nil)   ⟶   T
36.    eqval(COMP(x, e, xses))   ⟶   (x><e) & eqval(xses)
37.    sub(l(y), nil)   ⟶   l(y)
38.    sub(l(y), (x @e) ++ xses)   ⟶   if(x=y, e, sub(l(y), xses))
39.    sub(d0, xses)   ⟶   d0
40.    sub(d + e, xses)   ⟶   sub(d, xses) + sub(e, xses)
41.    sub(d - e, xses)   ⟶   sub(d, xses) - sub(e, xses)
42.    sub(e, (x @l(x))++xses)   ⟶   sub(e, xses)
43.    sub(T, xses)   ⟶   T
44.    sub(F, xses)   ⟶   F
45.    sub(e <= d, xses)   ⟶   sub(e, xses) <= sub(d, xses)
46.    sub(b1 & b2, xses)   ⟶   sub(b1, xses) & sub(b2, xses)
47.    sub(b1 | b2, xses)   ⟶   sub(b1, xses) | sub(b2, xses)
48.    sub(not(b1), xses)   ⟶   not(sub(b1, xses))
49.    sub(nil, xses)   ⟶   nil
50.    sub((y @d)++ysds,xses)   ⟶   (y @sub(d,xses))++sub(ysds,xses)
51.    eqiden(xses, xses)   ⟶   true
52.    eqiden(x @e, y @d)   ⟶   if(x=y, true, false)
53.    eqiden((x @d)++ysds, (x @e)++xses)   ⟶   eqiden(xses, ysds)
54.    eqiden((x @e) ++ xses, nil)   ⟶   false
55.    appear(x, l(y))   ⟶   (x=y)
56.    appear(x, e0)   ⟶   false
57.    appear(x, d + e)   ⟶   appear(x, d) | appear(x, e)
```

```
58.   appear(x, d - e) ⟶ appear(x, d) | appear(x, e)
59.   union(embed(x), embed(x)) ⟶ embed(x)
60.   appear(x, T) ⟶ false
61.   appear(x, F) ⟶ false
62.   appear(x, e <= d) ⟶ appear(x, d) | appear(x, e)
63.   appear(x, b1 & b2) ⟶ appear(x, b1) | appear(x, b2)
64.   appear(x, b1 | b2) ⟶ appear(x, b1) | appear(x, b2)
65.   appear(x, not(b1)) ⟶ appear(x, b1)
66.   free(x, STOP) ⟶ false
67.   free(x, SKIP) ⟶ false
68.   free(x, ABORT) ⟶ false
69.   free(x, 1(input⁻ y)) ⟶ (x=y)
70.   free(x, output ! e) ⟶ appear(x, e)
71.   free(x, asn((y @e) ++ ysds))
                        ⟶ appear(x, e) | (x=y) | free(x, asn(ysds))
72.   free(x, IFF((b1≫p)++gs))
                        ⟶ appear(x, b1) | free(x, IFF(gs)) | free(x, p)
73.   free(x, SEQ(1(p) ++ ps)) ⟶ free(x, SEQ(ps)) | free(x, p)
74.   free(x, end(embed(y))) ⟶ (x=y)
75.   free(x, end(union(embed(y), V1))) ⟶ (x=y) | free(x, end(V1))
76.   free(x, INT(y, p)) ⟶ if((x=y), false, free(x, p))
77.   p |< p ⟶ true
78.   ABORT |< p  ⟶ true
79.   (((p |< q) & (q |< r) => (p |< r)) ⟶ true
80    IFF((F≫p)++gs) ⟶ IFF(gs)
81.   IFF((T≫p)++gs) ⟶ p
82.   IFF(b1 ≫ STOP) ⟶ STOP
83.   IFF((b1≫p)++(not(b1)≫IFF(gs))) ⟶ IFF((b1≫p)++gs)
84.   IFF(((b1≫p)++(b2≫p))++gs) ⟶ IFF(((b1 | b2)≫p)++gs)
85.   IFF(((b1|b2)≫IFF((b1≫p)++(b2≫q)))++(b3≫r))
                        ⟶ IFF(((b1≫p)++(b2≫q))++(b3≫r))
86.   asn(nil) ⟶ SKIP
87.   asn((y @1(y)) ++ xses) ⟶ asn(xses)
88.   IFF((eqval(xses)≫SEQ(1(asn(xses)) ++ 1(p))) ++ gs)
                        ⟶ IFF((eqval(xses)≫p) ++ gs)
89.   SEQ(nil) ⟶ SKIP
90.   SEQ(1(p)) ⟶ p
91.   SEQ((ps ++ 1(SEQ(qs))) ++ rs) ⟶ SEQ((ps ++ qs) ++ rs)
92.   SEQ(1(IFF((b1≫p)++(b2≫q)))++qs)
                        ⟶ IFF((b1≫SEQ(1(p)++qs))++(b2≫SEQ(1(q)++qs)))
93.   SEQ(1(asn(xses))++1(IFF((b1≫p)++(b2≫q))))
                        ⟶ IFF((sub(b1,xses)≫SEQ(1(asn(xses))++1(p)))
                              ++(sub(b2,xses)≫SEQ(1(asn(xses))++1(q))))
94.   SEQ(1(asn(x @e)) ++ 1(1(input⁻ x))) ⟶ 1(input⁻ x)
95.   1((input⁻x)++(input⁻y)) ⟶ SEQ(1(1(input⁻x))++1(asn(y @1(x))))
96.   SEQ(1(1(input⁻x))++1(asn(y@1(x))))
                        ⟶ SEQ(1(1(input⁻x))++1(1(input⁻y)))
97.   SEQ(1(ABORT) ++ 1(p)) ⟶ ABORT
98.   SEQ(1(asn(xses)) ++ 1(ABORT)) ⟶ ABORT
99.   SEQ(1(end(V1)) ++ 1(end(V2))) ⟶ end(union(V1, V2))
100.  SEQ(1(asn(x @e)) ++ 1(end(embed(x)))) ⟶ end(embed(x))
101.  SEQ(1(end(V1)) ++ 1(ABORT)) ⟶ ABORT
102.  SEQ(1(end(V1)) ++ 1(STOP)) ⟶ STOP
103.  INT(x, p) |< INT(x, SEQ(1(asn(x @1(y))) ++ 1(p))) ⟶ true
104.  p |< p ⟶ true
```

105. ABORT $|<$ p $\longrightarrow$ true
106. $((p |< q) \And (q |< r)) => (p |< r) \longrightarrow$ true

2. THE ORIGINAL SPECIFICATION OF PL_0^+

Notation: b, c, b_i are variables ranging over Boolean expressions, p, q, r, p_i are variables ranging over PL_0^+ processes, x, y, x_i are variables ranging over identifiers, e, e_i are variables ranging over expressions. An underlined variable denotes a (finite) sequence of variables of that type, for example $\underline{gc} = (b_1 \to p_1, \ldots, b_n \to p_n)$. Finally the notation $b[\underline{e}/\underline{x}]$ is used to denote the Boolean expression obtained by replacing each occurrence of b_i in b by e_i, $1 \le i \le n$. The following laws are reproduced from [15].

Law 2.1 $\text{IF}(b \to p, \underline{gc}) = \text{IF}(b \to p, \neg b \to \text{IF}(\underline{gc}))$

*Law 2.2 $\text{IF}(b_1 \to p_1, \ldots, b_n \to p_n) = \text{IF}(b_{\pi(1)} \to p_{\pi(1)}, \ldots, b_{\pi(n)} \to p_{\pi(n)})$,
for any permutation π of $\{1, \ldots, n\}$ provided that $b_i \wedge b_j \equiv \text{FALSE}$ whenever $i \ne j$.

Law 2.3 $\text{IF}(b \to p, c \to p, \underline{gc}) = \text{IF}(b \vee c \to p, \underline{gc})$

Law 2.4 $\text{IF}(\text{FALSE} \to p, \underline{gc}) = \text{IF}(\underline{gc})$

*Law 2.5 $\text{IF}(\underline{gc}, b \to \text{STOP}) = \text{IF}(\underline{gc})$

Law 2.6 $\text{IF}(\text{TRUE} \to p, \underline{gc}) = p$

Corollary $\text{IF}(b \to p, \neg b \to p, \underline{gc}) = p$

Law 3.1 $() := () = \text{SKIP}$

**Law 3.2 $(x_i \,|1 \le i \le n) := (e_i \,|1 \le i \le n) = (x_{\pi(i)} \,|1 \le i \le n) := (e_{\pi(i)} \,|1 \le i \le n)$,
for any permutation π of $\{1, \ldots, n\}$.

*Law 3.3 $(x \cdot \underline{y} := e \cdot \underline{y}) = \underline{x} := \underline{e}$

*Law 3.4 $\text{IF}(\wedge_i(x_i \to e_i) \to p, \underline{gc}) = \text{IF}(\wedge_i(x_i \to e_i) \to \text{SEQ}(\underline{x} := \underline{e}, p), \underline{gc})$

Law 4.1 $\text{SEQ}() = \text{STOP}$

Law 4.2 $\text{SEQ}(p) = p$

Law 4.3 $\text{SEQ}(\underline{p}, \text{SEQ}(\underline{q}), \underline{r}) = \text{SEQ}(\underline{p}, \underline{q}, \underline{r})$

Corollary $\text{SEQ}(\text{SKIP}, \underline{p}) = \text{SEQ}(\underline{p}) = \text{SEQ}(\underline{p}, \text{SKIP})$

*Law 4.4 $\text{SEQ}(\text{IF}(b_1 \to p_1, \ldots, b_n \to p_n), q)$
$\qquad = \text{IF}(b_1 \to \text{SEQ}(p_1, q), \ldots, b_n \to \text{SEQ}(p_n, q))$

Corollary $\text{SEQ}(\text{STOP}, p) = \text{STOP}$

*Law 4.5 $\text{SEQ}(\underline{x} := \underline{e}, \text{IF}(b_1 \to p_1, \ldots, b_n \to p_n))$
$\qquad = \text{IF}(b_1[\underline{e}/\underline{x}] \to \text{SEQ}(\underline{x} := \underline{e}, p_1), \ldots, b_n[\underline{e}/\underline{x}] \to \text{SEQ}(\underline{x} := \underline{e}, p_n))$

Corollary $\text{SEQ}(\underline{x} := \underline{e}, \text{STOP}) = \text{STOP}$

Law 4.6 $\text{SEQ}(\underline{x} := \underline{e_1}, \underline{x} := \underline{e_2}) = \underline{x} := \underline{e_2}[\underline{e_1}/\underline{x}]$

Law 4.7 $SEQ(x := e, \text{input}?x) = \text{input}?x$

*Law 4.8 $SEQ(\text{input}?x, y := x) = SEQ(\text{input}?y, x := y)$

Law 4.9 $SEQ(ABORT, p) = ABORT$

Law 4.10 $SEQ(x := e, ABORT) = ABORT$

Law 4.11   (1) $SEQ(\cap\{q_n \mid n \geq 0\}, \underline{p}) = \cap\{SEQ(q_n, \underline{p}) \mid n \geq 0\}$
$\qquad\quad$ (2) $SEQ(\underline{p}, \cap\{q_n \mid n \geq 0\}) = \cap\{SEQ(\underline{p}, q_n) \mid n \geq 0\}$

Law 5.1 $SEQ(end_{V_1}, end_{V_2}) = end_{V_1 \cup V_2} = SEQ(end_{V_2}, end_{V_1})$

*Law 5.2   (1) $SEQ(x := e, end_x) = end_x$
$\qquad\quad$ (2) $SEQ(y := e, end_x) = SEQ(end_x, y := e)$
provided that $x \neq e$ and x does not appear in e.

Law 5.3 $SEQ(end_V, ABORT) = ABORT$

Law 5.4 $SEQ(end_V, STOP) = STOP$

Law 6.1 $INTx : p = p,$ $\qquad$ if x is not free in p.

Law 6.2   (1) $SEQ(p, INT(x : q)) = INTx : SEQ(p, q)$
$\qquad\quad$ (2) $SEQ(INT(x : p), q) = INTx : SEQ(q, p)$
provided that x is not a free variable of p.

Law 6.3 $(INTx : p) \sqsubseteq (INTx : SEQ(x := y, p))$

Law 6.4 $(INTx : x := e) = SKIP,$ $\qquad$ if x does not appear in e.

Law 7.1 $WHILE(b, p) = \cap q_n$

Law 7.2 $\mu X.F(X) = \cap\{F^n(ABORT) \mid n \geq 0\}$

Law 7.3 $WHILE(b, p) = \mu X.IF(b \rightarrow SEQ(p, X), \neg b \rightarrow SKIP)$

Law 7.4 $\mu X.F(X) = F(\mu X.F(X))$

Law 7.5   if $F(q) \sqsubseteq q$ then $\mu X.F(X) \sqsubseteq q$

Corollary $SEQ(WHILE(b, p), WHILE(b \vee c, p)) = WHILE(b \vee c, p)$

The implemented versions of Laws marked * /** are slightly/very different, respectively, from the originals. All the other Laws have been implemented directly except for Law 4.11 and Laws 7, which have not been implemented at all. (Laws 7 are discussed in [20])

Semantic Analysis of Larch Interface Specifications

Yang Meng Tan

(ymtan@lcs.mit.edu)

Laboratory for Computer Science

Massachusetts Institute of Technology

545 Technology Square

Cambridge, MA 02139.

Abstract

A concept, called *claim*, is introduced to support checking of a formal specification. Claims are logical assertions about a specification that must follow semantically from the specification. Claims can be used to debug formal specifications, help readers better understand a formal specification, highlight important features of a software design, support program verification, and help generate test cases.

Claims are described in the context of the Larch/C interface language, LCL.

1 Introduction

Given a formal specification, does the specification say what is intended? When a change is made to a specification, what can be done to minimize inadvertent consequences? This paper describes preliminary work towards addressing these questions.

Executable specification languages are designed to address these problems by allowing specifiers to run specifications [16]. Larch specification languages are designed to be simple and expressive, rather than executable. In place of executing specifications as a means of testing them, logical conjectures about the specification can be stated and checked at specification time. A Larch specification provides a logical theory. The conjectures about Larch specifications are called *claims*. The checking process may yield useful insights about the specification. Failures to prove some claims can help locate errors in the specification. These claims can also express properties that should follow from the *intended* specification. A specifier can be more confident that the specification is the intended formalization if he is able to prove such claims. To increase a specifier's confidence that changes do not have undesirable consequences, the specifier should try to re-prove the claims when a change is made.

This approach leads to some open problems: First, what kinds of claims are worth making and checking? This paper gives our thoughts on this issue. Second, what aids can be given to help specifiers discharge claims? Our approach is to build a tool to translate Larch specifications into inputs for LP, a proof checker [5]. This tool will help us answer a related question: What strategies can be used to prove claims? Experimentation is needed to address this question.

Research in the past looked at generic properties of formal specifications. Two of these properties stand out. We certainly would like our specifications to be consistent. Second, we would like to know when our specification is complete. These are interesting and useful properties to check. Checking these properties are, however, impossible in general and very difficult in practice. While we know what it means for a logical specification to be consistent, what constitutes a complete specification is not clear [15]. Where checking for the consistency and completeness of formal specifications are possible, they still do not address the original problem we have: how do we know that the specification describes our intent?

We take a different but complementary approach: we focus on problem-specific claims. It is frequently easier to state and prove such claims. It also helps address the original problem of formal specification validation. A claim language can be designed to facilitate the expression and proof of problem-specific claims.

Besides using claims to help debug and validate formal specifications, claims can be used in other ways. The author of a specification can use claims to highlight important or interesting properties of the specification. Claims can serve as useful lemmas in program verification. They can also be used to suggest useful test cases. Our work can also be viewed as exploring the use of formal specification to detect design errors [6, 10, 11].

Our focus is on checking Larch interface specifications; complementary work has been done on checking Larch Shared Language specifications [12]. We introduce claims in the context of a Larch/C interface language, LCL, a language for specifying ANSI C programs [7]. We describe LCL in the next section. In Section 3 we describe the concept of claims, explain how they can be used, and illustrate the different kinds of claims expressible in LCL by example. In Section 4 we define when a claim is valid in an LCL specification. The research issues yet to be addressed by this work are discussed in Section 5. In the last section we sketch the current status of this work.

2 Larch/C Interface Language

LCL version 1.0 was designed by Guttag and Horning [7]. The version of LCL described here is called LCL 1.1; it incorporates some changes made to LCL 1.0. The only change germane to this paper is the addition of claims; this will be described in later sections.

LCL was designed with several goals in mind: First, LCL provides a language to formally specify ANSI C programs [1]. LCL specifications will be useful as precise and formal documentation of C programs. Second, tools can be built to analyze LCL specifications and to check aspects of C programs against their LCL specifications. The former is achieved by a program that checks the syntax and static semantics of LCL specifications. A program called *LCLint* can be constructed to perform the usual checks that a good lint program does, and in addition, to check that certain constraints implied by the specifications are obeyed. Besides providing a specification language, an important goal of the LCL effort is to design a simple, modular, and effective style of programming that combines the strengths of abstract data types and the popularity and portability of C.

There are a few distinguishing features of LCL:

Module Orientation: Users organize a design around software modules. A module defines the operations that can access the data encapsulated by the module. LCL is intended to be used in a programming style in which abstractions play a key role. Besides providing a way to specify the function abstraction provided by the C programming language, LCL allows users to define abstract data types within a module.

Pre and Post States: The specification of a procedure is modeled as a predicate on a sequence of states. In the case of sequential programs, this is a relation between two states, the state before and after the execution of the procedure.

Composability and Reuse of Specifications: Specifications are built up in a modular fashion, by combining different specifications.

Extensive Tool Support: Even before a specification is sent to implementors to be constructed, the specifier can analyze the specification to minimize errors in the specification.

Two-Tiered Approach: A formal specification in LCL is composed of two parts, one part is specified in the Larch Shared Language (LSL) [9] and the other in LCL. LSL is used by all Larch interface languages. It is used to capture mathematical abstractions that are programming language independent. At the interface level relations on program states, exceptions, and other programming language dependent features can be specified.

Modification Assertions: Each function specification must indicate which of the input objects and global variables may be modified by the function. All other objects not mentioned in the modifies clause must not be modified. This modification assertion is easy to write and can enable a number of LCLint checks.

Figure 1 shows an example of an LCL specification. This is the specification of a function in a module defining a mutable bag of integers.

```
mutable type bag;
uses bag(bag for C, int for E);

void bag_delete(bag b, int i) {
  requires true;
  modifies b;
  ensures b' = delete(i, b^);
}
```

Figure 1: Example of an LCL Specification

The first line in the LCL specification declares **bag** to be a mutable abstract type. This adds an additional requirement on the implementation of bags in C: the representation type must be such that assigning a bag to another in C corresponds to sharing the bag, i.e., assignments of mutable values have sharing semantics rather than the usual copying semantics of C. A consequence of this is that mutable values are effectively passed around in function calls by reference.[1] The next line in the specification indicates what LSL traits are used

---

[1] A mutable type can be implemented via a pointer or a handle.

```
bag (C, E): trait
  includes integer
  introduces
    { }: → C
    insert, delete: E, C → C
    count: E, C → int
    size: C → int
    __ ∈ __: E, C → bool
    { __ }: E → C
    __ ∪ __, __ - __: C, C → C
  asserts
    C generated by {}, insert
    C partitioned by count
    ∀ e, e1: E, b, b1: C
      count(e, {}) == 0;
      count(e, insert(e1, b)) == count(e1, b) +
                                  (if e = e1 then 1 else 0);
      count(e, delete(e1, b)) == count(e1, b) ⊖
                                  (if e = e1 then 1 else 0);
      { e } == insert(e, {});
      e ∈ insert(e1, b) == e = e1 ∨ e ∈ b;
      size({}) == 0;
      size(insert(e, b)) == succ(size(b));
      count(e, b ∪ b1) == count(e, b) + count(e, b1);
      count(e, b - b1) == count(e, b) ⊖ count(e, b1)
```

Figure 2: An LSL bag trait

by the current specification. The operator **delete** used in the ensures clause is
defined in the bag trait shown in Figure 2.

The syntax for the function specification is borrowed from the syntax of
C functions. The specification says that the **bag_delete** procedure takes in a
bag and an integer and returns nothing. The requires clause indicates that no
preconditions are needed. In such cases, the requires clause may be omitted.
The modifies clause specifies which of the input objects may potentially be
modified. In this case, it says that the bag object may be modified. The
ensures clause describes the effects this function is supposed to carry out. In
LCL specifications. The symbol ^ is used to extract the value of an object in
the pre state, and the symbol ' is used to extract its value in the post state.

Figure 2 shows an example of an LSL trait. Details about the semantics of
LSL specifications are described in [8].

3 Claims: What and Why

Claims are logical assertions about a Larch specification that must follow semantically from the specification. A Larch specification specifies a logical the-

ory, and claims are conjectures in such a theory. Besides providing a language for writing claims, we will also build a program, *lcl2lp*, that translates LCL specifications and claims into proof obligations in the input language of a proof checker, LP [4]. In this way, the user can check that all claims indeed follow from the specifications.

A claim language allows us to state redundant information. This redundancy brings about the following benefits:

Support Debugging and Check Understanding: An author of a specification can check his understanding of the specification, by stating some claims that he believes should follow from the specification, and by trying to prove the claims. Failure to prove a claim should alert the author to potential bugs in the specification. Failures in the proof process can also help indicate the potential locations of bugs.

This is useful in Larch specifications because of the separation of interface and shared specifications. Thus, one key use of claims is to validate the specifier's understanding of the relationships between LSL traits and interface specifications.

Highlight Properties: There are infinitely many true logical consequences in a logical theory. Most of them are neither interesting nor useful. It can be difficult for readers of a specification to pick up the important or useful properties of the specification. Specifiers can use claims to highlight these properties.

Support Program Verification: Claims are properties of a specification. Since specifications are abstract, claims are properties that must be true of any valid implementation. As such, they can serve as useful lemmas in program verification.

Generate Test Cases: When claims state important properties of a specification, these are likely to be properties that should be checked in an implementation. Thus claims can be used to motivate test cases.

To illustrate the above benefits, the next few subsections show some examples of the kinds of claims that can be expressed in LCL. The examples also serve to describe the claim language.

3.1 A Simple Claim

Figure 3 shows a simple example of a claim within a procedure specification. This specification is identical to the one shown in Figure 1, except for the addition of the claims clause. The claim says that at most one copy of i is removed from b, and other members of b are not removed.

```
void bag_delete(bag b, int i) {
 modifies b;
 ensures b' = delete(i, b^);
 claims ((i ∈ b^) ⇒ count(b', i) = count(b^, i) - 1)
       ∧ ∀ x: int ((x != i) ⇒ count(b', x) = count(b^, x));
}
```

Figure 3: Example of an LCL Claim

In order to show that the claims are true, we need to consult the bag trait. The third equation in Figure 2 shows the meaning of **delete(b1, e2)**: it deletes one copy of **e2**, not all copies of **e2**.

3.2 Module Claims

If a data abstraction is just a collection of related procedures, then it will not be very interesting. A data abstraction is intended to be a *coherent* set of operations on some data. A key aspect of a data abstraction is the provision of a data type induction principle which can be used to prove properties of all objects of the module. These properties are useful for understanding and using the module. Some of these induction principles can be automatically deduced from a module specification. LCL supports claims about the invariants that must be true of the objects defined by the module, called module claims.

The previous example of a claim is a logical conjecture about one function specification. In this section we show two examples of claims that apply to an entire LCL module. The module claims in Figure 7 express two invariants about the **dbase** module taken from [7]. The dbase module consists of a number of functions that add and delete employees in a database that is encapsulated by the module. There are also operations for modifying attributes of employees and for querying the database.

```
dbaseAssumptions: trait
  job enumeration of MGR, NONMGR, job_ANY
  gender enumeration of MALE, FEMALE, gender_ANY
  employee tuple of ssNum: int, name: employeeName,
                    salary: int, gen: gender, j: job
  dbase_status enumeration of dbase_OK, salERR, genderERR,
                    jobERR, duplERR
  dbase_query tuple of g: gender, j: job, l: int, h: int
```

Figure 4: Background for Examples of Claims

The LSL trait in Figure 4 models some of the basic abstractions needed in the dbase module. The first line in Figure 4 says that **job** is an enumeration of the three values shown. Similarly, **gender** and **dbase_status** are modeled as enumeration types. The third line in the figure says that **employee** is modeled as a tuple with a number of fields. The fields of a tuple can be accessed in the usual way, e.g., if **e** is an employee, then **e.ssNum** is the **ssNum** field of the employee tuple. **[ssNum: 123456789, name: "tan", salary: 9, gender: FEMALE]** constructs an employee. The relevant part of the dbase module is shown in Figure 5. The supporting dbase LSL trait is given in Figure 6.

The first claim in Figure 7 says that the social security number (the **ssNum** field of an employee) is the unique identifier in the database **d**. The symbol ~ is analogous to those of ^ and ' , but it extracts the value of an object in any state. It is used for stating module invariants and claims. The second claim says that if an employee **e** is in the database **d**, its gender and job cannot be unknown and its salary must be non-negative.

```
   ...
spec immutable type dbase;
spec dbase d;

uses dbase;

void dbase_initMod(void) dbase d; {
   modifies d;
   ensures d' = new;
}
dbase_status hire(employee e) dbase d; {
   modifies d;
   ensures (if result = dbase_OK then d' = hire(d^, e)
             else d' = d^)
         ∧ result = (if e.gen = gender_ANY then genderERR
                      else if e.j = job_ANY then jobERR
                      else if e.salary < 0 then salERR
                      else if employed(d^, e.ssNum) then duplERR
                      else dbase_OK);
}
bool fire(int ssNum) dbase d; {
   modifies d;
   ensures result = employed(d^, ssNum)
         ∧ (if result then d' = fire(d^, ssNum) else d' = d^);
}
int query(dbase_q q, empset s) dbase d; {
   modifies s;
   ensures s' = s^ ∪ query(d^, q) ∧ result = size(s' - s^);
}
bool promote(int ssNum) dbase d; {
   modifies d;
   ensures result = (employed(d^, ssNum)
         ∧ find(d^, ssNum).j = NONMGR)
         ∧ (if result then d' = promote(d^, ssNum) else d' = d^);
}
bool setSalary(int ssNum, int sal) dbase d; {
   modifies d;
   ensures result = employed(d^, ssNum)
         ∧ (if result then d' = setSal(d^, ssNum, sal)
            else d' = d^);
}
```

Figure 5: Part of dbase Module Specifications

```
dbase: trait
  assumes dbaseAssumptions
  introduces
    new: → dbase
    hire: dbase, employee → dbase
    fire, promote: dbase, int → dbase
    setSal: dbase, int, int → dbase
    find: dbase, int → employee
    employed: dbase, int → bool
    query: dbase, dbase_q → empset
  asserts
    dbase generated by new, hire
    dbase partitioned by query
    ∀ e: employee, k, sal: int, g, gq: gender,
            j, jq: job, q: dbase_q, d: dbase
      fire(new, k) == new;
      fire(hire(d, e), k) == if e.ssNum = k then fire(d, k)
                                else hire(fire(d, k), e);
      promote(new, k) == new;
      promote(hire(d, e), k) == if e.ssNum = k then
                                    hire(promote(d, k), set_j(e, MGR))
                                else hire(promote(d, k), e);
      employed(new, k) == false;
      employed(hire(d, e), k) == if e.ssNum = k then true
                                    else employed(d, k);
```

Figure 6: Part of dbase LSL Trait

The uniqueness of the value of the **ssNum** field of employees in the dbase module is a useful property: in looking for an employee with a matching **ssNum**, once a matching employee is found, there is no need to look any further. The need for this module claim became apparent when we attempted to verify an implementation of **promote** in which we search for the employee to be promoted in the dbase and we quit right after we have found the first match. This example illustrates how claims can help support program verification.

While attempting to prove the second claim by hand, we found an error in the specification given in Figure 5: the specification for the **setSalary** function did not ensure that the input salary is non-negative. This allows a user to set the salary of an employee to some negative number, and hence violates the second claim. The failure to prove this claim leads us to the source of the error.

Both module claims can be used to support regression validation of this module: the proofs of these claims rely on all the exported functions of this module. If the specification of one of the functions is modified, the proofs of module claims must be repeated.

```
claims HasKey (employee x, employee y) dbase d; {
    ensures (x ∈ d~ ∧ y ∈ d~ ∧ x.ssNum = y.ssNum) ⇒ (x = y);
}

claims WellFormed (employee x) dbase d; {
    ensures x ∈ d~ ⇒ (x.job != job_ANY
           ∧ x.gender != gender_ANY ∧ x.salary ≥ 0);
}
```

Figure 7: Examples of Module Claims

3.3   Inter-Procedural Claims

We have so far seen claims that apply to a single function specification and those that apply to an entire module. In this section we show some examples of claims that relate different functions in a module.

Figure 8 shows two examples of inter-procedural claims. There are three clauses in each claim. The requires clause specifies the conditions assumed by the claim. The ensures clause states what must be true after executing valid implementations of the functions shown in the body clause of the claim. For now, we will consider only procedures that terminate. There is an implicit assumption in an LCL function specification that it will terminate if its requires clause is satisfied in the pre state.

```
claims Inter1 (employee e) dbase d; {
    requires not(employed(d^, e.ssNum));
    body { hire(e); fire(e.ssNum)}
    ensures d' = d^;
}

claims Inter2 (int pay, employee e, empset s) dbase d; {
    requires employed(d^, e);
    body {setSalary(e.ssNum, pay);
          query([g: e.gen, j: e.job, l: pay, h: pay], s)}
    ensures e ∈ s';
}
```

Figure 8: Examples of Inter-Procedural Claims

First note that the claims in Figure 8 are intended to be written within the dbase module (shown in Figure 5). d is the dbase that is private to the dbase module, but global to each of the procedure specification in the module. Thus, even though d appears free in the claims in Figure 8, it is the same private d in the dbase module. In the body of the first claim, semi-colons are used to express sequencing of function calls. This claim says that if someone is hired and then fired, the database is not changed, provided that the person was not in the dbase at the beginning of the action sequence. Because of the way hire is specified, if the precondition that e is not in the dbase is omitted, then the conjecture is false. hire is a no-op if e is already in the dbase, and firing e will remove it from the dbase.

The second claim in Figure 8 says that if an employee exists in the database, changing its salary using **setSalary** changes its salary as observed by **query**. Note that $^\wedge$ and ' refer to the start and the end state of the procedure call sequence, and not to any intermediate states. In this example, if the claim had been **s'** = {**e**} instead of **e** $\in$ **s'**, then it cannot be proved since there can be another employee with the same salary, gender and job. Alternatively, if the precondition **employed(d$^\wedge$, e)** has been left out, the claim cannot be proved because the query set would be empty.

The claim language allows some program schemas to be expressed. These program schemas can be used to show the intended usage of modules and for generating test cases.

3.4 Other Kinds of Claims

The kinds of claims expressible depend on the claim language provided. Part of this research is to find out what kinds of claims are most likely to be useful to practicing specifiers. In this section, we describe the directions we are pursuing by giving a few examples of other kinds of claims.

```
claims idempotent (employee e) dbase d; {
  requires not(e ∈ d^);
  body { (hire(e); hire(e)*) | hire(e) }
  ensures d' = hire(d^, e);
}
```

Figure 9: Other Kinds of Claims

In the body clause of an LCL claim, the function calls between the braces, together with some regular expression-like operators can be used to express some computation. The $*$ is a shorthand for executing the function any number of times, including zero times. The vertical bar is the alternate construct, indicating that the program fragment on either side of the vertical bar can be used to achieve the ensures clause. The claim in Figure 9 expresses the idempotency of the hire procedure: calling more than once achieves the same results as calling it once.

A loop invariant needs to be provided for each loop in order to prove the claim. This is identical to the need for loop invariants in program verification. In general it is impossible to generate such loop invariants automatically. As such, the user should be prepared to provide one. In this case, the following invariant suffices for the loop (**hire(e)***) in the claim: $\forall$**e** : **employee**, **d** : **dbase**(**d**$^\sim$ = **hire(d0, e)**). **d0** refers to the value of the dbase object at the start of the program fragment; it is a constant in the above assertion.

Claims can also be used to check ordering constraints on operations in a module. Ordering constraints can be used to highlight some typical combinations of module operations. For example, a module may need to be initialized before any operations it exports can be invoked. In a set module, we may want to specify that there must be at least one insert operation prior to each delete operation. This class of claims corresponds to legality traces in trace specifications [2]. Trace specifications are meant to define the behavior of software modules by giving traces, or sequences of function calls. Claims, on the other hand, are meant to help validate Larch specifications.

Another kind of claim that can be useful involves the determinism of results returned by a C procedure. A procedure specification P(x) is deterministic if the results of calling P twice with the same arguments are provably equal. That is, given x1 = x2, all results of P(x1) (including side-effects) are pairwise equal to those of P(x2). An example of a non-deterministic procedure is a set-choose procedure: it only constrains the result to be a member of the given set without specifying which one. A common specification error is to assume that a procedure returns a deterministic result when it does not.

4 Semantics of LCL Claims

In this section we give a sketch of the semantics of LCL claims. The formal semantics of LCL can be built up from viewing a specification for a C function as a relation between two states, in a style similar to that used to define the Larch/CLU interface language [14]. However, given that LCL claims consist essentially of sequences of function calls, a weakest precondition (wp) style semantics [3] is more intuitive and simpler for checking if claims logically follow from an LCL specification. As such, we define the specification of a function as a wp assertion, and provide a translation from LCL claims into wp predicates.

We illustrate our approach by showing the translation of the **Inter1** claim shown in Figure 8. First we show the translations for the LCL specifications of **hire** and **fire** in Figure 10.

The usual syntax of a wp predicate consists of a program fragment and a predicate that is true after the program fragment has been executed. To make global variables explicit, we extend this syntax to take a list of global variables which may be modified by the function call. Q is the predicate we are interested in proving; it may be expressed in terms of the inputs and outputs of the functions appearing in the program fragment, including global variables accessible by the functions. In the example shown in Figure 10, d0 and u0 are the values of d and u in the pre state and d1 and u1 are their respective values in the post state.

The modifies clause is translated into the logical statement "the value of any dbase object not equal to d is unchanged." Next, the ensures clause and the modifies clause are conjoined together; they are jointly implied by the requires clause. This implication assertion then implies Q with appropriate renaming. Both the hire and the fire procedures in the dbase module do not have requires clauses, so they do not appear in the translation in Figure 10.

A modifies clause also adds a frame axiom not shown here: all mutable objects of other types not mentioned in the modifies clause of a function are not modified by the function. Such a frame axiom is not easily expressible in the current logical language supported by LCL, but whenever they are needed, specific assertions can be generated. One aspect of this work is to explore how such frame axioms can be automatically generated on demand to complete the proofs of LCL claims.

```
let EnsuresHire(d0, d1, e) ==
   ((if result = dbase_OK then d1 = hire(d0, e) else d1 = d0)
   ∧ result = (if e.gen = gender_ANY then genderERR
               else if e.j = job_ANY then jobERR
               else if e.salary < 0 then salERR
               else if employed(d0, e.ssNum) then duplERR
               else dbase_OK));
let EnsuresFire(d0, d1, ssNum) == (result = employed(d0, ssNum)
          ∧ (if result then d1 = fire(d0, ssNum) else d1 = d0));

wp(result = hire(e), {d}, Q(e, result, d, u)) =
   (d0 = d^ ∧ d1 = d' ∧ u0 = u^ ∧ u1 = u')
   ⇒ (((u != d ⇒ u1 = u0) ∧ EnsuresHire(d0, d1, e))
      ⇒ Q[d0/d^, d1/d', u0/u^, u1/u'])

wp(result = fire(ssNum), {d}, Q(ssNum, result, d, u)) =
   (d0 = d^ ∧ d1 = d' ∧ u0 = u^ ∧ u1 = u')
   ⇒ (((u != d ⇒ u1 = u0) ∧ EnsuresFire(d0, d1, ssNum))
      ⇒ Q[d0/d^, d1/d', u0/u^, u1/u'])
```

Figure 10: Translations of the Specifications of **hire** and **fire**

Figure 11 shows the translation of the **Inter1** claim. In wp tradition, the desired assertion $d' = d^$ is pushed backwards through the body of the claim. Since the conjecture does not involve u we drop assertions involving u to simplify the proof obligation here. Note that the value of d in the state between the function calls is d1, its value at the beginning of the body is d0, and its value at the end of the call sequence is d2. The proof obligations are shown in stages in Figure 11.

Using the definitions of **employed**, **hire** and **fire** in the dbase trait, and a few case analyses, the above proof obligation can be shown to reduce to **true**. This establishes the validity of the claim.

It is easy to rewrite an intra-procedural claim as a simple inter-procedural claim involving only one function call, with no requires clause. For example, Figure 12 shows how the claim about the **bag_delete** function can be rewritten.

Similarly, each module claim can be translated into a set of inter-procedural claims. For each function specification **F** in the module a new inter-procedural claim is added: The claim has a requires clause formed from the module claim by replacing ~ with ^, and an ensures clause formed from the module claim by replacing ~ with '. For example, the inter-procedural claim corresponding to the **hire** function generated by **HasKey** is given in Figure 13. The **HasKey** claim also generates similar inter-procedural claims for the other functions in the dbase module.

5 Discussion

Our preliminary exploration suggests that claims can be useful in helping specifiers identify errors in specifications. This work also highlights other ways

```
claims Inter1_temp (employee e) dbase d; {
  requires not(employed(d^, e.ssNum);
  body { result2 = hire(e) }
  ensures (d1 = d' ∧ ssNum = e.ssNum
        ∧ result1 = employed(d1, ssNum)
        ∧ (if result1 then d2 = fire(d1, ssNum) else d2 = d1))
          ⇒ (d2 = d^);
}

not(employed(d^, e.ssNum))
⇒ (d0 = d^
    ⇒ (((if result2 = dbase_OK then d1_1 = hire(d0, e)
        else d1_1 = d0)
      ∧ result2 = (if e.gen = gender_ANY then genderERR
                   else if e.j = job_ANY then jobERR
                   else if e.salary < 0 then salERR
                   else if employed(d0, e.ssNum) then duplERR
                   else dbase_OK))
      ⇒ ((d1 = d1_1 ∧ ssNum = e.ssNum
        ∧ result1 = employed(d1, ssNum)
        ∧ (if result1 then d2 = fire(d1, ssNum) else d2 = d1))
        ⇒ (d2 = d0))));
```

Figure 11: Translation of the Inter1 Claim

redundancy in a formal specification can be put to good use. Many of the interesting questions in this work are empirical in nature. Some of them are as follows:

What kinds of claims are useful? We have suggested some ways claims can be put to use. Which of these are useful in practice? What other ways can claims be used?

How to motivate claims in a design? Some heuristics for finding claims in a design have been given in this paper. Further experience in using claims can suggest other ways of motivating interesting or useful claims about specifications.

What kinds of claims can be proved easily or automatically proved? While we expect most claims to highlight important properties of a specification, some claims may be used mainly for debugging purposes. Such claims will be useful if the cost of checking them is small. On the other hand, properties like the logical consistency of specifications, though important to designers, are difficult to prove. As such they are less useful to a software designer.

What kinds of claims can be disproved easily or automatically? Formal specifications are complex logical objects. We expect many initial attempts to write claims will fail because the claims are false. Given a claim, we may want to attempt to disprove it first by finding some counter-examples. It is useful to discover false claims quickly.

How to reuse proofs? If a small change is made to a specification, what can be done to reuse proofs about the old specification in the new one? Eventually

```
claims bag_delete_claim (bag b, int i) {
 body { result = bag_delete(b, i) }
 ensures (i ∈ b^) ⇒ count(b', i) = count(b^, i) - 1
       ∧ ∀ x: int ((x != i) ⇒ count(b', x) ≤ count(b^, x));
}
```

Figure 12: Translation of the bag_delete Claim

```
claims HasKey_claim1 (employee e) dbase d; {
   requires ∀ x, y: employee
        ((x ∈ d^ ∧ y ∈ d^ ∧ x.ssNum = y.ssNum) ⇒ (x = y));
   body { hire(e) }
   ensures ∀ x, y: employee
        ((x ∈ d' ∧ y ∈ d' ∧ x.ssNum = y.ssNum) ⇒ (x = y));

}
```

Figure 13: Translation of the HasKey Claim

we want to integrate LCL and LP well so that the specifier can interact with LCL alone. This solution, however, requires significant development effort. It is unwise to spend too much effort on the interface aspect of this issue until we have the opportunity to address the other pressing open problems. An intermediate solution is to allow specifiers to annotate LCL claims with proof hints that are translated by the *lcl2lp* translator into LP proof commands. In the absence of true integration, a specifier will use *lcl2lp* to translate LCL specifications into LP inputs. He will then attempt to prove some LCL claim. If the attempt succeeds, he will transfer the proof steps from LP into LCL proof hints. If the attempt fails, we hope that there is enough correspondence between the LP commands generated by *lcl2lp* and the input LCL specification that the specifier can debug the LCL specification or the proof effectively.

This approach raises other questions: What kinds of proof hints need to be specified in LCL claims in order to prove them automatically in LP? How many of these are LP-specific? Without LP, can a human follow the proof hints sufficiently to understand the proof of an LCL claim?

If a conjecture can be stated either as an LSL implies claim or an LCL claim, how do we decide which is the better one to use? A heuristic is to prefer the language that is more convenient for stating the intended claim. There are, however, tradeoffs to be considered.

If the conjecture is likely to be reusable, it should be put in an appropriate LSL trait. For example, the HasKey claim about the dbase example could have been incorporated into the dbase trait. On the other hand, the WellFormed module claim in that example involves error values that are not likely to be reusable; it should be stated as an LCL claim.

However, when the conjecture is placed in an LSL trait, its use in an interface specification becomes implicit. For example, the intra-procedural claim in the bag_delete procedure could be placed in the bag trait. If claims are used to highlight important properties of specifications, then putting them in LSL may help to obscure them.

There is also an issue of robustness to consider. If strong module claims are kept in the LSL tier, they can easily lead to inconsistencies which may not be easily detected. This makes the specification less robust. The HasKey module claim is a case in point. This module claim is useful for identifying unintended logical consequences when changes are made to the dbase module, i.e., for regression testing.

More experimentation is needed to help answer these questions.

6 Current Status and Other Work

We have made a number of changes to the original LCL language (version 1.0), including the addition of claims. Some of these changes have been incorporated into an existing checker. Other language extensions are being designed and a new program will be built to translate LCL claims into LP commands. This requires formalizing the semantics of the LCL language and this work is in progress. Some case studies are being planned and will be carried out when the translator is ready.

Another goal of our research is to study how higher-order functions may be specified, and how properties of such specifications can be checked. This additional language feature motivates new kinds of claims that can be checked. For example, a claim may relate the legality of using some specified function as an input function argument. More description about this work is given in [13].

Acknowledgements

I would like to thank John Guttag, Dick Waters, Jeannette Wing and members of the Systematic Programming group for their help and suggestions in this work.

Support for this research has been provided in part by the Advanced Research Projects Agency of the Department of Defense, monitored by the Office of Naval Research Research under contract N00014-88-K-0487 and N00014-89-J-1988, in part by the National Science Foundation under grant 9115797-CCR, and in part by the Mitsubishi Electric Research Laboratory Inc, Cambridge, MA.

References

[1] *American National Standard for Information Systems – Programming Language C.* American National Standards Institute, 1989. X3.159-1989.

[2] W. Bartussek and D.L. Parnas. Using assertions about traces to write abstract specification for software modules. In *Proc. 2nd Conf. European Cooperation in Informatics, LNCS 65*, pages 211–136, Springer-Verlag, 1978. Also in Software Specification Techniques, N. Gehani and A.D. McGettrick (ed.) Addison-Wesley, 1986.

[3] Edsger W. Dijkstra. Guraded commands, nondeterminacy and formal derivation of programs. *Comm. ACM*, 18(8):453–457, August 1975.

[4] S.J. Garland and J.V. Guttag. *A Guide to LP, The Larch Prover*. TR 82, DEC SRC, December 1991.

[5] S.J. Garland and J.V. Guttag. An overview of LP, the Larch Prover. In *Proc. 3rd Intl. Conf. Rewriting Techniques and Applications*, pages 137–151, 1989. LNCS 355.

[6] J.V. Guttag and J.J. Horning. Formal specification as a design tool. In *7th Annual ACM Symp. on Principles of Programming Languages*, pages 251–261, 1980. Also in Software Specification Techniques, N. Gehani and A.D. McGettrick (ed.) Addison-Wesley, 1986.

[7] J.V. Guttag and J.J. Horning. *LCL: A Larch Interface Language for C*. TR 74, DEC SRC, July 1991.

[8] J.V. Guttag, A. Modet J.J. Horning (eds.) with S.J. Garland, K.D. Jones, and J.M. Wing. *Larch: Languages and Tools for Formal Specification. Texts and Monographs in Computer Science*, Springer-Verlag, 1993.

[9] J.J. Horning J.V. Guttag and Andrés Modet. *Report on the Larch Shared Language: Version 2.3*. TR 58, DEC SRC, April 14, 1990.

[10] Richard A. Kemmerer. Testing formal specifications to detect design errors. *IEEE Trans. Software Engineering*, 11(1):32–43, January 1985.

[11] Piotr Rudnicki. What should be proved and tested symbolically in formal specifications? In *Proc. 4th Int. Workshop on Software Specifications and Design*, pages 42–49, April 1987.

[12] J.V. Guttag S.J. Garland and J.J. Horning. Debugging Larch Shared Language specifications. *IEEE Transactions on Software Engineering*, 16(9):1044–1075, September 1990.

[13] Yang Meng Tan. Role of formal specifications in software development. MIT EECS Dept PhD thesis proposal, in preparation.

[14] J.M. Wing. *A Two-Tiered Approach to Specifying Programs*. Technical Report MIT/LCS/TR-299, MIT, 1983. Ph.D. thesis, MIT EECS, May 1983.

[15] Kaizhi Yue. What does it mean to say that a specification is complete? In *Proc. 4th Int. Workshop on Software Specifications and Design*, pages 42–49, April 1987.

[16] P. Zave. An operational approach to requirements specification for embedded systems. *IEEE Trans. Software Engineering*, 8(3):250–269, May 1982.

Optimizing Programs with Partial Specifications

Mark T. Vandevoorde

Massachusetts Institute of Technology

Cambridge, MA 02139 USA

Email: mtv@lcs.mit.edu

Abstract

This paper describes a compilation method that exploits formal specifications to optimize programs. The method performs optimizations that are impossible using techniques based purely on code analysis because formal specifications contain information that either (1) cannot be deduced from code, or (2) can in theory be deduced from code but is too costly to deduce.

The method supports modular optimization in the presence of partial specifications: most calls to specified procedures may be optimized, even when the calling program calls unspecified or partially specified procedures.

To demonstrate the method, I built a prototype compiler for an imperative programming language called Speckle, which is based on CLU and uses Larch specifications.

1 Introduction

This paper describes a compilation method that exploits formal specifications, written in Larch [6], to optimize programs. Because formal specifications contain information that cannot be deduced and information that is too costly to deduce from code, the method performs optimizations that are not possible using techniques based purely on code analysis, e.g. [5]. The classes of optimizations that the method performs include eliminating redundant code, moving code out of loops, identifying dead code, and performing user-defined specializations (e.g., eliminating run-time checks).

Fig. 1 is a high-level sketch of the compilation method, which has two basic components. The System Builder constructs a logical system from a module M to be compiled, the specifications of procedures called by M, axioms for data types used by M, and the semantics of the programming language. The Optimizer then uses the logical system to perform both standard optimizations, e.g., eliminating redundant code, and specializations defined by the modules that M uses.

The implementor of M need not write any specifications. Thus, the local cost of specifying a module yields a global benefit: once a module is specified, all programs that use the module obtain improved optimization.

Like conventional compilation methods, my method only performs optimizations that are *sound*, i.e., program Unopt is only replaced by program Opt when the specification of Opt is stronger than the specification of Unopt. Both

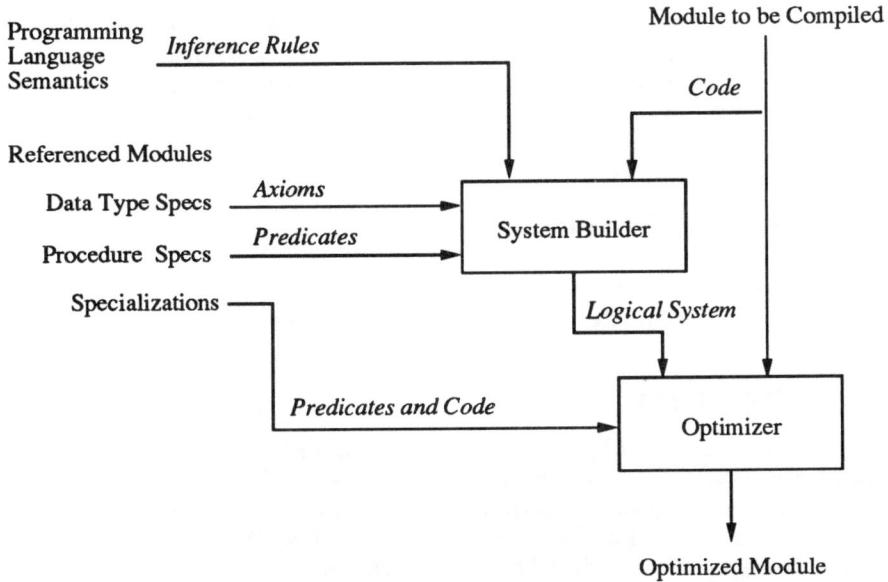

Figure 1: Sketch of Compilation Method

methods deduce a conservative estimate for the specification of Unopt. Conventional compilers use the input-output function, as determined by code analysis, as the deduced specification that must be preserved. My method uses a weaker deduced specification because it relies on the formal specifications, rather than the implementations, of called procedures. Thus, my method is free to change implementation-specific behavior concealed by the specifications.

The compilation method supports modular optimization in the presence of partial specifications. A procedure specification is a predicate on program states; a *partial specification* is a weaker predicate. Partial specifications arise when formal specifications are written incrementally. The goal of *modular optimization* is to be able to optimize most uses of a procedure once it is formally specified, even when the calling program calls unspecified or partially specified procedures. In contrast, approaches based on user-supplied program transformation rules are not modular, e.g. [7].

Given formal specifications, the method is more general than code analysis techniques that do not handle pointers [2, 4, 12], restrict pointers to at most one level of indirection [11], or do not allow procedures [8]. The compilation method can afford to let programmers use pointers and procedures freely because specifications contain useful information about the effects of procedure calls and about the possible aliases in a program.

I implemented the ideas in this paper in a prototype compiler for Speckle, a strongly-typed, imperative language based on CLU [10]. The prototype uses the theorem prover LP [13] to identify optimizations that are provably sound assuming the specifications are correct.

Section 2 is a discussion of the relative merits of optimization based on specifications versus optimization based only on code analysis. In section 3, I present the semantics of Larch/Speckle and Speckle and use them to define the deduced specification of a program. In section 4, I give a definition of soundness for a program optimization and explain how my method relies on the semantics of Speckle to construct logical systems for detecting sound optimizations. Conclusions appear in section 5.

2 Relative Merits

There are several advantages and disadvantages to using formal specifications to optimize programs instead of traditional techniques based on code analysis.

2.1 Advantages

A first advantage is that specifications contain information that cannot be deduced from code. Only a specification can conceal implementation details that are irrelevant to program correctness. Thus, when specifications are available, a compiler can perform optimizations that alter these irrelevant details. Such optimizations are impossible without specifications.

For example, consider the code sequence

```
read d1, d2
i1 := Relation_get_image(r, d1)
Relation_add_image(r, d2, i1+1)
i2 := Relation_get_image(r, d1)
print i1, i2
```

Suppose the specification of **Relation_get_image** is non-deterministic: a correct implementation is free to return any image of the domain element **d1** in the relation **r**. The code above can be optimized by replacing the second call to **Relation_get_image** by i1. This optimization is sound because the code should rely only on the specification of **Relation_get_image**, which allows any image to be returned. The fact that i1 is an image of **d1** in **r** follows from the unshown post-condition of **Relation_get_image** and from the unshown specification for **Relation_add_image**, which only allows it to add an image to **r** for d2.

Without specifications the optimization might be impossible. Suppose the actual implementation always returns the image for d1 last added to **r**. Thus, i2 = i1 when d1 $\neq$ d2, and i2 = i1+1 when d1 = d2. Because the optimization changes the input-output function of the program by making i2 = i1, a conventional compiler cannot determine that the optimization is sound.

A second advantage is that formal specifications make it easy to perform optimizations that, while theoretically possible by analyzing code, are too costly to perform. For example, consider the code sequence

```
Map_define(m, k, v1)
v2 := Map_lookup(m, k)
```

where **Map_define** is a procedure that extends (or alters) a mapping **m** to bind **k** to **v1**, and **Map_lookup** returns the image of **k** in **m**.

Given the axiom about mappings

$$\forall\ m: mapping,\ k: key,\ v: value\ [\ image(bind(m,\ k,\ v),\ k) = v\ ]$$

and formal specifications that relate the procedure **Map_define** to the function *bind* and **Map_lookup** to *image*, it is easy to determine that the call to **Map_lookup** can be replaced by **v1**.

Without the axiom about mappings or the specifications for **Map_define** and **Map_lookup**, it is still theoretically possible for a compiler to recognize the optimization, but in practice it is infeasible. The compiler would have to reason at the more complicated level of a mapping's representation, e.g., a hash table. Furthermore, some form of inductive reasoning would be necessary since the implementations of **Map_define** and **Map_lookup** might each use a loop or make recursive calls.

A third advantage is that formal specifications make it possible to express and perform user-defined optimizations not possible using code analysis. Specializations are one form of user-defined optimization. A *specialization* is a faster but less general implementation of a procedure plus a precondition describing when the faster version can be substituted for the general one. The precondition must be stated formally so that it can be discharged mechanically by the compiler during program optimization.

For example, consider an implementation of mappings represented as unsorted lists of key-value pairs where each key appears at most once. In general, the **Map_define** procedure, which sets the value of a key, must first check if the key already has a definition. However, this check is unnecessary when **Map_define** is called in contexts where the key is guaranteed to be undefined in the mapping. Hence, a specialization of **define(m, k, v)** is to omit the check when the precondition $k \notin m$ can be proved.

To prove the precondition, the compiler relies on other formal specifications. For example, in the code below which uses **Maps**

```
if not Map_is_defined(m, k)
   then Map_define(m, k, v)
        redefined := true
   end
```

the proof of $k \notin m$ follows from the specification of **Map_is_defined** and the semantics of **if**.

Finally, a pragmatic advantage of specification-based optimization is that it supports separate compilation. The callers of a procedure P must be recompiled only when P's specification changes or, if P is specialized, when a precondition of a specialization changes.

Interprocedural analysis, on the other hand, requires the whole program. For example, to compile a program using the interprocedural methods in [9, 3], the program's call graph is combined with the control flow graphs of all procedures used. Furthermore, the time required for analysis is polynomial in the size of the combined graph, so full interprocedural analysis is impractical for large programs.

2.2 Disadvantages

The primary problem of relying on formal specifications is that they may be incorrect, in which case the compiler may perform unsound optimizations. Furthermore, such errors may be difficult to debug.

A second disadvantage is that users must write specifications. However, this burden is reduced by allowing partial specifications, and the cost of writing specifications is amortized by their other uses, e.g., documenting interfaces and serving as inputs to advanced bug-detectors.

Finally, because my method uses theorem-proving techniques to justify optimizations, it is much slower than conventional optimizers that support separate compilation. On the other hand, it performs optimizations which they cannot perform.

3 Language Semantics

In this section I present the specification and programming languages. I assume the reader is familiar with the Larch Shared Language (LSL) [6] for writing algebraic specifications in first-order, multisorted predicate logic. First I describe Larch/Speckle, the Larch interface language for Speckle. Next, I give the semantics of Speckle.

3.1 Larch/Speckle

Larch/Speckle is similar to other interface languages, but it is most like the Larch/CLU interface language [14] since Speckle is a derivative of CLU.

A Speckle program state consists of an environment and a store:

$$Prog\ State = Env\ X\ Store$$
$$Env\qquad\ = Ident \rightarrow (\ ImmValue + Loc\ )$$
$$Store\qquad = Loc \rightarrow MutValue$$

The environment of program state σ is written as σ^{Env}, and its store is written as σ^{Str}.

Values are divided into three domains. An ImmValue is used to represent the value of an immutable data structure, i.e., one whose value can never be changed by the program.[1] A Loc represents the location (address) of a mutable data structure. The value of a mutable data structure, i.e., one which can be changed by the program, is represented by a MutValue. A Loc is *modified* by a procedure if its value in the store of the post-state differs from its value in the store of the pre-state.

There may be several aliases for a given Loc. The environment may map any number of Idents to the same Loc. Also, any MutValue in the range of the store or any ImmValue in the range of the environment may contain the Loc. For example, a value for an array of Loc contains each element Loc in the array. A tuple value contains each Loc that is a field of the tuple.

Aliasing is not possible for Idents because ImmValues and MutValues may not contain Idents.

---

[1] For example, integers and bignums are immutable in Common LISP, but cons cells are mutable.

```
Map = mutable type spec
   based on Map from Mapping(String, Int)
   contains --

   define = proc (m: Map, s: String, i: Int)
      requires --
      modifies m
      ensures m' = bind(m^, s, i)
   lookup = proc (m: Map, s: String) returns (i: Int)
      requires --
      modifies --
      ensures i = image(m^, s)
      except signals missing when ¬(s ∈ m^)
```

Figure 2: Map Interface Specifications

3.1.1 Data Type Interfaces

A data type interface names a sort used to represent values of the type and indicates whether the sort should be an ImmValue or a MutValue. For example, the interface for Map in Fig. 2 specifies that Maps are mutable and that the sort Map from Fig. 3 should be used as the MutValue to represent Maps. The unshown interfaces for String and Int specify that these types are immutable.

When a type is specified as mutable, a *location sort* is implicitly defined for the type, e.g., $MapLoc$ for locations of Maps. Larch/Speckle also defines a sort $LocSet$ for sets of locations. These sets are heterogeneous because they may contain values of different location sorts.

Location sorts can be used to represent arbitrary uses of pointers. For example, to specify a type for sets of pointers to Maps, one would use the $MapLoc$ sort to define a $MapLocSet$ sort. Location sorts can also be used to specify cyclic data structures.

Larch/Speckle is novel in that the interface for data type T must give an upper bound on the set of locations directly accessible through values of T. These bounds are used later to restrict the side-effects of unspecified or partially specified procedures.

Bounds on accessibility are specified using a contains clause. If any location of a value of T_2 is directly accessible through some value of T_1, T_1 is said to *contain* T_2, and T_1 must specify "contains T_2" in its interface. For example, a type for arrays of Maps would contain type Map; this would be written as "contains Map" in the interface of the array type.

Note that the expressive power of a contains clause is rather limited because it is not possible to distinguish different locations of values of the same type. Future versions of Larch/Speckle may allow the user to specify the set of locations contained by an instance of T.

Mapping (Dom, Ran): Trait

   Introduces

empty:		$\rightarrow$ Map
bind:	Map, Dom, Ran	$\rightarrow$ Map
image:	Map, Dom	$\rightarrow$ Ran
$\_\in\_$:	Map, Dom	$\rightarrow$ Bool

Asserts for all (m: Map, d1,d2: Dom, r: Ran)

   Map generated by (empty, bind)
   Map partitioned by (defined, image)

   $d1 \in empty == false$
   $d1 \in bind(m, d2, r) == (d1 = d2) \lor (d1 \in m)$
   $image(bind(m, d1, r), d2) ==$
        $if\ d1 = d2\ then\ r\ else\ image(m, d2)$

Figure 3: Mapping Trait

$\forall\ \sigma_{pre},\ \sigma_{post}:\ Prog\ State,\ m:\ MapLoc,\ s:\ String,\ i:\ Int$

Map_define:

   $Req(\sigma_{pre}^{Str}, m, s, i) ==\ true$

   $Norm(\sigma_{pre}^{Str}, \sigma_{post}^{Str}, m, s, i) ==$
      $\sigma_{post}^{Str}(m) = bind(\sigma_{pre}^{Str}(m), s, i) \land$
      $\forall\ l:\ MapLoc\ (l \neq m \Longrightarrow \sigma_{post}^{Str}(l) = \sigma_{pre}^{Str}(l))$

Map_lookup:

   $Req(\sigma_{pre}^{Str}, m, s) ==\ true$

   $Norm(\sigma_{pre}^{Str}, \sigma_{post}^{Str}, m, s, i) ==\ i = image(\sigma_{pre}^{Str}(m), s, i) \land \sigma_{post}^{Str} = \sigma_{pre}^{Str}$

   $Excpt(\sigma_{pre}^{Str}, \sigma_{post}^{Str}, m, s) ==\ \sigma_{post}^{Str} = \sigma_{pre}^{Str}$

   $Guard(\sigma_{pre}^{Str}, m, s) ==\ \neg(s \in \sigma_{pre}^{Str}(m))$

Figure 4: Procedure Predicates

3.1.2 Procedure Interfaces

Specifications of procedures, which may signal exceptions, are written as pre- and post-conditions in a stylized fashion. The **requires** clause defines the pre-condition, *Req*. The **modifies** clause restricts the side-effects of the procedure by defining the set of locations the procedure is allowed to modify; this restriction is part of every post-condition. The post-condition for a normal return, *Norm*, is further specified by the **ensures** clause, which typically defines the results in terms of the arguments. All procedures are assumed to terminate.

For the sake of brevity, here I allow at most one exception. The **when** clause defines a second condition on the pre-state, *Guard*. The procedure must signal the exception exactly when *Guard* is true. The post-condition for an exceptional return, *Excpt*, is defined by the **modifies** clause and an optional **ensuring** clause.

Fig. 4 lists the result of translating the interface specifications of Fig. 2 into predicates when **Map** is the only mutable type used by the program. For every other mutable type T, the assertion "$\forall$ *l: TLoc* $(\sigma_{\text{post}}^{\text{Str}}(l) = \sigma_{\text{pre}}^{\text{Str}}(l))$" would be added as a conjunct to the *Norm* post-condition for **Map_define**. Note that the post-conditions define only the store of the post-state; the environment will be defined by the semantics of the programming language.[2]

3.1.3 Partial Specifications

Larch/Speckle supports partial specifications by allowing any clause except **contains** to be omitted or to use "?". When a **requires**, **ensures**, or **when** clause is omitted or uses "?", the definition of the corresponding predicate is weakened to use $\Longrightarrow$ in place of $==$. For example, the clause "**requires** a & ?" is translated to the partial definition "$Req(\sigma_{\text{pre}}^{\text{Str}}, a) \Longrightarrow a$".

When the **modifies** clause is omitted or uses "?", a conservative estimate is computed from the types of the procedure's arguments. Because Speckle does not allow global variables, the only locations that a procedure may modify are those accessible from its arguments. The upper bound is the union of

- the set of locations of mutable arguments and

- the set of locations reachable from the values of the arguments.

A location L is reachable from a value V if L's type is reachable from V's type. Type T_2 is reachable from type T_1 if T_2 is in the irreflexive transitive closure of the contains relation on the set $\{T_1\}$.

When the **modifies** clause is estimated, the definitions of all post-conditions are weakened to use $\Longrightarrow$ in place of $==$.

3.2 Speckle

The semantics of Speckle defines the strongest specification deducible from a well-formed program using the specifications of called procedures rather than their implementations. A program is *well-formed* if, when its pre-condition is

---

[2]Pre- and post-conditions may not refer to environments because Speckle does not allow global variables.

satisfied, it terminates and it only calls procedures whose pre-conditions are satisfied.

The semantics also provides rules for proving that a property, e.g., the pre-condition of a procedure, holds at a given point in a program. Both the proof rules and the definition of deduced specifications are used in the next section to identify sound optimizations.

Because Speckle allows procedures to signal exceptions, it is convenient to view a program as a control flow graph (CFG). Each program has a unique entering edge labeled *enter*, one or more exiting edges, and zero or more internal edges. There are five kinds of nodes: assignment, procedure call, branch, merge, and loop. The meaning of program Prog, written $[\![Prog]\!]$, is a predicate on an edge, a pre-state, and a post-state. The way to interpret $[\![Prog]\!]$ is

$[\![Prog]\!](e, \sigma_{\text{pre}}, \sigma) = $ *If control enters Prog when the program state is σ_{pre}, control may reach edge e with the program state σ.*[3]

Note that the specification may be non-deterministic: for a given initial state, $[\![Prog]\!]$ may be allow different exiting edges and different post-states.

The predicate $[\![Prog]\!]$ is the strongest post-condition deducible from Prog. The deduced post-condition at exiting edge e is

$$\text{ProgPost}_e(\sigma_{\text{pre}}, \sigma_{\text{post}}) \equiv [\![Prog]\!](e, \sigma_{\text{pre}}, \sigma_{\text{post}})$$

$\text{ProgPre}(\sigma_{\text{pre}})$ is the weakest pre-condition that ensures Prog is well-formed.

$[\![Prog]\!]$ is defined indirectly by defining a theory[4] for each edge; this is convenient because the semantics of LSL and the interface tier define theories. The theory $\mathcal{T}_e$ of edge e defines how a program state σ_e at edge e must relate to the program state σ_{enter} which entered the program. For example, if the program is a single assignment x := y, the theory of the exiting edge *exit* would contain the formula $\sigma_{\text{exit}}^{\text{Env}}(\text{'x'}) = \sigma_{\text{enter}}^{\text{Env}}(\text{'y'})$.

Def.: $[\![Prog]\!](e, \sigma_{\text{pre}}, \sigma) \equiv $ *Formula $\sigma_{\text{pre}} = \sigma_{\text{enter}} \wedge \sigma = \sigma_e$ is consistent with $\mathcal{T}_e$.*

Formula F is *consistent with* theory $\mathcal{T}$ if "true = false" is not in the consequence closure of $\mathcal{T} \cup \{F\}$.

For the assignment example, if σ_{pre} is the state where 'x' is 0 and 'y' is 1 and σ is the state where 'x' is 5 and 'y' is 1, $[\![Prog]\!](exit, \sigma_{\text{pre}}, \sigma)$ is false: given the values of σ_{pre} and σ and axioms about program states, the assertions $\sigma_{\text{pre}} = \sigma_{\text{enter}} \wedge \sigma = \sigma_{\text{exit}} \wedge \sigma_{\text{exit}}^{\text{Env}}(\text{'x'}) = \sigma_{\text{enter}}^{\text{Env}}(\text{'y'})$ lead to the inconsistency $5 = 1$.

The relation $\in$ is used to define the theories at each edge; $F \in \mathcal{T}_e$ means that formula F is in theory $\mathcal{T}_e$. The relation is defined inductively using inference rules. Thus, the theory associated with each edge exiting a Prog is defined using the theory of the entering edge.

The theory of the entering edge $\mathcal{T}_{\text{enter}}$ comes from the specifications of Prog. $\mathcal{T}_{\text{enter}}$ is the consequence closure of the union of: the theories of LSL specifications used by Prog; the theory of the program state, location sets, and procedure predicates defined by Larch/Speckle; and the precondition for calling Prog specified by the user, if any.

---

[3] $[\![Prog]\!](e, \sigma_{\text{pre}}, \sigma) \equiv $ *false* when e is not an edge of Prog.

[4] A theory is an infinite set of formulae.

$$\frac{F \in ConsequenceClosure(T_e)}{F \in T_e}$$

$$\frac{F \in T_i \quad\quad Edge\ i\ dominates\ edge\ j}{F \in T_j}$$

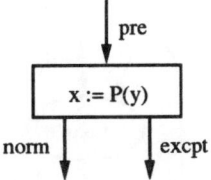

$\sigma_{post}^{Env}(\text{'x'}) = \sigma_{pre}^{Env}(\text{'y'})$	$\in T_{post}$
$\forall var : Ident[var \neq \text{'x'} \Longrightarrow \sigma_{post}^{Env}(var) = \sigma_{pre}^{Env}(var)]$	$\in T_{post}$
$\sigma_{post}^{Str} = \sigma_{pre}^{Str}$	$\in T_{post}$

$Norm(\sigma_{pre}^{Str}, \sigma_{norm}^{Str}, \sigma_{pre}^{Env}(\text{'y'}), \sigma_{norm}^{Env}(\text{'x'}))$	$\in T_{norm}$
$\neg\, Guard(\sigma_{pre}^{Str}, \sigma_{pre}^{Env}(\text{'y'}))$	$\in T_{norm}$
$\forall var : Ident[var \neq \text{'x'} \Longrightarrow \sigma_{norm}^{Env}(var) = \sigma_{pre}^{Env}(var)]$	$\in T_{norm}$
$Excpt(\sigma_{pre}^{Str}, \sigma_{excpt}^{Str}, \sigma_{pre}^{Env}(\text{'y'}))$	$\in T_{excpt}$
$Guard(\sigma_{pre}^{Str}, \sigma_{pre}^{Env}(\text{'y'}))$	$\in T_{excpt}$
$\sigma_{excpt}^{Env} = \sigma_{pre}^{Env}$	$\in T_{excpt}$

Figure 5: Semantic Rules for Speckle

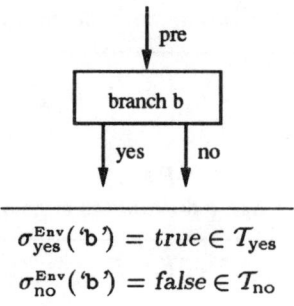

$$\sigma_{\text{yes}}^{\text{Env}}(\text{`b'}) = true \in \mathcal{T}_{\text{yes}}$$
$$\sigma_{\text{no}}^{\text{Env}}(\text{`b'}) = false \in \mathcal{T}_{\text{no}}$$

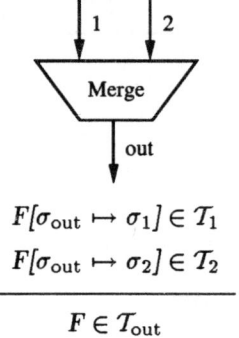

$$F[\sigma_{\text{out}} \mapsto \sigma_1] \in \mathcal{T}_1$$
$$F[\sigma_{\text{out}} \mapsto \sigma_2] \in \mathcal{T}_2$$
$$\overline{F \in \mathcal{T}_{\text{out}}}$$

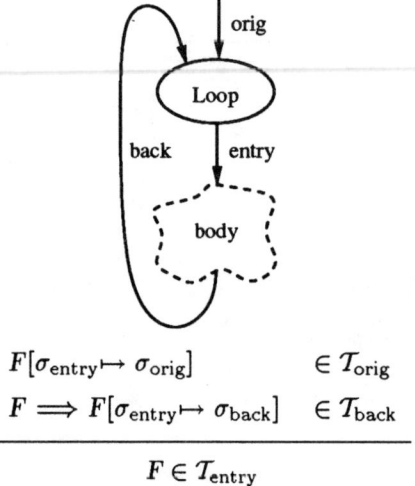

$$F[\sigma_{\text{entry}} \mapsto \sigma_{\text{orig}}] \qquad \in \mathcal{T}_{\text{orig}}$$
$$F \implies F[\sigma_{\text{entry}} \mapsto \sigma_{\text{back}}] \quad \in \mathcal{T}_{\text{back}}$$
$$\overline{F \in \mathcal{T}_{\text{entry}}}$$

Figure 6: Semantic Rules for Speckle, continued

Fig. 5 and Fig. 6 list the semantic rules for Speckle. I extend the notation for the hypothesis of an inference rule to include a template of a subgraph appearing in Prog. The first semantic inference rule is that each theory is closed under the usual inference rules of predicate logic.

The second semantic rule is that the theory of an edge j is an extension of the theories of each edge i that dominates j.[5] This rule propagates the formulae defining σ_i in T_i to T_j, so it allows T_j to define σ_j in terms of σ_i. In particular, the rule allows the semantics of a CFG node with edges *in* and *out* to define σ_{out} in terms of σ_{in} in T_{out}, for without the rule, σ_{in} would be undefined in T_{out}. The rule also propagates the formulae in T_{enter}, e.g., LSL axioms, to every theory.

The rule for an assignment states that the only variable affected by the assignment is the one named on the left of ":=", so assignment to 'x' never affects 'z'. Furthermore, the store is unchanged.

The rule for a procedure call node[6] uses the predicates from the procedure's specification to define the post-state in terms of the pre-state. When procedure returns normally, the only variable affected by a call is the one that is assigned the result of the call. If the procedure signals an exception, the environment is unchanged. Note that the theories of the exiting edges contain control-dependent information derived from the exception guard.

Because the effect of a procedure call is determined only by its specification, the deduced specification does not contain implementation details concealed by the specification. This makes optimizations like the **Relation** example on page 3 possible.

Branch nodes are a notational convenience for conditional branches; any branch node "**branch b**" can be replaced by a call node to the procedure

```
branch = proc (b: Bool)
   requires --
   modifies --
   ensures --
   except signals then_arm when b
```

Like a procedure call node, a branch node introduces control-dependent information in the theories of the exiting edges.

Unlike assignment, procedure call, and branch nodes, merge and loop nodes have more than one entering edge and have exactly one exiting edge. Loop nodes have exactly two entering edges, one forward edge and one back edge. (A back edge is an edge whose target node dominates its source node.) Back edges are only allowed in the position labeled "back" on the loop node, so all cycles in a CFG pass through a loop node.

The merge and loop rule rules correspond to the familiar rules for proof-by-cases and proof-by-induction. The notation $F[\sigma_i \mapsto \sigma]$ denotes F with σ substituted for σ_i and with bound variables renamed to avoid capture.

Note that the theory of an edge is inconsistent precisely when the edge is unreachable at run-time. For example, if a procedure is called in a context where it cannot signal an exception, i.e., $\neg Guard \in T_{pre}$, T_{excpt} is inconsistent because

---

[5] Edge i dominates edge j if every path from the entering edge to j must pass through i. Every edge dominates itself.

[6] The rule shown is for a procedure with a single argument and result. I rely on the reader's intuition to extend the rule for different numbers of arguments and results.

it contains both *Guard* and ¬*Guard*. The second semantic inference rule propagates the inconsistency to each edge dominated by *excpt*, but this is correct: *excpt* is unreachable, so any edge dominated by *excpt* is also unreachable.

4   Detecting Sound Optimizations

Using the semantics from the previous section, I now define what it means for a program optimization to be sound, and I use the definition to justify the proof obligations for four classes of optimizations. Next, I describe how the prototype compiler uses the theorem-prover LP [13] to discharge these proof obligations.

4.1   Soundness

The soundness criterion for replacing a program Unopt by a program Opt is the usual one: Opt must have a stronger specification than Unopt.

Def.: It is sound to substitute program Opt for Unopt if

$$\mathrm{UnoptPre}(\sigma_{\mathrm{pre}}) \implies \mathrm{OptPre}(\sigma_{\mathrm{pre}})$$

and if forall edges e exiting Opt

$$[\![\mathrm{Opt}]\!](e, \sigma_{\mathrm{pre}}, \sigma_{\mathrm{post}}) \implies [\![\mathrm{Unopt}]\!](e, \sigma_{\mathrm{pre}}, \sigma_{\mathrm{post}})$$

The first conjunct requires that Opt have a weaker pre-condition than Unopt; the second conjunct requires that Opt have a stronger post-condition than Unopt for each exiting edge in Opt.

The definition of soundness allows Opt to omit an exiting edge e that, according to $[\![\mathrm{Unopt}]\!]$, may be reached but need not be reached. In this case, Opt is a more deterministic implementation of Unopt's deduced specification.

4.1.1   Classes of Optimizations

Given the definition of soundness and the semantics of Speckle, it is easy to give proof obligations for four classes of optimizations: dead code elimination, specialization, reuse of available expressions, and reuse of loop-invariant expressions. In each case, the proof obligation is a sufficient condition for transforming an initial program, Unopt, into an optimized program, Opt.

The proof obligation for dead code elimination is straightforward: a node in Unopt corresponds to dead code if the theories of its source edges are inconsistent. Thus, if the compiler can prove $true = false \in T_e$, it can eliminate all edges and nodes dominated by e from Unopt to yield Opt. OptPre, the weakest pre-condition that ensures Opt is well-formed, is the same as UnoptPre since only dead code is removed. Similarly, the deduced post-conditions for Opt are the same as those for Unopt.

Another easy class to consider is specializations. A call to a procedure P at edge e can be replaced by a call to P′, a specialized verion of P, when $Special \in T_e$, where $Special$ is the (stronger) pre-condition for P′. Recall that by definition, the implementation of P′ has the same specification as P except for the stronger pre-condition, so every edge will have the same theory as before.

Thus, OptPre is the same as UnoptPre because the stronger pre-condition is satisfied, and the deduced post-conditions are the same.

A more interesting class of optimizations is reusing an available expression by replacing a procedure call with an assignment. It is sound to replace the procedure call $x := P(y)$ of Fig. 5 by the assignment $x := z$ when the following are true

- $\neg Guard(\sigma_{\mathrm{pre}}, \sigma_{\mathrm{pre}}^{\mathrm{Env}}(\text{'}y\text{'})) \in \mathcal{T}_{\mathrm{pre}}$

  This guarantees that deleting the call does not alter the program's control flow: the call to P never signals an exception because $Guard$ is false. Furthermore, because $Guard$ is false, $(true = false) \in \mathcal{T}_{\mathrm{excpt}}$, so dead code elimination is possible on edge Excpt.[7]

- $Norm(\sigma_{\mathrm{pre}}^{\mathrm{Str}}, \sigma_{\mathrm{pre}}^{\mathrm{Str}}, \sigma_{\mathrm{pre}}^{\mathrm{Env}}(\text{'}y\text{'}), \sigma_{\mathrm{pre}}^{\mathrm{Env}}(\text{'}z\text{'})) \in \mathcal{T}_{\mathrm{pre}}$

  This guarantees that the value of z before the call satisfies the **ensures** clause of P. The condition above can only be met if P modifies nothing since $\sigma_{\mathrm{pre}}^{\mathrm{Str}}$ is used as both the pre- and post-stores. Thus, when the call to P is deleted, no changes to the store are lost.

  Note that the value of z need not be equal to that returned by the call to P. Thus, optimizations like the **Relation** example from page 3 are possible.

The conditions above guarantee that the consequences of the semantic rule for the assignment imply the consequences of the semantic rule for the procedure call for a normal return. Therefore, the theory of each edge in Opt must be a superset of the edge's theory in Unopt, so the deduced post-conditions for Opt are at least as strong as those of Unopt. Furthermore, an assignment has no pre-condition and always terminates, so OptPre is no stronger than UnoptPre.

Finally, a sufficient condition for identifying loop-invariant expressions is to prove that a call to procedure P in the loop body modifies nothing and that the result of P does not depend on the loop body, i.e., that the result is equal to a term that contains no program state symbols or that contains only program state symbols σ_e such that e dominates the entire loop.

When the compiler identifies a loop-invariant procedure call, it can transform the program to reuse the result from the first iteration on all subsequent iterations. OptPre is the same as UnoptPre since no new calls or loops are introduced, and Opt has the same deduced post-conditions as Unopt.

4.2   Detecting Optimizations with LP

My compilation method, which has been implemented in a prototype Speckle compiler, uses the theorem-prover LP [13] to identify sound optimizations. LP is particularly well-suited for my purpose because it was designed to work with LSL and because it fails quickly when trying to prove a difficult conjecture rather than attempting expensive proof strategies. This is particularly important because most conjectures a compiler wants to prove are false, e.g., most procedure calls cannot be replaced by an assignment.

---

[7] $(true = false) \in \mathcal{T}_{\mathrm{excpt}}$ follows from $Guard \in \mathcal{T}_{\mathrm{excpt}}$, which comes from the semantic rule for a procedure call, and $\neg Guard \in \mathcal{T}_{\mathrm{excpt}}$, which follows from the second semantic rule.

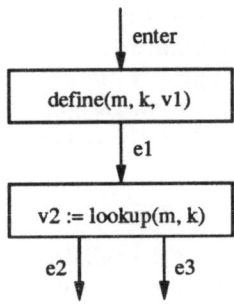

Figure 7: A Simple Program

I first consider programs that do not use merge or loop nodes, i.e., programs whose CFGs are trees. Next, I introduce automated proof-by-cases and proof-by-induction to support merge and loop nodes.

4.2.1 Programs with only Assignment, Procedure Call, and Branch Nodes

My method is to construct, for each CFG edge e, a logical system that conservatively approximates $\mathcal{T}_e$. These logical systems are then used to try to discharge the proof obligations for performing various optimizations. For example, for each procedure call that modifies nothing and returns a value of type T, the prototype attempts to prove that the value in an existing variable of type T can be substituted for the result of the call.

Because LP is primarily based on conditional term rewriting, each theory $\mathcal{T}_e$ is approximated as a term rewriting system $\mathcal{R}_e$. (A term rewriting system is a set of rewrite rules; each rule is used to reduce terms to simpler terms, e.g., $x * 0$ might reduce to 0. A rewriting system can be used to prove a conjecture by reducing the conjecture to *true*. See [13] for more information.) In general, $\mathcal{R}_e$ is only an approximation to $\mathcal{T}_e$ because rewriting systems are usually incomplete: some formulae in $\mathcal{T}_e$ are not reduced to *true* by $\mathcal{R}_e$.

The first step is to construct $\mathcal{R}_{\text{enter}}$, the rewriting system for the entering edge. $\mathcal{R}_{\text{enter}}$ is derived mechanically from the LSL specifications referenced by the program using the LSL Checker, which automatically translates LSL specifications into LP input, which LP then converts into a rewriting system. The Speckle compiler also adds rewrite rules to axiomatize program states, location sorts, and predicates derived from Larch/Speckle specifications.

The next step is to construct rewriting systems for the other edges in the program in depth-first order. When edge e exiting node n is visited, $\mathcal{R}_e$ is constructed by extending the rewriting system of the edge entering n. The extensions are determined by n: if n is an assignment node, the conclusions from the assignment semantic rule in Fig. 5 are added to $\mathcal{R}_e$; if n is a procedure call node, the procedure call semantic rule is used; if n is a branch node, the branch semantic rule is used. To add the conclusion $F \in \mathcal{T}_e$, the rewrite rule $F \rightarrow \textit{true}$ is added to the rewriting system.

Fig. 8 lists some of the rewrite rules in $\mathcal{R}_{\text{e1}}$ for the program in Fig. 7. Rules 1-3 come from the LSL Mapping trait. Rules 4 and 5 come from post-condition *Norm* for **Map_define** shown in Fig. 4. LP splits the conjunction of the **ensures**

	Guard	LHS	RHS
1		$d1 \in empty$	$\rightarrow$ $false$
2		$d1 \in bind(m, d2, r)$	$\rightarrow$ $d1 = d2 \lor d1 \in m$
3		$image(bind(m, d1, r), d2)$	$\rightarrow$ $if\ d1 = d2$
			$then\ r$
			$else\ image(m, d2)$
4		$\sigma_{e1}^{Str}(\sigma_{enter}^{Env}(\text{'}m\text{'}))$	$\rightarrow$ $bind(\sigma_{enter}^{Str}(\sigma_{enter}^{Env}(\text{'}m\text{'})),$
			$\sigma_{enter}^{Env}(\text{'}k\text{'}),$
			$\sigma_{enter}^{Env}(\text{'}v1\text{'})\ )$
5	$loc \neq \sigma_{enter}^{Env}(\text{'}m\text{'})$	$\sigma_{e1}^{Str}(loc)$	$\rightarrow$ $\sigma_{enter}^{Str}(loc)$
6		$\sigma_{e1}^{Env}(var)$	$\rightarrow$ $\sigma_{enter}^{Env}(var)$

Figure 8: Rewrite Rules

and **modifies** clauses in *Norm* into rules 4 and 5 because it converts all rules of the form $T1 \land T2 \rightarrow true$ into the pair of rules $T1 \rightarrow true$ and $T2 \rightarrow true$ and promotes rules of the form $T1 = T2 \rightarrow true$ into either $T1 \rightarrow T2$ or $T2 \rightarrow T1$. Rule 6 follows from the fact that **Map_define** has no results to assign to variables.

Given the rewriting system of Fig. 8, it is easy prove by rewriting that the call to **Map_lookup** can be replaced by **v1**. The first requirement is to prove that **Map_lookup** cannot signal an exception, i.e.,

$$\neg Guard(\sigma_{e1}^{Str}, \sigma_{e1}^{Env}(\text{'}m\text{'}), \sigma_{e1}^{Env}(\text{'}k\text{'}))$$

Given the definition of *Guard* for **Map_lookup** in Fig. 8 this becomes

$$\neg\neg(\sigma_{e1}^{Env}(\text{'}k\text{'}) \in \sigma_{e1}^{Env}(\text{'}m\text{'}))$$

which reduces to true.

The second requirement is to find a variable whose value satisfies the *Norm* post-condition for **Map_lookup**. The Speckle compiler tries all variables (of the proper type) appearing to the left of ":=" in nodes dominating the call node. For the variable **v1**, the goal is

$$Norm(\sigma_{e1}^{Str}, \sigma_{e1}^{Str}, \sigma_{e1}^{Env}(\text{'}m\text{'}), \sigma_{e1}^{Env}(\text{'}k\text{'}), \sigma_{e1}^{Env}(\text{'}v1\text{'}))$$

Given the definition of *Norm* this becomes

$$\sigma_{e1}^{Env}(\text{'}v1\text{'}) = image(\sigma_{e1}^{Str}(\sigma_{e1}^{Env}(\text{'}m\text{'})), \sigma_{e1}^{Env}(\text{'}k\text{'})) \land \sigma_{e1}^{Str} = \sigma_{e1}^{Str}$$

which reduces to *true*. Thus, the optimization is sound.

4.2.2 Programs with Merge and Loop Nodes

Proofs using term rewriting rely on showing that equal terms have identical terminal forms. When programs are restricted to only assignment, procedure call, and branch nodes, the rewriting systems of each edge reduce terms containing an internal program state symbol to terms containing σ_{enter}, the program state

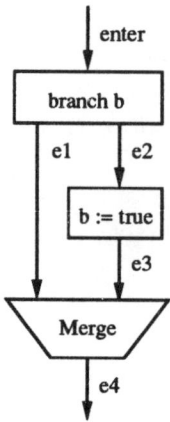

Figure 9: Proof by Cases

symbol of the entering edge. For example, in Fig. 8, rules 4-6 reduce terms containing σ_{e1} to terms containing σ_{enter}.

The difficulty in handling merge and loop nodes is that the semantic inference rules for these nodes cannot be expressed as rewrite rules because the hypotheses and conclusions involve the theories of different edges. Thus, if e is an edge exiting a merge or loop node, ordinary rewriting cannot reduce a term containing σ_e to a term containing σ_{enter}.

My approach for incorporating the merge and loop rules is to extend ordinary rewriting to attempt automated proof-by-cases and proof-by-induction. As before, a rewriting system is first constructed for each edge. When an edge exiting a merge or loop node is encountered, the rewriting system of its immediate dominator (as in [1]) is used.

When the compiler tries to discharge the proof obligation of an optimization, the compiler first tries to prove the conjecture by term rewriting. If the conjecture reduces to *true*, the optimization is sound. However, if the conjecture reduces to a term containing the program state symbol of an edge exiting a merge node, the compiler attempts a proof by cases using the semantic inference rule for merge nodes. Similarly, if the conjecture reduces to a term containing the program state symbol of an edge exiting a loop node, the compiler attempts a proof by induction.[8] In both cases, the compiler recursively tries to discharge the subgoals.

Fig. 9 is the CFG for the trivial program

```
if b then /* skip */ else b := true end
```

To prove that the value of b is *true* at edge e4, the compiler first tries to reduce $\sigma_{e4}^{Env}(\text{'b'})$ using $\mathcal{R}_{e4}$, but the term is irreducible. Since σ_{e4} exits a merge node, the compiler next tries proof-by-cases. The subgoals are to prove $\sigma_{e1}^{Env}(\text{'b'})$ at edge $e1$ and to prove $\sigma_{e3}^{Env}(\text{'b'})$ at edge $e3$. Both subgoals are proved by rewriting using $\mathcal{R}_{e1}$ and $\mathcal{R}_{e3}$.

---

[8]The induction is over the body of the loop, not over the generators of a sort as in LP.

To avoid excessive recursion when attempting proofs by cases or induction, the compiler places an lower bound and an upper bound on the edges whose program state symbols can trigger proof by cases or induction. Initially, when trying to prove a conjecture at edge e, the lower bound is the entering edge and the upper bound is e. Before starting a proof by cases to try to reduce a term that uses σ_j, the compiler first checks whether j is within the bounds; where edge e_2 is *within bounds* e_1 and e_3 if e_1 strictly dominates e_2 and e_2 dominates e_3. For the subgoals, the lower bound is raised to the immediate dominator of j and the upper bound is lowered to j. Proof by induction is restricted in a similar fashion.

The effect of the restrictions is to try to reduce terms backwards over conditional statements and loop statements one at a time. Recursion is allowed for nested statements, e.g., a conditional within a loop, but not for statements earlier in the program, e.g., a conditional statement before a loop. Without restrictions, the number of proofs by cases attempted might be exponential in the number of **if** statements in a program. Worse, proofs by induction might recurse infinitely.

4.2.3 A Bigger Example

Fig. 10 is an example of a procedure to compile. Given formal specifications and specializations of **IntSet**, a data type for mutable integer sets, and **IntArray**, a data type for integer arrays that can grow and shrink dynamically, the prototype which implements the method identifies the following optimizations

1. The expressions a[i] on lines 5 and 6 can be replaced by the value computed for a[i] on line 4. a[i] is a shorthand for IntArray_fetch(a,i).

   This optimization relies on the **modifies** clauses of **member** and **insert** to show that a is unchanged, and the specification of **fetch**.

2. The call to **insert** need not check whether a[i] is in s. This is a specialization defined by **IntSet**.

   This optimization relies on the semantics of **if**, the **modifies** clause of **fetch** to show that s is unchanged, and the specification of **member**.

3. The bounds checks for a[i] on line 4 are unnecessary. This is a specialization defined by **IntArray**.

4. The two expressions a.low on line 10 can be replaced by the value computed for a.low on line 1.

5. The bounds checks for a[j] on line 6 can be eliminated.

Note that the compiler handles iterators, which were not discussed here. Larch/Speckle allows the implementor of an iterator to supply a lemma which, when proved by the compiler, is likely to be useful in identifying other optimizations. For the **IntArray_indexes** iterator, the lemma is that the body of the loop does not alter the bounds of the array. The prototype automatically discharges this lemma using proof-by-cases and proof-by-induction and uses it for optimizations 3-5.

```
remove_duplicates = proc (a: IntArray)
  1  j: Int := a.low
  2  s: IntSet := IntSet_create()

  3  for i: Int in IntArray_indexes(a) do
  4      if not IntSet_member(s, a[i])
  5          then IntSet_insert(s, a[i])
  6              a[j] := a[i]
  7              j := j + 1
  8          end
  9      end

 10  IntArray_trim(a, a.low, j - a.low)
     end remove_duplicates
```

Figure 10: A Sample Procedure

5 Conclusion

Formal specifications can make programs run faster. Because specifications contain information not found in code, specifications enable optimizations that are either hard or impossible by analyzing only code. Furthermore, specifications make it possible for users to express new optimizations.

I have presented a method that uses specifications to optimize imperative programs. The method uses general-purpose formal specifications that can also serve as the only documentation of a program's interface. Furthermore, the method supports modular optimization in the presence of partial specifications. Thus, the investment of specifying a module, e.g., a library routine, benefits all programs that use the module.

I implemented the method in a prototype compiler, and my preliminary experience is encouraging: the prototype identifies optimizations that conventional compilers cannot or do not find. More work is needed to assess how significant such optimizations are in real programs and how much additional compilation time is required.

Acknowledgements

John Guttag made many useful suggestions for both improving this work and improving this paper. Jeannette Wing read a draft of this paper on short notice and made many useful suggestions. Jim Horning and Daniel Jackson have given useful feedback on the ideas presented here. Steve Garland and John Guttag designed and implemented LP.

Support for this research has been provided in part by the Advanced Research Projects Agency of the Department of Defense, monitored by the Office of Naval Research Research under contract N00014-89-J-1988, and in part by the National Science Foundation under grant 9115797-CCR.

References

[1] A. Aho, R. Sethi, and J. Ullman. *Compilers: Principles, Techniques, and Tools*. Addison-Wesley, 1986.

[2] J. P. Banning. An efficient way to find the side effects of procedure calls and the aliases of variables. In *Proceedings of the 1979 Conference on Principles of Programming Languages*, pages 29–41. ACM, January 1979.

[3] D. R. Chase, M. Wegman, and F. K. Zadeck. Analysis of pointers and structures. In *Proceedings of the 1990 Conference on Programming Language Design and Implementation*, pages 296–310. ACM, June 1990.

[4] K. D. Cooper. Analyzing aliases of reference formal parameters. In *Proceedings of the 1985 Conference on Principles of Programming Languages*, pages 281–290. ACM, January 1985.

[5] J. Ferrante, K. J. Ottenstein, and J. D. Warren. The program dependence graph and its use in optimization. *ACM Transactions on Programming Languages and Systems*, 9(3):319–349, July 1987.

[6] J. Guttag and J. Horning (eds.) with S. Garland, K. Jones, A. Modet, and J. Wing. *Larch: Languages and Tools for Formal Specification*. Texts and Monographs in Computer Science. Springer-Verlag, 1993.

[7] A. Hisgen. *Optimization of User-Defined Abstract Data Types: A Program Transformation Approach*. PhD thesis, Carnegie-Mellon University, 1985.

[8] N. D. Jones and S. S. Muchnick. Flow analysis and optimization of LISP-like structures. In *Program Flow Analysis: Theory and Application*, pages 102–131. Prentice-Hall, 1981.

[9] J. R. Larus and P. N. Hilfinger. Detecting conflicts between structure accesses. In *Proceedings of the 1988 Conference on Programming Language Design and Implementation*, pages 21–34. ACM, June 1988.

[10] B. Liskov and J. Guttag. *Abstraction and Specification in Program Development*. The MIT Electrical Engineering and Computer Science Series. MIT Press, Cambridge, Ma, 1986.

[11] A. Neirynck, P. Panangaden, and A. J. Demers. Computation of aliases and support sets. In *Proceedings of the 1987 Conference on Principles of Programming Languages*. ACM, 1987.

[12] B. K. Rosen, M. N. Wegman, and F. K. Zadeck. Global value numbers and redundant computations. In *Proceedings of the 1988 Conference on Principles of Programming Languages*. ACM, 1988.

[13] S.J. Garland and J.V. Guttag. A guide to LP, The Larch Prover. TR 82, DEC Systems Research Center, Palo Alto, CA, December 1991.

[14] J. M. Wing. A two-tiered approach to specifying programs. Technical Report MIT/LCS/TR-299, MIT, 1983.

A new Front-End for the Larch Prover

Frédéric Voisin

Laboratoire de Recherche en Informatique,
C.N.R.S. U.R.A. 410, Université de Paris-Sud,
Bât. 490, 91405 Orsay Cedex, France.

Abstract

We describe in this paper a new front-end for the "Larch Prover". The front-end, acting as a proof manager, provides the user with a greater flexibility for completing a proof, by relaxing the order in which subgoals are proved and by keeping track of the progress of the proof. It also supports the introduction of alternative attempts for proving a subgoal: the user can switch back and forth among them and the system records which attempts are completed or not. We give a general description of the front-end, sketch its current architecture and discuss some remaining problems.

1 Introduction

The mechanization of the proofs of conjectures, or the design of tools to make them easier, is a long-standing objective of research in formal aspects of computer science with several applications: the proof of correction of software or hardware components, computer-aided deductions, Artificial Intelligence, etc. Several systems, either prototypes or more advanced, have been designed, among which stand, for instance, AFFIRM [9], the Boyer-Moore prover [2], the LCF/PPML system [14], and the "Larch Prover" (hereafter called LP) [7]. References to newer releases, and to other systems like HOL, IMPS and Isabelle, can be found in [3, 4]. While the underlying logic of the system, its proof mechanisms, heuristics and tactics, and its explanation capability are of primary importance for the support provided for proving conjectures, "software engineering" aspects must also be considered. Efficiency and support of large-scale problems are definite concerns, but so is the existence of a convenient user-interface. The latter term is to be given a broad acceptation that includes the way the user interacts with the proof engine and how the information coming from the prover is displayed but also the proof management aspects, i.e. the temporal and logical sequence of steps for completing a proof.

In this paper we present an enhanced front-end for LP, which is a system for proving properties expressed in a subset of multisorted first-order logic. The new front-end offers an improved flexibility for working on a conjecture, by relaxing the order in which subgoals must be proved while keeping track of the parts that remain incomplete, by allowing independent strategies for proving a given formula, and by providing new mechanisms for replaying a proof. These new facilities are of interest both for those who prove large and complex conjectures and for the beginners to LP who will find additional support for performing experiments.

Plan: In Section 2 we recall some aspects of LP. In Section 3 we describe the features provided by the new front-end, whose architecture is sketched in Section 4.

Section 5 includes a description of the status of the current prototype and a list of the problems that need to be solved in order to have a more general system.

2 The Larch Prover

The "proof-debugger" LP is part of the Larch project. It has been designed to help reasoning about algebraic specification written in the Larch specification language [11], by making it easier to prove properties of such specifications [10]. LP has also been applied successfully to other domains such as the proof of circuits or software components and the mechanical checking of proofs expressed in a different formal language. We will not give a general description of the system here, but will focus on the aspects pertaining to the proof management. Interested readers may find a complete description of LP in [7, 8], and a selection of current and future applications of LP in [13].

Conjectures and Logical Systems: The conjectures, and the "subgoals" involved in their proofs, are formulas expressed in a subset of first-order logic. Each of these formulas is proved in a context that consists of a signature, which describes the names known by the prover, and of a logical system, which contains the facts invocable in the proof. The contexts are computed by LP, starting from an initial formalization of the problem provided by the user, and according to the proof commands already executed.

Proof Methods: Apart from commands for customizing parameters, LP's commands are divided in two classes: On the one hand, "backward inference" commands aim at proving a formula by reducing its proof to those of some finite set of other formulas: its subgoals. The context for each subgoal is the context of its parent formula, possibly enriched by some hypotheses and some symbols associated with the proof method. Typical examples of backward inference commands are the "proof by induction" and the "proof by cases". On the other hand, "forward inference" commands do not modify the formula to be proved but modify the associated logical system, by stating explicitly some logical consequence of the facts in the initial system. Typical examples are the introduction of new equations by instantiation of variables in existing equations, or the "critical pairing" between rewrite rules in the system.

Proof Management: In LP the user has no control over the order in which the subgoals are proved. This order is fixed and follows a stack discipline: Each subgoal must be proved as soon as it is introduced, and the relative order of the subgoals originating from a given command is imposed by the system. If the user is stuck in the proof of some subgoal, there is no possibility of switching to another subgoal, for instance for gaining some experience. Moreover, once a subgoal has been proved, it is discarded together with its logical system which is no longer accessible to the user. This makes apparent the next subgoal to be proved but hinders the comparison of similar proofs.

The "Proof-Debugging" Approach: LP is usually presented as a proof-debugger. To quote its designers: " LP carries out easily understood, though perhaps computationally difficult, steps". The underlying belief is that most proofs will fail, because of an incorrect formalization, of an imprecise conjecture or of the choice of an inadequate proof strategy, and that they should fail both quickly and gracefully. Hence, LP is not an automatic theorem-prover but is guided by the user and oriented towards the use of "scripts" and "logs". Scripts are structured lists of commands either written by the user or recorded by the system during an interactive session. Logs are complete records of what happens during a session and include both input from the user and feedback from the system. The user is encouraged to write scripts, to run them under LP and debug its proof strategy by scrutinizing the current logical systems and subgoals, to test some additional proof commands, then to correct the script and run it again ....

3   The new front-end

In addition to implementing new ways for interacting with LP, the front-end embeds a proof manager. Like other proof managers, its goal is to provide the user with a hierarchical organization of the proof; to allow proofs to be initiated, worked on, suspended and resumed; to record the theory associated with each part of the proof and to maintain the status of the proof. Differences between proof managers mainly lie in the flexibility offered to the user for wandering through the proof and for editing the proof structure. We first evoke some "weaknesses" of LP, before discussing our proposals and the constraints for implementing them. Our objectives were threefold:

1. *To offer a control on the order of proof steps*, either to let the user prove the subgoals in the order that is the most natural for him, or as a means to skip whole parts of the proof. The last point can be justified for efficiency purposes, by writing separate scripts for different parts of a proof before merging them into a unique script, or by focusing on a subpart of a larger proof.

   The benefit for the user of having the control over the order of proof steps is best described by considering two examples for which a fixed order is not convenient. The first example is the one of the "prove by cases": Would you prefer to start with the simplest case or with the most intricate ? Without discussing what "simple" and "intricate" mean, let us say that the answer depends largely on the confidence one has on the validity of the conjecture or the proof strategy ! When highly confident, one will often prefer to start with the most involved cases, expecting the other ones to go quite smoothly. When less confident, one could prefer to start with the simplest cases, because they can be incorrect or unprovable, or for gaining some experience by proving them; Alternatively one could prefer to still start with the most intricate cases, foreseeing a quick failure ! A similar example occurs with the use of "lemmas", or when one proves a sequence of intermediate results before proving the main conjecture. Then again, the natural order for proving the conjecture or lemma depends on the gain expected from using the lemma: A lemma, although useful, is sometimes almost as difficult to prove as the original formula, suggesting to prove it first; However, not all lemmas are valuable, so why should we always work on a lemma before knowing if it is worthwhile proving it ?

   A first-come, first-served discipline is not convenient, prompting for the possibility of a control by the user, with a default strategy, like LP's stack discipline, when the order does not matter. When it does matter, the decision is best left to the user.

2. Another objective is *to ease the comparison of various strategies* for proving a subgoal. As explained in [5], apart from a clever use of the *freeze/thaw* com-

mands, the main mechanism for testing alternative ways of proving a subgoal consists in cancelling the current commands up to a certain level in the stack, and entering a new list of commands. But if the new attempt is no better than the previous one, there is no automatic way to restore the cancelled attempt and one is forced to run the original script, or to issue the cancelled commands, again. Even then, the comparison of two attempts is not easy since it amounts to a scan of the whole log to find the parts corresponding to the two strategies, before comparing the subgoals and the logical systems associated with them.

Clearly, some direct and more advanced way to compare strategies is missing in LP.

3. *Make LP easier for the beginners*: First we should insist that LP is rather easy to start with, thanks to the intuitive semantics of its proof commands, to the clarity of their feedback and to the absence of hidden tactics. However, LP could still be made simpler to beginners. The above objectives are important for a new user, since they allow a proof to be treated in a natural order and since the effect of commands can be easily compared. This also corresponds to a more interactive use of LP, natural when learning a new system, than the script-oriented use, more efficient for working on large conjectures. Writing scripts from scratch is not easy for beginners who have to figure out how the contexts will look like. The same is true of logs which are perhaps too verbose and not structured enough for a novice. The structure of the proof is reflected in the log by the way subgoals are named, and by the explicit indication of when a proof succeeds. However, since a proof step, with its many subgoals, can cover several pages of output, logs often have to be read while making some parallel hand-drawing to reflect more abstractly how things go. The verbosity of logs is increased for beginners, who ask for a lot of displays of the current state of the proof or of the logical system: This mixes with the proof information and loosens the structure of the log file.

Our proposal for meeting this informal objective is to emphasize the structure of the current proof, by making explicit the "drawing" that most users do and by having a sharper separation between displays and proof actions. Displaying explicitly the proof structure reduces the need for displays, and some of them could be considered as temporary: Some displays do not need to appear into the log file, their insertion is rather the user's responsibility. A sharper separation between what is really the proof-engine and what is a user-interface can help a beginner.

An explicit tree structure: As mentioned above, the overall principle is quite simple and has already appeared in other systems [6, 1]: to make explicit the tree that is the natural representation of a proof and to let the user manipulate it. The tree structure closely reflects how proofs proceed: An intuitive link exists between a formula and the subgoals occurring in its proof; The signature and the logical system of the original formula are inherited along that link, with the addition of some local information. Let us emphasize that the subgoals of a conjecture are not independent, but must be viewed as glued together by the proof command that introduced them. No individual insertion or deletion can happen. Our display of the proof reflects this constraint: We display it as a hyper-graph whose vertices are the formulas to be proved and whose arcs are labeled by proof commands and join each formula to its subgoals. A context is associated with each node, which includes the logical

286

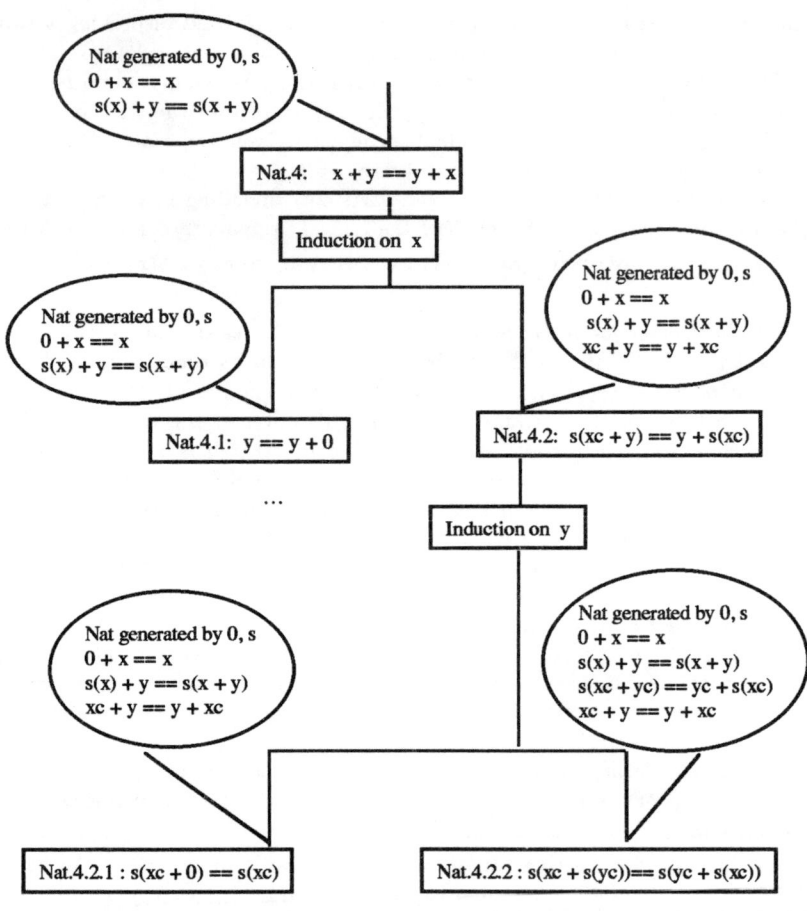

Figure 1: A tree for a partial proof

system and the increments in signature and theory provided by the command that introduced the node. This locality of logical systems ensures the soundness of the proof, by making sure that a fact is not used in a context where it has not been proved, whatever the temporal progression of the proof.

We show in Figure 1 how such a proof tree looks like: The figure illustrates a proof of the commutativity of the addition in some formalization of the natural numbers that is not given here. To keep the figure clear, the representation of contexts is sketchy. Unproved subgoals are indicated by a "..." symbol. Note that the partial proof in Figure 1 cannot exist in LP, since subgoal *Nat.4.1* is still pending. A stack discipline would have forced us to prove that subgoal first. The new front-end keeps track of which subgoals have been proved, and which ones are still unproved.

New commands allow to display information, to move in the proof structure, either to induce some display or to put the focus on another part of the proof, to edit the

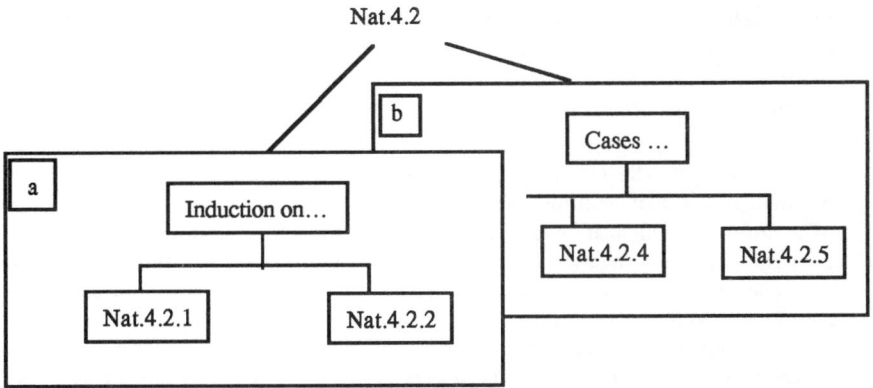

Figure 2: A proof tree with variants

proof by cancelling some commands, or to produce of a script for some part of the proof. As an example of a new command, the user can request a move to a subgoal by typing the *select-context* command with the name of that subgoal, as in *select-context Nat.4.2.2* .

Variants: the introduction of variants is a generalization of the tree structure, where nodes have more than one outgoing arc. Each arc corresponds to a different strategy for proving the formula at that node. Note that any variant at a node is logically compatible with any variant at a node in an independent subtree: The validity depends only on the formulas in the subgoals. Variants can be left incomplete, and the user can switch back and forth among them. They are parallel in the sense that none of them depends on the others being completed, but not in the sense that the user can work on them in parallel: there is always one current attempt, and commands are interpreted with respect to it. Switching attempts is done on user request only. This limitation has been introduced to limit the risk of having the user being confused by work done on parallel attempts: for instance, when an attempt succeeds, should the front-end select the next attempt at the same subgoal or switch to another part of the tree ? Therefore, in Figure 2, which illustrates variants, the correct view is a pile of attempts at node *Nat.4.2*, where only the current attempt is accessible without prior selection.

Making the tree structure accessible to the user also induces some drawbacks:

1. On the prover's side, a first problem is that contexts are no longer discarded when the subgoals succeed. This is useful for investigating the corresponding logical systems, but the impact on memory management and performances has to be evaluated in realistic examples. Alternatively, we could decide when contexts will be discarded, or provide the user with a command for that purpose. Some extra work is also performed by the system to record the logical status of proof: which subgoals or attempts are incomplete, which conjectures use unproved lemmas, etc. Propagation of logical inconsistencies in the proof tree is also slightly more complex in proofs by induction or by lemma: It relies on having some basic steps proved. Depending on the order the user chose to

prove subgoals, the propagation of an inconsistency can be either immediate or postponed until some other subgoal is proved. The user is warned of any postponed propagation of inconsistency, so that he can decide if the current attempt is worthwhile pursuing.

2. On the user's side, extra controls must be performed to prevent unexpected behaviors, since the validity of a command at a node can now depends on the moment it is issued. For instance, it makes no sense to modify the logical system of a node for which subgoals already exist, since the modification would not propagate to its subgoals; Forward-inference commands are therefore rejected on such a node. Some tuning is also needed to decide how automatically things should go: When switching to a node in the tree, what should happen to the contexts between the source and target nodes of the switch ? If one thinks of a script as a sketch of proof, where details are left out, one could expect LP to proceed the corresponding contexts automatically. Alternatively, if one thinks of a switch as a mere way to change the focus in the proof, then nothing should we done on skipped nodes. Experiments will provide some answers to these questions.

A "proof-editor" ? Once an explicit proof structure is built and made available to the user, one can think of using it as a basis for a proof-editor, with more semantic commands. This challenging system could, for instance, offer high-level commands for restructuring or for completing a proof, while ensuring the soundness of the resulting proof. Such commands could move some lemma higher in a proof tree to make it more general, or could duplicate, with suitable modifications, the strategy used at one node to prove another formula. We hope that our prototype will be a first step in that direction, but there are two kinds of problems. First, there are logical constraints to be respected, to ensure the correctness of the commands: One can safely move a lemma higher in a proof tree only if its (present) proof does not depends on some hypotheses now introduced below it ! Some mechanisms have to be provided by the proof engine to allow this property to be checked. Second, there are also operational problems, pointed to us by J. Guttag and S. Garland, that have to be overcome. A first point is the dependence of commands on names generated by LP (constants introduced in hypotheses, names of facts in the system, names of contexts, ...). Another point is that a proof, when moved to a different context, can be logically valid without being "operational", i.e. replayable, due to some confluence or terminaison problems associated with rewriting systems.

4   Architecture of the new front-end

Before describing the architecture of our current prototype, we list some of the constraints we had in mind during its design:

1. A major criterion has been the necessity of being compatible with LP, which is a quite large and complex piece of software. To be really useful, our prototype must accept all the commands, abbreviations, and ways of naming objects that LP currently accepts. It must also provide full support for scripts and logs. The same is true for outputting, and more precisely for the pretty-printing of formulas. This requirement of compatibility is important if we wish people to make experiments, and was not so easy to meet because of sophisticated aspects of the communication between LP and the user.

2. Another technical requirement was the independent development of extensions to LP on geographically distant sites. Changes to the structure of the system should be minimized, to help future integration of versions.

3. A last, important, criterion is a sharper separation between the user-interface aspects and the proof machinery than the one that exists in LP. This is needed for implementing local displays and for accepting new commands or new ways of interacting with the user. It can also help in interfacing LP with other environments. In such a case, LP would appear as a proof-engine, included in another system and depending on it for the user syntax or for the way of interacting.

   It should be noted that this last requirement is partly incompatible with the two previous ones, since it calls for major restructuring or recoding of the system, to be properly implemented: All communications between LP and its environment must be quite formal and abstract. Our current prototype presents some trade-off: The separation with the proof-engine is not so clear-cut, and some code is duplicated in LP and in the front-end. This should be viewed as a first step towards a cleaner separation.

The architecture of the new system is illustrated in Figure 3. Its design has been partly borrowed from an experimental "graphic" version of LP: XLP [5], allowing most code for input-output to be left unchanged.

LP appears as a component of a larger system, with which the user interacts. LP has its I/O channels redirected to pipes connected to the front-end. Communication between the user and LP goes through the first two channels, via the front-end. The last channel, at the bottom of the picture, is used by LP to send feedback on the proof commands to the front-end. Examples of feedback are indications that a subgoal is proved or the number of subgoals introduced by a backward-inference command. All this information is hidden to the user: it is the front-end's responsibility to transmit that information in a way or another. Graphical front-ends could update the proof tree, while line-oriented front-ends would rely on LP's output to keep the user aware of the progress of the proof. An abstract protocol allows the front-end to know on which side the next input will come from: either from the user or on one of the two LP's output pipes.

As mentioned in Figure 3, the two components are coded in different programming languages, with LP being in Clu. The choice of a different language for the front-end has been motivated by the connection of LP to different front-ends: not any front-end will be written in Clu ! More precisely, the objective of a front-end integrated with current windows management systems made the choice of the C language quite natural.

Where to put What ? In this paragraph we give some hints on the work done by each part of the system, distinguishing between what happens to be a natural separation of work, and what is the result of the trade-off evoked above.

1. The proof-engine implements the whole logical machinery: computation of the contexts, conjectures, theories, ordering of rules, etc. It also detects when a proof succeeds and when an inconsistency arises. For every proof action, it sends some feedback to the front-end, which will propagate it to the user. It should

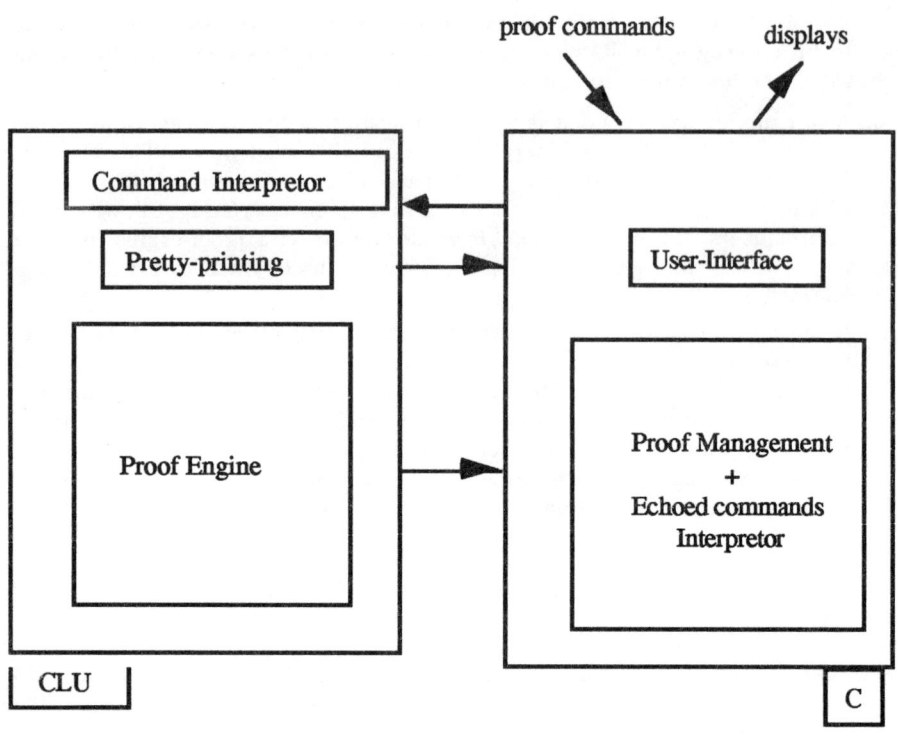

Figure 3: Architecture of the new system

be noted that it is based on some abstract notion of contexts and that it no longer has a global knowledge of the proof, nor does it have some mechanism for selecting contexts automatically: It simply performs computation on contexts.

To meet the compatibility requirement, all command analysis, prompting and pretty-printing has also been left on LP's side, although it should have fitted more naturally in the front-end. This guarantees that any regular input to LP is accepted. New commands exist, for instance to switch contexts or create attempts. Some commands can also no longer be handled by LP, like the one for checking the status of a conjecture. Hence, an extension of the LP's command interpreter has been realized that echoes these commands to the front-end on the third channel; they are deciphered there, and either they are executed by the front-end, or a similar "private" command is sent back with extra arguments to LP for processing. For that purpose, command analysis in LP has two modes: public or private. Private commands can only be sent by the front-end in answer to echoed commands, to prevent the user from entering unsound commands. This seemingly complex scheme allows to re-use LP's user interface with external transparency and minimal recoding, while transferring the commands related to proof management from LP to the front-end.

2. The front-end records the status of the proof from the information provided by LP, and handles requests from the user related to proof-management. It also disambiguates commands, maps user-oriented names to abstract contexts and handles the proof management: the selection of contexts by the proof-engine, either on user request or by mimicking LP's default strategy. Finally, using the proof tree, it handles requests for the proof history or for producing scripts. This can be viewed as a structural processing, while LP does the same but on a temporal basis: LP produces on-line scripts, while the front-end produces off-line, structural, scripts, freed of any hesitation and change of mind of the user. Only the commands necessary for reconstructing the proof in its current form are listed in these scripts, possibly for some attempts only.

In addition the front-end takes care of all user interaction, although it does it quite blindly. The commands and arguments are read from the user and sent to LP without any processing, even for new commands. Only the commands that have been echoed by LP are interpreted. The same is true for the output, which is produced by LP and propagated by the front-end without any processing, other than removing protocol messages. In future versions, the command analysis will be performed by the front-end, as it should be. Pretty-printing is more of a open problem: On the one hand, the front-end can adapt more easily to the environment (for instance, when changing the size of the display, or zooming in or out), but, on the other hand, the pretty-printing of logical formulas is an art that is maybe better kept with the rest of the logical machinery.

5   Current status and open problems

A first version of the system described in the preceding sections runs on Sun workstations, and experiments with it will start in the near future. We have added to LP the code for implementing abstract contexts, as well as an extension of the current line-oriented interface of LP that accepts the commands related to contexts and performs all the extra checks required by the front-end. New options to existing commands to account for the fact that more than one conjecture can exist at the same time.

Besides modifications to LP, an experimental proof manager has been designed that provides the functionalities described in the previous section. The effect of a few LP commands still has to be implemented, but most scripts already run, making the compatibility requirement a reality.

Independently, an extension has been made on top of this first prototype and integrated with the X-Windows system, to obtain a very experimental version of a graphical front-end. This graphical front-end uses the new proof-manager to interact with LP, while providing more elaborated displays and ways of interaction for the user: explicit display of the proof-tree, separate display of contexts, contexts selection by mouse clicking. This separate work is described in [12].

Future work and open problems: In addition to the new commands that experiments will probably suggest, and to the tuning that is necessary before having a user-friendly system, we would like to end this presentation with a few open problems that this first prototype has revealed. Some of them are related to the current implementation of LP, others are related to the front-end itself:

1. The Proof-Engine: there are currently three main problems. The first two ones are related to names and to the way they are generated and used in LP. The last problem is related to the difference between forward- and backward- inference commands:

   (a) Scoping of Names: Names in LP have a global scope and are not reusable. This situation was not too annoying as long as proofs proceeded sequentially. This is no longer true with the front-end, where attempts represent parallel developments of a proof. In our prototype, names of subgoals are generated by LP and are numbered sequentially in parallel attempts, when the user expects numbering of subgoals to be independent in alternative attempts. The numbering should reflect the order of subgoals in a proof step, without being mixed with some historical side-effects. The same situation occurs when wandering through the proof tree. A name like *Nat.4.1* stands for either the first subgoal in a proof of conjecture *Nat.4*, or for a new fact derived from it, as after an instantiation. If one first derives *Nat.4.1* from *Nat.4*, before working on the proof of the latter, then the numbering of subgoals will started with *Nat.4.2*, despite the fact that *Nat.4.1* is not visible inside the proof of *Nat.4*. A finer notion of scope is needed for names in LP; the problem will be addressed in the future.

   (b) Robustness of Names: Another problem with names in LP is that they are produced automatically and they are therefore quite sensible to a change in the proof environment: they are not robust with respect to embedding in a new context. More precisely, there is no guaranty that a script that works for a given conjecture will still work for proving the same conjecture if it is embedded in another script. The reason is that the script may need to reference some objects by a name that can represent a different object when scripts are embedded. That situation already exists in LP for the constants introduced by a proof method or for the names of facts, but it is made more frequent with the new front-end: In a script representing a proof tree with pending nodes, *select-context* commands with subgoal names have to be included to skip the missing parts and this introduces a new way to depend on names. Introducing some scoping mechanism in LP can help solve this problem.

   (c) Forward-inference commands are not undoable ! Recall that backward-inference proof methods are the ones that introduce subgoals. In general, each such subgoal receives a new copy of its parent's context, to be enriched with additional hypotheses. On the contrary, forward-inference commands and changes of settings update the logical system used for proving the current subgoal, without copying the original system. Since the effect of such a command is hardly undoable, we have reflected this behavior by not creating a new node in the proof tree when a forward-inference command is applied: Forward-inference commands have no counterpart in the proof tree; They are only recorded in a list attached to each node. That feature, altogether with the check that prevents forward-inference commands from being applied to contexts with subgoals, implies that all attempts start with the same logical system. For the moment there is no better way for undoing some forward-inference command than to start a new attempt one level higher in the tree and replay some of the commands.

This can be automated by a new specialized command, as a temporary solution.

Allowing any command to be undone, and to be associated with a separate node in the proof tree, would also have some drawbacks, since the names of subgoals would become very long, as shown by some experiments. The resulting proof tree would also easily become unreadable.

2. The Front-End: We list some points that will probably need some more reflexion:

(a) The first problem for the front-end concerns performances on large proofs. This has still to be evaluated. The management of abstract contexts adds some overhead to the proof processing, as does our way of interpreting commands. However, the main problem may be the impact on memory management of recording proved contexts and attempts. Experiments suggest that some decision has to be taken on when to discard proved contexts, either automatically or on user command. There is no reason for keeping forever every information about a proof, when one is interested only in the resulting theory !

(b) The next problem is related to partial scripts and to how automatic a proof should go. We mentioned at the beginning of this paper that a user control on the ordering of proof steps can be used as a way to write "sketches of scripts", *i.e.* scripts not intended to work on all subgoals. Such a script could be viewed as indicating "hints" on the proof, the prover either being able to prove the subgoals using these hints (in conjunction with the mechanism of automatic proof commands that exists in LP), or using them to perform as much work as possible before selecting the next subgoal for further work. Partial scripts would be a way to built a skeleton of the proof tree that can be completed during an interactive session. Another use of partial scripts is to accelerate the proof-debugging, by discarding parts of the proof, and focusing automatically on a sub-part. Writing a sequence of partial scripts, each for a different part of the proof, can permit to jump directly to the proof of interest, without having to spend time during debugging on parts that will be processed by other scripts or having to rely on *freeze/thaw* commands.

In the current prototype, it is possible to produce such scripts, starting from an incomplete proof tree. This possibility will be granted to the user, but with a suitable syntax for scripts that is still under investigation. In Figure 4 we give a partial script obtained from a proof tree, and how such a script could be written by the user in future versions of the system.

(c) Finally, the architecture of the system should be simplified, by moving some components from the prover to the front-end while keeping the same level of compatibility with LP. In particular, some code is presently duplicated in both components of the system to avoid excessive traffic on pipes, resulting in an unwanted coupling of the two parts.

294

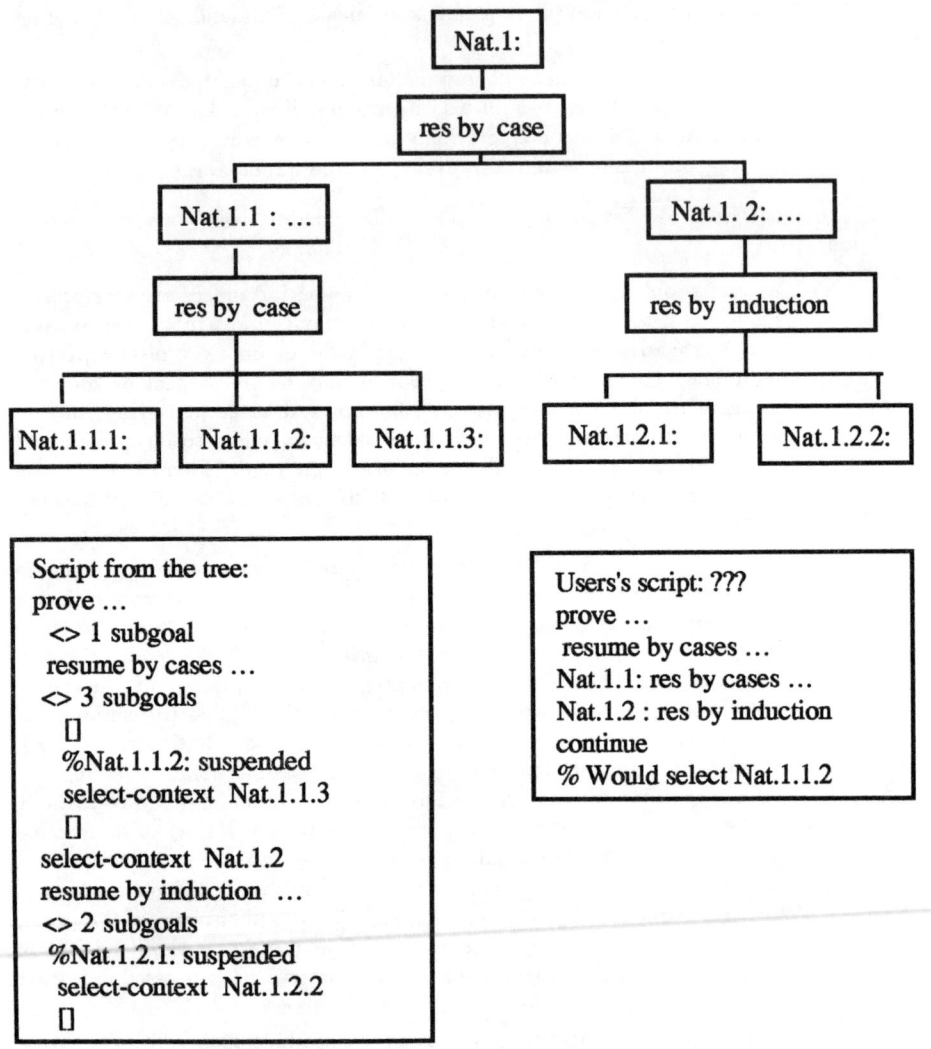

Figure 4: partial scripts

Conclusion: We have presented a new front-end for LP that acts as a proof manager. It lets users work on their proofs in the order that is the most natural for them, implements new support for trying alternative ways of proving formulas, and offers new facilities for producing scripts. The front-end also works as a user-interface, and we intend to extend it with more powerful display and interaction mechanisms, which will provide additional support for working on large procedures with LP. Although the new front-end may suggest a more interactive use of LP, a neither bad nor good bias, we think it is still compatible with the "proof debugging" approach: scripts can be written, run, tested and edited, but it provides new support for the debugging activity and less need for manual editing of scripts. We hope that incoming experiments will confirm that belief.

Acknowledgements: The work described here was started at M.I.T. during a stay in mid 1991, and benefited from early discussions about its objectives with J. Guttag and S. Garland. A special mention is due to S. Garland for his collaboration on the logical aspects of the front-end and for his explanations about the internal structure of LP. Finally, I would like to thank M. Bidoit and C. Choppy for the encouragements they provided me while I was working on this project.

References

[1] Bidoit M., Choppy C. and Voisin F. : *the Asspegique Specification Environment: Motivations and Design*. In Proc. of the Third Workshop on Theory and Applications of Abstract Data Types, Bremen, 1984, Informatik FachBericht 116, pp. 54-72, Springer Verlag.

[2] Boyer R. S. and Moore J. S. : *A Computational Logic*. Academic Press, New-York, 1979.

[3] CADE 90 : Proceedings of the 10th Conf. on Automated Deduction, Kaiserslautern, Germany, 1990. M. Stickel editor, Lecture Notes in Artificial Intelligence 449, Springer Verlag.

[4] CADE 92 : Proceedings of the 11th Conf. on Automated Deduction, Saratoga Springs, New York, U.S.A., 1992. D. Kapur editor, Lecture Notes in Artificial Intelligence 607, Springer Verlag.

[5] Edmunds M. V. : *A Tree-Based Proof Management System and User Interface for the Larch Prover*. Bachelor Thesis, M.I.T., Cambridge, U.S.A., 1989.

[6] Erickson R. D., and Musser D. R. : *The AFFIRM Theorem Prover: Proof Forests and the Management of Large Proofs*. In Proc. of the Fifth Conference on Automated Deduction, Lecture Notes in Computer Science 87, Springer Verlag, 1980.

[7] Garland, S. J. and Guttag J. V. : *An overview of LP, the Larch Prover*. In Proc. of the Third International Conference on Rewriting Techniques and Applications, Dijon, France, 1989. Lecture Notes in Computer Science 355, Springer Verlag, pp. 137-151.

[8] Garland, S. J. and Guttag J. V. : *A Guide to LP, the Larch Prover*. Technical Report 82, DEC SRC, Palo Alto, U.S.A., 1991.

[9] Gerhart S. L., and al. : *An Overwiew of AFFIRM: a Specification and Verification System*. Technical Report RR-9-81, USC Information Science Institute, U.S.A., 1980.

[10] Guttag J. V., Garland S. J. and Horning J.J. : *Debugging Larch Shared Language Specifications.* IEEE Transactions on Software Engineering, 16(9), pp. 1044-1075, Sept. 1990.

[11] Horning J.J., Guttag J. V. and Wing J. M. : *Larch in Five Easy Pieces.* Technical Report 5, DEC SRC, Palo Alto, U.S.A., 1985.

[12] Kaufman E. : *A Graphical Front-Ent to an enhanced Proof Management System for the Larch Prover.* Master Thesis, the Hebrew University of Jerusalem, Israel, 1992.

[13] Larch 1992 : *Proceedings of the first International Workshop on Larch.* U. Martin and J. Wing Editors, Dedham, Mass., U.S.A., 1992.

[14] Paulson L. C. : *Logic and Computation: Interactive Proof with Cambridge LCF.* Cambridge University Press, U.K., 1987.

Thoughts on a Larch/ML and a New Application for LP

Jeannette M. Wing, Eugene Rollins, and Amy Moormann Zaremski

School of Computer Science

Carnegie Mellon University

Pittsburgh, PA 15213 USA

Abstract

We describe a preliminary design for a Larch interface language for the programming language ML.[1] ML's support for higher-order functions suggests a need to go beyond the first-order logical foundations of Larch languages. We also propose a new application, *specification matching*, for the Larch Prover, which could benefit from extending LP to handle full first-order logic. This paper describes on-going work and suggests a number of open problems related to Larch/ML and to LP as used for specification matching. We assume rudimentary knowledge of Larch, its languages and two-tiered approach.

1 Introduction

1.1 ML

ML is a "mostly-functional," strongly-typed, polymorphic programming language with a published formal semantics [8]. On top of ML's small core language is a *module* facility that supports the incremental construction of large programs. An ML program is a collection of self-contained program units with explicitly-specified interfaces. ML programmers define interfaces, called *signatures*, separate from their implementations, called *structures*. Structures define environments (*i.e.*, bindings between identifiers and values); they are ML's way of encapsulating sets of variable, function, and type definitions. *Functors* are parameterized structures and are used to create and compose structures: application of a functor to a structure that matches a given signature yields a structure. ML supports separate compilation through its ability to export and import functors.

A Larch/ML specification extends the information contained in an ML signature. Like other Larch interface specifications, it associates ML types with Larch Shared Language (LSL) sorts and uses pre- and post-conditions to specify the behavior of declared functions. It adds semantic information to the syntactic information contained in a signature, but abstracts from the details of data representation and specific algorithms that would be found in the structures or functors that implement it.

---

[1] Since this design covers only a subset of Standard ML, we will refer to our interface language as Larch/ML rather than Larch/SML.

1.2   Why Larch and ML?

Larch complements ML. The Larch and ML communities both advocate taking a rigorous approach to software development. Larch is particularly well-suited for specifying properties of data types. Whereas precise static and dynamic semantics have been given for ML, they have assumed a set of basic types from which more interesting data types are built. Semantic properties of even the basic types in ML are left unspecified; hence, Larch provides a way to specify these properties.

Though most ML programmers strive to write code in a purely functional style, the ML community is not dogmatic about it. For example, in the Venari Project at Carnegie Mellon we are addressing issues like concurrency and persistence, and have found the existence of "impure" features critical, not just for performance, but for expressibility (*e.g.*, the Threads interface to ML exports sharable mutex locks and adds a notion of process state [1]). Larch addresses state changes like side effects and resource allocation (*e.g.*, creation of new objects) explicitly in interfaces. Larch interfaces highlight potential state changes that an ML programmer might otherwise miss when reading just the code.

Since Larch interfaces are defined in terms of the target programming language's model of state, to define a Larch/ML formally one needs to write an ML "state" trait. Writing such a "state" trait has always been a difficult exercise in designing other Larch interface languages since most programming languages do not come equipped with a formal semantics and/or their model of state is complex. Fortunately ML has both a formal semantics and a straightforward notion of state, so writing the Larch traits for ML state should be simpler than doing so for other programming languages (like C).

In Section 2 we give two examples of Larch/ML interface specifications and discuss some open problems.

1.3   A New Application for LP: Specification Matching

We are working on the design of Larch/ML in the context of the Venari Project's application of interest: searching large software libraries. We would like to be able to use specifications as search keys and do *specification matching* to determine whether a module should be returned as a result of a query [14]. We assume a specification, s_i, is associated with each component, p_i, in a software library of i components. For example, a procedure's specification might be a Larch interface describing the procedure's behavior. Specification matching is the process of determining whether for a given query, q, and specification, s_i, s_i *satisfies* q. If we assume the query and specification language are both drawn from the same logical language then *satisfies* is logical implication; specification matching is the process of showing an implication holds.

In Section 3 we discuss how we might use the Larch Prover as the backend "theorem prover" to do specification matching and suggest some extensions to LP that would make our task easier.

2 Larch/ML Examples

2.1 Queue

2.1.1 A Specification

Figure 1 shows an example Larch/ML specification of a queue type. We elaborate the ML signature module, QUEUE, with Larch/ML specification information, delimited by (*+...+*). Since ML comments are delimited by (* ... *), we can compile a Larch/ML specification as a normal signature, using the ML compiler without preprocessing.

```
signature QUEUE = sig
  (*+ using Que +*)
  type 'a t  (*+ based on Que.E Que.C +*)
  exception Deq  (*+ raised by deq +*)
  val create: unit → 'a t
     (*+ create ( ) = q
         ensures q = Que.new +*)
  val enq: 'a t * 'a → 'a t
     (*+ enq (q,e)
         ensures result = Que.insert(q,e) +*)
  val deq: 'a t → ('a * 'a t)
     (*+ deq q = (e, q1)
         ensures if Que.isEmpty(q) then raise Deq
                   else (e = Que.first(q)) and (q1 = Que.rest(q)) +*)
  val len: 'a t → int
     (*+ len q
         ensures result = Que.size(q) +*)
  end
```

Figure 1: Larch/ML Specification of an Immutable Queue

The specification begins with a **using** clause, which lists traits used by the Larch/ML interface. QUEUE uses the Que trait (Figure 2).

A **based on** clause may be attached to any type declaration to associate ML types with LSL sorts. In Figure 1, the **based on** clause associates the ML type t with the sort C from the Que trait. It also states that in any use of the type constructor t, the instance for the type variable 'a must be associated with a sort that can substitute for the sort E from the Que trait.[2] Later we explain how we type check specifications.

An ML signature declares exception values that may be raised in the module; the **raised by** clause enables specifiers to name the functions that may raise a particular exception. In QUEUE, Deq is the only exception value and deq is the only function that may raise it.

---

[2] In ML, type variables like 'a begin with a prime and are used for defining polymorphic types.

```
Que(E,C) : trait
   includes Integer
   introduces
       new: → C
       insert: C, E → C
       first: C → E
       rest: C → C
       isEmpty: C → Bool
       size: C → Int
   asserts
       C generated by new, insert
       ∀ q: C, e: E
          first(insert(q, e)) == if isEmpty(q) then e else first(q)
          rest(insert(q, e)) ==
             if isEmpty(q) then new else insert(rest(q), e)
          isEmpty(new)
          ~ isEmpty(insert(q, e))
          size(new) == 0
          size(insert(q,e)) == succ(size(q))
```

Figure 2: Que Trait

The specification for each function begins with a *call pattern* consisting of the function name followed by a pattern for each parameter, optionally followed by an equal sign (=) and a pattern for the result. In ML, patterns are used in binding constructs to associate names to parts of values (*e.g.*, (x, y) names x as the first of a pair and y as the second). ML programmers typically use patterns in function implementations to bind names to parameters and subcomponents of parameters; we borrow this ML feature as a way to introduce names in specifications. We adopt the convention that if the result pattern is not given, the default name for the result value is "result" (*e.g.*, as used in the enq and len functions in QUEUE).

Like other Larch interfaces, the **requires** clause specifies the function's precondition as a predicate consisting of trait operators and names introduced by the call pattern. Similarly, an **ensures** clause specifies the function's postcondition. If a function does not have an explicit **requires** clause, the default is **requires true**. In the QUEUE example, none of the functions have explicit **requires** clauses.

In QUEUE, the create function returns an empty queue; enq returns a queue that is a result of inserting an element in a given queue; deq raises the exception Deq if the queue is empty and otherwise returns a tuple whose respective values are the first element of the queue and the rest of the queue; finally, len returns the size of a given queue.

2.1.2   Type-checking

In type-checking a function specification, we assign the names in the call pattern ML types based on the type of the function. These ML types are associated with LSL sorts according to the **based on** clauses (or built-in associations for base types). We type check the **requires** and **ensures** clauses using the sorts associated with the types of the pattern names and the signatures of trait operators and interpreting the resulting type expression. For example, suppose the following were part of the QUEUE specification in Figure 1.

val convert: int t → bool t
    (*+ convert q
        ensures Que.first(q) = Que.first(result) +*)

This function specification contains a type error, discovered upon type checking: In step 1, we list the names used in the **ensures** predicate, along with their types, and substitute (⇒) associated sorts for ML types. In step 2, we substitute sort expressions for names within the **ensures** predicate, then simplify in step 3 and note the type error.

1) q   : int t (substitute sorts) ⇒ Int C
     result   : bool t (substitute sorts) ⇒ Bool C
     first   : (E C) → E

2) ((E C) → E) (Int C) = ((E C) → E) (Bool C)

3) Int = Bool

This next example converts a queue to a stack. It shows how type checking works in the presence of type variables and multiple type constructors; it uses sorts from two different traits, Que and Stk.

signature StackToQueue = **sig**
(*+ **using** Que, Stk +*)
type 'a t (*+ **based on** Que.E Que.C +*)
type 'a s (*+ **based on** Stk.A Stk.S +*)
val convert: 'a t → 'a s
    (*+ convert q
        ensures Que.first(q) = Stk.top(result) +*)

This example type checks successfully. In the second step below, the type checker unifies E of (E C) with the 'a of ('a C), which implies that any type that substitutes for 'a must be associated with a sort that can substitute for E in Que; the A of (A S) unifies with the 'a of ('a S), with a similar implication.

1) q   :'a t   (substitute sorts) ⇒ 'a C
     result   :'a s   (substitute sorts) ⇒ 'a S
     first   : (E C) → E
     top   : (A S) → A

2) ((E C) → E) ('a C) = ((A S) → A) ('a S)

3) 'a = 'a

The expression Que.first(result) would not type check. Substituting sort expressions gives us ((E C) → E) ('a S), but (E C) does not unify with ('a S).

2.1.3 Example Implementations

Figures 3 and 4 show two different ML implementations that satisfy the QUEUE specification. The first implementation represents a queue as a list, where the head of the list is the first element. The second implementation represents a queue as a pair of lists, where the head of the first list is the first element and the head of the second list is the last element. If a dequeue is performed when the first list is empty, the second list is reversed to form a new first list.

2.2 Symbol Table

Although most ML programs are purely functional, ML programmers do use imperative constructs (*i.e.*, refs, arrays, and commands for input and output). Thus, we do need to be able to specify side effects. Larch is particularly appropriate for dealing with the impure aspects of ML; in contrast, Sannella and Tarlecki's Extended ML specification language [11], also based on algebraic axioms, handles only the purely functional subset of ML.

The symbol table example in Figure 5 shows a Larch/ML interface used to specify a mutable symbol table. It uses the SymTab trait in Figure 6.

The **based on** clause states that objects of the ML type table range over values denoted by the terms of sort S specified in the SymTab trait. Each **modifies** clause lists those objects whose value may possibly change as a result of executing the corresponding function; lookup is not allowed to change the state of its symbol table argument, but insert and delete are. In an **ensures** clause we use t% to stand for the value of the table in the final state and simply t for the value in the initial state. The clause **fresh**(t_{obj}) in the init function specifies that the object t_{obj} is newly created.

This example shows how in ML a signature may contain substructures, e.g., Key and Value, and hence refer to names they export, e.g., key and value. For this reason, to avoid possible name conflicts in the pre- and post-conditions, we qualify each operator name with the name of the trait in which it is introduced; alternatively, we could name for each trait listed in the **using** clause the sort and operator names explicitly "imported" from that trait.

2.3 Open Problems

2.3.1 Handling higher-order functions

ML functions typically take functions as arguments and return them as results. Since the assertion language of Larch interfaces is first-order, we cannot write in the post-condition of function P the assertion "apply(Q, A)" where "apply" is a higher-order function, Q is the functional argument to P and A is some list of arguments for Q. We do not necessarily even want to state this kind of assertion since the interface should specify only the effects of P, not how to achieve them (*e.g.*, by applying Q). In principle, since P's implementor is not required to call Q, but only to ensure P's effects are as if P called Q, P's implementor is free to completely ignore Q.

Our current design of Larch/ML mimics other Larch interface languages by handling functional arguments using a "macro-substitution" approach. Instead of writing "apply(Q, A)" we would write in P's post-condition something

```
structure Queue : QUEUE =
  struct
     type 'a t = 'a list

     exception Deq

     fun create ( ) = [ ]

     fun enq ([ ],x) = [x]
       | enq ((hd::tl),x) = hd::(enq(tl,x))

     fun deq [ ] = raise Deq
       | deq (hd::tl) = (hd,tl)

     fun len q = length q

  end
```

Figure 3: A Queue Implemented by a List

```
structure Queue : QUEUE =
  struct
     datatype 'a t = Q of {front: 'a list, rear: 'a list}

     exception Deq

     fun create () = Q{front=nil,rear=nil}

     fun enq ((Q{front=f,rear=r}),x) = Q{front=f,rear=(x::r)}

     fun deq (Q{front=(hd::tl),rear=r}) = (hd,Q{front=tl,rear=r})
       | deq (Q{front=nil,rear=nil}) = raise Deq
       | deq (Q{front=nil,rear=r}) = deq(Q{front=rev r,rear=nil})

     fun len (Q {rear,front}) = length (rear) + length (front)
  end
```

Figure 4: A Queue Implemented by a Pair of Lists

```
signature SYMBOLTABLE = sig
  (*+ using SymTab +*)
  structure Key: KEY
  structure Value: VALUE
  type table  (*+ based on SymTab.S +*)
  val init: unit → table
     (*+ init () = t
        ensures t = SymTab.emp and fresh(t_obj) +*)
  val insert: table * Key.key * Value.value → unit
     (*+ insert (t, k, v)
        modifies t
        ensures t% = SymTab.add(t, k, v) +*)
  val lookup: table * Key.key → Value.value
     (*+ lookup (t, k) = v
        requires SymTab.isin(t, k)
        ensures v = SymTab.find(t, k) +*)
  val delete: table * Key.key → unit
     (*+ delete (t, k)
        requires SymTab.isin(t, k)
        modifies t
        ensures t% = SymTab.rem(t, k) +*)
end
```

Figure 5: Larch/ML Specification of a Mutable Symbol Table

```
SymTab: trait
  introduces
     emp: → S
     add: S, K, V → S
     rem: S, K → S
     find: S, K → V
     isin: S, K → Bool
  asserts
     S generated by (emp, add)
     S partitioned by (find, isin)
     ∀ (s: S, k, k1: K, v: V)
        rem(add(s, k, v), k1) == if k = k1 then rem(s, k)
          else add(rem(s, k1), k, v)
        find(add(s, k, v), k1) == if k = k1 then v else find(s, k1)
        isin(emp, k) == false
        isin(add(s, k, v), k1) == (k = k1) ∨ isin(s, k1)
  implies
     converts (rem, find, isin) exempting ∀ k: K (rem(emp, k), find(emp, k))
```

Figure 6: SymTab Trait

like "Q.spec **with** (A **for** F)," which refers to Q's specification, Q.spec, with appropriate renamings of actuals, A, for formals, F.

For example, in Figure 7, the function map takes a function convert as an argument. The specification of map refers to the specification of convert as convert.spec. We can think of these references as follows. For each application of map, the specification clause of the actual parameter for convert is macro-expanded into the specification of map. In the call pattern for map, we give the argument of convert a local name, x, which stands for the argument of any function passed as an actual parameter for convert. Renaming of the local name stands for renaming of the argument within the specification of any function passed as an actual parameter for convert. The local name result is given to the result of all function parameters. Note that the specification of map refers to itself. If we assume that macro expansion is lazy, a recursively-defined specification is well-formed if a base case is given.

```
signature Q = sig
    (*+ using Que +*)
    type 'a t  (*+ based on Que.E Que.C +*)
    val map: ('a → 'b) → 'a t → 'b t
        (*+ map (convert(x)) q
            ensures
                convert.spec with
                    (Que.first(q) for x, Que.first(result) for result)
            and
                map.spec with
                    (convert for convert, Que.rest(q) for q,
                    Que.rest (result) for result)  +*)
end
```

Figure 7: Specification of a Higher-Order Function

This solution is not entirely satisfying. Aside from the cumbersome syntax,[3] the thorniest technical problem is in dealing with functional arguments with side effects. Since an interface denotes a predicate over two states, in specifying the behavior of a function P with a side-effecting functional argument Q, we cannot explicitly assert anything about the intermediate states that P would see in calling Q, but be hidden from P's caller. The semantics of Larch interface languages designed so far (*e.g.*, for C [3], CLU [13], and Modula-3 [6]) have either ignored or have been limiting in their way of handling functional arguments. The advantage of looking at this issue in ML is that ML's formal semantics makes it possible to talk precisely about state and side effects. On the flip side, ML naturally pushes Larch to deal with higher-order functions as "first-class citizens" rather than as at the fringes of more traditional imperative programming languages; this push may be sufficient impetus for going beyond Larch's first-order restriction.

---

[3]which would be especially annoying to ML programmers who use functional arguments as the norm rather than the exception.

2.3.2 Sharing

In ML it is possible, and sometimes necessary, to allow sharing of types and even substructures between different program modules. For example, in building a compiler, a parser module and an abstract syntax tree module might need to share a symbol table. ML has a facility for letting programmers specify *sharing constraints* between types and between structures. Checking whether a constraint is met is determined by type or structure equality, as the case may be, since this check is easily computable. In a more complete Larch/ML we would like to allow the specifier to attach additional semantic constraints (*e.g.*, expressed as equations or a trait) on a shared type or structure. We would view these constraints as a shared theory in the sense of Larch.

2.3.3 Polymorphism

ML functions and structures can be defined using type variables. The closest that previous Larch interface languages have come to dealing with type variables is with CLU's parameterized modules. Again, the Larch treatment was syntactic in nature. Unlike for functional arguments, however, the syntactic approach to dealing with type variables should suffice for a Larch/ML, which we have done in our current design. However, we need to do a more careful semantic analysis to support this claim.

2.3.4 Other "types" of types

Features of ML we have not touched on in this paper include: *equality types*, *strong* versus *weak* types, **datatypes**, and **abstractions**. We have not at all addressed the semantics of Larch/ML with respect to these features; some (equality and weak types) raise new questions and others (datatypes and abstractions) raise issues already addressed in other Larch interface languages.

In ML the equality test is defined for values constructed of integers, reals, strings, booleans, tuples, lists and datatypes. Equality testing is not possible for function types and abstract types. Therefore ML supports the notion of *equality* types, types that admit equality testing, which users may define through an **eqtype** declaration. Just as for a **type** declaration, Larch/ML allows a **based on** clause attached to an **eqtype** declaration.

ML's reference values denote store locations that can be updated. Since ML's basic type checking algorithm does not cope with assignments to polymorphic references, ML provides a class of type variables called *weak* type variables (*e.g.*, 'la), which offer a limited degree of polymorphism. Larch/ML allows weak type variables in function declarations and relies on the ML type checker to ensure that the rules applied are the same as those for checking a plain ML signature module.

In Larch/ML we treat ML's **datatype** declarations as "exposed" (concrete) types (à la Larch/C) since defining a **datatype** in a signature module is like exposing the representation of an abstract type to the module's client.

ML supports abstract data types through **abstraction** modules.[4] An abstraction, **abstraction** S: SIG = **struct** ... **end**, is a special kind of structure

---

[4] In our design of Larch/ML we choose to ignore **abstypes** since they have been supplanted by **abstractions**.

in ML that limits the view of the structure to be exactly what is specified in the signature SIG of the abstraction S. Thus Larch/ML interfaces might very well be implemented by abstractions. Rules for determining when an abstraction satisfies a Larch/ML interface would extend existing ML rules for determining when an abstraction satisfies an ML signature.

3 A New Application for LP

3.1 Specification Matching

We are exploring the idea of using the Larch Prover to do specification matching. In general we need to prove some formula that looks like:

$$s_i \ satisfies \ q$$

Consider the specification of the symbol table in Figure 5 to be the query q. We might want to retrieve different symbol table implementations that satisfy q. Suppose there are four implementations, each (informally) specified to have the following properties:

1. s_1 stores its entries in an order based on the lexicographic ordering of keys. No duplicates are stored.

2. s_2 stores its elements in insertion order. No duplicates are stored.

3. s_3 retains multiple, possibly duplicate, bindings to the same key, but upon lookup always returns the value most recently bound to the given key.

4. s_4 retains multiple, possibly duplicate, bindings to the same key, and upon lookup returns any one of the values bound to the given key.

Intuitively, the first three, and not the fourth, satisfy the query q and hence should be retrieved. (q maintains an unordered set of keys to which values are bound, and lookup always returns the most recently bound value.)

To make this intuition more concrete, let us first assume that the specification and query languages are drawn from the same logical language. Let this logical language be a first-order predicate language over equality, where terms are drawn from the term language of LSL, equality is defined as in LSL, and quantifiers are over state variables. We now need to show for a given module specification s_i:

$$s_i.Th \supseteq q.Th$$

where $s_i.Th$ stands for associated theory of the ith specification and $q.Th$ stands for associated theory of the query q. It is beyond LP's ability to handle the above formula since it is a statement about theory containment.

However, now consider a subproblem–that of matching an individual function's specification–which would be necessary to partially prove the above. For retrieving ML functions whose specifications, s_i, are written in terms of pre- and post-conditions (as in Larch/ML), we need to match the corresponding pre- and post-condition predicates of a given function query q. A pre-condition is satisfied if the pre-condition of the query implies the pre-condition of the ML function. That is, the function's pre-condition can be weaker than the query's pre-condition, meaning that the function can be called in any context required by the query as well as other contexts. A post-condition is satisfied if the post-condition of the ML function implies the post-condition of the query. That is, the function's post-condition can be stronger than the query's post-condition, meaning that the function may produce results for any context required by the query as well as other contexts. We capture these ideas in terms of LP commands as follows:

> ... % other declarations and assertions
> **assert S generated by** emp, add
> ... % other declarations and assertions
> **prove** $q.pre \Rightarrow s_i.pre$ **by induction**
> **prove** $s_i.post \Rightarrow q.post$ **by induction**

where $x.pre$ and $x.post$ stand for the pre- and post-conditions of component x. Among the declarations and assertions in ..., we assert (as in the SymTab trait) that terms of sort S are generated by operator symbols emp and add. We then tell LP to prove the two implications by induction.

For example, suppose we want to retrieve the ML functions that assume an element e is in a collection c upon invocation and ensure that it no longer is upon return. That is,

$$q.pre \equiv isin(c, e), \text{ and}$$
$$q.post \equiv \sim isin(c\%, e).$$

Then looking at the delete function of Figure 5,

$$delete.pre \equiv isin(t, k), \text{ and}$$
$$delete.post \equiv t\% = rem(t, k).$$

To show that $isin(c, e) \Rightarrow isin(t, k)$ LP needs to do appropriate renaming of variables. More subtly, LP needs to show (or more realistically, to be told by the user through LSL's **includes** construct) that the theory of elements is included in the theory of keys and the theory of collections is included in the theory of symbol tables. To show $t\% = rem(t, k) \Rightarrow\sim isin(c\%, e)$ (*i.e.*, that an element removed from a collection implies that it no longer is a member of the collection when that collection is a table), LP needs to do equational reasoning. Figure 8 shows a proof sketch of what LP would need to prove given the appropriate human guidance.

3.2 Open Problems

3.2.1 Re-engineering LP's interface

We begin with some obvious limitations of LP with respect to its user interface, rather than its functionality.

Translating a Larch/ML specification into LP input. As for other Larch interfaces, associated with a Larch/ML specification is a set of predicates. These predicates along with any of the trait theories the Larch/ML interface uses can be stored in a file in a format that LP interprets as commands. LP already

Prove: $t\% = rem(t, k) \Rightarrow\sim isin(c\%, e)$.

Rename $c\%$ to be $t\%$ and e to be k by the same reasoning above about theory inclusion.

Then we need to show:

$$t\% = rem(t, k) \Rightarrow\sim isin(t\%, k).$$

Assume $t\% = rem(t, k)$. Show $\sim isin(t\%, k)$.

Hence, show $\sim isin(rem(t, k), k)$ by substitution for $t\%$.

> **Proof:** By induction on t.
> Base: $t = emp$
> > $\sim isin(rem(emp, k), k)$. Exempt case
> > since $rem(emp, k)$ is **exempt**.
>
> Ind. step: Assume for all $t1, k$. $\sim isin(rem(t1, k), k)$. (IH)
> > Let $t = add(t1, k1, v1)$.
> > Show $\sim isin(rem(add(t1, k1, v1), k), k)$.
> > > Case 1: $k = k1$. From the **then** part of equation
> > > for rem, we get:
> > > > $\sim isin(rem(t1, k), k)$ which is true by IH.
> > >
> > > Case 2: $k \neq k1$. From the **else** part of equation
> > > for rem, we get:
> > > > $\sim isin(add(rem(t1, k), k1, v1), k)$
> > >
> > > By the last equation in SymTab trait, we have:
> > > > $\sim isin(rem(t1, k), k)$ which is true by IH.

Figure 8: A Proof Sketch for Specification Matching

---

has an **execute** command that has the effect of reading in a list of commands from a file.

User Interaction. Once the translation from a Larch/ML specification to LP input is done, then LP can essentially take over. Here is where the crux of the problem lies. LP is designed to be a proof checker, not an automatic theorem prover. Hence, the human user must painstakingly guide it into finding the proof of a formula. Though LP does invoke some built-in rules of inference automatically, the human user plays a critical role in seeing a proof to completion. Given the goal of retrieving software components from a program module library through specification matching, for typical queries, such interaction with LP would be an unacceptably high price to pay.

However, given a sufficiently restricted specification and query language, it is possible to do specification matching automatically. As a feasibility study, we recently experimented with using λProlog [7] to show the use of specifications as search keys [10]. Our implementation encodes both LSL traits and Larch interfaces into λProlog clauses. We used our λProlog version of Larch as a specification language to describe a toy library of ML functions. We relied on λProlog's built-in higher-order unifier to do the *satisfies* check "for free" (*i.e.*, no theorem-proving or user interaction is needed). In support of our hypothesis, we found that including more semantic information in the search key increases precision of a match. However, the primary limitation of our λProlog experiment is λProlog's inability to deal with equality; our specifications were similarly limited in expressibility.[5]

Vandevoorde uses LP as a backend to his Speckle checker [12]. He restricts his input to LP to that which LP can handle automatically. His work suggests that with similar kinds of restrictions, we can use LP as a backend for a restricted form of specification matching.

3.2.2 Extending LP's functionality

The problem of specification matching raises the following issues with respect to the current functionality of LP. These issues are orthogonal to the interface issues described above. and hence can be pursued in parallel. Extending LP's underlying logic would benefit not just our own research, but the Larch specification community and the theorem proving community in general.

Algorithmic. LP supports a limited form of universal quantification through its **deduction** rules. Every Larch interface language needs to be able to handle not just universal quantification in a more general form, but existential quantification as well. Other users of LP have also suggested adding existential quantification to support proofs of (bounded) liveness properties of concurrent systems.

For a Larch/ML interface, we need to be able to specify higher-order functions. If we were to extend the assertion language of an interface to support higher-order logic, then we would need to understand how to extend LP similarly. This extension would push against some known theoretical boundaries (*e.g.*, unification is known to be undecidable for orders greater than two and the result is unknown for order equal to two when variables are restricted to range over only types [5]); however, there exists a complete second-order matching algorithm [4]. Performing even first-order unification over equational theories raises some interesting issues. For example, EQLOG [2], which is based on Horn clause logic with equality rather than full first-order predicate calculus with equality, uses the technique of *narrowing* as a means of exploiting unification and term rewriting in one system. It would be interesting to explore the design of efficient algorithms for performing (first-order) unification modulo "small" (application-specific) equational theories.

Finally, in order to perform the kind of specification matching suggested by the symbol table example, in principle we need to show that some theory includes another. A certain kind of theory containment (specifically, conservative extensions) was once considered in the design of LSL (*i.e.*, through the **imports** clause) but was recently discarded; one of the reasons was that LP cannot in general be used to check for conservative extension nor can reasonable sufficient conditions be found for any but the most trivial examples. It would be interesting to revisit this issue given a different motivating application.

Methodological. In reality, an LP proof of whether specification s_i satisfies a query q might best be broken into smaller subproofs. For example, a proof that a symbol table ML implementation satisfies the symbol table specification is necessarily going to depend on the proofs of each of the individual functions defined (*e.g.*, insert and delete). LP comes with limited facilities to help users

---

[5]Sometimes a library component may satisfy a query, but without equality it cannot be proved. Thus, the query processor may miss some library components that would be of interest to the user.

manage proofs through a proof stack. A logically tree-structured proof is thus flattened into the LP-imposed linear structure of a stack. One possible extension to LP would be to let users maintain and traverse a proof tree, rather than a stack, to reflect more naturally proof structures and proof development.

LP's interface with the file system can be extended to support a library of proofs. The proof and specification subdirectories included with the sources to LP are a step in this direction. Organizing proof and specification libraries so they can be accessed from LP smoothly would be convenient for users.

4   Status of Design and Tools

We are in the midst of designing Larch/ML and have only been speculating on the use of LP for specification matching.

We are building a checker/translator for Larch/ML. Since a Larch/ML specification is an ML signature with specification clauses included as special comments, an ML compiler can check and compile a Larch/ML specification as a regular ML signature. The Larch/ML translator parses, checks, and translates the specification clauses. To check a Larch/ML specification fully, we first run an ML compiler over it and then run the Larch/ML translator over it.

Since we can use names from the ML signature in the specification clauses, the Larch/ML translator processes the ML signature, noting identifiers defined in the signature and their types. In processing the specification clauses, the translator does structural checks (*e.g.*, a **based on** clause follows a type declaration), namespace checks (*e.g.*, all identifiers are uniquely defined), and type checks (*e.g.*, all clauses are well-typed).

For a given specification, the Larch/ML translator generates a fully-checked abstract syntax tree that can be deposited into a persistent object base [9]. Then to search a software library, the Larch/ML translator would convert a specification query to an abstract syntax tree, which would be matched against all trees in the persistent object base. To match a query tree against a library component tree, we would first signature match on the trees. If this succeeds, we would then match each function in the query against a function in the component, and then specification match on their specifications using the Larch Prover as indicated in Section 3.

To date, we have completed structural and namespace checking for the Larch/ML translator and are implementing type checking. We have already added the capability of using a persistent object base to an ML compiler. We have implemented signature matching (on ML function types), but not yet specification matching.

Acknowledgments

We thank Greg Morrisett and Scott Nettles for their feedback on our design of Larch/ML and Stephen Garland for his help with using LP.

This research was sponsored by the Avionics Lab, Wright Research and Development Center, Aeronautical Systems Division (AFSC), U. S. Air Force, Wright-Patterson AFB, OH 45433-6543 under Contract F33615-90-C-1465, Arpa Order No. 7597.

References

[1] Eric C. Cooper and J. Gregory Morrisett. Adding Threads to Standard ML. Technical Report CMU-CS-90-186, School of Computer Science, Carnegie Mellon University, December 1990.

[2] J. A. Goguen and J. Meseguer. Eqlog: Equality, types, and generic modules for logic programming. In D. DeGroot and G. Lindstrom, editors, *Functional and Logic Programming*, pages 179–210. Prentice-Hall, 1986.

[3] J.V. Guttag and J.J. Horning. Introduction to LCL: A Larch/C Interface Language. Technical Report 74, DEC/SRC, July 1991.

[4] G. Huet and B. Lang. Proving and applying program transformations expressed with second-order patterns. *Acta Informatica*, 11:31–55, 1978.

[5] G.P. Huet. A unification algorithm for typed λ-calculus. *Theoretical Computer Science*, 1:27–57, 1975.

[6] K. Jones. Lm3: A Larch Interface Language for Modula-3. Technical Report 72, DEC/SRC, June 1991.

[7] D. A. Miller and G. Nadathur. Higher-order logic programming. In *Third International Conference on Logic Programming*, London, July 1986.

[8] R. Milner, M. Tofte, and R. Harper. *The Definition of Standard ML*. MIT Press, 1990.

[9] Scott M. Nettles and J.M. Wing. Persistence + Undoability = Transactions. In *Proc. of HICSS-25*, January 1992.

[10] E.R. Rollins and J.M. Wing. Specifications as search keys for software libraries. In *Proceedings of the Eighth International Conference on Logic Programming*, Paris, June 1991.

[11] D. Sannella and A. Tarlecki. Program specification and development in Standard ML. In *Proceedings 12th ACM Symp. on Principles of Programming Languages*, pages 67–77, New Orleans, January 1985.

[12] M.T. Vandevoorde. Exploiting formal specifications to produce faster code. MIT Ph.D. dissertation in progress, 1993.

[13] J.M. Wing. *A Two-Tiered Approach to Specifying Programs*. PhD thesis, MIT, May 1983. Available as MIT-LCS-TR-299.

[14] Amy Moormann Zaremski. Using semantic information to find program modules. CMU Ph.D. dissertation in progress, 1993.

Author Index

Published in 1990–91